CONSUMER SOCIETY: CRITICAL ISSUES & ENVIRONMENTAL CONSEQUENCES

CONSUMER SOCIETY: CRITICAL ISSUES & ENVIRONMENTAL CONSEQUENCES

Editor

Irena Kucera

Socialy PRESS
AN IMPRINT OF SCITUS ACADEMICS

Consumer Society: Critical Issues & Environmental Consequences

Edited by **Irena Kucera**

This Book is Printed on Acid-Free Paper. ♾

ISBN: 978-1-68117-836-3

Library of Congress Control Number: 2017938867

Socialy Press

(An Imprint of Scitus Academics),

616, Corporate Way, Suite 2, 4766,

Valley Cottage, NY 10989

www.scitusacademics.com

Notice

Printed in United States of America.

Preface

Our consumption of goods obviously is a function of our culture. Only by producing and selling things and services does capitalism in its present form work, and the more that is produced and the more that is purchased the more we have progress and prosperity. Consumption is the process by which goods and services are, at last, put to final use by people. Consumption is at the end of the line of economic activities that starts with an evaluation of available resources and proceeds through production of goods and services and distribution of goods and services (or the means to acquire them) among people and groups. At last, the goods and services themselves come to be used. The effect of this consumption, including depletion of resources and generation of waste as well as enhancement of human survival and flourishing, determines the resource base for the next round of economic activity. Consumption is the sole end and purpose of all production and the welfare of the producer ought to be attended to, only so far as it may be necessary for promoting that of the consumer. Consumption activities most directly address living standard (or lifestyle) goals, which have to do with satisfying basic needs and getting pleasure through the use of goods and services. However, the production, processing, and consumption, of commodities requires the extraction and use of natural resources (wood, ore, fossil fuels, and water); it requires the creation of factories and factory complexes whose operation creates toxic byproducts, while the use of commodities themselves creates pollutants and waste. Yet of the three factors environmentalists often point to as responsible for environmental pollution — population, technology, and consumption — consumption seems to get the least attention.

Consumer Society: Critical Issues & Environmental Consequences compiles together a huge set of resources for thinking about consumer culture and examining its geneses and concerns worldwide. Decades of relatively steady growth have changed the way we live. We produce and consume more goods and services. We travel more and live longer. But the environmental impacts of our economic activities at home and abroad have become bigger and more visible. Environmental legislation, when implemented thoroughly, achieves results on the ground. This book will be of beneficial for all those interested in global culture of consumption including students of sociology, social geography and cultural studies.

Table of Contents

1

CHAPTER

Positioning Food Cultures: 'Alternative' Food as Distinctive Consumer Practice

Jessica Paddock

Sustainable Consumption Institute, University of Manchester, UK

ABSTRACT

Many sociological studies to date have explored the role of food in marking distinctions between groups. Less well understood is how 'alternative' means of food consumption become figured in such relations. Drawing on accounts of food practice derived from 20 in-depth interviews and a two-year period of participant observation, this article considers the role of class culture in the practice of alternative food consumption. As participants speak their position, expressions of class arise through discussions of food practice. Having explored how food plays a part in marking boundaries of distinction between foods 'for us' and 'for them', we are reminded that in reproducing certain ideas about proper eating, we confine our imagining of alternative food futures to a limited politics of the possible. The article highlights implications for future development of equitable alternatives to conventional foodways.

INTRODUCTION

As awareness of the environmental effects of advanced capitalism grows, we witness the progression of 'ethical' (Harrison et al., 2005), 'alternative' (Goodman and Goodman, 2009) or 'sustainable' (Jackson, 2006) consumption movements. Here, the promise of fairer conditions of trade between consumers and producers has also come to ground food in questions that seek to realise global social justice (Lyon and Moberg, 2010), while shortening food supply chains and grounding them within local economies has become a core focus for the wider project of sustainable development (Arce and Marsden, 1993). Although each movement appeals to consumers' ethical dispositions, their sense of what is moral, good and responsible, they do so with differing emphasis upon abstinence from or modification of existing consumption practices (Sassatelli and Davolio, 2010). For Littler (2009), ethical consumption is considered an act of sanctimonious shopping, which she describes as a means of extolling one's moral virtues and displaying the ethical self to others. This article argues that there is a further element playing out through such practices where alternative food consumption is figured in processes that demarcate social groups. Class is one way through which such boundary formation can come to be understood.

This line of argument has deep roots in the sociology of consumption, from Veblen (1994), Douglas and Isherwood (1996) and Bourdieu (1984) to Slater (1997), Warde (1997) and Bennett et al. (2009), to name but a few. Across the sociology of food there is a great deal of consideration given to the analysis of the social dimensions of eating and differentiation, focused both in and around the home. Studies reported by Murcott (1983), DeVault (1991), Southerton (2002), Bugge and Almås (2006), Mellor et al. (2010), Evans (2011) and Wills et al. (2011) are but a few examples. Moreover, Warde and Martens (2000) consider the symbolic significance of eating out, while Elias (1978) and Mennell (1985) chart such changes in eating over time. Following such lines of inquiry, the article takes a Bourdieusian theorisation of social classification of difference between groups understood as 'position', which is taken as an axis around which to understand how and where social actors locate themselves in relation to others, who they are and how they live and want to live within the society in which they operate. Expressions that reveal such positions may be fractured and fragmented, but are nevertheless a means of anchoring an aspect of one's self in relation to others. Consistent with Bourdieusian methods for recognising positions or indeed class identities we may look to the performance of social practices such as eating, and the acquisition of resources such as food, demanded by these practices. This does not necessarily assume class identification and awareness – class for itself – but considers a class identity as recognisable, among many other possible markers, by preferences for certain cultural goods over others, and the discursive techniques of separation that mark the preferred from the undesirable. The schemes of the habitus operate below the level of consciousness or language (Bourdieu, 1984: 466); for social actors do not create dispositions, worldviews, or indeed 'habitus', but acquire them.

What has been less fully explored by the sociology of consumption and the cultural geographies of agri-food networks is the extent to which alternative food consumption in the UK figures in reproducing social, cultural and economic divisions. There is a growing literature in this area (Adams and Raisborough, 2008), but this has mostly focused upon FairTrade consumption in general (Wheeler, 2012). This article draws on insights derived from a case-study involving a two-year period of participant observation at a farmers' market and at a community food co-operative located within the same neighbourhood of a UK city, developing a sociological perspective with regard to spaces of alternative food consumption. While alternative food supply chains have a long developmental history, with roots in the anti-slavery boycotts of the 1700s and later the co-operative movement (Nützenadel and Trentmann, 2008), it is a contemporary incarnation of the farmers' market and community food co-op that inspires this study. Here, the valorisation of the embeddedness of local foods (Murdoch et al., 2000), of the connections between producer and consumer (Kneafsey et al., 2008), and the aesthetic of foods positioned as 'slow' (Miele and Murdoch, 2002) characterise this the contemporary manifestation of alternative food.

Field notes, 20 in-depth interviews, a survey and documentary analysis reveal how particular ideas about 'good', and this case, 'alternative' food consumption are used as a means of drawing boundaries between social groups as distinctions are made in talk between foods that are for 'us' and those that are for 'them'. This is noted as particularly characteristic of British ethical consumer movements, which Varul (2009) finds is less pervasive in a German context. Finding such differences across national and cultural contexts may suggest we exercise caution in generalising findings to a wider context. However, Slocum (2008), Guthman (2008a) and Zukin (2008) argue that alternative food initiatives in the US enlist different people in particular moral projects that are socially exclusive and thus ineffectual in bringing about change towards more sustainable ways of procuring, preparing and eating food. While we should expect such cross-cultural variation in the expression of boundary formation and processes of exclusion – such process in the US were grounded in race – this should not deter wider consideration of their implications for the development of equitable alternatives to conventional foodways.

DISTINCTION: FOOD FOR DIFFERENTIATION

With the onset of post-modernity, consumer choices are thought to be influenced less by social groups and more as the result of self-determination (Harvey, 1990). Questioning the extent to which the consumer experience is characterised by such freedom, Warde (1997) studies the effects of social and cultural change on British food habits between 1968 and 1992, finding persistent and shared patterns of preference and expenditure across groups. This is much akin to Bourdieu's (1984) seminal study of French eating habits in the 1960s, where necessity imposes a taste for the necessary; working-class meals are 'elastic' and 'abundant' with avoidance of dishes requiring careful measurement of portions. For the bourgeoisie, the meal marks aesthetic refinement and is premised upon quality over quantity, and style over function. More recently, Lamont (1992) provides a startling portrait of successful French and American upper-middle-class men and their means of forming boundaries between themselves and others, while Southerton (2002) finds that economic, cultural and social resources are central to explaining the accord between respondents in constructing boundaries of separation and alignment between actors. However, Bennett et al. (2009) suggest that while the exercised and cultivated body is an instrument of social classification – through sport, exercise, diet management and maintenance – the practice of eating, particularly within the home, is not found to play a part in this, stating that 'symbolic distinction finds little place in family dining' (Bennett et al., 2009: 168). This finding warrants further investigation, particularly given lack of consideration of differences in the form and quality of such foods.

For Sayer (2005b) the privileged have access to goods that are valued by all, and are not only a means of expressing superiority and distinction. A large home does not always simply have an exchange value based solely on conspicuous display, but is also inherently 'good', it has a *use* value – it is warm, has enough space to accommodate people and their different needs for sleeping, studying and playing. These are things that matter to people (Sayer, 2011) but, in Bourdieu's terms, those who are refused such goods come to refuse them. Their exclusion is internalised as a dislike. Alternative food, this article argues, offers one such example of a highly moralised terrain where it is not so simple to argue that a preference for one sort of food is relative to any other. In other words, alternative food may not simply be 'posh', it may also have the potential to be 'good'. Exploring participants' talk of alterative food and the practices associated with its consumption, the article explores such dynamics of misrecognition, considering how these might come to shape the development of equitable and socially inclusive alternatives to conventional foodways.

Positioning: Distinction in Quality Foods?

Emerging from the data is an understanding of participants as constructing positions relative to 'others'. For Bourdieu, 'it is clear that tastes in food cannot be considered in complete independence of other dimensions of the relationship to the world, to others and to one's own body, through which the practical philosophy of each class is enacted' (Bourdieu, 1984: 193). That is, we may gain a sense of our place and that of others within wider relations of order via practical knowledge of resource distribution between groups. Through the habitus, the structures of everyday life interplay, providing unconscious rules that perpetuate its conditions over time. As a structured cultural grammar, the habitus produces a number of possible, although limited, practices. It inculcates 'reasonable' and 'common sense' social action (Bourdieu, 1990: 55) such as taste, through which we may come to 'sense or intuit what is likely to befall – and therefore benefit – an individual occupying a given position in social space' (Bourdieu, 1984: 466). The habitus is the disposition from which one acquires tastes and preferences, from which we can delineate the 'things and people that go together' (Bourdieu, 1984: 241). In the way that 'taste classifies the classifier' (Bourdieu, 1984: 6) food may bear the signs of vulgarity as well as distinction, but only when perceived relationally. It is through the conscious or unconscious projections that individuals or groups make with regard to these distinctions that class can potentially come to be understood. Building on Bourdieu's concept of class as a relative position, Southerton (2002), Sayer (2005a), Lawler (2005) and Lamont (1992) consider the moral dimensions of this process. This is significant when considering the practice of 'alternative' food consumption, for not only is food in its most conventional form a first need of the human body, but in its 'alternative' form, appears to become figured in evaluative judgements about what is good or bad, both morally and aesthetically. By paying attention to what matters to people, we are able to discern normative manifestations of social position, or indeed, class identities, as opposed to commenting solely upon recognition of or affiliation with objective class categories (Payne and Grew, 2005).

The task at hand is thus not classificatory, but an exploration of the dynamics of relational position in the 'dialectic of competition, distinction and differentiation which is central to symbolic domination' (Sayer, 2005a: 80). Here, class is considered a relational social position, which can be understood through participants' normative account of the struggle for resources, namely foods they value in upholding their ways of life. Taste, then, serves the perpetration of symbolic violence as those with the symbolic power to do so judge those who fall short of their ideas of what is right and proper (Skeggs, 2004). Those without symbolic power are ridiculed and shamed for their tastes through these very imaginaries of otherness. Recognising these processes at work is important, for without appreciation of tensions between groups in delineating rules of 'proper eating' (DeVault, 1991) we entrench what Hinrichs and Kremer (2002) term a socially homogenised and exclusionary form of sustainable place-making. That is, while Murdoch et al. (2000) suggest that concern for food quality empowers at the local level, this article argues that such a realignment and turn to local embeddedness – as represented by the farmers' market studied here – can reproduce a balance of power that favours well-to-do consumers (Nygård and Storstad, 1998).

METHODS

Chosen for their situation within the same community, the research sites comprise a farmers' market (the 'market') and a community food co-operative (the 'co-op') located on the outskirts of a city in South Wales. The co-op and the market are supported by the same umbrella organisation, yet there is a clear demarcation in their customer profile. A survey (n = 300) of customers at both sites provided indicative socio-demographic data as to gender, age, postcode, ethnicity and income, and served mainly to recruit interviewees (see Table 1 for an outline of the dimensions of the sample). While making no claims as to the representativeness of the findings beyond this case, market customers sampled tend to visit from more affluent wards within the county, to earn a net income over £30,000 a year, to have secured postgraduate qualifications, and to have parents who held professional and managerial positions. In contrast, most customers of the co-op live either within the ward or in neighbouring deprived wards (as measured by the Welsh Index of Multiple Deprivation), while 58 per cent earn less that £10,000 per annum, and tend to hold school-leaver qualifications, much like their parents.[1] Given these marked differences, a case study research strategy suits the imperative to explore the dynamic relationship between these sites, each of which professes to offer the means of connecting consumers with quality food. The market typically comprises 20 stalls staffed by farmers themselves selling produce, meat, and value-added products such as chutneys, pies and cakes. Food and drink is also available for on-site consumption every Sunday morning. The co-op pre-orders fresh produce from a wholesaler and distributes from a local community centre every Tuesday morning. Volunteers then distribute produce into fruit and vegetable bags for collection by local residents who place a further order for the following week.

Table 1. List of participants.

Name	CFC/FM	Gender	Age Group	Occupation
Catherine	FM	Female	31–40	Manager
Rhydian	FM	Male	31–40	Graphic designer
Adam	FM	Male	21–30	Student/works for a charity
Karen	FM	Female	51+	University lecturer
Trevor	FM	Male	51+	Retired
Valerie	FM	Female	51+	Art student (retired)
Ronald	FM	Male	31–40	Scientist
Charlie and Sophie	FM	Male and female Couple	31–40	Both civil servants in local government
Robert	FM	Male	51+	Story-teller
Niamh	FM	Female	21–30	Physiotherapist
Samantha	CFC	Female	31–40	Administrator
Julianne	CFC	Female	51+	Unemployed
Bev	CFC	Female	31–40	Administrator
Victoria	CFC	Female	51+	Administrator
Gina	CFC	Female	31–40	Teacher (part time)
Claire	CFC	Female	21–30	Massage therapist
Emily	CFC	Female	21–30	Unemployed
Ken	CFC	Male	41–50	Unemployed
Vera	CFC	Female	51+	Administrator
Sheila	CFC	Female	51+	Sales assistant
Marina	CFC	Female	31–40	Housewife

Interviewees directly quoted in the article are in **bold**.
CFC = Community Food Co-op.
FM = Farmers' Market.

A sustained period of observation behind the stall-face while 'participating as volunteer' (Atkinson and Hammersley, 1994) underscores on-site ethnographic interviews, documentary analysis, survey and 20 in-depth semi-structured interviews lasting between one and two hours, which sought to elicit narratives of everyday food shopping and consumption routines. In speaking their food routines and practices, participants state their position in a field of cultural goods, their likes/dislikes for particular foods and products, and the people that go with them. Due to constraints of space, a proportion of the data gathered from in-depth interviews form the empirical focus of the article, which are chosen because they provide illustrative examples of themes emerging across the data. The article explores 10 participant narratives (five from each site) with the use of pseudonyms to protect the anonymity of interviewees. While narratives elicited from female participants dominate the article, they do so because they capture succinctly the talk of alternative food and its role in reproducing and even destabilising particular ideas of 'proper' eating. Reflection upon any potential gendered difference in accounting for taste is best reserved for fuller consideration elsewhere.

A Field of 'Alternative' Food Consumption

A 'Hugely Different Attitude to Life'

Exploring means of position-taking, this section introduces five farmers' market customer narratives. Marking the legitimacy of her food practice, Karen positions herself in contrast to her working-class neighbours. Karen consolidates this distinction by reference to consumer culture more generally, and alternative food politics more specifically. This position is then anchored by articulating her vision of the 'good life', thus providing a platform for the pejorative judgement of others. Crucially, explicit categories of class are employed when describing herself in relation to other community members who:

K: ... think we're a bit weird I think.

I: In what way do you think?

K: Just a sort of, you know, 'middle-class English people' really, you know [laughter]. This is the sort of working class white [name of City] people who've just lived there always, and their families are all linked.

(Karen, market customer)

Rather than claiming 'ordinariness' (Savage et al., 2001), Karen judges negatively the stasis of family ties that are historically characteristic of working-class families (Young and Willmott, 1957). This is compounded by later discussions of food practice perceived as characteristic of these very neighbours:

> They're very uncritical about that sort of things I'm criticising in terms of the consumerist culture, cheap food, not worrying about where the stuff comes from how far it's come or how it's produced and just saying well something's cheap and that's great and bigger cars and going on foreign holidays and thinking that's you know, taking the attitude that that's the good life. (Karen, market customer)

Importantly, class differences are not framed as economically determined, for those to whom she refers are believed to have more money than her. They are instead, as Bourdieu argues, separated by degrees of cultural capital; a different idea of the 'good life' that involves adopting a critical attitude to cheap food. Defining the 'good', Karen contrasts her food politics with working-class consumption practices deemed inadequate, including the preference for cheap food, 'bigger cars' and 'foreign holidays'.

Similarly, Catherine emphasises her commitment to an ethos of *terroir*,[2] which she claims is practiced by shopping at a farmers' market, through organic box delivery schemes and eating seasonally. Describing her view of good food is also accomplished by somewhat jovially juxtaposing these foods with those less favourable, and the people that go with them. Indeed, her family eats fresh organic produce, purchased through an organic box delivery scheme or at the farmers' market, while her friend's husband 'was brought up on Findus[3] pancakes so we always joke about that'. Catherine then goes further by positioning her food preferences in contrast to imagined others, presented as being incapable of delaying gratification:

> ... but people don't think anything of going out and spending [money] on pints of cider, or, do you know what I mean, we don't do, we choose, we don't do that, we want to go and enjoy our food, and it depends on what people want. (Catherine, market customer)

Here, the imperative to consume in one way rather than another is attributed as a rational choice – 'it depends on what people want'. Similarly, Valerie's account of working-class caring practices within the home is cause for some concern. Drawing on her professional experience as a health visitor, Valerie speaks of encounters with working-class families:

> The problem *is*, unless it [class] fades away completely you're going to get an increasing division between those who've received lots of health education and have the finances to support it and the sort of under-proletariat who can't afford it and don't have that sort of information and don't believe the information, the problem is *believing* the information [...] Breast feeding is a good example erm I can remember erm in [a privileged area] everybody breast feeds for years and years and years. In [a deprived area], everybody thought it was disgusting, you know, absolutely disgusting and I remember one woman said she wouldn't breast feed because she'd been told if [she] did her breasts would shrivel up, you know. There's this horror; horror of bodies really. (Valerie, market customer)

While Valerie recognises a 'huge social class divide in nutrition', this is attributed to bad choices characterised firstly as information deficit, before moving on to undermine her analysis by invoking visceral responses such as a 'horror of bodies' – they *choose* not to believe the information. Moreover, Valerie goes on to speak of families who have 'allowed their children's teeth to go black' in their refusal to accept guidance regarding 'proper nutrition', and is similarly astounded that such families do not have 'cooking pots'. However, despite attempts made to sympathise with structural constraints faced, we detect a discourse prevalent across the interview data with farmers' market customers: a particular view of the 'good' life is upheld in opposition to that which is presented as unsavoury. While Bourdieu argues that expressions of taste betray social position, we see the other side of the coin wherein 'disgust is one manifestation of a bourgeois project to distinguish the middle class from its others, a means of self-constitution' (Lawler, 2005: 443).

So far, we see these market customers making some headway in carving out what they consider to make up the rules of 'proper eating'. Indeed, alternative food as experienced at the farmers' market is central to framing their ideas about 'good food' and the 'good' people that partake in its consumption. Problematising this framing, the following section explores a disjuncture between these professed ideas and their practice, highlighting the symbolic violence produced by such misrecognition of class (Skeggs, 2004).

Disjuncture in Practice: A 'Good' Means of Thinking About Food

Despite suggesting that the consumption of quality food from the market forms a core strategy for enacting their ideas of good practice, market customers also speak of the structural constraints faced in doing so. While shopping at the market is presented as ideal, Catherine admits to shopping regularly at a supermarket. Separation from other supermarket customers is accomplished via reflection over what she describes as the trappings of consumer culture, and her ability to see through promotional deals that encourage unplanned purchases:

> I think the supermarkets have a very bad effect on local communities in many ways really, but making that critique of it is very hard not to be drawn into it yourself [...] and you see all this stuff that you don't actually need, but because of the way that they market it, you think 'oh it might be nice to try that', 'that looks that's new that's different' or 'there's an offer on this' and you buy all this stuff that you don't really, you didn't intend to buy it wasn't on your list [...] 'oh, well that's cheap' you know, 'shall I get a *golf club*' or something (laughter) what am I doing! You know. And I think it's very easy for people to sort of get drawn in to this habit of consumption. Erm, I do get to, you know, buy free range meat at our local butchers occasionally so that's an option. (Catherine, market customer)

Through such self-critique, these narratives suggest discursive means of critically separating their inevitable engagement with oligopolistic market forces and the 'others' who are deemed to engage in such consumer culture due to being simply 'uncritical of cheap food'. Several participants mark their position by virtue of a claim to a taste for a particular aesthetic and feeling of connection attached to local food (Kneafsey et al., 2008), the enjoyment of the atmosphere at the market and their support for local economic development. Indeed, we see that the embeddedness (Murdoch et al., 2000) of local foods plays into dynamics of distinction, achieved not necessarily by practice, but through a different means of *thinking* about food. That is, the farmers' market studied here is not so much a space for the purchase of a substantial proportion of household groceries, but a source of enjoyment and occasional indulgence:

Int: So what brings you to this market then to do your shopping?

S: Sunday dinner mostly isn't it.

C: Yeah, we like the Saturday morning slow meander, do a bit of shopping get a paper,that sort atmosphere, and yeah, nice Sunday dinner. It's a weekend treat.

S: Like what we're doing now.

C: Supplies are running low, we do our shopping on a Monday.

(Sophie and Charlie, market customers)

Taking pleasure in a 'slow meander' through the market is common for market customers. What is being problematised is not the enjoyment experienced via a re-engagement with food, especially given the widely perceived disenchantment with a global food supply chain (Nygård and Storstad, 1998), but the unintended consequences for such alternative food developments. That is, the relative success of this market and other similar initiatives such as box schemes and farm shops brings with it the conflation of particular ideas of 'good' food with a narrow imagining of alternatives to conventional foodways as less privileged consumers are thought to be beyond the pale of inclusion. That is, the dearth of working-class presence in 'alternative' spaces (Guthman, 2008a) is thought to result from financial exclusion (Zepeda, 2009) coupled with disinterest in the wider politics of food.

The following section explores a deeper component of this perceived absence through an examination of talk surrounding food practice among five co-op customers. Just like the market customers, they do not always present a simple class identity, but a narrative of class belonging peppered with references to those from whom they distinguish themselves. Their class position is, then, determined by relational identifications. Much akin to Southerton's (2002) findings, food continues to figure as a resource, marking what is considered reasonable for 'us' relative to 'them'.

Subjects of Disgust: Contesting, Resisting and Compensating

Ken identifies as working class by virtue of his belonging to a 'proper working-class community', and his work in semi-skilled manufacturing. Being a 'down to earth working-class guy' he is separate from the 'poshies' who are characterised as the 'bosses', and who represents typical market customers:

> So when you're in a room of people and they're talking a certain way, you know they're the poshies and they're the middle classes and you shouldn't really be there sort of thing you know that's my feeling. (Ken, co-op customer)

In contrast to Savage et al. (2001), Ken not only articulates an overt class position, but draws a clear boundary between spaces that are 'for' one class and not another, reminding us not to throw out the classed baby with the proverbial bathwater. Rather, we can see that there is recourse to support arguments that class identities are expressed through boundary marking (Bourdieu, 1984; Lamont, 1992; Southerton, 2002) between what is considered appropriate for 'us' and 'them':

> I went round there [the market] one time, like, because I thought they'd have interesting food and stuff, but it was really quite expensive a lot of the stuff it was quite strange I mean even though it's in the [local] area. Most of the people there were quite middle class and it seemed more aimed towards them than the local people [...] I bought one or two things there but they were just, there was a lot of people there wearing afghan stuff and 'hello Rodney' and all this you know [laughs] and then there's me with my [local] accent like, there wasn't much evidence of a [local] accent there like you know and you did feel like, what's this doing? This is not for me, you know. (Ken, co-op customer)

Crucially, the middle-class 'poshies' are identified as the typical customer, inciting his discomfort with this space. Ken also resists the moralising discourse that Skeggs (2004) theorises as a reproachful middle-class gaze. In mocking the accent of market customers, Ken implies that the overt display of a sociality unfamiliar to him effectively undermines what he thought this market to be – 'what's this doing?' The market is not a space he recognises, it is not part of his cultural repertoire and therefore it is not considered 'for' him. In a similar way, Emily dismisses the benefits of consuming organic food by referring to scientific controversies. This dismissal is, however, blemished by admission that she would be 'more conscious' if she were financially able. The structural inhibitions Emily faces are thus compensated through a narrative of scepticism. Under this thick skin of compensation, Emily conflates 'exchange' with 'use' value (Sayer, 2005a), dismissing what may be 'good' and refusing what she is refused:

> A younger friend, they are quite well off financially, erm, so when I go there now she'll like 'oh you know what Helena says about this, well of course this has to be organic', yeah well if I'd had that, then maybe I would be more conscious about it, but I can't be, so let's not worry too much. At the end of the day we could all get sick through hormones in

> meat or whatever, but if it happens it happens. And I, I don't think I'm condemning myself by eating your normal, your average chicken or things like that. (Emily, co-op customer)

It is not so simple to say from this that Emily is a disengaged 'other' who is not interested in food, but that she has limited capacity to engage with alternative food as currently defined. Claire, also a co-op customer, explains her position on healthy eating, patently pointing out that speaking of such efforts is not an attempt at displaying that she is any 'better than anyone else', but suggests she is 'fussy' and 'suspicious' of pre-packaged meals. Indeed, Claire emphasises that she does not judge those who do not cook from scratch, for she used to eat microwave meals herself: 'you have to, life is manic'. Now, she nips in and out of local shops to secure bargains, and purchases meat from a local restaurant supplier. Through connections with friends and family, she provides at least one hot meal a day for herself and her daughter at an affordable price. The co-op presents opportunities for Claire to obtain affordable vegetables, and is also an occasion for her four-year-old daughter to be introduced to a world of food outside of supermarkets. At the co-op, she is able to resolve a perceived contradiction between differing qualities of food:

> All you can really do is try and shop as locally as possible to stop us ending up with a situation where everything is out of town. We do, I mean we should probably care a bit more about organic stuff than we do but I'm a bit cynical in my old age! I don't trust many retailers and I think unless you're growing it yourself then you can't really know that it is organic, sometimes I think in the supermarkets, I think why am I buying these organic runner beans form Kenya when I don't know how many air miles and stuff ... there are just so many things you're supposed to care about aren't there! (Claire, co-op customer)

Contrasting the imagery of working-class consumers put forward by market customers, supporting local enterprise is a theme that occurs across market and co-op customer narratives. Frequenting many different stores, knowing when fresh food will be reduced in price, and where they may secure the best value for their money does not resonate with the imagery of a disengaged food consumer. However, while as a public space the market does not refuse access to anyone per se, the interplay of social, cultural and economic dynamics combine, excluding some by fostering a feeling of discomfort. As Ken suggests, the absence of local accents and the sense that many of the other customers are acquainted brings with it a feeling of not belonging. Being excluded on the grounds of price is, then, but one part of this story.

Furthermore, Samantha grows her own food, a practice rooted in family tradition passed on from her grandfather. When speaking of composting waste and growing fruit and vegetables, she not only provides rebuttal to the imagery of the 'disgusting' (Lawler, 2005) working-class subject, but positions *her* way of engaging with contemporary 'food politics' (Micheletti and Stolle, 2007) as more genuine than her middle-class counterparts, whom she suggests engage merely 'to be trendy'. In laying the foundations for this appeal, Samantha brands 'alternative' consumers as 'worthies'; people who display and preach of their political efforts. Crucially, these 'worthies' are defined as those whom she imagines see themselves as superior to her position as a 'working-class girl':

> I think there's a whole kind of group of hidden green people who don't wear hemp and kind of [...] they're not overtly green, who make green choices *most* of the time but are quite pragmatic about it. I think I probably fall in that camp but you know [...] we don't kind of wear it on our sleeve literally. And you know therefore I just think I'm not going as far as some other people who are out there in kind of kaftans and long skirts and beads [...] there's a guy I used to work with that really is quite green and [...] he was quite critical and I was like 'for goodness sakes ... I compost, and you're criticising me for using a water-based paint with a tiny bit of solvent it in you know ... get a grip' so yeah he was interesting, one of those annoying types who's just *way* too worthy! (Samantha, co-op customer)

Recounting further experience of 'worthy' others, Samantha speaks of the 'yoga Mums' who contravene her pragmatic and private engagement with 'green' issues. While not speaking directly to issues of food, Samantha employs these examples in illustrating her position as a pragmatic rather than a 'worthy' consumer. Indeed, it is through this narrative – outlining her experience of this 'worthy' gaze – that she accomplishes her account of growing food and composting as a rebuttal to judgements made by those whom she suggests are concerned with display over substantive action:

> She [a 'Yoga Mum'] gets a bit kind of full on about re-usable nappies which is a bit of a cheek because she's only just started to use them [...] and well some of us have been using them quietly without making a big deal about it for months! [...] When she makes a green decision everybody knows about it and all of a sudden any other way is not right. (Samantha, co-op customer)

This appeal to authenticity (Vannini, 2009) acts as a tool for rebuttal, resisting the imagery of the inadequate consumer by pointing to the artificiality of the market. Skeggs (2004) might argue this is a tool of anti-pretentiousness, of refusing what we are refused. Rhydian is similarly critical of the farmers' market as a space for conspicuous performance of ideals, a claim he makes from observations as an occasional customer himself:

> It just feels stereotypical, people make an effort to go on their bikes, and I don't know many of those people go everywhere on their bikes or whether they just feel like '*oh you should*' and you take your plastic bags there and your recycled bags and make a bit of an effort there, and I don't know maybe if people carry that on in everyday of their life [...] It just feels a bit artificial I suppose, but maybe I'm just looking at myself, and everyone else lives their lives like that all the time. (Rhydian, market and co-op customer)

While such competing claims are part of the scene of everyday life and talk, with actors having what Potter (2010) terms their 'stake' in the matter of 'good food', this article seeks not to adjudicate such claims. The analysis serves to highlight spaces of alternative food consumption as such a contested and classed space, pointing to consequences for future alternative food developments. Indeed, is it so simple that excluded consumers are content to remain so, on the basis that they are refusing an affectation? This is problematised by the notion that somewhere underneath the 'thick skin' of compensation (Southerton, 2002) 'alternative' food is valued. The ways in which it has been appropriated by middle-class consumers, however, is not. In Sayer's (2005b) words, they may not be merely refusing what is 'posh' but also what is 'good'.

Conclusions: Separating the 'Posh' from the 'Good'

To recap, market customers present imagery of others as not wishing to engage with 'alternative' food practice as they are instead perceived as committed to a conspicuously consumptive vision of the 'good life' – they make *choices* between spending money on 'pints of cider' or 'good food'. Following the analysis of data presented above, we might consider another explanation for their absence: their discomfort with what is perceived as a space not 'for them' (Southerton, 2002). For market customers such as Sophie and Charlie, the market provides a space for sociality, while it is considered both laughable and uncomfortable for co-op customers such as Ken and Samantha. Although middle and working-class consumers each find some fault with the practices of the 'other' as either repugnant or ridiculous, we should take seriously that it is the derision expressed by middle-class consumers that goes hand-in-hand with the association of 'good' food with *their* food practices. It is this very insistence that resounds in the development of 'alternative' food initiatives such as the market studied here, driving a narrow view of future alternatives, which Guthman and DuPuis (2006) suggest reproduces a white, middle-class 'politics of perfection'. Having explored the accounts of co-op customers, it may not even be so simple as to suggest that working-class consumers may feel excluded culturally, but the compensatory strategies (Southerton, 2002) developed to cope with such exclusion render the idea of developing one all-encompassing strategy for 'alternative' food provision as incongruous; an argument I develop elsewhere more fully (Paddock, 2015).

Indeed, while Bourdieu (1984) argued that it is common for those who are refused certain goods to refuse what they are refused, it is not unreasonable to imagine the future refusal of alternative food developments. In refusing these goods that are culturally legitimised, they 'not only invite the scorn of the dominant in so doing, they also confirm their refusal of internal goods which are valuable regardless of whether the dominant happen to value them' (Sayer, 2005b: 121). Of sociological note here is that to imagine an equitable and sustainable food future, we might suggest that the 'posh' be separated from the 'good' by taking seriously the difference between 'use' and 'exchange' value in alternative food initiatives. Some goods are valuable not simply because others regard them so, but are 'good' because they offer nutrition, shelter or comfort. Recognising the field of alternative food consumption as a highly differentiated terrain may encourage a shift towards imagining alternatives that do not appeal solely to a middle-class realm of cultural comfort. To pursue strategies that create separations between what is considered food for 'us' and food for 'them' (Southerton, 2002) is to continue to misrecognise class in a way that secures, for the more privileged, practical advantages of the field of 'alternative' food consumption, of what is 'good' and not what is simply 'posh'. This is not to suggest that markets and community co-operatives do not have significant roles to play in providing a platform for community sociability and for providing a means to access fresh food. Rather, it remains to recognise whose communities are being served, whose are excluded, and to what effect.

Taking on board a critical amendment of Bourdieu's approach as proposed by Sayer (2005a), this article considers class as a normative expression of position. That is, in exploring what *matters* to people, we are able to discern normative manifestations of class culture, rather than commenting only upon affiliation with class categories (Payne and Grew, 2005). Not only a first need of the human body, the moralised terrain surrounding consumption lays bare the highly charged nature of food as a carrier of our culture (Douglas and Isherwood, 1996), embodying more or less what Sennett and Cobb (1972) describe as the hidden injuries of class. In moralising the 'other' for not consuming 'good' food, we misrecognise the harsh realities faced by many in feeding themselves and their families. Indeed, watching and listening to people go about their food shopping, it becomes clear that food carries along with it the hopes and desires about how we would like to live, while the imagined food practices of 'others' can become the subject of pride, envy, discomfort and derision. Competing claims as to the authenticity of one's food practice make fertile ground for further research.

In this way, a Bourdieusian conceptualisation of 'position' is useful in highlighting the nuances of uptake and discomfort at work in a field of alternative food consumption. Exploring such nuances, albeit through one case study, begins the process of recognising class difference and its role in mediating the development of alternative, more sustainable and inclusive food practices for the future. This article provides some armoury to this call, and points towards a future research agenda concerned with exploring the potential to realise a more reflexive form of localism (DuPuis and Goodman, 2005) that takes into account the diversity of positions, tastes and worldviews that shape what may come to be considered reasonable food. Indeed, we may move beyond a limited 'politics of the possible' (Guthman, 2008b), recognising that farmers' markets provide a means of engaging predominantly white middle-class consumers. It might not be sufficient to expect that diverse populations can or will engage on these same terms. Recognising this dynamic is one step in lifting the symbolic violence governing alternative food developments. As Lawler (2005: 443) observes, 'It is important, in other words, to challenge an unmarked and unproblematized middles classness which claims a monopoly on true humanity'.

FUNDING

This research was funded by the ESRC (PTA031200600081) doctoral research programme, which was completed at Cardiff University's School of Social Sciences. I would particularly like to thank Susan Baker and Bella Dicks who supported this work from inception. I am also grateful to two anonymous reviewers for their insightful observations, and to Alan Warde for commenting on final drafts of this paper.

NOTES

1. Space for discussing the survey data is limited, and given the intention of this article to explore position-taking through talk, survey data briefly introduces the socio-demographic composition of each site.
2. 'Terroir' indicates the specificity of place, and often translates into the practice of matching the foods and wines of a region's complete environment.
3. A brand of frozen convenience food.

REFERENCES

1. Adams M, Raisborough J (2008) What can sociology say about FairTrade? Class, reflexivity and ethical consumption. Sociology 42: 1165–1182.
2. Arce A, Marsden TK (1993) The social construction of international food: A new research agenda. Economic Geography 69: 293–311.
3. Atkinson P, Hammersley M (1994) Ethnography and participant observation. In: Denzin NK, Lincoln YS (eds) The Handbook of Qualitative Research. London: Sage.
4. Bennett T, Savage M, Warde A, Gayo-Cal M, Wright D (2009) Culture, Class, Distinction. London/New York: Routledge. Bourdieu P (1984) Distinction: A Social Critique of the Judgement of Taste. Cambridge, MA: Harvard University Press.
5. Bourdieu P (1990) The Logic of Practice. Cambridge: Polity Press.
6. Bugge AB, Almås R (2006) Domestic dinner representations and practices of a proper meal among young suburban mothers. Journal of Consumer Culture 6: 203–228.
7. DeVault ML (1991) Feeding the Family: The Social Organization of Caring as Gendered Work. Chicago, IL: University of Chicago Press.
8. Douglas M, Isherwood B (1996) The World of Goods: Towards an Anthropology of Consumption. London: Routledge.
9. DuPuis EM, Goodman D (2005) Should we go 'home' to eat? Toward a reflexive politics of localism. Journal of Rural Studies 21: 359–371
10. Elias N (1978) The Civilizing Process. New York: Urizen Books.
11. Evans D (2011) Blaming the consumer – once again: The social and material contexts of everyday food waste practices in some English households. Critical Public Health 21: 429–440.
12. Goodman D, Goodman MK (2009) Food networks, alternative. In: Thrift RK (ed.) International Encyclopedia of Human Geography. Oxford: Elsevier, 208–220.
13. Guthman J (2008a) Bringing good food to others: Investigating the subjects of alternative food practice. Cultural Geographies 15: 431–447.
14. Guthman J (2008b) Neoliberalism and the making of food politics in California. Geoforum 39: 1171–1183.

15. Guthman J, DuPuis M (2006) Embodying neoliberalism: Economy, culture, and the politics of fat. Environment and Planning D 24: 427–448

16. Harrison R, Newholm T, Shaw D (2005) The Ethical Consumer. Thousand Oaks, CA: Sage.

17. Harvey D (1990) The Condition of Postmodernity: An Enquiry into the Origins of Cultural Change. Oxford: Blackwell

18. Hinrichs C, Kremer KS (2002) Social inclusion in a Midwest local food system project. Journal of Poverty 6: 65–90.

19. Jackson T (2006) The Earthscan Reader in Sustainable Consumption. London/Sterling, VA: Earthscan.

20. Kneafsey M, Cox R, Holloway L, Dowler E, Venn L, Tuomainen H (2008) Reconnecting Consumers, Producers and Food Exploring Alternatives. Oxford: Berg

21. Lamont M (1992) Money, Morals, and Manners: The Culture of the French and American Upper-Middle Class. Chicago, IL: University of Chicago Press.

22. Lawler S (2005) Disgusted subjects: The making of middle-class identities. The Sociological Review 53: 429–446.

23. Littler J (2009) Radical Consumption: Shopping for Change in Contemporary Culture. Maidenhead: Open University Press/McGraw-Hill Education.

24. Lyon S, Moberg M (2010) Fair Trade and Social Justice: Global Ethnographies. New York: New York University Press.

25. Mellor J, Blake M, Crane L (2010) 'When I'm doing dinner parties I don't go for the Tesco's cheeses': Gendered class distinctions, friendship and home entertaining. Food, Culture & Society 13: 115–134.

26. Mennell S (1985) All Manners of Food: Eating and Taste in England and France from the Middle Ages to the Present. Oxford/New York: Blackwell.

27. Micheletti M, Stolle D (2007) Mobilizing consumers to take responsibility for global social justice. The Annals of the American Academy of Political and Social Science 611: 157–175.

28. Miele M, Murdoch J (2002) The practical aesthetics of traditional cuisines: Slow food in Tuscany. Sociologia Ruralis 42: 312–328.

29. Murcott A (1983) The Sociology of Food and Eating: Essays on the Sociological Significance of Food. Aldershot: Gower.

30. Murdoch J, Marsden T, Banks J (2000) Quality, nature, and embeddedness: Some theoretical considerations in the context of the food sector. Economic Geography 76: 107–125.

31. Nützenadel A, Trentmann F (2008) Food and Globalization: Consumption, Markets and Politics in the Modern World. Oxford: Berg.

32. Nygård B, Storstad O (1998) De-globalization of food markets? Consumer perceptions of safe food: The case of Norway. Sociologia Ruralis 38: 35–53.

33. Paddock J (2015) Invoking simplicity: 'Alternative' food and the reinvention of distinction. Sociologia Ruralis 55(1): 22–40.

34. Payne G, Grew C (2005) Unpacking 'class ambivalence': Some conceptual and methodological issues in accessing class cultures. Sociology 39: 893–910.

35. Potter J (2010) Representing Reality: Discourse, Rhetoric and Social Construction. Thousand Oaks, CA: Sage

36. Sassatelli R, Davolio F (2010) Consumption, pleasure and politics: Slow Food and the politico-aesthetic problematization of food. Journal of Consumer Culture 10: 202–232.

37. Savage M, Bagnall G, Longhurst B (2001) Ordinary, ambivalent and defensive: Class identities in the Northwest of England. Sociology 35: 875–892.

38. Sayer A (2005a) Class, moral worth and recognition. Sociology 39: 947–963.

39. Sayer RA (2005b) The Moral Significance of Class. Cambridge: Cambridge University Press.

40. Sayer A (2011) Why Things Matter to People: Social Science, Values and Ethical Life. Cambridge: Cambridge University Press.

41. Sennett R, Cobb J (1972) The Hidden Injuries of Class. New York: Knopf.

42. Skeggs B (2004) Class, Self, Culture. London: Routledge.

43. Slater D (1997) Consumer Culture and Modernity. Cambridge: Polity Press.

44. Slocum R (2008) Thinking race through corporeal feminist theory: Divisions and intimacies at the Minneapolis Farmers' Market. Social & Cultural Geography 9: 849–869.

45. Southerton D (2002) Boundaries of 'us' and 'them': Class, mobility and identification in a new town. Sociology 36: 171–193.

46. Vannini P (2009) Authenticity in Culture, Self, and Society. Farnham: Ashgate.

47. Varul MZ (2009) Ethical selving in cultural contexts: Fairtrade consumption as an everyday ethical practice in the UK and Germany. International Journal of Consumer Studies 33: 183–189.

48. Veblen T (1994) The Theory of the Leisure Class. New York: Dover Publications.

49. Warde A (1997) Consumption, Food, and Taste: Culinary Antinomies and Commodity Culture. London: Sage.

50. Warde A, Martens L (2000) Eating Out: Social Differentiation, Consumption and Pleasure. Cambridge: Cambridge University Press.

51. Wheeler K (2012) Fair Trade and the Citizen-Consumer: Shopping for Justice? New York: Palgrave Macmillan.

52. Wills W, Backett-Milburn K, Roberts M-L, . (2011) The framing of social class distinctions through family food and eating practices. The Sociological Review 59: 725–740.

53. Young M, Willmott P (1957) Family and Kinship in East London. London: Routledge and Kegan Paul.

54. Zepeda L (2009) Which little piggy goes to market? Characteristics of US farmers' market shoppers. International Journal of Consumer Studies 33: 250–257.

55. Zukin S (2008) Consuming authenticity: From outposts of difference to means of exclusion. Cultural Studies 22: 724–748.

56. Jessica Paddock joined the University of Manchester's Sustainable Consumption Institute in 2014 from Cardiff University. Her research explores inequalities, cultural differentiation and food security in the context of environmental change. Previous projects have included the study of alternative food networks in the UK and social-natural scientific research on the links between ecosystem services and food security in the Caribbean. Current research is exploring changes and continuities in patterns of eating out in the

UK over the last 20 years, gathering insights as to how systems of food provision may be re-configured to be more sustainable.

2

CHAPTER

Household Consumption and Environmental Change: Rethinking the Policy Problem through Narratives of Food Practice

Jessica Paddock

Sustainable Places Research Institute, Cardiff University, UK;

Sustainable Consumption Institute, The University of Manchester, UK

ABSTRACT

Central to debates concerned with societal transition towards low-carbon living is the imperative to encourage individual subjects to shift their behaviours to support less consumptive ways of life: eating less meat, consuming less energy and water, and wasting less of what we do consume. Exploring narratives derived from 30 interviews with householders living in and around a UK city, this article considers the dynamics surrounding consumption, unpacking the notion that consumers act as agents of choice. Drawing on accounts of daily routines, the article pays close attention to the complexity of social, cultural and material factors that shape narratives of daily life, where food emerges as a core organising principle. This suggests that food practice provides a nexus point around which change can be more effectively conceptualised for public policies aimed at inculcating more sustainable ways of life. That is, through an understanding of food practice, we can explore means of locking and unlocking wider practices deemed unsustainable.

Keywords Consumption, sustainability, food, practice, policy

INTRODUCTION

Evidence presented by the United Nation's Intergovernmental Panel on Climate Change (UN IPCC) Fifth Assessment Report (IPCC, 2013) points to the unequivocal warming of the climate system. As planetary boundaries are increasingly transgressed, thus threatening humanity's safe operating space (Rockström et al., 2009), the sustainable development agenda (Bruntland, 1987) gathers momentum in integrating environmental, economic and social concerns into a new development paradigm (Baker, 2006), especially as Sustainable Development Goals replace Millennium Development Goals (Leach, 2013).

Extensive works in environmental social science (Macnaghten, 1998; Pretty et al., 2007; Redclift and Woodgate, 2010) undertaken over the last three decades are testament to a mounting contribution, which leads Wainwright (2011) to suggest that sociology is 'warming' to the study of climate change. Indeed, Urry (2011) makes the case for turning the sociological imagination towards issues of global environmental change that have until now been largely debated by the behavioural and natural sciences (Yearley, 2009), where the focus tends to lie with the relationship between attitudes and actions of individual social actors (Anable et al., 2006; Lorenzoni and Pidgeon, 2006). This article unpacks this problem framing by turning to an alternative conceptualisation as offered by theories of practice (Warde, 2005). Having outlined the methodological approach, the article then presents 10 consumer narratives pertaining to daily routines, thus adding further insight as to the location of food practices as a nexus point around which further daily life practices coalesce. Around such a nexus point, it is argued that change towards more sustainable ways of accomplishing daily life may be better understood. Such an alternative problem representation (Bacchi, 2009) offers a novel approach for public policy seeking to inculcate changes in the face of numerous sustainability challenges presented by a changing climate.

THE UNSUSTAINABLE CONSUMER AS A PUBLIC POLICY PROBLEM

Central to debates concerned with societal transition towards low-carbon living is the imperative to encourage individual subjects to shift their behaviours to support more sustainable ways of life. Changing the landscape of political participation is the citizen-consumer who translates moral virtues into marketplace activities. They are thought to represent a new mode of governance for the consumer age (Ryan, 2001; Trentmann, 2007) where interventions such as green labelling allow for engaged public participation (Boström, 2008). Should such ethical and political consumerism offer, as Soper (2007) argues, a means for realising an alternative vision of consumption as the 'good life', political consumerism comes to represent an *individualised form of collective action* (Micheletti, 2003).

Stemming a critique of this approach, Miller and Rose (1997) find in their case study of archives from the Tavistock Institute of Human Relations – for whom a key concern throughout the post Second World War was to understand what mobilises consumers towards a fulfilment of needs via certain consumer products – that the struggle to 'make-up' and comprehend the consumer was no simple matter of understanding rational choices. Rather,

> in order for a relation to be formed between the individual and the product, a complex and hybrid assemblage had to be inaugurated, in which forces and flows imagined to issue from within the psyche of persons of particular ages, genders or social sectors were linked up to possibilities and promises that might be discerned within particular commodities, as they were organised within a little set of everyday routines and habits of life. (Miller and Rose, 1997: 41)

In other words, the consumer represents a highly problematic entity, whose actions result from the dynamic interaction of agency and structure (Giddens, 1984; Bourdieu, 1990). From the data analysed, this article takes forward this conceptualisation by drawing upon sociological framings of everyday life practices (Reckwitz, 2002; Schatzki, 2010; Shove et al., 2012) and the 'ordinary consumption' entailed (Gronow, 2001). Doing so critically explores a dominant framing in public policy, that poor choices made by individuals are at the root of the problem of unsustainability. Indeed, current policy interventions such as 'nudge', as championed by Sunstein and Thaler (2008), have taken the individual as the root of the problem to be solved. As Bacchi (2009) argues, how a problem is represented shapes the policy response, and over time, the very problem itself (Billings and Hermann, 1998).

Many authors, including Warde (2005) and Shove (2010), argue for a practice orientation in exploring consumption, which offers an alternative means of framing the problem of the unsustainable consumer. A practice is understood a routinised behaviour made up of several interconnecting elements: bodily actions, mental activity, emotional meaning, materials 'things' and background knowledge or 'know-how' (Reckwitz, 2002). A practice-theoretical lens offers a means of exploring the interaction between our attitudes and the world around us, understood as producing particular ways of acting, saying and doing. Thus, we refocus away from individual behaviours, attitudes and mental processes of rational calculation as the engine of social life. For example, domestic technologies themselves such as washing machines, tumble dryers and cooking devices have been understood to reconfigure and reproduce practices over time. For Hand et al. (2005) domestic technologies become implicated in 'the choreography of things and people in time and space' (p. 680). Here, the material, spatial and temporal organisation of the home affects what people come to *do* within their home, shaping what becomes normal over time – washing and drying clothes more often, purchasing and freezing larger amounts of food. In asking how it is that a group of office dwellers might be dislodged from the expectations of having an ambient and controlled indoor temperature at work, Hitchings (2011) suggests that it is not so simple as to frame such expectation as a matter of individual choice. Rather, 'as a consequence of being recruited into particular patterns of comparatively habitual behaviour' (Hitchings, 2011: 2839), these office dwellers interact with embodied sensibilities (the proclivity to appropriate work attire), habitual modes of thought (social context) and physical infrastructure (the ambient environment itself). Arguing for a fuller account of how these elements combine in producing everyday actions – embodied sensibilities, habits and infrastructure – it becomes nascent to think of individuals as addicted to thermal standards, but to think of a wider system that guides and shapes such ideas of comfort.

Within the home, Truninger (2011) explores changing competences in the kitchen, where cooks are recruited to the practice of cooking with 'Bimby' – a multi-functional 'Thermomix' food processor. Here, the interplay between images or 'embodied sensibilities', technologies and competences afford new possibilities for cooking in daily life. Similarly, Wheeler (2012) employs a practice-theoretical approach in exploring preference for Fairtrade goods via interviews facilitated with a collection of respondents' shopping receipts. Here, Wheeler (2012) argues that consuming Fairtrade is enacted as a bundle of 'doings and sayings' (p. 132). Just as Reckwitz (2002) points to the nature of individuals as the 'crossing points' of practices, the purchase of Fairtrade goods forms part of a wider comingling of routines, preferences and social norms that produce a moment of consumption as part of wider practice performances. With further regard to food, Evans (2011) suggests that household food waste is a product of particular social and material conditions that have become culturally, socially and materially embedded in day-to-day life. For example, conventions that surround feeding the family include adherence to rules around the constitution of a 'proper' meal (DeVault, 1991) and conventions as to how ingredients are safely stored. In preparing such a meal, food packaging norms may restrict our ability to select exactly the amount required, leading to overprovision.

Given that the experience-oriented narratives elicited in this study often turn without prompt to the topic of food, this article argues that food provides a nexus point around which policy interventions towards sustainability may be better understood. This is not to say that judgements are being made as to what sorts of consumption practices are better than others. Indeed, Born and Purcell (2006) and Edwards-Jones et al. (2008) each make a strong case that local food, for example is not necessarily more sustainable than their global counterpart. Nor is it possible to distinguish easily between the merits of alternative and more conventional mechanisms of food supply, as argued by Sonnino and Marsden (2006). Moreover, while food has received much empirical and theoretical attention with regard to food production and supply chains (Goodman, 2003), Eden et al. (2008) suggest that studies have tended to focus heavily on production and points of consumption, while largely neglecting consumers themselves. This article explores and embraces this notion of complexity and contradiction, and in so doing, continues to problematise the notion of consumer choice by drawing on accounts of daily routines and the connections between them. Here, food figures as a prominent organising principle in daily life, suggestive of a fertile ground for research that seeks to go beyond debate over the advantages of a particular logic of production or supply over another, and instead looking at consumers as the carriers of practices. Exploring food as a nexus thus furthers understandings of how practices come to be locked and unlocked by virtue of their interaction with wider rhythms of daily life.

METHODS

Statistics compiled from the 2001 census are used to identify areas of different demographic composition: students, families, retired, unemployed or professional residents as well as differences in the housing itself; semi-detached, terraced, apartments. Leaflets were distributed through letterboxes, followed by door-knocking, recruiting 30 participants in total. While we would expect there to be class differences across households, and that these would affect the organisation of food practices, discussion of this is reserved for elsewhere, for this article makes no comparisons between households and their householders at this stage. Instead, the paper concentrates upon the broader themes that emerged from the data, and across all types of households and areas sampled. It is around each of these three themes that the empirical section of this article is organised in order to allow space to more fully explore the food practices themselves, regardless of social and cultural differentiation at this stage.

During interview, participants were asked to speak of daily routines, from which we gain an insight not only as to how participants speak of habitual practices, but also of the sets of relationships and structures around which daily life becomes organised, understood and reproduced. That is, we address the semantics of narrated 'experience', and not the syntax of 'storied' events (Andrews et al., 2008: 41). Moreover, by focusing upon routines centred in and around the home, this analysis makes a contribution to work that seeks to rescue understandings of household consumption from being reduced to either the mundane act of provisioning the home (Lunt and Livingstone, 1992) or at the other extreme, as a political act (Micheletti and Stolle, 2007). Instead, consumption is a 'moment' in almost every practice (Warde, 2005). The 'stuff' (Miller, 2010) that we accumulate is more than the realisation of what may widely be considered superficial consumerist frenzy, but as materials figured in the accomplishment of practices that make up social life. From the equipment necessitated by leisure pursuits such as Nordic walking (Shove and Pantzar, 2005), different cycling practices and ways of doing dinner parties (Mellor et al., 2010), consumption comes to be seen as less about the meaningless accumulation of goods by disaffected consumers and more as the embodiment of social life in material culture.

From this perspective, it is therefore imperative to understand how, for example, carbon emissions reductions are to be met not through the chastisement and penalisation of high consumption of goods and services, but to understand the practices that *demand* consumption. Supporting comprehensive work that seeks to re-frame policy responses to consumer behaviour (Spurling et al., 2013), we look at such complex dynamics between social meanings, competencies and material culture through narratives that highlight both the fixity and interconnectedness of daily routines as well as accounts of changed practices hinged upon shifts in the life course. While Wheeler (2012) encouraged discussions of daily routines via the use of shopping receipts, this study interviewed people in their homes in order to facilitate dialogue concerning around household provisioning as then related to activities outside of the home. Doing so is an established means of discovering the contexts in which change occurs in daily life, as participants reflect on present as well as the past in speaking through biographical transitions (Southerton, 2006). In this way, the qualitative interview reconstructs practice through the participants' narrative, that is, as they make sense of their daily lives and routines through talk (Holstein and Gubrim, 2004; Mason, 2002). While such an approach may invite criticism on the grounds that narrative methods privilege the voice of the individual and neglects the materiality of the world around them, Riessman (2008) reminds us that narrative is as much about making sense of how the world around us shapes our practices and experiences as well as making sense of how we experience this world. Understanding the location of the individual experience within a practice is not the same as taking a methodologically individualistic ontological view. While care is taken here to suggest any generalisability of these findings, I stress that the narratives discussed provide an avenue for further exploration. Exploring in detail the accounts of 10 out of 30 participants allows for insights as to how they make sense of change in their lives, the potential for success in these endeavours and the internal as well as external the conflicts associated with them. Conversely, we then explore narratives that account for life-course changes and critical 'moments' (Hards, 2011), such as becoming a parent or moving home that ripple across a number of interlocking practices, highlighting the temporality and rhythm of food practice that render them both resistant and open to changes in practice. The decision to select narratives from 10 out of 30 participants is made on the basis that these participants express most succinctly a dynamic prevalent across the data, that food-related practices figure prominently in the organisation and patterning of daily life. There is simply too little space to explore fully the multitude of ways in which such dynamics find expression. However, the three themes below arise from analysis of all 30 interviews, which were coded in Nvivo as a means to organise the data. The following themes are the richest and the most prominent codes to emerge from the data.

NARRATIVES OF ROUTINE

Fixity and fluidity

Alan is a research assistant in his late twenties lodging in a terraced suburb of the city. He feels he is stuck in a 'bad routine'. Having spent years attempting to 'live better' Alan speaks of his struggle to live up to how he feels his life should be organised, finding it difficult to put his ideal lifestyle into practice. Indeed, Alan highlights how change requires a number of elements to each fall serendipitously into place with one another:

> Well because first of all it's a symptom of being disorganised and in a bad routine of, probably going to bed too late and getting up too late and

> if I just decided to ... I mean I having said that I tend to go through periods of living really well and really disciplined with a good routine. There might be a few months where I basically wake up in the morning have a couple of apples for breakfast after that when I'm in work, use the gym at work and then feel really good and have a small lunch and usually rustle up a fairly healthy dinner but other times if for some reason I let it go a little bit and tumble into a bad routine again. At this point now in order to become a creature of routine I try to actually arbitrarily say right, this is gonna be my week. So in that respect it's a schedule that I hope will become routine.

Here, Alan even begins to suggest that he might learn to be a little less disorganised if only he had the impetus to decide to do so, before recounting periods in which he considers himself to have succeeded. In teasing out what it is that knocks Alan from these newly formed routines, he speaks of periods of illness, changing work patterns and moving house. Living with different people, for Alan, has inspired changes in ways of eating in the past, such as eating predominantly vegan food while living with vegan housemates. Once he moved on from this house-share, he also slid back into eating meat, fish and dairy. While he might have possessed the social impetus to eat vegan while living with vegan housemates, this embodied sensibility did not travel with him, nor did the knowledge of vegan cooking practices carried by his past housemates. Therefore, we might suggest that the decision to live more healthily is not sufficient enough a motivation to drive such a lifestyle change. As Mylan (2014) argues, based on her analysis of laundry and lighting, elements of a practice interconnect with other practice elements and do so in a manner that can be described as tightly or loosely coupled, with differing outcomes in the uptake of innovations in these fields. In this case, we can see that elements of Alan's vegan practice are only loosely coupled with interconnecting practices related to housing dynamics and infrastructure, work and emotional associations. From this, it is argued that exploring the number of elements holding together a routine, we can see both the potential steadfastness and fragility of practices as tied temporally to daily rhythms and life-course events, depending on the strength of the relationship between interconnecting practice elements.

Similarly for Francesca, a radiographer in her mid-twenties, living in a rented terraced home, daily life is arranged around work-shift patterns. Rotas for clothes washing and drying, vacuuming and cleaning the bathroom clearly mark responsibilities for chores shared with her housemates. Cooking remains an individual undertaking. Indeed, her set daily routine allows for the successful enactment of the many practices that support her way of life, such as cooking and freezing meals in individual portions ready to be defrosted and re-heated upon her return from work.

Without the freezer, Francesca suggests she would be at a loss as to how to negotiate the various pressures and demands upon her time. If this routine is disrupted, Francesca tends to opt for 'take-aways and stuff, when I just can't face cooking, or forgot to prepare in advance'. The social conventions of shared living, knowledge of food preparation and storage, coupled with the convenience offered by supporting technologies such as the slow-cooker and the freezer together produce a repeated pattern of activities that in time have developed into routines that might prove difficult to undo.

Similarly, Connie and William – a retired couple in their late eighties living in terraced house within a residential zone of the city – speak of changes and continuities across their lifetime. Connie and William speak of life lived together over the last 60 years in their house, which they claim has 'not changed much over the years'. Their house has not undergone structural alteration, and their furnishings have been acquired over time, necessitating very little in the way of replacement and refurbishment. Much like the other three elderly couples interviewed, their retirement period has cemented a set of routinised practices: exercise classes, lunch with friends in a local club, time with grandchildren, and walks around the park and going out for Sunday dinner. They eat 'full hot meals' at their social club, and tend only to prepare small or cold meals at home: 'sandwiches, soup, or a jacket potato'. Each activity has a set day and time allocation, and its repetition seems only to be at risk in the case of ill-health. Crucially, the only interruptions capable of dislodging and forming new routines, or the slippage into old ones noted across the sample, are those brought by wider shifts in the life course, generally shaped by life events such as marriage, divorce, the arrival of a child or moving home.

Moments for change

As well documented in social scientific research, life-course events provide fertile ground for changes in practices (Marshall and Anderson, 2002; Plessz et al., 2014; Shirani and Henwood, 2011). For Samantha, having a child 'changed everything'. While working professionals, she and her partner were well practised in arriving home late in the evening, eating take-away food or 'something quick' like a ready-bought microwaveable meal or an omelette. They now eat home-cooked food 'from scratch'. Indeed, the time at home afforded by a period of maternity facilitated local shopping at several points throughout the week. Importantly, Samantha's ability to structure childcare around local food shopping is made possible by her location. Living on the outskirts of the town centre, she is situated near to a number of grocers, small supermarkets, butchers and delicatessen. Walking to local shops is built into wider daily routines of visiting the park, attending appointments and meeting friends. As noted by Halkier (2009), each cooking performance may play out differently as the practitioner enacts different styles of cooking in different contexts: the improvised, the planned, the healthy or the manageable meal. Indeed, Samantha does not visit local shops everyday. While such performances may vary, the ways in which such performances rely upon interconnecting elements and wider interconnecting practices is, however, unfaltering.

In contrast to Samantha, Lydia makes trips by car to an out-of-town supermarket to provision her home. These are trips made while her daughter is taking part in play clubs and at nursery school, afforded also by the flexibility of working as a self-employed physiotherapist. This contrasts to her routine prior to motherhood of provisioning the home through one large weekly shop at a supermarket, which she is now unable to complete, for her child, she claims, will 'act up' if too long a time is spent on one activity. To satisfy these needs, Lydia makes several short trips to the supermarket in conjunction with the completion of further daily tasks such as visiting parents living in a nearby village, tending to clients and caring for her child. It is clear that any shift in behaviour is hinged upon the coming together of several elements of other daily routines and practices. This dynamic is familiar to Jenny, another first-time mother living in the same area:

> now that I'm at home more, I do a lot more cooking. When we were working we didn't need a fridge full, we would just nip across the road and get dinner, and now we have a big fridge full.

Indeed, being at home makes planning meals easier, and a bigger shop at a supermarket fills the fridge with ingredients for meals planned and prepared in advance to enable its eating to coincide with their young baby being asleep. However, 'before we'd have more things like stir-fry's and quick-to-cook things when I come in from work. Now I can turn it on and leave it on, but I can't be at the cooker, cooking all the time'. Just as Alan and Francesca have negotiated moments in which food preparation and consumption takes place in relation to their work day, Samantha and Lydia achieve similar tasks in different ways. Crucially, in each case, practices of food consumption are always but an element of wider set routines geared towards childcare, work as well as social and family commitments, highlighting the social flow of food-related practices, which arguably cannot be understood as contingent entirely upon individual agency and choice. We also see that different infrastructures are implicated in reproducing routines of food procurement, preparation and consumption. Cars play lesser or more prominent roles depending on location relative to the city as well as the presence and efficacy of public transport infrastructure. Changing cooking practices is therefore clearly linked to life-course events such as changing work patterns, cohabitation, and the arrival of a child. Cutting across such moments are altered driving patterns, the purchase of new domestic technologies such as a tumble dryers or a larger fridge/freezer. Concurrent with the findings of Butler et al. (2014) in their analysis of energy consumption and daily life, such shifts are not, however, presented as rational decisions to drive more or to consume more energy, but appear to be considered as the consequence of their daily life demands. Resources, skills and standards are reconfigured, renegotiated and reconsidered as part of the recruitment to new practices and/or their defection from another. The practice 'block' (Reckwitz, 2002), therefore, is undone by the loss of connection between different elements of that routine. While Alan reflects on his routines as locked because he finds it difficult to achieve changes he would like to make to his daily routines, we see here that practices are also somewhat fluid. Under certain circumstances, they would be entirely unlocked and reconfigured.

For example, following separation from her partner, Mary moved from the inner city to the outer suburbs. While Mary purports to have always been interested in 'green living', she has found that previously entrenched practices were uprooted when, having split from her partner, she moved house. Mary attributes the different supporting infrastructure now surrounding her in accounting for her lapse in commitment to local food shopping, for example,

> What else do I do? I've been doing it so long, I don't even think about it. I used to be far more extreme in terms of not wanting to go to supermarkets and stuff but here it's much more difficult. When I lived in town it would be easier, I could go to the market and stuff, but I try and think about producers rather than big supermarkets.

While Mary lived near the city centre, she was able to undertake a degree of local shopping as part of a wider routine involved in the travel to and from her place of work. Her daily routines would take her past a number of independently owned shops and grocers, meaning that a visit to the supermarket was but a rare event, performed monthly in order to stock the store cupboard. However, the routines that worked together in upholding the practice of home cooking have fallen away with following a separation from her partner. To inculcate a new set of routines, Mary is re-imagining not just what she cooks, but of the temporality of cooking and shopping alongside their interconnection with other routines such as exercise, meditation, travel to and from work. Indeed, the loss of the shared meal with a loved one has disrupted embodied sensibilities and meanings that worked together in holding fast the practices of home cooking and local shopping. Indeed, the adoption of new technology has facilitated this transition to a new routine:

> When I lived with my partner I loved cooking but since I've lived on my own I got quite lazy but I've got a slow cooker and that's been fantastic

> as I'll often buy some nice meat and then just make a big curry or big stew or something and get that to last me three or four nights with something different on the side.

The slow-cooker allows for a compromise between Mary's lost fervour for cooking, her daily commute to the suburbs of the city and her social life that now includes new hobbies alongside her ambition to eat more healthily. While provisioning the home with the necessary ingredients to prepare a meal now requires a designated trip to a supermarket, the decision to do so is not taken lightly. Mary agonises over the contradictions evident in her desire to avoid supermarkets on account of her opposition to oligopolistic market forces, underlined by reference to her following of activist texts and online blogs. Despite her rebuttal of supermarkets in principle, Mary is unable to put this sentiment into practice, for she is locked into routines and infrastructures that do not support this lifestyle.

Similarly, Rhys' move away from the city to a village on the outskirts of the city and its suburbs city has enabled the interlocking of new commuting, shopping and cooking practices. Crucially, Rhys' village is situated alongside a river path with a dedicated cycle lane. Commuting to work by bicycle, the additional exercise afforded enabled Rhys to cancel his now redundant gym membership, reducing the number of car journeys made for both work and leisure. While we are not able here to explore the carbon footprint of these shifting practices in order to make a clear judgement about the relative benefits of a changed routine – does Rhys now eat more meat to compensate for the energy spent commuting by bicycle? However, we are able to see that any account of changes to routine practices is contingent upon wider practices and shifts in the daily or life-course path, as conceptualised by Pred (1981). Thus, practices are not independent of one another. There is a temporality and rhythmic order to routines made up of interconnecting practices (Shove et al., 2012) that make up everyday life. Indeed, as the everyday 'establishes itself, creating hourly demand, systems of transport, in short, its repetitive organisation' (Lefebvre, 2004: 7) we are reminded that we are not so much the carriers of routines, habits and practices, as much as we are captured and carried along by them.

Carried by practice

A recurrent theme throughout the data is represented by further discussion of decision-making processes with regard to meals prepared at home. Indeed, meals are not planned, but are guided by the contents of store cupboards that hold ingredients for a repertoire of dishes that are repeatedly made and adapted over time. Becca, who is in her mid-30s and cohabits with her boyfriend near the city centre, speaks of how meals are decided upon in her home. The decision to prepare 'spaghetti bolognaise, she suggests, is guided by the contest between ingredients in stock and their potential to be put together into a reasonable and coherent dish. Having spaghetti, onions, tinned tomatoes, dried herbs and a third of a bottle of left-over red wine from a previous meal or occasion, here guides the ruling to 'pop in to the shop on the way home from work to get some mince, or maybe add some veg I have left in the fridge'. Had there been no spaghetti, a different meal altogether may have come to fruition via the meeting of available ingredients, and the know-how and cultural comfort afforded by her culinary repertoire. This is not to say that this is necessarily a rational choice made, but the coming together of practice elements that Shove et al. (2012) refer to as materials, infrastructure and meaning. They have the appropriate materials and competencies (e.g. spaghetti, tinned tomatoes and the know-how of how to prepare a dish that incorporates them), the infrastructure that interlocks with other practices (a route of commuting to work that takes Becca past a small supermarket) and the meanings or, indeed, the culturally embedded notion that cooking spaghetti in this way is appropriate. They are not flouting social conventions or acting outside of the norm, but are building on traditions and embodied sensibilities associated with a comforting, nutritious, affordable week-day meal.

With regard to lunchtime food provisioning, Gemma prepares a packed lunch for her family each morning. Recruiting her 3-year-old son as a helper, sandwich rolls are laid out and fillings rarely deviate from the regular appearance of ham and cheese, cheese and pickle, or tuna and onion, with a piece of fruit and a small chocolate-based treat. Not solely a food preparation activity, Gemma claims this is part of educating her son about not eating 'rubbish' bought in canteens or from vending machines. Gemma suggests that by becoming involved in food preparation, she hopes this practice will become normal for him. Indeed, as we saw above with Becca's usual way of forming a typical evening meal, Gemma recognises the temporally layered nature of food practice, and the difficulty of uprooting habitual and culturally resonant practices later on in life. Like Alan, changing undesirable food practices is not easy, as it involves unlocking oneself from a suite of interconnected practices. One can imagine from such accounts that people are not so much carriers of these practices, but rather, that practices are governed via their interconnections.

Illustrating this dynamic further is Victoria, who is in her mid 60s and lives in one of the city's less affluent neighbourhoods. She speaks of a collection of meals that are prepared and repeated weekly in tandem with her responsibilities at work, caring for elderly family members and occasionally her visiting children. Having clear preferences for foods that have been part of her culinary repertoire since childhood, Victoria is fervently opposed to trying new foods or recipes. Delving further into her account, it becomes clear that such vehemence is not solely the result of a visceral dislike of particular foods, but is tied to further constituent elements upholding this particular way of eating. Speaking of the routines that puncture her day, Victoria presents herself and her husband as having developed a strict repertoire of dishes that are cooked on set evenings of the week, which she sometimes delivers to her brother living nearby. Her husband cooks 'sausage and mash on a Wednesday' and a 'full cooked dinner on a Sunday', which they describe as the 'major meals' of the week. In addition, Victoria makes 'macaroni cheese on pasta night, and something with fish every Friday'. Vegetables are missing from this repertoire, for even as a child, she refused to eat them, a trend repeated by her children. However, since her eldest son began living with his girlfriend, he has now had vegetables introduced to his diet, and has even attempted to inspire change in his mother's eating habits, albeit unsuccessfully:

> I don't like it, I, you know, as a child my mother sat me down and said 'you're eating that or you're not having anything else' and I was still there at bed time, and I just sat there saying 'I'm not gonna eat it, no way', always hated, I mean, you know, I went on a sort of diet at one time where I was trying to eat much more, my sons came and made me, a what was it, some sort of pesto with things you know, pesto pasta with erm a mixture to make it a sort of dip and they even brought carrots to eat it with because he was trying to convince me that it's a better way of eating you know I ate 'em but that was it, they were saying 'go on Mam you can do it', and it's funny him saying that 'cause it's only 'til he went and lived with girlfriend who did like veg, all his younger life he was murder to feed, he was as bad as me when I was a kid.

Victoria's aversion might not be so easily attributed simply to her dislike of vegetables or lack of knowledge as to their health benefits, but could result from the entrenchment of distaste over time, making it unreasonable to now consider incorporating them into her gamut of established recipes. While there is a daily and weekly order to meals shopped for, prepared and consumed, there is also a temporal sequence ordered at the level of the life course. Indeed, the change in her son's vegetable eating had only begun once he was co-habiting with a girlfriend who 'did like veg'. Vegetable thus became part of the cultural repertoire of what comprises a 'proper meal' (DeVault, 1991), suggesting that changes in food practice are facilitated by shared daily routines. That is, a life-course event, such cohabiting with a partner for the first time can facilitate recruitment to a new practice of eating vegetables through the interlocking of elements in new ways. However, just as Alan did not continue eating a vegan diet, Victoria's son might not carry with him this new practice should current arrangements change, as element of that practice might then connect differently.

FOOD AS A NEXUS POINT FOR POLICY INTERVENTION

Exploring the complexity of factors shaping everyday life, this article highlights the constraints faced by individuals in putting choices into practice. That is, despite their best will, individuals face difficulties in realising changes in their daily lives – healthy eating, shopping locally or preparing meals 'from scratch' all serve as examples of changes desired. From the narratives explored above, it seems that difficulties faced in overturning old practices need not be theorised as a lack of individual will, but the result of a combination of social, cultural and material factors. Such factors combine in ways that both deeply entrench undesirable practices, while at other times, the complementarities of other daily routines combine in supporting the inculcation of new practices. These examples may serve as reminders not only of a limited capacity for particular attitudes of beliefs to bring forth changes in the ways on which we go about our daily lives – a belief may indeed act as inspiration, but cannot 'do' – but of the inter-dependency of practices, routines and rhythms that interlock in making-up daily life. It is not as individuals that we enact change. Rather, it is the carriers of routines and practices that we become figured in transformations of social and technical orders as we know them. It is a contention of this article, therefore, that it not us as individuals, nor as collectives that should form the focus of analysis when seeking to understand what is necessary to inculcate the social changes necessary to face environmental challenges, but the practices around which daily life coalesce.

This article goes further than supporting a practice theory orientation by suggesting that we might not only focus upon the practices themselves, but the relationship between practices. Food provides one such nexus around which appropriate intervention points for a public policy geared towards carving pathways towards more sustainable ways of life may be identified. As a first need of the human body, food implicates many social, technical, biological and ecological processes in its lifecycle that interact in complex ways, thus necessitating context-specific policy responses (Ericksen, 2008). For this reason, issues surrounding food production and provision have been explored from a wider system-based perspective (Heller and Keoleian, 2003) where global trends in production, distribution and consumption pose multiple policy challenges (Lang and Heasman, 2004). These accounts often presume an active consumer who chooses what to consume from a market of variable goods. Consumption thus arises from the presence or absence of a well-intended belief, attitude or value. If we were to take the view that consumption is a 'moment' in almost every practice (Warde,

2005), the policy problem is framed entirely differently, with practices and their interconnections serving as the unit of analysis.

From the data presented in this article, we can see that narratives of daily life routines coalesce around food practices. These are not made sense of in isolation from a suite of further interconnecting practices, for food practices are clearly embedded in materiality (housing, technology), infrastructure (transport, amenities) and cultural notions of appropriateness (ideas about proper eating, care and convenience). They are also susceptible to either reproduce or rupture due to smaller changes in the temporal organisation of daily life and/or due to the life-course events such as birth, death, marriage and divorce. This suggests that it is at the nexus of practices that we might conceive of unlocking or locking practices.

While consumer narratives explored here suggest that practices are a useful means of understanding daily routines and their persistence, much further work is to be done to identify points for intervention that encourage the evolution of new and more sustainable pathways. Indeed, this article is not alone in agreeing with Warde (2005) that the external linkages between practice elements are under-researched (Mylan, 2014). As a starting point, this article first contributes to the body of work that identifies practices as a more useful unit of analysis than consumer choices. Employing a practice-oriented approach thus reframes the 'problem' of the unsustainable consumer, while empirical data explored highlight food practice as a nexus around which to think differently about interconnections between related practices. It is in thinking about the nexus of practices that we might come to more novel and dynamic policy interventions for sustainable consumption.

ACKNOWLEDGEMENTS

I am grateful to Susan Baker and Bella Dicks for their support throughout the research and writing process, and to two anonymous reviewers for their insightful comments.

FUNDING

This paper is based on research conducted as part of an ESRC funded doctorate (PTA031200600081) which was completed at Cardiff University's School of Social Sciences. This paper also builds on work developed while funded by the Climate Change Consortium of Wales, Cardiff University.

REFERENCES

1. Anable J, Lane B, Kelay T (2006) An Evidence Base Review of Public Attitudes to Climate Change and Transport Behaviour, London: Department for Transport.

2. Andrews M, Squire C, Tamboukou M (2008) Doing Narrative Research, Thousand Oaks, CA: Sage.

3. Bacchi C (2009) *Analysing policy: What's the problem represented to be?* Frenchs Forest, NSW: Pearson.

4. Baker S (2006) Sustainable Development, London; New York: Routledge.

5. Billings R, Hermann C (1998) Problem identification in sequential policy decision making: The re-representation of problems. In: Sylvan D, Voss J (eds) Problem Representation in Foreign Policy Decision-Making, Cambridge: Cambridge University Press, pp. 53–79.

6. Born B, Purcell M (2006) Avoiding the local trap scale and food systems in planning research. Journal of Planning Education and Research 26: 195–207.

7. Boström MKM (2008) Eco-Standards, Product Labelling and Green Consumerism, Basingstoke: Palgrave Macmillan.

8. Bourdieu P (1990) *The Logic of Practice.* Cambridge, UK: Polity Press.

9. Bruntland G (1987) Our Common Future: The World Commission on Environment and Development, Oxford: Oxford University Press.

10. Butler C, Parkhill KA and Pidgeon NF (2014) Energy consumption and everyday life: Choice, values and agency through a practice theoretical lens. *Journal of Consumer Culture*. Epub ahead of print 19 October. DOI: 10.1177/1469540514553691.

11. DeVault ML (1991) Feeding the Family: The Social Organization of Caring as Gendered Work, Chicago, IL: University of Chicago Press.

12. Eden S, Bear C, Walker G (2008) Mucky carrots and other proxies: Problematising the knowledge-fix for sustainable and ethical consumption. Geoforum 39: 1044–1057.

13. Edwards-Jones G, Milà i Canals L, Hounsome N, (2008) Testing the assertion that 'local food is best': The challenges of an evidence-based approach. Trends in Food Science & Technology 19: 265–274.

14. Ericksen PJ (2008) Conceptualizing food systems for global environmental change research. Global Environmental Change 18: 234–245.

15. Evans D (2011) Blaming the consumer – Once again: The social and material contexts of everyday food waste practices in some English households. Critical Public Health 21: 429–440.

16. Giddens A (1984) The Constitution of Society: Introduction of the Theory of Structuration, Oakland, CA: University of California Press.

17. Goodman D (2003) The quality 'turn' and alternative food practices: Reflections and agenda. Journal of Rural Studies 19: 1–7.

18. Gronow JWA (2001) Ordinary Consumption, London; New York: Routledge.

19. Halkier B (2009) Suitable cooking? Performances and positionings in cooking practices among Danish women. Food, Culture and Society 12: 357–377.

20. Hand M, Shove E and Southerton D (2005) Explaining showering: A discussion of the material, conventional, and temporal dimensions of practice. *Sociological Research Online* 10. Available at: http://www.socresonline.org.uk/10/2/hand.html.

21. Hards S (2011) Social practice and the evolution of personal environmental values. Environmental Values 20: 23–42.

22. Heller MC, Keoleian GA (2003) Assessing the sustainability of the US food system: A life cycle perspective. Agricultural Systems 76: 1007–1041.

23. Hitchings R (2011) Researching air-conditioning addiction and ways of puncturing practice: Professional office workers and the decision to go outside. Environment and Planning A 43: 2838–2856.

24. Holstein JA, Gubrim JF (2004) The active interview. In: Silverman D (ed.) Qualitative Research: Theory, Method and Practice, London: SAGE, pp. 140–161.

25. IPCC (2013) Summary for policymakers. In: Stocker TF, Qin D, Plattner G-K, et al. (eds) *Climate Change 2013: The Physical Science Basis. Contribution of Working Group I to the Fifth Assessment Report of the Intergovernmental Panel on Climate Change.* Cambridge, UK: Cambridge University Press, pp. 3–29.

26. Lang T, Heasman M (2004) Food Wars: The Global Battle for Mouths, Minds and Markets, Oxon: Earthscan.

27. Leach M (2013) Democracy in the Anthropocene? Science and sustainable development goals at the UN. *The Huffington Post UK*, 27 May. Available at: http://www.huffingtonpost.co.uk/Melissa-Leach/democracy-in-the-anthropocene_b_2966341.html.

28. Lefebvre H (2004) Rhythmanalysis: Space, Time and Everyday Life, London: Continuum International Publishing Group.

29. Lorenzoni I, Pidgeon N (2006) Public views on climate change: European and USA perspectives. Climatic Change 77: 73–95.

30. Lunt PK, Livingstone SM (1992) Mass Consumption and Personal Identity: Everyday Economic Experience, Buckingham; Philadelphia, PA: Open University Press.

31. Macnaghten PUJ (1998) Contested natures. Available at: http://search.ebscohost.com/login.aspx?direct=true&scope=site&db=nlebk&db=nlabk&AN=45515.

32. Marshall DW, Anderson AS (2002) Proper meals in transition: Young married couples on the nature of eating together. Appetite 39: 193–206.

33. Mason J (2002) Qualitative interviewing: Asking, listening, interpreting. In: T M (ed.) *Qualitative Research in Action*. London: Sage, pp. 225–241.

34. Mellor J, Blake M, Crane L (2010) When I'm doing a dinner party I don't go for the Tesco cheeses. Food, Culture and Society 13: 115–134.

35. Micheletti M (2003) Political Virtue and Shopping: Individuals, Consumerism, and Collective Action, New York: Palgrave Macmillan.

36. Micheletti M, Stolle D (2007) Mobilizing consumers to take responsibility for global social justice. The Annals of the American Academy of Political and Social Science 611: 157–175.

37. Miller D (2010) Stuff, Cambridge: Polity Press.

38. Miller P, Rose N (1997) Mobilizing the consumer: Assembling the subject of consumption. Theory, Culture & Society 14: 1–36.

39. Mylan J (2014) Understanding the diffusion of sustainable product-service systems: Insights from the sociology of consumption and practice theory. *Journal of Cleaner Production*. Epub ahead of print 15 February. DOI: 10.1016/j.jclepro.2014.01.065.

40. Plessz M, Dubuisson-Quellier S, Gojard S, et al. (2014) How consumption prescriptions affect food practices: Assessing the roles of household resources and life-course events. *Journal of Consumer Culture*. Epub ahead of print 4 February. DOI: 10.1177/1469540514521077.

41. Pred A (1981) Social reproduction and the time-geography of everyday life. Geografiska Annaler. Series B. Human Geography 63: 5–22.

42. Pretty J, Ball A, Benton T, (2007) The SAGE Handbook of Environment and Society, Thousand Oaks, CA: Sage.

43. Reckwitz A (2002) Toward a theory of social practices A development in culturalist theorizing. European Journal of Social Theory 5: 243–263.

44. Redclift MR, Woodgate G (2010) The International Handbook of Environmental Sociology, Cheltenham: Edward Elgar Publishing.

45. Riessman CK (2008) Narrative Methods for the Human Sciences, Los Angeles, CA: Sage.

46. Rockström J, Steffen W, Noone K, (2009) A safe operating space for humanity. Nature 461: 472–475.

47. Ryan N (2001) Reconstructing citizens as consumers: Implications for new modes of governance. Australian Journal of Public Administration 60: 104–109.

48. Schatzki TR (2010) Site of the Social: A Philosophical Account of the Constitution of Social Life and Change, University Park, PA: Penn State University Press.

49. Shirani F, Henwood K (2011) Taking one day at a time: Temporal experiences in the context of unexpected life course transitions. Time & Society 20: 49–68.

50. Shove E (2010) Beyond the ABC: Climate change policy and theories of social change. Environment and Planning A 42: 1273–1285.

51. Shove E, Pantzar M (2005) Consumers, producers and practices: Understanding the invention and reinvention of Nordic walking. Journal of Consumer Culture 5: 43–64.

52. Shove E, Pantzar M, Watson M (2012) The Dynamics of Social Practice: Everyday Life and How It Changes, Thousand Oaks, CA: Sage.

53. Sonnino R, Marsden T (2006) Beyond the divide: Rethinking relationships between alternative and conventional food networks in Europe. Journal of Economic Geography 6: 181–199.

54. Soper K (2007) Re-thinking the good life: The citizenship dimension of consumer disaffection with consumerism. Journal of Consumer Culture 7: 205–229.

55. Southerton D (2006) Analysing the temporal organization of daily life: Social constraints, practices and their allocation. Sociology 40: 435–454.

56. Spurling N, McMeekin A, Shove E, et al. (2013) Interventions in practice: Re-framing policy approaches to consumer behaviour. Available at: http://www.sprg.ac.uk/uploads/sprg-report-sept-2013.pdf.

57. Sunstein CR, Thaler R (2008) Nudge: Improving Decisions about Health, Wealth, and Happiness, New Haven, CT: Yale University Press.

58. Trentmann F (2007) Citizenship and consumption. Journal of Consumer Culture 7: 147–158.

59. Truninger M (2011) Cooking with Bimby in a moment of recruitment: Exploring conventions and practice perspectives. Journal of Consumer Culture 11: 37–59.

60. Urry J (2011) Climate Change and Society, Cambridge: Polity Press.

61. Wainwright SP (2011) Review Essay: Is sociology warming to climate change? Sociology 45: 173–177.

62. Warde A (2005) Consumption and theories of practice. Journal of Consumer Culture 5: 131–153.

63. Wheeler K (2012) The practice of fairtrade support. Sociology 46: 126–141.

64. Yearley S (2009) Sociology and climate change after Kyoto: What roles for social science in understanding climate change? Current Sociology 57: 389–405.

AUTHOR'S BIOGRAPHY

Jessica Paddock, joined the University of Manchester's Sustainable Consumption Institute in 2014 from Cardiff University. Her research explores inequalities, cultural differentiation and food security in the context of environmental change. Previous projects have included the study of alternative food networks in the UK and social-natural scientific research on the links between ecosystem services and food security in the Caribbean. Current research is exploring changes and continuities in patterns of eating out in the UK over the last 20 years, gathering insights as to how systems of food provision may be re-configured to be more sustainable.

3

CHAPTER

An Analysis of Dee's Identity Construction from the Perspective of Consumer Culture

Qian Zhang[1], Haimei Liu[2]

[1]*Foreign Language Department, Baoding University, Baoding, China*

[2]*School of Foreign Languages and Literature, Yan Shan University, Qinhuangdao, China*

ABSTRACT

This paper will focus on the role of the consumer culture in Dee's identity construction in *Everyday Use*. Dee's identification with the female image and her aestheticization of the reality and the history of African American reflect consumer culture acts as the "Other" in the Dee's identity construction. However, consumption culture also serves as the domain where Dee establishes her self-identity as a black female in a white-dominant world. Through the exploration of the double role of consumer culture in Dee's identity construction, this thesis advocates that in *Every Use* Walker presents the new black women dilemma in white-male consumer society and her thought on how to construct black female identities under the invasion of consumer culture into the American South, so that to some extent it makes certain contribution to the issue how women construct their own identity in the consumer society full of survival anxiety.

Keywords: Everyday Use, Dee's Identity Construction, Consumer Culture

1. INTRODUCTION

1.1. The Research Significance

Everyday Use, written by black female American writer Alice Walker, is an excellent short story published in 1973, some nine years before she won Pulitzer Prize for *The Color Purple*. Since it was published, this short story has gained great popularity. Many scholars have done many researches on this short story. As for the interpretation of theme, many critics focus on the writer's view on ethnical cultural identity and how to inherit the heritage. Many critics praise Mother and Maggie's loyalty to their ethnic identity and cultural heritage, but condemn Dee's betrayal of black cultural heritage. Some critics advocate the necessity and feasibility of fusion between white and black cultures. As for the characters, some studies are done in light of the psychology and feminism. As for the artistic features of this short story, symbols and irony have gained the deep analysis from the perspective of formalism. Moreover, some research deals with narrative strategy from the perspective of feminist narratology or spatial narratology. Another research deals with this short story in light of the consumer culture. The aestheticization of everyday life is a cultural strategy adopted by the mainstream society to control rigorously the black community. However the studies on this story from this perspective are rarely available. As for the character Dee, the previous research presents Dee confronts dilemma of self identity in the multi-cultures for Dee knows a little about the past and loses her own identity in pursuit of the black people's independent culture. On the base of these studies, this paper tends to answer what role consumer culture plays in Dee's constructing her identity as a black female in American in the 1960s-1970s. The analysis will be made on the basis of related consumer culture theory in the following three aspects: the female images, the aesthetic concept and fashion implied in *Everyday Use*.

1.2. The Research Background

Generally speaking, consumer culture is "a social arrangement in which the buying and selling of goods and services is not only a predominant activity of everyday life but also an important arbiter of social organization, significance and meaning" (from wikipedia). Some scholars think that consumer culture refers to material activity and the accompanying psychological process, which influence the consumer's interests, tastes, thoughts and morality, even the consumer's daily consumptive behaviors and the way of life (Li &Wang, 2012: p. 99). In this paper, consumer culture refers to a type of material culture, that is, a culture of the use or appropriation of objects or things. Consumer culture is a type of material culture in which the consumer emerges as a master category of collective and individual identity (Lury, 2011: p. 9).

Among various studies on consumer culture, there are three main perspectives on consumer culture: Marxism, semiotics, together with anthropology and sociology. The earliest research in consumer culture can date back to Karl Marx who put forward the notion of "commodity fetishism" and "alienation of labor". Based on the Marx's thought, later the neo-Marxist schools especially the Frandkfurt School have made significant research on the consumer culture. To study the cultural meaning of things many scholars turn to semiotics. Roland Barthes is the first person who introduces semiotics into the consumer culture in his *Mythologies* (1957). Jean Baudrillard (1929-2007), the French social theorist, contributes a lot in interpreting modern and post-modern consumer cultures in his *The System of Objects* (1968) and *The Consumer Society* (1970). In the study of consumer culture in light of anthropology and sociology, Pierre Bourdieu proposes theories of social stratification based on aesthetic taste in *Distinction: A Social Critique of the Judgment of Taste.*

In this paper, much attention will be paid to the consumer culture in 1960s-1970s in America South. The reason is that the exact historical setting of the story is not indicated, but a number of details point to a period covering part of 1960s-1970s in the American South. For example, the narrator mentions a television show and Johnny Carson, host of "Tonight Show" at the zenith of his career. American society has "shifted from a productive society to a consumer society in the late nineteenth century and the early twentieth century", (Jiang, 2004: p. 73) but consumer culture in the American South has been developing lower than the American north. Historically, the South relied heavily on agriculture with sharecropping and tenant farming as a dominant form, and was highly rural until after 1945. It has since become more industrialized and urban but the process of industrialization and urbanization in the South is quite lower than the North for the historical factors. The South has the highest percentage of African Americans in the country and in the 1960s-1970s the consumption culture expands its power to the rural area in America South.

2. DEE'S FEMALE IDENTITY AND FEMALE IMAGE IN CONSUMER CULTURE

According to the Belgian sociolinguist Jan Blommaert, identity is who and what you are. He proposes that we can see identity as particular form of semiotic potential, organized in a repertoire which is conditioned by dynamics of access (Blommaert, 2005: p. 203). The gender researchers also point out the gender identity is the result of social construction. The feminist Simone De Beauvoir's statement can be strong evidence: "One is not born a woman, but becomes one" (Beauvoir, 1952: p. 295). Her analysis focuses on the Hegelian concept of the other. It is the social construction of Woman as the quintessential other that Beauvoir identifies as fundamental to women's oppression. This part will focus on female image of Dee in *Everyday Use* and her experience and try to explore the role of the consumer culture as the role of the Other in Dee's female identity construction.

2.1. The Conflict of the Female Image in Mrs. Johnson and Dee

At the beginning of the story, Mrs. Johnson deliberately chooses to wait for her daughter Dee's coming home in the yard. Mrs. Johnson, the narrator in Alice Walker's *Everyday Use,* lives in and feels comfortable with the Southern tradition of farming life. However, in the third and fourth paragraph of this short story, Mrs. Johnson dreams a dream in which Dee and she are suddenly brought together on a TV program hosted by Johnny Carson. Here we see the consumer culture in the urban has invaded into the comfortable country life for TV is an important media to spread the mass and consumer culture. In the TV programs the children who have made success embrace and express thanks for their parents. But the mother thinks that such kind of touching scene can never happen between herself and her daughter, The reason is that the image of Mrs. Johnson is far from the one required by Dee and the TV program.

In real life, the narrator is "a large, big-boned woman with rough, man-working hands", wears loose clothes such as flannel nightgowns and overalls and worked hard to make a living such as slaughtering mercilessly like a man, "breaking ice to get water for washing" in winter. She can eat "pork liver cooked over the open fire minutes after it comes steaming from the hog" (Guerin et al., 2004: p. 389). Here it depicts a typical image of African American woman living in the rural area of American South. Such kind of African-American women possess more masculine traits. From the narrator's description, we do not see any sign of self-depreciation but a sense of pride for her masculinity. There are two reasons for the narrator's perception of beauty and body. First, African-American women believe that African-American males prefer larger women, so they have no reason to lose weight and think their large figure more attractive. Another reason is that the age-old agrarian African American way of life requires lots of manual labor. Women have to do lots of things by their own hands so that women develop big figure to support their labor both on land and at home.

However the popular TV programs and Dee want her to be: a hundred pounds lighter, her shin like an uncooked barley pancake. Her hair glistens in the hot bright light and. Johnny Carson has much to do to keep with her quick witty tongue. The image of African American women required by the TV programs and Dee conforms to the standard of body size and beauty for the female required by the consumption culture especially by the dominant white culture. Such kind of women have a small and thin figure, a special taste for the clothing and hairstyle, and possess more feminine traits, which is quite different from image of African American woman living in the rural area of American South. African American women experience greater social mobility, they may be especially at risk, due to the exposure to white women preferences, attitudes, and ideals about beauty, weight, and food... Dee represents a small group of African-American women who identify more with the dominant culture than with their racial or ethnic culture.

The conflict of the female image in Mrs. Johnson and Dee in fact reflects the conflicts in cultures: the Southern tradition of farming life in rural area and the thriving consumer culture in the urban. At the same time there is an emerging consciousness that the African-American are not necessarily destined to subsistence living but to enjoy the advantage and convenience brought by technology and science.

2.2. Dee's Identification with Female Image in Consumer Culture

For African America women like Dee, consumer culture acts as the dual "Other" in gender and race. Unlike her mother, a typical image of black women, "a large, big-boned woman with rough, man-working hands" who construct herself to meet the gaze of African American males, Dee constructs herself like white woman on the basis of white man's preference for the small figured and thin female. Dee is subject to "male gaze" and becomes the object of white men's desires.

Her willingness to obey the standard of body and beauty established by the consumer culture will be discussed in the following two aspects: First, Dee, as a young girl, shares the same nature with the white woman that women cannot resist the allure of beautiful commodities. Such notion of womanhood has been discussed by Jennifer Jones. In his *Coquettes and Grisettes*, it is argued that "women's psychology and sensory apparatus made them ideally suited to consume, and their passivity rendered them particularly vulnerable to capture by their sensual delight in agreeable and frivolous objects" (Jones, 1996: p. 36). In *Everyday Use*, when Dee is a little girl, she likes nice things. She is so sensitive to the color that she has natural ability to dress herself in a suitable and new way without her mother's guidance. For example, she chose "a yellow organdy dress to wear to her graduation from high school; black pumps to match a green suit she'd made from an old suit... at sixteen she had a style of her own and know what style was" (Guerin et al., 2004: p. 390). As a young girl, she does get great pleasure in decorating herself with the colorful and nice things, so she is open and easily captured by the agreeable things. Second, her identification with the ideal female image of white man reflects her political aspiration. As a black girl in rural area of American South, she is lucky enough to get high education, which germinates her dream to change the lower and despised situation and to gain due recognition in the white-dominated society. However she cannot change her skin color and birthplace. Maybe her mother has shared the same dream a dream which she think impossible to realize. Dee thinks marriage acts as a short cut to improve herself from lower position in marginalized minorities to the middle-upper class in the mainstream society. So she builds herself in the manner, language to meet the desired image by the white man. She succeeds in attracting the young and furtive boys: "Impressed with her they worshiped the well-tuned phrase, the cute shape, the scalding humor that erupted like bubbled in lye". When she established herself as an ideal figure in white man's eyes, she is brave enough to court Jimmy T. and "turn all her faultfinding power on him". But Jimmy T. does not accept her love and marry "a cheap city girl from a family of ignorant flashy people". Her failure in pursuing a white boy to some extent shatters her dream to integrate herself into the white society by construct herself on the standard of beauty and body advocated by the dominant middle class culture.

3. DEE'S RACIAL IDENTITY AND AESTHETIC PERCEPTION IN CONSUMER CULTURE

Consumer culture plays an important role not only in Dee's construct herself as the ideal female in the gaze of white man, but also in Dee's aesthetic perception. Under the influence of consumer culture, she perceives these everyday common things and the house in an aesthetic way. She constructed herself as a collector with an elegant taste and a recorder of the African America history. There are two ways for Dee to collect things: one is that Dee owns the common everyday objects as decoration in her house; the other is that Dee can collect the visual images of her family with the help of Polaroid. This part will explore how consumer culture influences Dee's aesthetic perception especially her perception on the suffering past and the survival reality of the black American and the role of consumer culture in constructing her racial identity.

3.1. The Conflict of Perception of Things in Mrs. Johnson and Dee

Jean Baudrillard thinks that there are four ways of an object obtaining value: the functional value of an object; the exchange value of an object; the symbolic value of an object; the sign value of an object. The sign value proposed by the Baudrillard is an important complement to the Marxist theory of the value of goods. In this short story, Mrs. Johnson and Maggie focus on the functional value and the symbolic value in the conventional things. Mama and Maggie are not only the users of these things but also heritor of these things, because they know how to use them in daily life and the historical and cultural meaning behind these conventional things. While Dee pays more attention to the sign value in these things. The function of common everyday objects collected by Dee is to highlight her improvement in social status from a lower black female to a member of middle class with elegant taste.

Take the old quilts for example, for Maggie and Mama, the old quilts can be put into everyday day to keep warm in functional value aspect; the symbolic value of the old quilts lies in that two old quilts can be regard as a token of a family's history of pride and struggle, and of the African American historical and cultural heritage in American. In Dee's eyes, for the exchange value, the old quilts are priceless for its rarity. Dee lives in the urban where many things belong to the mass production. Even her mother in country has the quilts stitched by the machine rather by the hands in their house. So the old quilts are rare and unique both in the Dee's world and Mother's world. More attention will be paid on the sign value rather than the other value of the old quilts. The only thing that Dee could do with quilts is not to use them but to hang them on the wall. The sign value of the old quilts lies in that it can serve as a decoration to display her taste as black women who has become a member of middle class.

The conflict of perception of things between Mrs. Johnson and Dee in fact reflects their different social status of the black woman and different attitudes towards the suffering history of the black American: Maggie and Mama who have a lower social status has a better understanding of their own history in America, while Dee who improves herself form a lower position to a middle class only sees the oppressive side of history imposed by the white and wants to break with the past of the social, psychological hardship.

3.2. Dee's Identification with Aesthetic Perception in Consumer Culture

In the process of Dee's constructing herself as a desired female by white man, aesthetic perception in consumer culture also acts as the "Other" in her constructing her racial identity. The French sociologist Pierre Bourdieu in *Distinction: A Social Critique of the Judgment of Taste* points out that the elite in society define the aesthetic values like taste and the different levels of the exposure to these aesthetic values can results in the social stratification. In Dee constructing herself as a collector with an elegant taste, she loses her racial identity for she does not understand historical and cultural meaning embodied by the conventional things and the function of common everyday objects collected by Dee is to highlight her improvement in social status from a lower black female to a member of middle class with elegant taste. She becomes the other of her mother and sister who stick to their racial culture. The influence of aesthetic perception in consumer culture on her constructing her racial identity will be discussed in the following two aspects.

Firstly, Dee constructs herself as a collector by owning the common everyday objects to decorate her house. What Dee collects is common everyday objects rather than the things in museum or works of art in exhibition reflects not only the effacement of the boundary between art and everyday life in modern consumer culture but also Dee's aestheticization of the harsh reality of the black female in American South. In *Consumer Culture and Postmodernism*, Mike Featherstone has pointed out that the inherent meaning of the aesthetic in consumer age refers to the aestheticization of everyday life. One meaning of the aestheticization of everyday life is that art can be anywhere or anything. The detritus of mass culture, the debased consumer commodities, could be art (Featherstone, 2000: pp. 95-96). When Dee enters in the house, she was attracted by those conventional items found in the house such as the quilts, the benches used in place of chairs, the churn, and the dasher. Everything in the house delights her for she thinks of the artistic value in them. For example, she wants to use the churn top as a centerpiece for the alcove table. All these common things in the house everyday life have become a kind of art in Dee's eye. However, the conventional items such as the quilts, the benches used in place of chairs, the churn, the snuff in the shabby house represent the lower economic situation of rural blacks and social status. To some extent, her effacement of the boundary between art and everyday life reflects her aestheticization of the harsh reality of the black female in American South.

Secondly, Dee constructs herself as a recorder of the African America history by collecting the visual images of the traditional house with the help of Modern Polaroid. When she returns home, she is eager to "line up picture after picture" that shows her mother in the front of the house. She carefully manages to get her mother, Maggie, house and the nibbling cow all in the same shot. The narrator tells us that "she never takes a shot without making sure the house is included". Here Dee's action of taking photos of the house is meaningful in consumer culture. Mike Featherstone has argued that another sense of the aestheticization of everyday life refers to the rapid flow of signs and images which saturate the fabric of everyday life (98). In Dee's eyes, the existence of the house as a preserver and protector of the age-old African American way of life is not a living thing but a series of images and pictures. Another meaning of Dee's action is that Dee turns the suffering history of African American represented by the house into a visual image. Jean Baudrillard points out that the modern culture built on the advanced media means supported by high technology is endowed with a new property—simulacra. The sign and simulacra are widely spread by the science and technology, as result, art and aesthetic are expanded drastically from the traditional art into every corner of society, which effaces the image and the reality. In this short story, the narrator tells us that Dee once hated the old house and wanted to tear the reconstructed house down, for she does not face their oppressive history imposed by the white man. To the mother's surprise, Dee takes pictures of the house and do not show her dislike. Dee takes advantage of the Polariod to visualize the suffering history into "simulacra" where the time is fixed. She perceives the house not in the reality bur in its image. Therefore, the image of the house not only relives Dee' shameful and painful feeling of African America history but also adds some poetic color to their history.

In Dee constructing herself as a collector with an elegant taste, the aesthetic perception consumer culture acts as the other in Dee's constructing her racial identity, for such aesthetic perception results in Dee's aestheticization of the reality and the history of African American. On the one hand, she constructed herself as a collector with an elegant taste to display her social status as one member of the middle-upper class in the mainstream society and her aestheticization of the harsh reality of the black female in American South. One the other hand, Dee constructs herself as a recorder of the African America history with the modern Polaroid who is enchanted by the image rather than the real history.

4. FASHION AND DEE'S IDENTITY

In the former part, consumption culture acts as the "Other" in the Dee's identity construction through the female image and the aesthetic concept. However, consumption culture also serves as the domain where Dee establishes her self-identity as a black female in a white-dominant world. French scholar Michel de Certeau in *The Practice of Everyday Life* points out that despite repressive aspects of consumer culture, the consumer can reverse the function of the available source and materials to satisfy their own needs in practice, posing a challenge to the established order of society. In Dee's constructing her identity, there exists some creative resistance to the repressive power of the consumer culture. The subject construction of Dee will be discussed from the African fashion and car as a form of space in the context of consumer culture.

4.1. African Fashion and Dee's Identity

Fashion as an important part of the consumer culture plays an important role in Dee's constructing her identity. Before this, our attention will be paid to the social motive and function of fashion. German sociologist Georg Simmel in *The Philosophy of Fashion* argues that fashion is a form of a social relationship. On the one hand, fashion allows someone to conform to the standard of a group so as to make the members of certain group more intimate. On the other hand, fashion can be used by certain group to distinct itself from other groups. In other words, fashion allows some to be unique and special by deviating from the norm. For an individual, fashion can satisfy one's desire both to belong to a group and to be individual. In this story, Dee lives in the United States 1960s-1970s. At that time, there is a political movement called "Black Power" expressing a new racial consciousness among blacks. Under the slogan of "Black is beautiful", many black women and men use their special clothing style and other decorations to establish a collective identity. The African fashion was used to express the political desire of Africa Americans at that time. Therefore, when Dee imitates African fashion established by Africa Americans, Dee gains a sense of belonging which makes her feel not lonely on the process of seeking her identity as a black female in America and a sense of security which relives her responsibility and guiltiness for her different appearance, taste and manner in white-dominant society. However, what is more important for Dee is that African fashion can serve as an outlet to satisfy her desire to be herself as a black female. In the part two and three, Dee's struggles to construct her identity as an ideal female on the standard of white man and a collector with the same elegant taste as a member of middle class does not make herself different from the white people. Therefore, fashion can be an alternative way to express Dee's desire for self-identity unrealized in mainstream society.

In following African fashion in 1960s-1970s, Dee is creating a new image of black women. Such kind of black women do not construct themselves on the standard of beauty, body size, taste advocated by the dominant middle class culture as the gazed object of the white man. In contrary, new black women manage to construct themselves on their ethical culture. Names, the use of words, clothing and decorations can be regarded as different ways of creating identity. In this story, Dee replaces her earlier name with "Wangero". For Dee, her earlier name represents the oppressive culture of the dominant majority, so she gives it up and chooses an African pattern to display the transformation of her identity. In language, Dee greets her mother with an African dialect salutation "Wa-su-zo-Tean-o". In clothing and decoration, she wears an impressively long and bright dress, with her hair "straight up like the wool on a sheep", earrings gold "hanging down to her shoulders", bracelet "dangling and making noise when she moves her arm" (Guerin et al., 2004: pp. 389-390). From the names, the use of words, clothing and decorations, we can see Dee is constructing a perfect example of the black women who turns their eyes on Africa to create fashion to construct their own identity. The uniqueness of African fashion lies in that it is hard to be imitated by the white people for example, African hairstyle, so that we can say that African fashion highlights the distinctive difference between African American and the white people and that African fashion to some extent can be used to make Dee's identity as an African American more stable.

4.2. Car as a Form of Space and Dee's Identity

Car is undoubtedly one of the most important goods which represent consumer culture in America in twentieth century. In this story, the first appearance of Dee in this short story is that she comes out of the car and the last scene is that Dee and her friends drive a car away while Maggie and her mother watch the car dust settle. Here the car is not only a moving and fashionable vehicle but also a form of space which displays the culture Dee belongs. If the house and the garden are the space Maggie and the mother belongs to, car can be regarded as the space which Dee belongs to in this story. French philosopher Henri Lefebvre in *The Production of Space* says "(Social) space is a (social) product… the space thus produced also serves as a tool of thought and of action… in addition to being means of production it is also a means of control, and hence of domination, of power" (Lefebvre, 1991: p. 158). Every society produces a certain space. Space does have its own cultural and ideological meanings in certain society. So their difference of belonging spaces reflects their different economic conditions, cultures and social status. What role the car as a form of space plays in the process of Dee's construction of her identity will be discussed in two ways: comparison with Dee's space and Maggie and their mother's space and the position of the car in female's consumption.

First, comparison with Dee's space and Maggie and their mother's space will be made to show the role of car in Dee's construction of self identity. The house and the garden represent simple traditional agrarian life. Maggie and mother are strictly confined to their house. Their identity is basically defined as mothers and wifes who are supported to their nurturing gifts and exert their influence on their children and husbands. They are living in simple and poor living conditions at the bottom of society. While the car serve as the representative of a complex and turbulent consumer culture in modern life. Unlike Maggie and mother confined themselves in their house in a small country, many new black women like Dee make best use of car to get rid of the constraint of their narrow domestic sphere and to get freedom to go where they want according to their plans. Compared with Mother and Maggie, Dee has the chance to define herself in public space because the car makes it easier for her to go the public space and it also reflects Dee's wealthy economic conditions and Dee's consuming power.

Another perspective is from the position of the car in female consumption. The study done by Emily S. Rosenberg shows that when the car initially occurred, the female was regarded unsuitable for driving because of emotional personality and fragile constitution. However in the late 1920s Dee represents a small group of African-American women who identify more with the dominant culture than with their racial or ethnic culture. When the car entered into the overproduction, the car companies changed marketing strategies and began to advocate that the female is portrayed as the suitable driver of the car. Under the influence of the mass media especially the advertising, the female is considered as the potential buyer and driver of a car. As a result, the car is no longer goods exclusive to men but an object endowed with rich cultural meaning. The car becomes a symbol of independence and freedom of woman.

5. BLACK FEMALE DILEMMA IN WHITE-MALE DOMINANT SOCIETY

In the earlier 20th century, the shift from an agrarian to an industrial-commercial society took place in American society. At that time because of mass production, the new technology of and the development of the mass media, American society has "shifted from a productive society to a consumer society". For Black Americans, the shift had occurred at a markedly slower pace. However, in the 1960s-1970s the consumption culture expands its power to the rural area in America South. Many black females like Dee and Maggie seem unwilling to participate in that shift. While, some new black women like Dee is longing for it.

In the process of Dee constructing her identity as a black woman in white-dominant society, consumer culture acts as the double role. In fact, the double role of consumer culture reflects the new black female dilemma in white-male dominant society. On one hand, under the influence of consumer culture, Dee identifies herself with the female image in the gaze of white man and deals with the harsh social reality and the suffering history of Black American in an aesthetic way. Dee represents a small group of African-American women who may lose themselves for they identify more with the dominant culture than with their racial or ethnic culture when they struggle to establish themselves in white-dominant society in American in 1960s-1970s. On the other hand, under the influence of fashion, an important part of consumption culture, which shows itself in name, language, clothing, hairstyle and car, Dee establishes her self-identity as a black female in a white-dominant world for she began to identify her ethnic culture. Compared with her mother and sister who are confined in the house, Dee represents a kind of new black women who say goodbye to their traditional role as stay-at-home mother and wife and trying to redefine themselves in family and society.

Here for the character Dee, Alice Walker shows her worries about how some new black women construct their self identities without losing their own ethnic culture in white-male consumer society. For the mother and Maggie, should they stick to the simple and self-productive agrarian life regardless of the changes of time? Should they stay at home and play their traditional role as mother and wife? The author also implies her thought on how to construct black female identity under the invasion of consumer culture into the American South.

6. CONCLUSION

Through the exploration of the double role of consumer culture in female image, aesthetics and fashion in Dee's identity construction, this thesis advocates that in Every Use Walker presents the new black women dilemma in white-male consumer society and her thought on how to construct black female identity under the invasion of consumer culture into the American South. Hopefully this paper to some extent will make certain contribution to the issue how women construct their own identity in the consumer society full of survival anxiety.

REFERENCES

1. http://encyclopediajrank.org/articles/pages/6480/Consumer-Culture.html
2. Li, C. L., & Wang, X. M. (2012). An Analysis of the Consumerism in William Faulkner's Works. Foreign Literature Studies, 04, 99.
3. Lury, C (2011). Consumer Culture (2nd ed.). Cambridge: Polity Press.
4. Jiang, D. C. (2004). Consumer Culture, Identity Construction and Modernism——The Evolvement of the American Consumer Culture in the 20th Century. Foreign Languages Research, 2, 73.
5. Blommaert, J. (2005). Discourse: A Critical Introduction. Cambridge: Cambridge University Press. http://dx.doi.org/10.1017/CBO9780511610295
6. Beauvoir, S. D. (1952). The Second Sex (Translated by Parshley, H. M.). New York, NY: Random House.
7. Guerin, W. L., Labor, E., Morgan, L., &Reesman, J. C. (2004). A Handbook of Critical Approaches to Literature (4th ed.). Beijing: Foreign Language Teaching and Research Oxford: Oxford UP.
8. Jones, J. (1996). Coquettes and Grisettes Women Buying and Selling in Ancient Régime Paris. In V. de Grazia, & E. Furlough (Eds.), The Sex of Things Gender and Consumption in Historical Perspective (p. 36), Berkeley: University of California Press.
9. Featherstone, M. (2000). Consumer Culture and Postmodernism (Translated by Liu, J. M.). Nanjing: Yilin Press.
10. Lefebvre, H. (1991). The Production of Space (Translated by Nicholson-Smith, D.). Malden, MA: Blackwell Publishers Inc.

4

CHAPTER

Debtor Publics: Tracking the Participatory Politics of Consumer Credit

Joe Deville

Goldsmiths, University of London, London, UK

Current address: Lancaster University, Lancaster, UK

ABSTRACT

In the context of apparently ubiquitous relations of debt, it has been argued that the debtor possesses a unique, revolutionary potential. Why is this potential seemingly as yet unrealised? Where might nascent debtor publics be found? And what conditions, what infrastructures, might facilitate their emergence? In answering these questions, this paper argues that there are spaces where emergent "counter-*agencing*" debtor publics can be detected – however, these are organising less around the issue of (consumer credit) borrowing than default. By analysing a prominent online debtor's forum in the UK – the Consumer Action Group debt collection industry sub-forum – the paper argues that such spaces contain important insights into the politics of credit markets and debt default, collective practices of calculation, and the formation of publics.

Keywords: publics, debt, calculation, politics, markets, devices

INTRODUCTION

Alongside the global spread of ubiquitous debt and all the various iniquities in which it is implicated, new infrastructures are emerging around which debtors themselves are coming together to try to shift their conditions of market engagement. One such infrastructure, and the conversations and material devices that circulate around it, is this paper's object. It examines the Consumer Action Group, an online debtor forum in the UK, and, specifically, its debt collection industry sub-forum. This is a space where debtors can visit and anonymously share their debt-oriented concerns and ask for advice about how to deal with debt collection prompts. Similar sites can be found elsewhere: in the USA, for instance, in discussions on Reddit as well as on the Credit Info Centre, ExpertLaw and myFICO discussion boards.

Such forums stand as instances of debtors themselves trying to agence markets, to deploy the terminology of this Special Issue. Sometimes, simply in order to create better (economic/social) outcomes for themselves, sometimes with more collective ambitions in mind. Acts of attempted market agencing are understood in this paper as successful shifts in more or less stabilised conditions of market/organisational engagement, with consequences that can potentially have either market or non-market effects, and which operate at the level of an individual and/or the collective. In the dual sense of the term deployed by Franck Cochoy, this is about attending, on the one hand, to how specific socio-market arrangements (*agencements*) are produced and, on the other, to how distinct forms of agency are "[put] into motion" (2014, 117). Indeed, given that the activities being followed by this paper set themselves in direct opposition to the far more stable and dominant set of economic arrangements organised by the credit industry, they can perhaps be considered as not simply acts of *agencing* but (also) "counter-*agencing*". In analysing these processes, the paper also builds on work looking at the distinct modes of political and collective engagement that can be stimulated by online forums (e.g. Akrich and Méadel 2007; Freelon 2010), while additionally focusing on a much-neglected research object: consumer credit default (see Deville 2015). (Credit default is the condition of having broken the terms of a credit agreement by not having repaid a debt according to the agreed schedule.)

The paper highlights the variable co-articulation of both politics and market calculation in this space, in which the circulation of collections devices offers the potential for new forms of engagement and the emergence of nascent, if fragile and heterogeneous, debtor publics. It is thus not an examination of the way in which a well-defined social movement might succeed (or not) in effecting changes in the practices of one or more targeted organisations (see King and Soule 2007; Lounsbury, Ventresca, and Hirsch 2003; Rao, Morrill, and Zald 2000; Soule 2012; Weber, Rao, and

Thomas 2009). It is closer to work that has looked at how emergent collectivities, operating ostensibly beyond the concerns of powerful organisations, *themselves create and diffuse* new and potentially challenging organisational forms (Schneiberg 2013).

The paper also shows how devices used by debt collectors can, in combination with suitable infrastructural conditions/affordances (Star 1999), themselves unintentionally play a role in the market *agencing*, by acting as prompts for "novelty", pushing/pulling defaulting debtors towards new, differently formatted connections with other people and agencies. This paper is, therefore, about how objects *themselves*, and not just infrastructures, prompt participation (Marres 2012, 28–59). In this case, they have an impact on the political registers through which personal debt problems and the experience of confronting the debt collector are articulated. Finally, as I will also demonstrate, what these forums achieve is to turn what is posited as an individualised and "private" responsibility into a more (if not entirely) "public" issue.

Before proceeding, some brief methodological contextualisation may be helpful. The paper draws principally on an analysis of forum posts, while also, in the description of the experience of default, using data from a group of 20 interviews with defaulting UK debtors conducted in 2008. The forum posts range across a broad temporal spectrum, from 2008 and 2012. The focus of the analysis is on characteristic "modes" of interaction on the forum: the paper contrasts "Critique and collective resistance" to "The politics of the collections device", which stand for modes of engagement, and indeed politics, that are respectively explicit as opposed to practical. The significance of these modes emerged from many weeks spent reading the forum, rather than any quantitative analysis (the paper by no means offers a wholly comprehensive overview of the role played by this or other forums), from which it also became clear that the former is far rarer. A clear majority of the discussions on the forum concern the practicalities of default – about specific collections letters, collections companies, and debt issues – very much in line with the analysis presented in the second of the two sections in particular. Amongst the many other modes of interaction on the forum, the significance of critical forms of debtor engagement relates less to its quantity (even if, as I will discuss, a particular political trigger can generate voluminous discussion) than to the intensity of the forms of engagement that are solicited.

Debtor publics

We are dire need of debtor publics. This seems to be the consensus in some of the most influential analyses of the hold credit has on contemporary life.

Take the following from Maurizio Lazzarato's *The Making of the Indebted Man*:

> ... the only way to stop and turn back, not the "risks" of financialization, but the destructive power of debt [...], lies in the capacity of debtors to think and act collectively. Exactly as in industrial societies, "awareness" must be imposed on the institutions and structures of government through a struggle that divides society, that breaks the consensus. (2012, 157–158)

The debtor is posited as the subject with the greatest potential for forcing a widespread, revolutionary problematisation of contemporary capitalist economies. A similar sentiment can be found in David Graeber's *Debt: The First 5,000 Years*. For Graeber, the debt-driven financial crisis saw "the beginning of an actual public conversation about the nature of debt, of money, of the financial institutions that have come to hold the fate of nations in their grip" (2011, 15). The book would end up a part of this conversation (or, "counter-*agencing*"?), becoming adopted by the Occupy movement in which Graeber was also actively involved (see Graeber 2012).

However, it is not easy for debtors to coalesce into collectivities. Writing in the immediate aftermath of Occupy, Graeber sounds a note of caution. While observing that many social revolutions, including some of the most ancient, were rooted in relations of debt, "it's notoriously difficult", he also notes, "to assemble debtors into a coherent movement; indebtedness is isolating by nature, and the very feelings of anxiety and humiliation it sparks have made it a potent ideological tool" (Graeber). If we are on the brink of revolution, then we have not tipped over. Important reasons include the long-standing difficulty inherent in transforming an experience that has such a potent capacity to be understood as a private concern, to shame people into isolation, into an issue around which publics might be able to assemble. Such factors exert a strong performative drag against the very possibility that debt, and particularly personal debt, might become an issue of more widespread concern.

Writing in an earlier historical moment, Paul Rock focuses down on the difficulties, both practical and political, facing specifically defaulting debtors involved in routine confrontations with debt collectors. He notes that debtors in London in the late-1960s could "be manipulated because they are kept apart and without significant support" (Rock 1973, 8) and that "Debt collection is so organized that it contains very few of the *mechanisms* which can attract and hold the attention of people towards a social problem" (Rock 1973, 4, emphasis added). Among the reasons he identifies for the latter he includes that fact that the sanctions of debt collection tend to occur in private settings rather than in public, ritualised acts of censure (1973, 6–8) – an observation that is as relevant now as it was then – and that a public perception holds in which the causes of credit default are held to be individual rather than social in origin (Rock 1973, 15–18). His analysis thus foreshadows not only Graeber, but also both the post-Foucauldian analysis of the increasing individualisation of responsibility for everyday credit management (indeed for most of socio-economic life) (see Langley 2009; also Langley 2008, 2014; Marron 2009) and recent attention to the importance of attending to the (present or absent) *conditions* of issue formation (Latour 2007; Marres 2009, 2012).

That is not to say that there has been nothing in the way of a collective response to the global ubiquity of debt. Graeber himself has been involved in one of the most high profile: Strike Debt! Associated with Occupy, Strike Debt! published the *Debt Resisters' Operations Manual* (Strike Debt and Occupy Wall Street 2012) a prominent online text that highlights the forms of expropriation debt involves while providing information about how debtors can themselves escape its grasp. It also set up Rolling Jubilee, a movement that buys defaulting debt from creditors but with the intention not of collecting on it, but destroying it (Strike Debt! 2014). A more long-standing organisational response is the Jubilee Debt Campaign, which lobbies for debt forgiveness, in particular forgiveness of sovereign debt owed by developing governments (Jubilee Debt Campaign 2014). We can also add those various other organisations, both state led and not-for-profit, concerned with the potentially damaging effects of ubiquitous debt, but whose response is less radical – offering support and advice to debtors, or advocating if not for debt forgiveness then at least for better consumer protection (e.g. in the UK, the Citizens Advice service, StepChange, the Financial Conduct Authority; in the USA, the National Consumer Law Center, the more reputable credit counselling services, the Consumer Financial Protection Bureau).

It would thus certainly be wrong to conclude that the contemporary globally networked credit markets are devoid of either politics or collectively organised and/or mandated responses. These markets have clearly become, in certain instances and spaces, framed as a socio-economic "matter[s] of concern" (see Callon 2009; Callon, Méadel, and Rabeharisoa 2002), whether for organisations, states, or social theorists. It is also worth noting that other debtor collectivities exist in markets, even if this is often not recognised: debtors are routinely being assembled and acted upon *as* collective entities in and through sets of increasingly ubiquitous calculative, algorithmic apparatuses (see Marron 2009; Poon 2007). Seen from this perspective, what debtors share is their status as "calculated publics" (Gillespie 2014), publics that are the object of explicitly targeted processes of attempted "captation" (Cochoy 2007). Yet, these acts of collectivisation, these publics, are market-led and, for most at least, unseen. What seems so hard to achieve is a response to the iniquities of debt economics in which debtors themselves *recognise, act according to, and/or develop ongoing infrastructures to support* their collective self-presence. Strike Debt! managed this (see also McKee 2014; Ross 2013, 2014). And there are also historical examples (see Caffentzis 2013; Graeber 2011). However, at present, they are thin on the ground.

Emergent collectives, device-led politics

Politically salient publics do not necessarily, however, need to exhibit the qualities of conventionally conceived social movements. The politics of markets frequently operates within the shifting sands of fragile emergent alternatives, which is a register of the political that science and technology studies has been particularly good at detecting. This sees the precise way entities are brought into alignment with one another as part of the (cosmo)political composition of the world (see Latour 2007; Stengers 2003a, 2003b). Politics may therefore be found in the ways even mundane practices provoke some form of difference, some form of novelty, in the order of things. Groups of individuals may also exhibit variable moments of coherence: at times, despite sharing the same space, they act as apparently individualised and self-interested, while, in other moments, there are more or less fleeting recognitions of collective purpose and identity. Collectivity, then, can itself be an emergent property: blink, and you miss it; but just maybe it is there, nonetheless. It is this type of emergent, unstable, sometimes more and sometimes less coherent public that is the concern of this paper.

Furthermore, the "troubles" that prompt the formation of publics may ontological rather than epistemological in character (see Marres 2012; Mol 2002; Woolgar and Lezaun 2013). The routine life of default bears witness to this: it is an intimate, embodied experience in which the sense of life being out of balance emerges in particular from the intrusion of debt collection devices into the home (see Deville 2015). Once in default, debtors are likely to find aspects of their daily home life undergoing a shift. The telephone, perhaps also the mobile phone, formerly more or less benign carriers of conversation, become imbued with a new, unpredictable power, as each ring brings with it the possibility of uncomfortable questions about the status of their debt. The front door, meanwhile, actually always quite a porous thing, becomes the passage point for sequences of collection letters that slip through the letterbox to accumulate below, in a messy mix of bills, junk mail and an assortment of other letters. These objects, these devices, ("market devices"; see McFall 2009; Muniesa, Millo, and Callon 2007) themselves intersect with the sociocultural attachments that specific debts generate. Guilt about past spending, perhaps; a generalised sense of regret about unspecified past purchases,[1] maybe peaking into anger or self-blame.[2] Thrown into this mix is the perceived threat – that, in the UK, materialises far less often than debtors assume (Deville 2015) – of future domestic intrusion by a bailiff and the expropriation of property, an image cut through with the imagined possibility of violence.[3]

Such personally troubling situations provide particularly felicitous conditions for devices themselves to become involved in the formation of publics, as highlighted by Marres (2012). Many of Marres' case studies centre on the attempts to design participation through particular objects – such as, in relation to environmental politics, through devices like eco-kettles, smart electricity meters, and augmented teapots. Such devices aim to deliberately problematise everyday, domestic socio-material practices, to render visible and apparently modifiable otherwise under-articulated attachments between users and the (issue of the) environment.

This seems quite different from the devices that accompany the experience of default. These not only lack mechanisms of publicisation (Marres 2009), but actively seek to ensure the continued *privatisation* of the issue of debt (privatisation in the sense of individualisation). Rather than rendering debt default political, an issue requiring more public forms of intervention or solution, collections devices can be understood as potentially embodying powerful, performative *de-politicising* effects.

However, first, as Marres shows, material devices are particularly adept at being involved in the "co-articulation" of multiple registers of engagement; it is "an inherent feature" (2012, 71). "Which register of co-articulation ends up being predominant", she writes, "depends on *how devices are deployed*" (Marres 2012, 71, emphasis added). This means that devices that are formatted to prompt forms of political participation may end up, in practice, shaping forms of economic participation. This also holds out the possibility that, under certain conditions, devices formatted in such a way as to inhibit political engagement and to stimulate market attachment – market devices – might conceivably end up doing quite the opposite. And, second, devices do not operate in isolation. Their participatory effects are inhibited or stimulated by the settings into which they travel (Marres 2012, 113–123). It is this articulation *between* devices and settings, the latter of which incorporate the infrastructural, that I explore in what follows.

The consumer action group

The Consumer Action Group was founded in 2006. The forum originally aimed to provide support to those looking to challenge banks that, it was believed, were levying their customers with unfair charges (Davis 2009). Since then, it has become a major source of information for consumers in the UK seeking both advice and moral support in relation to a range of consumer rights issues. In particular, its "debt collection industry" sub-forum has become a highly active space where debtors routinely exchange stories and advice about each other's debts and dealing with debt collectors. Particularly common are discussions about debtors' own letters.

One rough indication of its success is that searching online for the name of almost any major UK debt collection agency combined with a term such as "debt collection" will return a high-ranking result pointing to a Consumer Action Group forum post. Another is to look at the debt collection industry sub-forum itself. In June 2014, it was hosting around 33,500 separate threads, stretching back to July 2006, each of which in turn might have generated many posts in reply (note the distinction between a "thread" and a "post").[4] One of the most viewed threads, a "sticky" on the front page, giving guidance on the enforceability of credit agreements, has registered over 235,000 views over six years (although this discussion was closed because of changes in the legal landscape).[5] Another popular sticky (124,000 views) gives details on how to deal with collectors' telephone calls.[6] Others include how to be removed from online telephone directories (149,000 views)[7] and a discussion of the regulator's official guidance for the debt collection industry (Office of Fair Trading 2012) (103,000 views).[8]

Despite the rudimentary architecture and aesthetic of the site, here is evidence of an apparently actively engaged issue public. What's more, it's clear that the forum's features – how easy it is to use, its increasing store of debtor-generated knowledge, the speed and reliability of replies to queries, how easy it is to come across when searching for collections companies online, its potential for anonymity – combine to create a set of affordances for participation: that is, the requisite socio-material scaffolding upon which a defaulting debtor public can crystallise.

How, then, do users themselves engage in the politics of consumer credit? Let us begin with how this can, in less common but nonetheless important instances, take the form of critique and collective resistance.

Critique and collective resistance

While critique of the credit and collections industry exists throughout the site in fragmentary form, there are occasions when this coalesces more clearly – in particular, there have been moments in the site's history when it has been suggested that the collections industry was either monitoring or trying to shut the forum down. This suggestion provided participants with the chance to reflect on the broader politics of debt and collection. The degree of interest in the topic is partially indicated by the fact that the longest such thread, titled "So – they don't like these forums !!", which became an extensive discussion about the ethics of collections work, attracted a total of 575 individual posts over 2 months. This is a particularly intense level of discussion on the site.

In such moments, it seems to users that the forum, which by and large focuses on individual problems, is potentially having a collective impact. This conclusion prompts a reflexive recognition amongst users that the site is apparently hosting a conversation that has an external audience and that their collective work may in fact have certain features of a social movement (the point is that it feels as such for participants). Take the following from the above-mentioned thread:[9]

[emmaf01]

The fact that the DCAs {i.e. Debt Collection Agencies} fear us is a mark of how important [The Consumer Action Group] is!  [10]

[babybear39]

Scared of us? They're positively sh****** {i.e. shitting} themselves  [11]

[sosumi]

I'm glad of it. People power. Woohoo!!![12]

Or take this from a poster called Mizunoboy1954, at the start of another thread:

Had to share this with members, you may have already seen it[,] but the Credit Services [Association][13] are complaining about sites like this that give advice about how to "combat" their illegal and bullying tactics to extort money from the unsuspecting public [a specific claim I will return to in the conclusion] [. A]re they for real!!!!!! Apparently, they are trying to stop us from operating or restraining what we can do?????????????? Just shows that a little bit of knowledge is power and they will never prevail over decent folk who just want to be treated as human beings and not hardened criminals. Three cheers for the consumer action group, hip hip hoorah!

 [14]

In each of these posts, it is clear that the site is being valued by participants for its ability to facilitate mutual support, but also for disrupting, for *agencing*, the operations of an oppressive industry (the mechanisms for doing so will be discussed below), with Mizunoboy1954 explicitly alleging the use of illegal and unfair tactics.

A particularly strident response, directed squarely at a collections industry imagined as listening, is made by a user called OnMyWayOut. This post is useful, as it encapsulates some of the implicit and explicit attacks made against the debt collection industry throughout the forum into one, manifesto-like statement:

The reason most of us are here is because we have been harassed, lied to, intimidated, threatened, coerced and treated like dirt by companies who assume that because we aren't paying them it's because we won't pay. Our personal situations mean nothing to them, in fact our human rights mean nothing to them. If they had made a reasonable approach and taken circumstances into account they probably wouldn't have ended up with such a fight on their hands.

Many people have found their way here because of their illegal, immoral and underhand tactics. Many people who were already in payment arrangements found this site when [Original Creditors] and DCAs started to demand increases in payments that the person could not meet. It is their own greedy fault that the worm has turned.

Debt-purchasing DCAs in particular have done nothing to earn the money they are demanding from us – it is merely speculation, hoping to make a quick buck out of people's unfortunate situations to maximise their profits.

If and when they learn to treat people with debt problems as people, not rogues, delinquents or cash cows and they also learn to keep 100% within the laws of the land, not to pick and choose which bits they want to comply with, then they might get a better response from us.[15]

Not only does the post also clearly invoke a collective ("The reason most of us are here ... ", "Our personal situation means nothing to them ... " etc.), it additionally captures justifications frequently made elsewhere for an adversarial tone and for the site's very existence – although this attitude is not shared by all. OnMyWayOut levels a series of accusations at collectors. These include profiteering, illegal practices, lack of attention to individual circumstance, and intimidation. Any moral obligations that may be held by the debtor to the creditor have been rendered void by the actions of debtors. Replete with political, even revolutionary overtones ("the worm has turned"), the collector, from this perspective, has forfeited the right to (economic) governance. At least one member of Lazzarato and Graeber's debtor public is, according to the post at least, to be found here.

Against what is this post being directed? While it addresses the specific practices of the debt collections industry, I suggest that it also attempts a more general (counter-) *agencing* of markets. Specifically, the market's current set of arrangements is framed as something that cannot be relied upon to be both a self-regulating economic and moral mode of organisation.

This is captured in the critique of the debt purchasing industry. Debt purchasers come in for particular criticism because they are seen as purely profit seeking. This is a common trope on the site. Take the following, excerpted from debates elsewhere about the ethics of debt purchase:

[the tinkerman]

I [t]hink Brig [it's] not the fact that we are looking for a way out of our obligations, I think what [NCM] is getting at is the fact that the [Original Creditor] is not just getting the 10 or 20p in the pound that they sell bulk debts for[,] but also the fact that the purchaser can then still claim the whole amount which surely is IMMORAL.[16]

[ScarletPimpernel]

Buying debt for a fraction of the book value and then collecting the full amount can realise very large profits – which is why investment companies have moved in to the sector […].

That it causes misery for many people doesn't matter to those involved in it; the drones who work for DCAs get commission, and the investors get dividends. This money no doubt eases their consciences no end. What they do is morally repugnant, but it's not illegal, even if it ought to be.[17]

In this same thread as ScarletPimpernel's post, the discussion of debt purchasing prompts another user to raise questions about the wider ethics of the collections and finance industries:

[spamheed]

I think if we examined the moral and ethical arguments surrounding the behaviour of the Financial Institutions and the links between them and the DCAs without looking at the laws which governed them, I think the whole lot would be shut down and disassembled.[18]

Not being the agency originally involved in lending the customer funds, debt purchasers "have done nothing to earn the money" that becomes legally owed to them after their purchases. In such critiques is an implicit recognition of the validity of some residual moral obligation to the creditor (albeit one that is, increasingly, being invalidated by the creditor's actions), but also of the illiquid nature of those obligations. The legal transfer of a debtor's account to an external agency does not, from this perspective, involve the transfer of moral obligations. The "value" of a debt on the open market, forum participants effectively argue, does not and cannot express the "values" that have become attached to that product over time (here including basic human rights, moral obligations, and fairness). Such posts in effect posit the idea that markets are "embedded" in social relations. Echoing themes that have a long sociological tradition (see Fourcade and Healy 2007), these authors are unwilling to see a market's ability to generate agreed prices (here: the price of a defaulting debt) as, in itself, a justification for the way that market is organised. In the case of a defaulting consumer credit debt, it is not just that price is socially embedded, but that the market is not an adequate mechanism for managing and "disentangling" this embeddedness (see Callon 1998).

The politics of the collections device

Such generalised critique can be contrasted to a much more specific mode of engagement which is targeted at quite particular debt collection devices. This is, as outlined in the introduction, a more common mode on the site. On the forum, there is one such device that, for a period, was especially amenable to scrutiny by participants: the use by collectors of "trading styles", which tailed off from around 2010 due to regulatory changes (see Credit Services Association and Office of Fair Trading 2010). At least until this point, this potent collections device was routinely materialised in collections letters and sometimes reinforced over the phone. It involved the creditor trying to exploit the potential for a debt being passed "externally" to a collections agency to shock a debtor into action (Deville 2015).

Collectors achieved this by creating new company identities from which letters were sent to debtors (Wonga, the high-profile UK payday lender, was recently opened up to compensation claims potentially amounting to £2.6million by the regulator for similar historical practices (The Financial Conduct Authority 2014)). The message, rendered explicit to varying degrees, was that the debt had been "passed" to this new company, away from the original creditor. Often, this was accompanied by company names and visual identities deliberately designed to communicate quasi-legal authority, or involving deliberately rough and ready branding. The intended message was clear: the debtor was perhaps closer to legal action, or had moved from dealing with a major banking establishment, to a small, perhaps amateurish operation that may have far fewer worries about pressing debtors harder for the money they owed.

One popular activity became the "unmasking" of trading styles. This is part of a broader set of activities within the forum dedicated to opening up collections devices, of all sorts, for scrutiny: text is copied out from letters, or documents are scanned and posted up in their entirety, including credit agreements and letters they have received from collectors. Devices that were intended as private thus quickly and easily begin to circulate in public. In the specific case of trading styles, such acts of publicisation often involved users paying a nominal fee of £1 to Companies House (the public register of companies in England and Wales) to obtain the accounts of named companies. In some cases, this could show up the organisation as a subsidiary or "dummy" company. In such instances,[19] users undertook activities that can be seen as part collective detective work – including carefully examining clues provided by the letter itself – and part quasi-sociological exposure (see Cochoy 2007), in a quite conventional way, of what might be glossed as the hidden structural relations that connect what previously seemed to be disconnected socio-economic entities.

The forum's work on collections devices is, however, routinely far less spectacular. While unmasking trading styles often involves groups of experienced users working together, more commonly, the dynamic is of a single, new user coming to the forum, hoping to find answers to a series of otherwise unanswerable questions posed by the domestic insertion of collections devices.

To get an insight into these practices, it is useful to follow a single post, started by a user called "Tally_69". He has an old debt owed to the British retail bank Halifax of £9000 that he has been paying off but which has not decreased as much as he expected.[20] He is now receiving, from a third-party collections agency called Robinson Way, "a load [of] letters from [...] nice to nasty". It is thus worth noting that his initial foray onto the Consumer Action Forum is prompted by the arrival of collections devices and that, as he suggests, these deploy a varied emotional repertoire. "My [head's] in pieces" he says in a later post. He's "confused and mixed up.  Causing bad temper tantrums and sleepless nights once again.." .[21] Later, he writes about visions of his fiancée ringing him and telling him "bailiffs are ransacking the house".[22] All this apparently speaks to the lived, domestic experience of default sketched earlier, in which engagement with the forum is explicitly prompted by the calculative and emotional confusion that collection devices generate.

The responses are numerous, the first being 14 minutes after his request for help and asking for more information. Over the course of a conversation that extends over many days, those that reply give him various options, some of which indeed do not mirror standard advice from a debt adviser (e.g. "[d]on't bother with [the Citizen's Advice service] as they tend to side with the creditor and don't always tell you ALL the options"[23] – this is advice he ends up ignoring), but some of which do (e.g. explaining his rights if he were to receive a home visit from a collector and the (lengthy) legal processes that need to be followed before any property could be removed from his home). The site also offers moral support. Take the following reply by Keefyboy:

As for losing sleep, we have all been there too, and I know it is easy for us to say to you don't worry, but try not to ... *we have people on here that KNOW the laws* and guide us on dealing with these scumbag companies, and if they decide to take you to court, (and [that's] a last resort for them and most bail out before going into the court), there are legal people on here that will buddy you, *so take note of what we tell you, ... you are in good hands*, don't be afraid to ask questions, *soon you will gain a lot of knowledge and you will be adding to other [people's] threads and feel a real part of this group*. So keep your head up and *do what we advise you* and you are on a safe journey.[24] (emphasis added)

Like many posts replying to less experienced members of the site, the tone is reassuring, foregrounding the capacity of the forum to act as a source of shared, communal experience. Part of this means having also lived the intimate, everyday life of default (e.g. lack of sleep, "we have all been there too"). At the same time, there is an explicit attempt to legitimate the advice being offered: the "newbie" is "in good hands", including people with legal expertise. Tally_69 is also encouraged to make the move to expert status ("soon you will gain a lot of knowledge and you will be adding to other people's threads"). This online space, while not a full scale "hybrid forum" of the kind identified by Michel Callon and colleagues (Callon, Lascoumes, and Barthe 2009), potentially containing an extensive range of interested/implicated stakeholders/spokespersons, nonetheless provides a stage for the performance of quite distinct forms of expertise, including offering a trajectory along which new members can in effect progress from being possessors of "lay" knowledge to "expert" (on which, see Irwin and Michael 2003; Michael 2006).

But follow this particular conversation to its conclusion and it is clear that the primary mode of interaction that Tally_69 is most looking for is that which will help him find a route through, what is to him, a bewildering array of calculative opacities. Some of these relate to particular terms being used on the site. Some relate to the new devices he is being asked to deploy against the collector, in particular letter templates provided by the site. Many, however, are those that are in specific response to the incursion into his life of collections devices. So, for instance:

HELLLLLLLPPPPPPPP [...] Robbers way *[i.e. Robinson Way]* have sent me a letter telling me if [that if] [I] [don't] [p]ay they will be sendin[g] me a DOORSTEP CALL if [I] [don't] respond within 12 days.

[...] What do [I] [d]o now.. [Should] I have the doorstep letter in the house just in case ??  *[i.e. a prepared letter to give someone who calls explaining the debtor's legal rights]*.[25]

A couple of days later:

I'm [c]onfused  [...] After being [harassed] by Robbers way and recently receiving a letter mentioning a Doorstep call [I] have received a letter this morning from [Halifax] saying basically [that] my accounts [are] in arrears[, but that] if [I'm already] making any payments to continue as [I] am. I'm not paying a penny yet[.] Waiting for a call back from [the Citizen's Advice Bureau] [to] see what they say. Does this mean Robbers way [don't have] this Debt  [26]

And then, around a week later:

RIGHT UPDATE [...] Looks like Robbers way have passed my debt onto a company called HORWICH FARRELLY SOLICITORS[.] Anyone heard of this company before[?] What do [I] do now[?] Info please. [I [j]ust read through [their] [l]etter. [The] [w]ebsite [is] www.robway.co.uk. Sounds [a lot] like robbersway lol *[i.e. laugh out loud].* [27]

Tally_69 here mirrors the tendency to often refer to collectors pejoratively on the site: Robinson Way here becomes "Robbers Way". But it is the calculative problems posed by some quite specific letters that trouble him. Going through the above three instances sequentially, these include: (1) concerns about a visit (it is quite possible that his capitalisation of "DOORSTEP CALL" is lifted directly from a collections letter);[28] (2) after previously having been contacted by the collector, being now re-contacted by the creditor, raising questions about who is responsible for collecting the debt; (3) being contacted by a solicitors – although there are suggestions, via the website address, that they may be connected to Robinson Way somehow.

Tally_69 presents the forum with a series of calculative problems prompted by the new arrival of collections devices. The group replies to each query in supportive, reassuring tones, frequently expressing solidarity and sometimes mocking the collections industry, while providing simple to follow practical advice and explaining his legal rights. They also allow him to solve the riddle of who Horwich Farrelly Solicitors are – they are, as he perhaps suspects, a trading style of Robinson Way. As user Debt4get puts it: "Just a different setting on the spamo-printer".[29]

In particular, when it comes to advice about a repayment strategy, the advice is not necessarily consistent: some suggest avoiding paying at all and that the collector will ultimately move onto "easier prey" (again, not advice a conventional debt counsellor might give),[30] some suggest contacting debt advice organisations and organising a repayment plan.[31] But whichever option he follows, he learns that the forum will offer practical and moral support, allowing some of the calculative and emotional indeterminacies of being a defaulter promise to be managed.

There are a number of important dynamics in play here. The first relates to the forms of economic qualification that are in evidence, as in many other examples that I could provide: what emerges is a practice of collective calculation, or what Cochoy (2008) refers to as practices of "calqulation". The term, rooted in the French verb *calquer*, speaks to mutual *collective* adjustment between human actors and material devices, moving together towards modes of both quantitative and qualitatively oriented calculation – or "qualculation" (see also Callon and Law 2005; Cochoy 2002). I mentioned earlier the ways that devices might offer possibilities for the co-articulation of logics. Here, we see this in action: devices that were aimed at prompting individual forms of engagement become the prompts for the constitution of a quite different kind of calculation – one that is distributed across forum members – as well as, simultaneously, for strengthening a particular form of social collectivity. The sense of solidarity on the forum and the consistency of emotional support are not thus just by-products, they are *preconditions* for collective calculation, they *emerge with it*, and this is in fact reinforced by the unceasing insertion into debtors' worlds of collections devices.

Second, this sheds important light on what the Consumer Action Forum, as a particular type of co-created setting, *is*: it is a dynamic, ongoing, socio-materially mediated cultivation of a shared calculative and affective sensibility (on the latter see Bennett 2001). It is this specific set of infrastructural conditions that allows collections devices to be deconstructed and ridiculed and, even if in a limited way, operating at the level of an intervention into an individual's conditions of engagement, this market to be *agenced.*

Third, debtors do, at in crucial instants, move towards the reflexive self-recognition of their status as a debtor public. Whether or not this newly recognised status is also recognised by those that exist beyond the confines of the forum is not the point; as noted earlier, publics are routinely being created without accompanying public recognition. It should instead be understood as a significant achievement in its own right, involving at once the infrastructural affordances of the forum, the troubling prompts of collections devices, and the actions of a debtor collective. This significance is not to be measured against the effects it has on the creditors and collections organisations against which the forum positions itself, but against the powerful performative forces arrayed *against this very possibility*.

CONCLUSION

The story that the Consumer Action Forum reveals is one of the co-emergence of calculative, emotional and collective participation, in which the agential mobilities of market actors within a particular market setting become the object of political and practical contestation. One of the achievements of a site like the Consumer Action Group is to open up for more public scrutiny some of the precise ways in which a set of commercial and organisational actors (creditors/collectors) are attempting to shape the conditions of market participation for the individuals who are their target (defaulting debtors). The forms of market *agencing* or even counter-*agencing* that can be observed therefore involve the terms of market engagement becoming recalibrated via users' routine participation in the forum, both in those moments when the forum succeeds in addressing some of the calculative problems of debt collection and when it allows debtors to find others who understand the intimate problematics of debt default. What this shows is that, when attending to the precise ways that markets are arranged, to their manner of *agencement*, it is important to focus not only on those socio-material infrastructures designed to stabilise and reinforce them – infrastructures towards which commercial organisations direct so much of their endeavour – but also on those emergent counter-infrastructures that can spring up around a market's fringe. The latter, by virtue of their paradoxical dependence on the market for their existence, cannot be external to the market in question but can nonetheless reveal some of its contingencies and areas of weakness.

An unexpectedly and unintentionally active agent in this process of counter-*agencing* is the market device itself. Collections devices – the collections letters, collections telephone calls, are designed as prompts for novelty (Fraser 2010). They aim, by inserting themselves into the home, to problematise the conduct of daily life and to shake debtors out of their routines in order to begin the process of addressing their debts. However, the presence of the forum-as-affordance can shift the results of such domestic problematisations. Debtors, rather than responding to collections prompts by first contacting creditors, instead find their way online, to then become guided into generating new connections to quite different set of people and agencies.

In the processes, we see new materially and affectively mediated debtor publics begin to crystallise. At times, these organise themselves around what appear to be more radical, critical engagements with the everyday politics of consumer debt. However, as a mode of doing politics, of responding to the forms of ontological trouble that actually living the everyday life of default entails, this mode of publicisation struggles to compete with the routine revelations involved in exposing the work of the collector. These mundane spectaculars repeatedly open up for view the strategy behind, and opacities within, debt collection technologies, in the process lending the forum both its political and practical relevance for users.

On the one hand, this does highlight the very real challenges facing the rise of explicitly politically engaged debtor publics. The forum would have a long way to go before it could be identified as regularly producing politically radical debtor subjectivities. On the other, and recalling Rock's earlier observations, by providing both a new source of peer-led support to debtors and a mechanism for opening up the everyday politics of indebtedness, it does open up a crack in how the issue of ubiquitous contemporary debt is *considered and acted upon by debtors*. The various interactions on the forum can be seen as constructing up a complex, messy public archive, not only available not to existing forum members, but also acting as an affordance to which new forum participants can become drawn with a simple search. This subtly reshapes the boundaries between the public and the private that are routinely being (re)stabilised by credit instruments of all sorts: debt shifts from something to be addressed individually to being potentially collectively solved.

And, at least in the UK, there is evidence that such actions have worried the industry, the debt collection industry in particular. There were complaints about the site in a number of interviews I conducted in 2009. In the same year, such concerns were repeated in a PowerPoint presentation that was leaked to *The Guardian* newspaper, which revealed that the industry trade body – the Credit Services Association (CSA) – had organised workshops for its members to assist them in "combating" forums such as the Consumer Action Group (Jones 2009). One charge was that such sites were actively "encouraging" debtors to evade their debts. The concern, in other words, is of the rise of what has been called "strategic default" (see Cooper 2014).

This points to the fact that the relations of debt and credit may well not be as stable as we often assume. Although the precise extent to which forums such as the Consumer Action Group have the potential to radically and permanently *agence* such relations remains an open question, with further research also certainly needed into the effects of such forums on the experience of problem debt, on the interaction between distinct modes of engagements, and on its effects on collections practices, what is important to hold in view for now is the very fact that such publics exist, that they are self-organising, and that they are having direct impacts on practical challenges of the life of default. Given the challenges of achieving even this, these new debtor publics at least demand our attention.

ACKNOWLEDGEMENTS

Many thanks for their helpful comments on earlier drafts to the editors, to all the participants at the *Agencing Markets* workshop that was held at Institut d'Etudes Scientifiques de Cargèse in September 2013 (in particular the commentators Luis Araujo and Hans Kjellberg), and to the two anonymous reviewers.

DISCLOSURE STATEMENT

No potential conflict of interest was reported by the author.

NOTES

1. Two different interviewees.
2. As expressed in different ways by multiple interviewees.
3. Again, a concern expressed by multiple interviewees.
4. All figures correct as of 30 June 2014. Unless otherwise indicated, all figures rounded to the nearest 10,000.
5. http://www.consumeractiongroup.co.uk/forum/showthread.php?171037-Multiple-agreements-falling-within-section-18-CCA-1974.
6. http://www.consumeractiongroup.co.uk/forum/showthread.php?99376-Telephone-harassment-an-action-plan.
7. http://www.consumeractiongroup.co.uk/forum/showthread.php?236913-192.com-people-finder(1-Viewing)-nbsp.
8. http://www.consumeractiongroup.co.uk/forum/showthread.php?84273-OFT-debt-collection-guidance.
9. To make these posts as readable as possible, spelling and punctuation mistakes have been corrected, abbreviations expanded, and words inserted on occasion to make the meaning clear, while at the same time trying not to change the tone of the extracts.
10. http://www.consumeractiongroup.co.uk/forum/showthread.php?158466-So-they-don-t-like-these-forums-!!&p=1701300&viewfull=1#post1701300.

11. http://www.consumeractiongroup.co.uk/forum/showthread.php?158466-So-they-don-t-like-these-forums-!!&p=1701367&viewfull=1#post1701367.

12. http://www.consumeractiongroup.co.uk/forum/showthread.php?158466-So-they-don-t-like-these-forums-!!&p=1701373&viewfull=1#post1701373.

13. The main industry body for the UK collections industry.

14. http://www.consumeractiongroup.co.uk/forum/showthread.php?369453-Credit-Services-Association&p=4019893&viewfull=1#post4019893.

15. http://www.consumeractiongroup.co.uk/forum/showthread.php?158466-So-they-don-t-like-these-forums-!!&p=1701570&viewfull=1#post1701570.

16. http://www.consumeractiongroup.co.uk/forum/showthread.php?387230-Debt-Questions.&p=4202253&viewfull=1#post4202253.

17. http://www.consumeractiongroup.co.uk/forum/showthread.php?373616-1st-Credit-Finance-Limited&p=4057573&viewfull=1#post4057573.

18. http://www.consumeractiongroup.co.uk/forum/showthread.php?387230-Debt-Questions.&p=4202872&viewfull=1#post4202872.

19. See for instance: http://www.consumeractiongroup.co.uk/forum/showthread.php?51651-Barclaycard-using-Mercers-Debt-Collection-Ltd-(who-have-quot-dormant-accounts-quot-)e&p=419954&viewfull=1#post419954.

20. Various indications on the site suggest that the poster is male, but it is not definitively clear.

21. http://www.consumeractiongroup.co.uk/forum/showthread.php?258952-Halifax-loan-under-Kensington-DMP-now-Robinson-Way-chasing&p=2767215&viewfull=1#post2767215.

22. http://www.consumeractiongroup.co.uk/forum/showthread.php?258952-Halifax-loan-under-Kensington-DMP-now-Robinson-Way-chasing&p=2770790&viewfull=1#post2770790.

23. http://www.consumeractiongroup.co.uk/forum/showthread.php?258952-Halifax-loan-under-Kensington-DMP-now-Robinson-Way-chasing&p=2767005&viewfull=1#post2767005.

24. http://www.consumeractiongroup.co.uk/forum/showthread.php?258952-Halifax-loan-under-Kensington-DMP-now-Robinson-Way-chasing&p=2770773&viewfull=1#post2770773.

25. http://www.consumeractiongroup.co.uk/forum/showthread.php?258952-Halifax-loan-under-Kensington-DMP-now-Robinson-Way-chasing&p=2784130&viewfull=1#post2784130.

26. http://www.consumeractiongroup.co.uk/forum/showthread.php?258952-Halifax-loan-under-Kensington-DMP-now-Robinson-Way-chasing&p=2788651&viewfull=1#post2788651.

27. http://www.consumeractiongroup.co.uk/forum/showthread.php?258952-Halifax-loan-under-Kensington-DMP-now-Robinson-Way-chasing&p=2806579&viewfull=1#post2806579.

28. On the use of capitalisation and a range of other textual and visual devices in collection letters, see Deville (2015Deville, Joe. 2015. *Lived Economies of Default: Consumer Credit, Debt Collection and the Capture of Affect.* London: Routledge.).

29. http://www.consumeractiongroup.co.uk/forum/showthread.php?258952-Halifax-loan-under-Kensington-DMP-now-Robinson-Way-chasing&p=2806629&viewfull=1#post2806629.

30. http://www.consumeractiongroup.co.uk/forum/showthread.php?258952-Halifax-loan-under-Kensington-DMP-now-Robinson-Way-chasing&p=2784622&viewfull=1#post2784622.

31. http://www.consumeractiongroup.co.uk/forum/showthread.php?258952-Halifax-loan-under-Kensington-DMP-now-Robinson-Way-chasing&p=2785751&viewfull=1#post2785751.

REFERENCES

1. Akrich, Madeleine, and Cécile Méadel. 2007. "De L'interaction a L'engagement: Les Collectifs Electroniques, Nouveaux Militants Dans Le Champ de La Sante." *Hermès* 38:145–154.

2. Bennett, Jane. 2001. *The Enchantment of Modern Life: Attachments, Crossings and Ethics.*Princeton, NJ: Princeton University Press.

3. Caffentzis, George. 2013. "Reflections on the History of Debt Resistance: The Case of El Barzón." *South Atlantic Quarterly* 112 (4): 824–830.

4. Callon, Michel. 1998. "Introduction: The Embeddedness of Economic Markets in Economics." In *The Laws of the Markets*, edited by Michel Callon, 1–57. Oxford: Blackwell.

5. Callon, Michel. 2009. "Civilizing Markets: Carbon Trading Between in Vitro and in Vivo Experiments." *Accounting, Organizations and Society* 34 (3–4): 535–548.

6. Callon, Michel, and John Law. 2005. "On Qualculation, Agency and Otherness."*Environment and Planning D: Society and Space* 23 (5): 717–733.

7. Callon, Michel, Cecile Méadel, and Vololona Rabeharisoa. 2002. "The Economy of Qualities." *Economy and Society* 31 (2): 194–217.

8. Callon, Michel, Pierre Lascoumes, and Yannick Barthe. 2009. *Acting in an Uncertain World: An Essay on Technical Democracy*. Cambridge, MA: MIT Press.

9. Cochoy, Franck. 2002. *Une Sociologie Du Packaging, Ou L'âne de Buridan Face Au Marché* [A Sociology of Packaging, or Buridan's Ass in the Face of the Market]. Paris: Presses Universitaires de France.

10. Cochoy, Franck. 2007. "A Brief Theory on the 'Captation' of Publics: Understanding the Market with Little Red Riding Hood." *Theory, Culture & Society* 24 (7–8): 203–223.

11. Cochoy, Franck. 2008. "Calculation, Qualculation, Calqulation: Shopping Cart Arithmetic, Equipped Cognition and the Clustered Consumer." *Marketing Theory* 8 (1): 15–44.

12. Cochoy, Franck. 2014. "A Theory of 'Agencing': On Michel Callon's Contribution to Organizational Knowledge and Practice." In *The Oxford Handbook of Sociology, Social Theory and Organizations Studies: Contemporary Currents*, edited by Paul Adler, Paul du Gay, Glenn Morgan, and Mike Reed, 106–114. Oxford: Oxford University Press.

13. Cooper, Melinda. 2014. "The Strategy of Default: Liquid Foundations in the House of Finance." *Polygraph: An International Journal of Culture and Politics*, 23/24: 79–96.

14. Credit Services Association, and Office of Fair Trading. 2010. Guidance Document: Use, Format and Content of Standard Debt Collection Letters. Newcastle upon Tyne: Credit Services Association.

15. Davis, Chris. 2009. "Interview: The Consumer Forums [Online]." Accessed July 19, 2011.http://www.sparkbb.com/free-forum-articles/interview-theconsumeractiongroup-forum.php.

16. Deville, Joe. 2015. *Lived Economies of Default: Consumer Credit, Debt Collection and the Capture of Affect*. London: Routledge.

17. Fourcade, Marion, and Kieran Healy. 2007. "Moral Views of Market Society." *Annual Review of Sociology* 33: 285–311.

18. Fraser, Mariam. 2010. "Fact, Ethics and Event." In *Deleuzian Intersections in Science, Technology and Anthropology*, edited by Casper Bruun Jensen and Kjetil Rödje, 74–82. New York: Berghahn Books.

19. Freelon, Deen G. 2010. "Analyzing Online Political Discussion Using Three Models of Democratic Communication." *New Media & Society* 12 (7): 1172–1190.

20. Gillespie, Tarleton. 2014. "The Relevance of Algorithms." In *Media Technologies: Essays on Communication, Materiality, and Society*, edited by Tarleton Gillespie, Pablo J. Boczkowski, and Kirsten A. Foot, 167–194. Cambridge, MA: The MIT Press.

21. Graeber, David. 2011. *Debt: The First 5,000 Years*. Brooklyn, NY: Melville House.

22. Graeber, David. 2012. "Can Debt Spark a Revolution?" *The Nation*, September 5. http://www.thenation.com/article/169759/can-debt-spark-revolution#.

23. Irwin, Alan, and Mike Michael. 2003. *Science, Social Theory and Public Knowledge*. Maidenhead: Open University Press/McGraw-Hill.

24. Jones, Rupert. 2009. "Money: Debt Agencies Look to Silence the Critics: Rupert Jones on a Move to Take on 'Irresponsible' Forums." *The Guardian*.

25. Jubilee Debt Campaign. 2014. *Campaigns*. Accessed December 12, 2014.http://jubileedebt.org.uk/campaigns.

26. King, Brayden G., and Sarah A. Soule. 2007. "Social Movements as Extra-Institutional Entrepreneurs: The Effect of Protests on Stock Price Returns." *Administrative Science Quarterly* 52 (3): 413–442.

27. Langley, Paul. 2008. *The Everyday Life of Global Finance: Saving and Borrowing in America*.Oxford: Oxford University Press.

28. Langley, Paul. 2009. "Debt, Discipline, and Government: Foreclosure and Forbearance in the Subprime Mortgage Crisis." *Environment and Planning A* 41 (6): 1404–1419.

29. Langley, Paul. 2014. "Consuming Credit." *Consumption Markets & Culture* 17 (5): 417–428.

30. Latour, Bruno. 2007. "Turning around Politics: A Note on Gerard de Vries' Paper." *Social Studies of Science* 37 (5): 811–820.

31. Lazzarato, Maurizio. 2012. *The Making of the Indebted Man: An Essay on the Neoliberal Condition*. Translated by Joshua David Jordan. Cambridge, MA: MIT Press.

32. Lounsbury, Michael, Marc Ventresca, and Paul M. Hirsch. 2003. "Social Movements, Field Frames and Industry Emergence: A Cultural–political Perspective on US Recycling." *Socio-Economic Review* 1 (1): 71–104.

33. Marres, Noortje. 2009. "Testing Powers of Engagement: Green Living Experiments, the Ontological Turn and the Undoability of Involvement." *European Journal of Social Theory*12 (1): 117–133.

34. Marres, Noortje. 2012. *Material Participation: Technology, the Environment and Everyday Publics*. Basingstoke: Palgrave Macmillan.

35. Marron, Donncha. 2009. *Consumer Credit in the United States: A Sociological Perspective from the 19th Century to the Present*. New York: Palgrave.

36. McFall, Liz. 2009. "Devices and Desires: How Useful Is the 'New' New Economic Sociology for Understanding Market Attachment?" *Sociology Compass* 3 (2): 267–282.

37. McKee, Yates. 2014. "Debt: Occupy, Postcontemporary Art, and the Aesthetics of Debt Resistance." *The South Atlantic Quarterly* 112 (4): 784–803.

38. Michael, Mike. 2006. *Technoscience and Everyday Life: The Complex Simplicities of the Mundane*. Maidenhead: Open University Press.

39. Mol, Annemarie. 2002. *The Body Multiple: Ontology in Medical Practice*. Durham, NC: Duke University Press.

40. Muniesa, Fabian, Yuval Millo, and Michel Callon. 2007. "An Introduction to Market Devices." *Sociological Review* 55 (s2): 1–12.

41. Office of Fair Trading. 2012. "Debt Collection: OFT Guidance for Businesses Engaged in the Recovery of Consumer Credit Debts." Accessed December 12, 2014. http://webarchive.nationalarchives.gov.uk/20140402142426/http://www.oft.gov.uk/shared_oft/consultations/OFT664Rev_Debt_collection_g1.pdf.

42. Poon, Martha. 2007. "Scorecards as Devices for Consumer Credit: The Case of Fair, Isaac & Company Incorporated." In *Market Devices*, edited by Michel Callon, Yuval Millo, andFabian Muniesa, 284–306. Oxford: Blackwell.

43. Rao, Hayagreeva, Calvin Morrill, and Mayer N. Zald. 2000. "Power Plays: How Social Movements and Collective Action Create New Organizational Forms." *Research in Organizational Behavior* 22: 237–281.

44. Rock, Paul. 1973. *Making People Pay*. London: Routledge & Kegan Paul.

45. Ross, Andrew. 2013. "Dossier from Strike Debt." *The South Atlantic Quarterly* 112 (4):782–783.

46. Ross, Andrew. 2014. "You are Not a Loan: A Debtors Movement." *Culture Unbound: Journal of Current Cultural Research* 6: 179–188.

47. Schneiberg, Marc. 2013. "Movements as Political Conditions for Diffusion: Anti-Corporate Movements and the Spread of Cooperative Forms in American Capitalism." *Organization Studies* 34 (5–6): 653–682.

48. Soule, Sarah A. 2012. "Social Movements and Markets, Industries, and Firms."*Organization Studies* 33 (12): 1715–1733.

49. Star, S. L. 1999. "The Ethnography of Infrastructure." *American Behavioral Scientist* 43 (3):377–391.

50. Stengers, Isabelle. 2003a. *Cosmopolitiques*. Vol. I. Paris: La Découverte, 2003.

51. Stengers, Isabelle. 2003b. *Cosmopolitiques*. Vol. II. Paris: La Découverte, 2003.

52. Strike Debt! 2014. "Initiatives." Accessed December 12, 2014. http://strikedebt.org/#initiatives.

53. Strike Debt, and Occupy Wall Street. 2012. "The Debt Resistors' Operations Manual. New York: Strike Debt / Occupy Wall Street." Accessed December 12, 2014. http://strikedebt.org/The-Debt-Resistors-Operations-Manual.pdf.

54. The Financial Conduct Authority. 2014. "Wonga to Pay Redress for Unfair Debt Collection Practices." Accessed December 12, 2014. http://www.fca.org.uk/news/wonga-redress-unfair-debt-collection-practices.

55. Weber, Klaus, Hayagreeva Rao, and L. G. Thomas. 2009. "From Streets to Suites: How the Anti- Biotech Movement Affected German Pharmaceutical Firms." *American Sociological Review* 74 (1): 106–127.

56. Woolgar, Steve, and Javier Lezaun. 2013. "The Wrong Bin Bag: A Turn to Ontology in Science and Technology Studies?" *Social Studies of Science* 43 (3): 321–340.

5

CHAPTER

A Carbon Consumption Comparison of Rural and Urban Lifestyles

Jukka Heinonen * and Seppo Junnila

Aalto University School of Engineering, P.O. Box 11200, 00076 AALTO, Finland

ABSTRACT

Sustainable consumption has been addressed from different perspectives in numerous studies. Recently, urban structure-related lifestyle issues have gained more emphasis in the research as cities search for effective strategies to reduce their 80% share of the global carbon emissions. However, the prevailing belief often seen is that cities would be more sustainable in nature compared to surrounding suburban and rural areas. This paper will illustrate, by studying four different urban structure related lifestyles in Finland, that the situation might be reversed. Actually, substantially more carbon emissions seem to be caused on a per capita level in cities than in suburban and rural areas. This is mainly due to the higher income level in larger urban centers, but even housing-related emissions seem to favor less urbanized areas. The method of the study is a consumption-based life cycle assessment of carbon emissions. In more detail, a hybrid life cycle assessment (LCA) model, that is comprehensive in providing a full inventory and can accommodate process data, is utilized.

Keywords: life cycle assessment; carbon; climate change; lifestyle; consumption; urban structure

1. INTRODUCTION

Cities have been both blamed for climate change [1,2] and defended [3] in comparison to rural and semi-urban areas. The per capita carbon emissions in cities have been reported as substantially lower than those of the surrounding rural and suburban areas and the country average in several studies [4-6]. In addition, high density areas, based on multi-storey buildings, have been reported to cause significantly less carbon emissions on a per capita basis than low-density low-rise areas [7]. However, almost completely opposite results have been reported recently [8].

Unquestionably, the importance of cities in the search for effective climate change mitigation strategies is high, as cities have been estimated to produce up to 80% of global greenhouse gases (GHGs) [9]. However, the approaches utilized in a vast majority of earlier studies are not sufficient to conclude cities or rural areas as more sustainable in preventing climate change. The approaches have two notable deficiencies. First, they have concentrated on the producer perspective, allocating the GHG emissions for a city or region that can occur inside the borders of the region. This seems to favor cities as heavy industries and energy production are often located outside of the city borders. Second, a relevant question left unanswered in them, is how the type of a region, city or rural, affects the consumption habits, *i.e.*, the lifestyle. If cities accommodate more consumption-intensive lifestyles, the possible advantage of high density and dwelling-based housing might easily be lost in comprehensive carbon emission calculations.

This paper presents an empirical consumption-based assessment of the carbon emissions caused by consumers living in different types of communities. We utilize the life cycle assessment (LCA) method to assess the GHGs (CO_2, CH_4, N_2O and HFC/PFCs) attributable to private consumption. This approach enables global comparisons as no regional borders need to be set. Also, the approach allows an analysis of the relations between consumption habits and the area or habitation type.

The study utilizes urbanization rate-based samples from rural to metropolitan areas taken from a large consumer survey representing different consumer profiles in Northern Europe. The consumer profiles offer a possibility to assess the carbon consumption, the GHG emission associated with consumption of commodities in carbon equivalents, related to the lifestyles in different area types.

In the paper we will demonstrate that, when a change from rural to urban area type leads to upgrade in the income level, and thus in the consumption volume, urbanization might lead to significantly higher carbon emissions instead of diminishing of the emissions. We argue that this perspective will be of high importance in the future in the search for effective climate change mitigation strategies. Together with the more common regional production-based assessments, the two perspectives provide sustainable basis for strategic decision making in an urban development.

2. METHOD

The study is conducted utilizing the LCA method. The method includes two main approaches: input-output-LCA (IO-LCA), process-LCA, and a combination of the two, namely hybrid-LCA. The three approaches together with the main solutions are shortly presented below.

The traditional way of conducting an LCA, process-LCA, assesses the emissions based on energy and mass flows in the production and supply chain processes inside the selected assessment boundaries [10-12]. The accurateness of the method is potentially very high as the emissions are measured as they are generated. However, even by including multiple upstream processes into the assessments, the approach suffers from truncation error from the boundary selection that always needs to be made. The amount of processes that add emissions to a certain good or service is normally very high if all production and supply chain processes are calculated. These boundary selection-based cutoffs may potentially significantly affect the result of the assessment [10]. Also, a comprehensive process-LCA is inherently laborious and time consuming to conduct [10,11] due to the described nature of the assessment.

IO-LCA, in turn, assesses the emissions based on monetary transactions, the basic idea being that every monetary transaction is related to production of a good or service that causes emissions [11]. The IO method is based on transaction tables that describe the connections between different industries, normally within a certain national economy [12]. The tables show the emissions that each sector causes related to a monetary transaction on one sector. The tables capture both the energy and non-energy related GHG emissions from each industry sector in the supply chain related to production and distribution of a product over its lifetime, thus including the embedded as well as the production phase emissions. Together these form a comprehensive carbon footprint of a certain good or service independent of the geographic place where the production or the consumption occurs. The carbon footprint referred in this paper is thus in accordance with several definitions, *i.e.*, Pandey *et al.* (2010) [13].

The IO method does not suffer from the truncation error described above. The method is comprehensive, always providing a full inventory of the emissions attributable to a certain good [11,14], except for the end of life stage, which should be added to the calculations [10]. Input output method is also quick and rather easy to use [11].

There are three types of inherent problems related to IO method. The first is a high level of aggregation of industry classifications. Even in the most disaggregated model, the number of industry sectors is less than 500 [15], significantly lower than in an economy in reality. The second include possible temporal (inflation and currency rate differences) and regional (industry structure differences) asymmetries between the data and the model. The models available are not updated annually, and the industry structure of the model might deviate from that of the region studied. Third, the models generally assume domestic production of imports, meaning that the emissions intensities are always the same for each sector [10,11,16].

Although both of the described approaches have weaknesses, the inherent problems differ from each other. This creates space for the approach combining the strengths of the two approaches and reducing the weaknesses related to them; hybrid-LCAs [10,17]. The hybrid-LCA method allows life cycle assessments with lacking information, and enables creation of models that significantly reduce the truncation error inherent in process-LCAs while reaching to process specificity. In addition, hybrid-LCAs suit well for assessments within the context of the built environment, where the studied systems tend to be complex in nature [18]. Three different approaches can be distinguished in hybrid-LCAs: tiered hybrid LCA, IO-based hybrid analysis and integrated hybrid analysis [10].

In this study we exploit an IO-based application of tiered hybrid-LCA, utilized also earlier by Heinonen and Junnila [8], to assess the GHGs related to private consumption. The model retains the comprehensiveness of IO approach while reaching for the accurateness of a process approach. The model is based on IO tables to maintain full coverage of the inventory. To increase the accuracy, the key emission sources are assessed with local process data. The utilized model and its construction is further described in the next section.

3. RESEARCH DESIGN

3.1. Rural, Semi-Urban, City and Metropolitan Consumers

Four representative samples of consumers from Finland were selected for the study covering a range of types of living from rural to metropolitan to assess the carbon consumption of an average consumer of each living type.

The first sample consists of consumers living in Finnish rural regions. These consist of regions where less than 60% of the inhabitants live in urban areas with the largest urbanization smaller than 15,000 inhabitants, or of regions where 60 to 90% of the inhabitants live in urban areas with a maximum of 4,000 inhabitants. The second sample, the semi-urban regions, comprises consumers from municipalities where 60 to 90% of the inhabitants live in urban areas with 4,000–15,000 inhabitants. The third sample, the cities, consists of consumers of municipalities where a minimum of 90% of the inhabitants live in urban areas, and those where the largest urbanization is larger than 15,000 inhabitants. The Helsinki metropolitan area forms the fourth sample. The region consists of the capital of Finland, Helsinki, and the three large cities surrounding Helsinki, the region together having around 1,000,000 inhabitants. In addition, the Finnish average carbon consumption was assessed to support the analysis.

The described selection of lifestyle-based samples enabled us to demonstrate the changes in carbon consumption from three perspectives: growth of the urban density, change in the dominant type of habitation from detached houses to apartment buildings, and growth in the income level. In rural areas, detached housing is dominating and the areal structures are loose. On the other end, in the Helsinki metropolitan area, the urban structure is substantially denser and apartment buildings dominate housing. Semi-urban areas and cities fall between the two extremes. In addition, the differences in the income levels and the consumption volumes are significant. In rural areas the annual consumption volume an average consumer is 12,200 € whereas that of an average consumer in the Helsinki metropolitan area is 17,600 €. Again, semi-urban areas and cities fall between these values [19]. Table 1 gathers together the important figures related to the four samples.

Table 1. The key figures of the four studied samples on the reference year 2006.

	Rural	Semi-urban	City	Metropolitan
Total population	1.120.000 inhab.	860.000 inhab.	3.210.000 inhab.	930.000 inhab.
Respondents in the sample	2.200 inhab.	1.600 inhab.	4.700 inhab.	1.100 inhab.
Level of urbanization	municipalities where <60% live in urban areas with <15,000 inhab. or 60–90% live in urban areas with <4.000 inhab.	municipalities where 60–90% live in urban areas with 4.000–15.000 inhab.	municipalities where >90% live in urban areas or with urbanizations with >15.000 inhab.	Helsinki, Espoo and Vantaa, the capital region
Dominant types of housing	mainly detached	detached and small apartment buildings	mainly apartment buildings	mainly apartment buildings
Average household size	2.33	2.27	2.01	1.93
Annual volume of consumption per capita	12.200 €	13.800 €	15.200 €	17.600 €

3.2. Input Data

The four samples forming the exploited input data were taken from the Finnish consumer survey 2006 [19]. The consumer survey 2006 data describes the consumption of an average Finnish consumer. The survey presents the consumption of an average consumer in very detailed form as it includes around 1,000 categories and sub-categories of goods and services. The sample size, nearly 10,000 participants on a national level (0.2% of the Finnish population), can also be considered representative. Smaller samples can be produced based on diverse variables, type of areal structure and region being the ones used in this study. This survey data were used as inputs in the carbon consumption assessments of the study.

The utilized process data include the average Finnish emissions of heat and electricity production, fuel combustion emissions of private driving and public transport, disaggregation of the public transport sector according to the local profiles of public transport use, and a regional price level correction on property prices. The data are described in more detail in the next section.

3.3. Tiered Hybrid-LCA Model

The study consists of two calculation phases, a direct IO assessment and a hybrid assessment. For the calculations, the original 1,000 categories were aggregated down to 43 consumption sectors representing the region and lifestyle-related consumption. After this, two different assessment models were utilized to calculate the carbon consumption of an average Finn: the Carnegie-Mellon EIO-LCA US Industry benchmark 2002 based model [15] as the primary model, and the Finnish ENVIMAT [20] to evaluate the result. The Finnish average consumption volumes in the above-mentioned 43 consumption sectors were utilized as inputs for both models. The overall results of the two assessments were very similar, within a 5% range of each other, supporting the use of the Carnegie Mellon EIO-LCA as the basis of our hybrid model. The EIO-LCA output matrices are publicly available, which enables construction of tiered hybrid applications. The emissions included in the model are CO_2, CH_4, N_2O and HFC/PFCs calculated in carbon equivalents (100 years equivalency). Furthermore, the model is the most disaggregated model available, providing output tables for 428 industry sectors, reducing thus the aggregation error inherent in IO approaches. This was given high importance as the input data utilized in the study is highly complex. The problem of high level of aggregation of the industry sectors, inherent in all IO models, has been addressed by a number of studies. Of these, Lenzen *et al.* (2004) state that the level of disaggregation has significant impact on the results and thus the most disaggregated model should be utilized [21]. The Finnish economy is also a small and open economy with over 50% of the value of total consumption oriented to import goods [22], a significant part of the emissions attributable to Finnish consumption thus originating abroad. Of the model dimensions, the first tier utilized to accommodate local process data, the production or combustion phase, complies the WRI (2009) [23] Scopes 1 and 2 definitions. The whole model, in turn, is in accordance with the Scope 3 definition.

The model selection includes some potential sources of bias in addition to those inherent for the IO approach in general. First, as in all IO-based LCA assessments, the number of included processes is infinite within the system boundary defined by the scope of the model [10]. However, the problem that arises is an assumption of domestic production of imports. In this study, this means US industry emissions intensities for all the commodities outside of the utilized Finnish process data. The potential industry structure and emissions asymmetry error between a US based model and Finnish consumption profiles was assessed as not very significant according to the comparative assessment with the ENVIMAT model. Larsen and Hertwich (2009) also employ the same type of EIO-

LCA based tiered hybrid LCA model in their study concerning the public sector in Norway arguing for the suitability of EIO-LCA in a similar northern country context [24]. However, Weber and Matthews (2008) report a 15% increase in the US household carbon emissions when the international trade is explicitly modeled [25]. This uncertainty is further discussed later in the paper.

Second, to decrease the temporal asymmetry problem arising from inflation and currency rate differences between the US and the Finnish economies, and the base years of the model and the input data, the model was adjusted with purchasing power parity (PPP) multiplier [26], a method that was utilized by Weber and Matthews in their fairly recent study of the global and distributional aspects of the American household carbon footprint [16].

Third, as inherent in all IO-based models, the output tables exclude the emissions from the use and the end of life phases. However, the use of total private consumption as the input data reduces this problem significantly. The costs related to these phases are embedded either in the consumer prices of goods and services or included in the input data as waste and recycling costs.

The final problem that needs to be assessed in IO method-based calculations is the accuracy problem arising from the use of the use of industry averages in the output matrices. In this study, the use of a hybrid assessment model reduces this problem as the utilization of the US industry averages can be avoided. The sectors enhanced with local process data cover more than 50% of the total carbon emissions, and all the most significant emission sources, as is further described below.

In the second phase the direct IO assessment was used for the design of the tiered hybrid-LCA model. In the tiered hybrid-LCA the most important processes creating carbon emissions according to the IO model were enhanced with local process data, but the rest of each output matrix, the EIO-LCA result matrices describing the emissions of each industry sector related to a monetary transaction on a certain sector, was left untouched to maintain the full coverage of the model.

In the direct IO assessment, four sectors were found to cover two thirds of the carbon consumption in all the samples. These four sectors were emissions related to housing energy use (heat and electricity), building related emissions and transport-related emissions divided into public transport and private driving. According to this assessment these four key sectors were enhanced with process data.

Concerning housing energy, the production phase emissions, the first tier in the output matrix, were replaced with process data. We utilized the average Finnish emission profiles for electricity, district heat and oil assessed with energy method, that allocates the production phase emissions of combined heat and electricity production directly according to the distribution of the total production between the two. According to Kurnitski and Keto [27] the carbon intensities in Finland are 240 g CO_2/kWh for electricity, 286 g CO_2/kWh for district heat and 267 g CO_2/kWh for oil. For private use of firewood, zero carbon emissions were assumed. The Finnish electric power production profile behind the figures is: nuclear power 28%, fossil fuels 36%, peat 8% and renewable energy sources 28%.

The consumption survey, the input data, distinguishes in detail the maintenance charges of privately owned detached houses, but the maintenance paid as housing management charges or rents are embedded within these costs. To increase the reliability of the assessment, the communal building energy, normally paid with rent or housing management charges in apartment buildings and row-houses, was added to the energy consumption of a consumer by disaggregating the consumption sectors of housing management charges and rents. The average shares of communal heat and electricity attributable to each inhabitant were calculated in a study including eight housing corporations from the Helsinki metropolitan area [28]. Furthermore, all the other operation and maintenance costs included in rents and housing management charges, water, waste, cleaning, maintenance and repair construction, *etc.*, were re-allocated under appropriate consumption categories according to the results of Kiiras *et al.* [29].

In private driving, the first tier emissions, the direct emissions from fuel combustion, were also replaced with process data. The process data utilized was taken from The Technological Centre of Finland's LIPASTO study, the emissions per passenger kilometer (pkm) being 179 g CO_2-eqv. [30].

Next, the emissions from expenditure on building and property were enhanced with regional data. These expenditures are separated from the management costs in the input data, except of the share embedded in the rental payments. The embedded share was distinguished from the rental payments by assuming that the division of the costs between management charges and payments of building and property is similar to the privately owned apartments. Of these, the share of the price of property has substantial regional variations, and as the emissions related to building and property differ heavily, regional price adjustments were utilized according to the property price statistics of The Housing Finance and Development Centre of Finland (ARA) [31]. After the adjustment, the building share of the expenditure was allocated to construction of residential buildings, whereas the emissions related to the property were assessed with a low-intensity office work sector.

Finally, while emissions related to public transport had minor significance in the IO calculation, they were enhanced with Finnish industry-based data as the sector forms an important substitute for private driving, and the emissions profile of EIO-LCA significantly differs from that of Finland. The enhancement method was full replacement of the EIO-LCA output matrix with that of the respective Finnish ENVIMAT study.

After the construction of the hybrid model, we further combined the 43 consumption categories down to 10 consumption areas, which indicate the type of region and income level-related carbon consumption. The utilized consumption areas are:

1. Heat and electricity;
2. Building and property;
3. Maintenance and operation;
4. Private driving;
5. Public transportation;
6. Consumer goods;
7. Leisure goods;
8. Leisure services;
9. Travelling abroad;
10. Health, nursing and training services.

Of the 10 consumption areas, Heat and electricity contain all housing energy use, including both household heat and electricity and the share of communal building energy. Building and property is dominated by construction, whereas Maintenance and operation comprise emissions of maintenance and repair construction, water and waste water, waste and cleaning. Private driving, in addition to gasoline combustion, includes all activities related to driving, purchases and maintenance of private vehicles. Public transportation mostly consists of travelling by coach or train.

Goods and services classes comprise daily consumption and consumption of durable goods, so that leisure-related expenses are separated for demonstration of the allocation of emissions and lifestyle differences. Travelling abroad include all private flying and accommodation abroad. Finally, health, nursing and training services are put together as they only include private services, which in Finland form a minor share of all the services of these sectors.

4. RESULTS

The study produced an unconventional but really interesting outcome. The results indicate that the level of carbon consumption is determined by income level and the area, and habitation types have little significance. According to the study, the carbon consumption of an average consumer in rural areas is 9.0 tons of carbon dioxide equivalents (t CO_2-eqv.), in semi-urban areas 9.9 t, in cities 10.9 t and in the Helsinki metropolitan area 12.5 t. The Finnish average was assessed as 10.3 t CO_2-eqv. It would thus seem that in rural areas, significantly less emissions are caused on per capita level compared to city living. Also, all the different types of areas studied follow the same pattern as the lifestyle of semi-urban and city consumers falls between rural and metropolitan lifestyles. Figure 1 shows the annual per capita carbon consumption of different lifestyles together with the private income and the consumption volume.

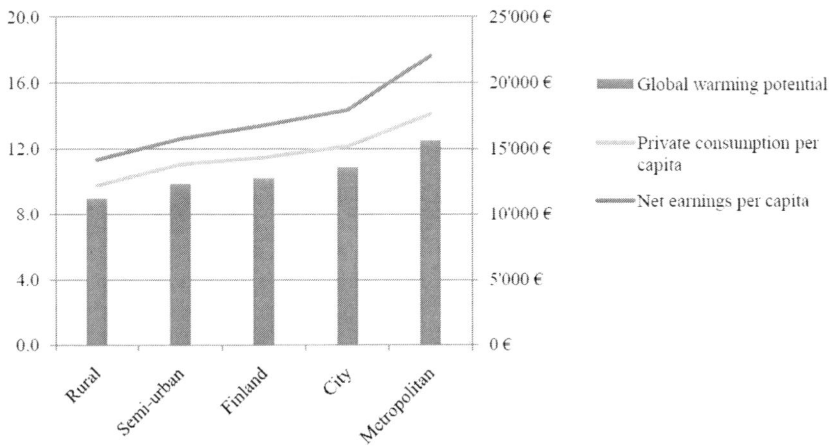

Figure 1. The annual per capita carbon consumption (t CO_2-eqv.) in the reference year 2006, together with net income (€) and the volume of private consumption (€) of the average consumers of the four area types.

As the Figure 1 shows, carbon consumption is closely related to the income level (the red line indicating annual net income per capita). However, as the green line of annual private consumption shows, only a diminishing share of the earnings is consumed as the level of earnings grow. This has an equaling effect on the carbon consumption of different lifestyles.

If we further analyze the components of the carbon consumption, very interestingly, the carbon emissions grow in each category but one as the degree of the urbanization grows. Energy related to housing is the largest single sector of carbon emissions. Quite surprisingly, it would seem that also the emissions related to housing energy grow as the type of region changes from detached house dominated rural regions to denser and more apartment building dominated city and metropolitan areas. The same 2.9 t CO_2-eqv. carbon emissions are caused by energy use in rural and semi-urban areas with 670 € and 650 € annual expenditures, whereas in cities the figure is 3.3 t and in the Helsinki metropolitan area 3.7 t with purchases of 630 € and 650 €. While the level of energy consumption varies only slightly between the different area types, the carbon content of the energy used is slightly better in rural and semi-urban area types explaining the result. Figure 2 presents the annual energy consumption in monetary terms divided according to the utilized fuels.

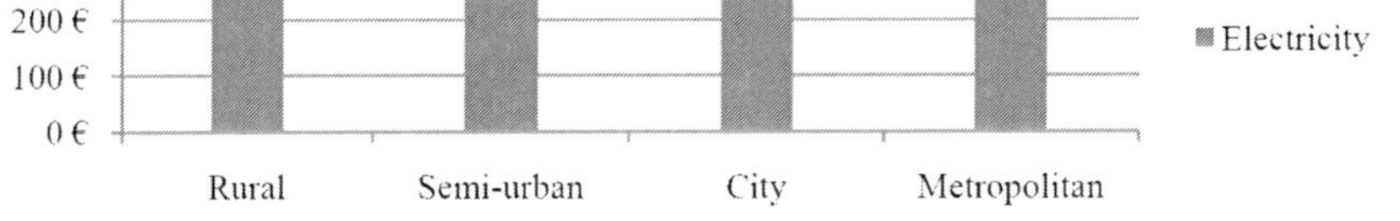

Figure 2. The annual per capita fuel purchases (€) in the reference year 2006 in the four area types.

Emissions from the construction and maintenance of the building (Building and property and Maintenance and operation) together form another significant entity of the total carbon consumption. In rural areas, 1.8 t CO_2-eqv. emissions relate to these two categories with annual purchases of 3,000 €, whereas in the Helsinki metropolitan area the figure is as high as 2.9 t the average consumer spending 5,200 € on the commodities of these categories. In semi-urban areas the carbon consumption in these categories is 2.3 t (3,790 €) and in cities 2.6 t (4,350 €). The spending on acquisition of homes is on a substantially higher level in more urbanized areas, and the same applies to a majority of all operation and maintenance costs, explaining the differences.

The only exception in the pattern are the emissions related to private driving, which follow earlier studies *i.e.*, [32,33] in having a growing tendency as the density of the region diminishes from the metropolitan to the rural type. In rural and semi-urban areas, the carbon consumption from private driving is 2.0 t, but in cities it is 1.6 t and in the Helsinki metropolitan area, only 1.4 t. The acquisition of vehicles equals the figures as the differences in the emissions from vehicle production are almost equal between the regions. The overall purchases on the category are 2,210 € in rural and 2,180 € in semi-urban areas, 1,910 € in cities and 1,860 € in the Helsinki metropolitan area.

Public transport slightly affects little the overall carbon consumption, but is an important low-carbon substitute for private driving. It would seem that a denser urban structure leads to higher level of public transport use, as the emissions grow from 0.05 (70 €) and 0.06 t CO_2-eqv. (80 €). in rural and semi-urban areas to 0.15 (200 €) and 0.24 t (320 e) in cities and the Helsinki metropolitan area.

The rest of the categories comprise carbon emissions from consumption on goods and services. The share of these of the total carbon consumption varies from 25% in rural areas to 33% in the Helsinki metropolitan area, and the consumption volumes from 6,260 € to 9,270 €. The high positive connection between income and carbon consumption is also seen in these categories. In fact, these are a key explanation as to the growth in carbon consumption as the income level grows despite the region type. The pattern is very clear, as Figure 3 shows. In Figure 3, the carbon consumptions of the average consumers of the four different area types are shown sector by sector. The figure demonstrates that the emissions increase, following the growth in the volume of consumption as the income increases together with the urbanization size, in virtually every consumption sector leading thus to substantially higher overall carbon consumption in larger urbanizations.

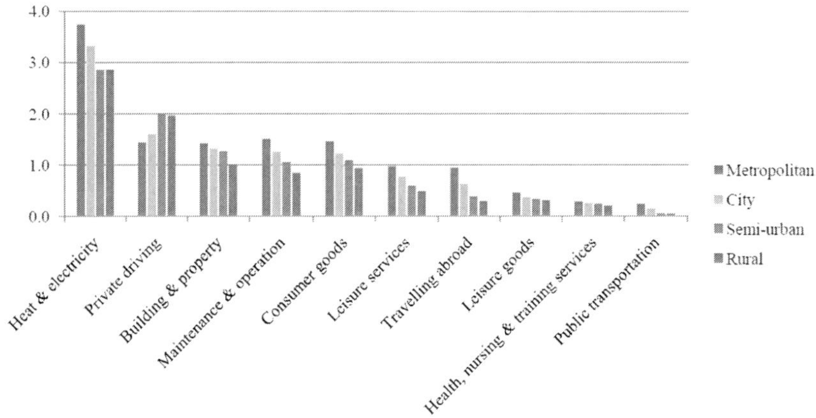

Figure 3. The annual per capita sectoral emissions (t CO_2-eqv.) in the reference year 2006 of the average consumers of the four area types.

5. DISCUSSION

The purpose of this study was to conduct a consumption-based analysis of consumer carbon footprints for comparing the carbon emissions of average inhabitants living in different types of urban structures. This was done with four samples of consumers from Finland representing types of regions from rural to semi-urban, city and metropolitan areas. The study was conducted utilizing an application of tiered hybrid-LCA method that notifies all life cycle emissions including production and delivery chains without boundary cutoffs. We argue that this type of consumption-based modeling of emissions is of high importance and adds valuable information to more common regional production-based assessments. Especially, when seeking solutions for low-carbon living and low-carbon areal structures, consumption-based assessments of the emissions are essential.

In the study we assessed the carbon consumption of the different area types and the Finnish average consumer with the hybrid model. This assessment showed slightly unconventional results, as an average consumer of rural areas seems to cause significantly less carbon emissions than a city resident. According to the assessment, in rural areas the annual carbon consumption of an average consumer is 9.0 t CO_2-eqv., in semi-urban areas 9.9 t, in cities 10.9 t and in the Helsinki metropolitan area 12.5 t.

The explanation for the unconventional result seemed to be twofold. First, it would quite unconventionally seem that the degree of urbanization, whether a rural region dominated by detached housing, or a city or metropolitan area dominated by apartment buildings, barely affects the overall emissions of an average consumer. Concerning energy consumption, which was considered to strongly favor apartment building-based city residents, the per capita monetary consumption seemed in the end to have only small variation between the different housing types. In addition, the pattern found was that the housing related emissions actually grow as the structure gets denser and housing more apartment building based due to rise in expenditure on building and maintenance following growth in the size of the urbanization. This contradicts some earlier studies, which have shown substantial differences between the carbon emissions of detached houses and apartment buildings. The explanations offered by the input data are clear, though. First, when also the communal building energy was allocated to the consumer in addition to household energy, the total amount of energy used was roughly equal in all types of regions. Second, the profile of energy sources explain the difference in emissions, as in areas with detached housing a significant amount of wood is used for heating. Also, as electricity dominates the total energy consumption in the rural areas, and has slightly better emissions profile than district heat and oil, the emissions in rural areas are lower with equal consumption volume. And third, the size of an average household is 2.33 persons in rural areas, 2.27 in semi-urban areas, 2.01 in cities and 1.93 in the Helsinki metropolitan area [22]. Even if there was difference in energy use on building level, the per capita perspective would diminish this.

The second explanation for the overall result lies in the consumption volume, 12,200 € in rural areas annually per capita, 13,800 € in semi-urban areas, 15,200 € in cities and 17,600 € in the Helsinki metropolitan area. An important pattern found in the study was that the income level and, following this, the level of consumption on goods and services grows together with the density of the structure. The consumption volume grows as the density and size of the urbanization grow in virtually all consumption sectors except private driving (see Figure 3). Now, as the volume of consumption grows, the emissions related to consumption grow. This study strongly indicates that this effect of income growth determines the volume of carbon consumption regardless of regional factors like density and housing type. Whether the more consumption-intensive lifestyle is a consequence of the growth in the size of the urbanization or not is not clear, however.

In private driving, the conventional, previously reported pattern, where emissions grow as the density decreases, was found. However, the effect on the overall carbon consumption per capita is quite weak when all the emissions related to driving are calculated, including car manufacturing, deliveries and maintenance of vehicles. According to the hybrid model, the share of fuel combustion of all private driving related emissions is 50 to 70%, the rest being dominated by car manufacturing-related emissions. Thus, growth in trip generation due to decline in the density of the city structure has only a relatively minor effect on the overall carbon consumption.

The reliability of the study was assessed from four perspectives. First, a positioning of the results among earlier applicable studies was made. Of these, calculation with the Finnish ENVIMAT study output tables showed an annual per capita carbon consumption of 10.1 t CO_2-eqv. for an average Finnish consumer, whereas the figure with the hybrid model of this study was 10.3 tons. Regarding the results and the conclusions, the authors have published similar results in other recent papers [8,34]. On the method level, a reference for the applicability of the method has been published quite recently by Weber and Matthews, who used the EIO-LCA approach to study the global and distributional aspects of the American household carbon consumption [16]. Furthermore, the usefulness of the consumption-based approach has been noted in several studies. Ramaswami *et al.* call for the importance of exceeding the regional boundaries [35], whereas Kennedy *et al.* also bring up the issue stating that "it is appropriate to attribute more than just the within-boundary emissions to cities, as the consumption activities located in the cities cause the emissions" [36]. The truncation error might also be significant, *i.e.*, [37], if boundary cutoffs are needed. Regarding this perspective the IO basis would seem very suitable for a carbon consumption assessment, as the truncation errors of all the commodities would accumulate. However, also the uncertainty (discussed further below) of the IO-based model from the utilization of industry average emissions accumulate, and create uncertainty to the results.

Second, as a test of the sensitivity of the results regarding the building-related emissions, which include some uncertainty on the allocation of the expenditure, we removed the Building and property category from the results. While the change decreases the overall emissions, the interpretation of the results remains the same. Without the sector the average annual per capita carbon consumptions of each area type are 7.3 t in rural areas, 8.0 t in semi-urban areas, 8.9 t in cities and 10.3 t in Helsinki metropolitan area.

The third source of possible biases is the hybrid model itself due to the inherent problems of all LCA approaches. Based on the assessments and amendatory actions described in the method and research design sections, we argue that we have substantially diminished these. However, especially concerning the goods and services sectors, the output sector choices include some uncertainties, as both the input data and the output sectors are quite diversified. However, the impact on the overall results is low, and no adjustments were seen to be necessary. In addition, the previously mentioned assumption of domestic production of imports is a potential source of bias. Regarding this study, this means the US industry GHG intensities for all the commodities outside of the scope of the local process data. A majority of the consumption commodities in Finland are imported, but a multi-regional model would be needed to explicitly assess the emissions. Weber and Matthews (2008) found a 15% increase in the US household carbon emissions when the imports were modeled in detail [25]. Larsen and Hertwich (2009) utilized the EIO-LCA model in Norway context, but without providing specific assessment of the potential bias of the results [24].

Finally, the reliability of the input data was assessed. In this study, the Finnish consumer survey provided the primary input data. The level of detail of the data is very high. The survey presents private consumption divided into more than 1.000 categories of goods and services, thus providing an excellent basis for IO based LCAs. Also, the sample size is representative, including roughly 10,000 subjects (0.2% of the Finnish population). In this study, the sub-samples remained sufficient (over 1,000 observations in each sample) and thus biases related to these were considered small.

Despite the very high quality input data, free public services and heavily subsidized services create a source of bias in the Finnish economy system, as these form a noteworthy share of the total private consumption. However, no amendatory actions were taken, since the assessment in the Finnish ENVIMAT study showed that the bias predominantly concerns our comprised consumption class "health, nursing and training services", which had minor significance in this study.

As the final test of the robustness of the results, we conducted a longitudinal study using preceding consumer survey data from 2001. The test results were very similar, except for a scale difference due to the change in the income levels between the two surveys. This test strongly supports the robustness of our findings.

6. CONCLUSIONS

The study demonstrated that cities may not be more sustainable in nature compared to the surrounding suburban and rural areas concerning climate change as is often suggested, when a demand-based approach is taken. In fact, the study showed that the per capita emissions related to city lifestyle are substantially higher than those related to rural and semi-urban lifestyles in the Finnish context. This notion is very important when sustainable climate change mitigation strategies are sought in the near future. However, it is very important to notify that this study only presents a static situation of the reference year, and concluding that rural living would always be less carbon intense would be misleading. Migration from city to rural areas would probably not have any carbon mitigation effect. Thus, the main issue is to understand the huge effect of income on the overall carbon consumption, and that the type of urbanization as such does not define the emissions. It should also be noted that a very important factor behind the results of this study is the pattern of growth in the average income as the size of the urbanization grows. There might be reverse situations on a global level which could limit the generalizability of the results.

Despite the limitations, we argue that the type of consumption-based assessment approach presented here should be given high value in national- as well as regional-level decision making regarding climate change. In the future, the accuracy of the model could be further increased. In addition, comparative global studies should be conducted to test the results in different contexts.

CONFLICT OF INTEREST

The authors declare no conflict of interest.

REFERENCES

1. Girardet, H. Sustainable cities: A contradiction in terms? In *Environmental Strategies for Sustainable Development in Urban Areas: Lessons from Africa and Latin America*; Fernandes, E., Ed.; Ashgate: Aldershot, UK, 1998.

2. Satterthwaite, D. The key issues and the works included. In *The Earthscan Reader in Sustainable Cities*; Satterthwaite, D., Ed.; Earthscan: London, UK, 1999; pp. 3–21.

3. Dodman, D. Blaming cities for climate change? An analysis of urban greenhouse gas emissions inventories. *Environ. Urban.* **2009**, *21*, 185–201.

4. Carney, S.; Green, N.; Wood, R.; Read, R. *Greenhouse Gas Emission Inventories for 18 European Regions*; University of Manchester: Manchester, UK, 2009.

5. Rauhala, K.; Mäkelä, K.; Estlander, K.; Tolsa, H.; Martamo, R.; Lahti, P.; Perälä, M. *Environmentally Favorable Urban form and Transport System*; Technical Research Centre of Finland: Espoo, Finland, 1997.

6. Glaeser, E.L.; Kahn, M.E. The greenness of cities: Carbon dioxide emissions and urban development. *J. Urban Econ.* **2010**, *67*, 404–418.

7. Norman, J.; MacLean, H.L.; Kennedy, C.A. Comparing high and low residential density: Life-cycle analysis of energy use and greenhouse gas emissions. *J. Urban Plan. Dev.* **2006**, *132*, 10–21.

8. Heinonen, J.; Junnila, S. Implications of urban structure on carbon consumption in metropolitan areas. *Environ. Res. Lett.* **2011**, *6*, 014018.

9. *City planning will determine pace of global warming, un-habitat chief tells second committee as she links urban poverty with climate change*; United Nations: New York, USA, 2007. Available online: http://www.un.org/News/Press/docs/2007/gaef3190.doc.htm (accessed on 7 April 2011).

10. Suh, S.; Lenzen, M.; Treloar, G.J.; Hondo, H.; Horvath, A.; Huppes, G.; Jolliet, O.; Klann, U.; Krewitt, W.; Moriguchi, Y.; Munksgaard, J.; Norris, G. System boundary selection in life-cycle inventories using hybrid approaches. *Environ. Sci. Technol.* **2004**, *38*, 657–664.

11. Junnila, S. Empirical comparison of process and economic input-output life cycle assessment in service industries. *Environ. Sci. Technol.* **2006**, *40*, 7070–7076.

12. Joshi, S. Product environmental life-cycle assessment using input-output techniques. *J. Ind. Ecol.* **1999**, *3*, 95–120.

13. Pandey, D.; Agrawal, M.; Pandey, J.S. Carbon footprint: Current methods of estimation. *Environ. Monit. Assess.* **2010**, *178*, 135–160.

14. Matthews, H.S.; Hendrickson, C.T.; Weber, C.L. The importance of carbon footprint estimation boundaries. *Environ. Sci. Technol.* **2008**, *42*, 5839–5842.

15. Carnegie Mellon University Green Design Institute. Economic input-output life cycle assessment (EIO-LCA), US 2002 industry

benchmark model [Internet]. Carnegie Mellon University Green Design Institute: Pittsburgh, USA, 2008. Available online: http://www.eiolca.net/ (accessed on 1 February 2010).

16. Weber, C.L.; Matthews, H.S. Quantifying the global and distributional aspects of American household carbon footprint. *Ecol. Econ.* **2008**, *66*, 379–391.

17. Sharrard, A.L.; Matthews, H.S.; Ries, R.J. Estimating construction project environmental effects using an input-output-based hybrid life-cycle assessment model. *J. Infrastruct. Syst.* **2008**, *14*, 327–336.

18. Crawford, R. *Life Cycle Assessment in the Built Environment*; Spon Press: London, UK, 2011.

19. Statistics Finland. *The Finnish Consumer Survey 2006, the Data not Publicly Available*; Statistics Finland: Helsinki, Finland, 2007.

20. Seppälä, J.; Mäenpää, I.; Mattila, T.; Nissinen, A.; Katajajuuri, J-M.; Härmä, T.; Korhonen, M-R.; Saarinen, M.; Virtanen, Y.; Koskela, S. *Assessment of the environmental impacts of material flows caused by the Finnish economy with the ENVIMAT model (Suomen kansantalouden materiaalivirtojen ympäristövaikutusten arviointi ENVIMAT-mallilla)*; Finnish Environment Institute (SYKE): Helsinki, Finland, 2009.

21. Lenzen, M.; Pade, L.-L.; Munksgaard, J. CO_2 multipliers in multi-region input-output models. *Econ. Syst. Res.* **2004**, *16*, 391–412.

22. Statistics Finland. Statistics Finland: Helsinki, Finland, 2009. Available online: http://www.stat.fi/ (accessed on 15 December 2009).

23. World Resources Institute. *Greenhouse Gas ProtocolInitiative: New Guidelines for Product and Supply ChainAccounting and Reporting*; World Business Council for Sustainable Development: Geneva, Switzerland, 2009.

24. Larsen, H.N.; Hertwich, E.G. The case for consumption-based accounting of greenhouse gas emissions to promote local climate action. *Environ. Sci. Policy* **2009**, *12*, 791–798.

25. Weber, C.L.; Matthews, H.S. Quantifying the global and distributional aspects of American household carbon footprint. *Ecol. Econ.* **2008**, *66*, 379–391.

26. International Bank for Reconstruction and Development, The World Bank. *Global Purchasing Power Parities and Real*

Expenditures; International Bank for Reconstruction and Development, The World Bank: Washington, DC, USA, 2008.

27. Kurnitski, J.; Keto, M. *Emissions from Building Energy Consumption and Primary Energy Use in Finland (Rakennusten energiankäytön aiheuttamat päästöt ja primäärienergiankäyttö)*. unpublished work.

28. Kyrö, R.; Heinonen, J.; Säynäjoki, R.; Junnila, S. Climate Impact of Housing Companies—A Hybrid LCA Approach. Proceedings of 2011 2nd International Conference on Environmental Science and Technology (ICEST 2011), Singapore, 26–28 February 2011.

29. Kiiras, J.; Saari, A.; Hyart, J.; Kammonen, J. *Property Maintenance Expenses in Finland 1992 (Kiinteistöjen ylläpidon kustannustieto 1992)*; Helsinki University of Technology: Espoo, Finland, 1993.

30. VTT Technical Research Centre of Finland. "LIPASTO—Unit emissions—Passenger traffic—Road traffic," 2010. VTT Technical Research Centre of Finland: Espoo, Finland, 2010. Available online: http://lipasto.vtt.fi/yksikkopaastot/ henkiloliik ennee/tieliikennee/henkilo_tiee.htm (accessed on 1 March 2010).

31. The Housing Finance and Development Centre of Finland (ARA). *Reports A 12/2006*; The Housing Finance and Development Centre of Finland (ARA): Lahti, Finland, 2006.

32. WSP Finland Ltd. Passenger Transport Survey 2004–2005. WSP Finland Ltd.: Helsinki, Finland, 2005. Available online: http://www.hlt.fi/english/index.htm (accessed on 7 April 2011).

33. Kivari, M.; Voltti, V.; Heltimo, J.; Moilanen, P. *Impact of the Type and Location of the Residentialarea on Travel Behaviour*; Finnish Road Administration: Helsinki, Finland, 2007.

34. Heinonen, J.; Junnila, S. Metropolitan Carbon Management, A Hybrid-LCA Approach. Proceedings of 2011 2nd International Conference on Environmental Science and Technology (ICEST 2011), Singapore, 26–28 February 2011.

35. Ramaswami, A.; Hillman, T.; Janson, B.; Reiner, M.; Thomas, G. A demand-centered, hybrid life-cycle methodology for city-scale greenhouse gas inventories. *Environ. Sci. Technol.* **2008**, *42*, 6455–6461.

36. Kennedy, C.; Steinberger, J.; Gasson, B.; Hansen, Y.; Hillman, T.; Havránek, M.; Pataki, D.; Phdungsilp, A.; Ramaswami, A.; Villalba

Mendez, G. Greenhouse gas emissions from global cities. *Environ. Sci. Technol.* **2009**, *43*, 7297–7302.

37. Huang, Y.A.; Lenzen, M.; Weber, C.L.; Murray, J.; Matthews, H.S. The role of input-output analysis for the screening of corporate carbon footprints. *Econ. Syst. Res.* **2009**, *21*, 217–242.

6

CHAPTER

Collaborative Consumption: Towards a Resource-Saving Consumption Culture

Kristin Leismann [1,*], Martina Schmitt [2], Holger Rohn [1,2] and Carolin Baedeker [2]

[1]*Trifolium–Beratungsgesellschaft mbH, Alte Bahnhofstraße 13, 61169 Friedberg, Germany*

[2]*Wuppertal Institute for Climate Environment and Energy, Döppersberg 19, 42103 Wuppertal, Germany*

ABSTRACT

Resource efficiency in production and technological innovations are inadequate for considerably reducing the current use of natural resources. Both social innovations and a complementary and equally valued strategy of sustainable consumption are required: goods must be used longer, and services that support collaborative consumption (CC) patterns must be extended. "Using rather than owning" strategies, such as product sharing, have the potential to conserve resources. Based on the results of different German studies, this article highlights the resource-saving potentials of CC patterns and recommendations proposed for policies and further research questions. The purpose of this paper is to show that a general resource-saving potential can be realized by "use rather than own" schemes, depending on the application field and the framework for implementation. CC is suitable for making a positive contribution to achieving the Factor 10 target by playing an important role in changing consumer patterns.

Keywords: collaborative consumption; resource efficiency; resource saving potential; rebound effects; product sharing; service; product service systems; ownership-substituting services; sustainable consumption patterns

1. INTRODUCTION

One of the major challenges currently facing academia, business, society and the political sector is the issue of resource efficiency and conservation. In this connection, the necessity to achieve an economic, effective use of natural resources—in order to continue to generate wealth in the future and to sustain human life in general—was recognized and analyzed by parts of the scientific community decades ago. Beyond this analysis, normative goals and implementation concepts to enhance resource efficiency were drawn up based on a certain target value. The concepts of “Factor 10” [1] and “Factor 4” [2] were relatively widespread in academic discourse and in parts of society; in addition, the “Factor 10” approach was operationalized in an application-oriented manner following the development of the MIPS concept (MIPS stands for material input per service unit) [1], which can be used to calculate the material input per service unit [3,4,5,6,7,8].

At the political level, resource efficiency was strategically anchored by the German Resource Efficiency Programme, “ProgRess” [9]. In its National Sustainability Strategy, the German government set the target of doubling energy and raw material productivity by 2020 compared to the base year, 1994 [10]. In this connection, doubling resource efficiency by 2020 can only constitute an intermediate step. In order to enable the economies of emerging and developing countries and future generations to gain needs-based access to resources, Western industrial societies must reduce their absolute resource consumption by a factor of 10 by 2050. In the case of Germany, for example, this would mean reducing the annual per capita resource consumption from the current figure of over 70 to a maximum of eight tons [1,11,12]. Enormous efforts must be made to create such an “eight-ton society”—not only on the part of business, which would have to make products and services along the entire value-chain considerably more efficient, consistent and adequate when it comes to resources, but also on the part of the State, which would have to create economic policy framework conditions that would be conducive to more sustainable production and consumption and that, in addition, would have to provide infrastructures resulting in the consumption of considerably fewer resources [13,14,15,16,17]. Ultimately, an eight-ton society would require consumers switching to resource-light patterns of consumption and lifestyles that would be marked to a lesser extent by consumption and flow rates than by benefit orientation and enjoyment in moderation. [11,12,13,18,19,20,21,22,23,13,18]. It would therefore appear that technological innovations alone are unable to bring about a substantial reduction in the consumption of natural resources (for example, abiotic and biotic raw materials, water and land). This can be better achieved by adding a further strategy: consumer goods must be used more intelligently, they must be kept longer in the use phase and must be reused. Services that foster "using rather than owning" need to be expanded. Product sharing [24,25], as well as new rental and collaborative models, have great potential for conserving natural resources [19,26]. This is where the concept of "using rather than owning" comes in, involving the prolongation of the use phase of products by pursuing a variety of strategies for action. For instance, the resource consumption of products that are material-intensive in the production phase can be optimized by prolonging the use phase. This paper focused the resource-saving potentials of "using rather than owning" schemes and recommendations proposed for policies and further research questions.

In the present analysis, "using rather than owning" is considered to concern all products and services that aim to achieve the prolongation and optimization of the product utilization phase. This is usually implemented in the form of services that replace products, for example, by rental or leasing models or forms of exchange. Commercial forms of "using rather than owning" are so-called product service systems. These systems offer a combination of products and services that are able to satisfy consumers' needs, offering an alternative to purchasing a product or purchasing a new product [22]. Precisely, the following aspects are involved: on the one hand, services for the provision of goods, such as rental systems for the shared use of goods (in the short- or long-term); on the other hand, services leading to the recovery and reuse of components and goods, such as exchange and donation systems, second-hand shops and so on.

However, the idea behind this is an "old" one: as early as over 15 years ago, the issue was broached under other names, such as "use-oriented economy", "new utilization concepts" [27,28], "ecological or ownership-substituting services", "product service-systems" [29,30] or "service-providing machines" [1,31,32,33,34,35,36,37,38]. In 1978, Felson and Spaeth from the University of Illinois published the "Community Structure and Collaborative Consumption: A Routine Activity". It was the first study that focused on collaborative consumption (CC) and defined collaborative consumption as "events in which one or more persons consume economic goods or series in the progress of engaging in joint activities with one or more others," such as drinking or eating together with friends and using a washing machine for the family. They describe those acts of collaborative consumption as routine activities [39]. In Germany, Schmidt-Bleek first describes in 1994 the potential for saving resources through the shared use of "service-providing machines" [1], and even back in 1996, the study entitled "Zukunftsfähiges Deutschland" (Sustainable Germany in a Globalized World) stressed that consumer societies that wish to remain sustainable "(...) will focus a large part of the logistics of their goods on use rather than ownership" [40]. Before Rachel Botsman and Roo Rogers spread the "Rise of collaborative consumption" [24] all over the world in 2008, followed by extensive PR, videos, interviews, events and lectures, there were few publications on the buying, sharing or renting of goods. Initial conceptual approaches towards this from the field of sustainability research were presented, e.g., in Germany by Stahel [41] and Schmidt-Bleek [1,8,26], focusing on reducing the quantity of resources used. A good overview of the international debate is given by T.S. Baines *et al.* (2007): "State-of-the-art in product service-systems" [29]. A. Tukker [30] in his article, "Eight Types of Product-Service Systems: Eight Ways to sustainability?" analyses sustainability effects and potentials that can be associated with different types of Product-Service-Systems (2004). This is also where the study underlying this article—"Nutzen statt Besitzen. Auf dem Weg zu einer ressourcenschonenden Konsumkultur" (Using rather than owning. On the way to a resource-conserving consumption culture)—by Leismann *et al.*, 2012, comes in [42]. The basic idea is as follows: "living lighter" or rather "a resource-light life" as a general principle for a new ownership-substituting use culture. After all, the transition to a sustainable society can only be achieved by applying a consistent resource efficiency and conservation strategy. In this connection, saving resources corresponds to a great extent on the ecological and economic understanding of efficiency, which is why it harbors virtually no conflicts of interests. However, a tendency towards limiting the term "resource efficiency" too strongly to a technical and economic understanding of efficiency can be discerned, which can lead to the creation of blind spots, such as with rebound effects. Rebound effects mean that more resource-efficient products and services, as well as the increase in resource efficiency in production do not lead to a decline in resource consumption in macroeconomic terms if they are overcompensated by volume effects or, in other words, when the rising demand for a product increases the volume of the products on the market. This is the case, for example, when the reduction in energy and water consumption of household appliances is overcompensated by additional sales and increased use [43,44]. However, absolute, rather than relative, resource consumption is decisive for the Earth's ecological sustainability. A sustainable social transformation requires more than just technological and organizational changes. In addition to these aspects, social change and adaptation and design processes must also be taken into consideration (for example, consumer behavior, policy frameworks) [15,29,30,36,37,45,46,47,48,49,50,51]. Established concepts for enhancing resource efficiency, such as the MIPS concept [1,3,4,5,6,29], take this circumstance into account, explicitly factoring in consumption. Changing individual lifestyles and levels of consumption is a key element in reducing absolute resource consumption [15,52]. The objective is to enable society, and hence business, to be resource-lighter, achieving a transition from previous styles of production and consumption in order to bring about an absolute reduction in resource consumption. Integrated sustainability strategies, such as the integration of efficiency, consistency and sufficiency in production and consumption, play a major role in the development of a resource-light society. Our survival and simultaneous prosperity can only be secured if resources are used as effectively as possible and the impact we have on the environment is lessened [1,13,14,53].

Similar to Schmidt-Bleek, who, in 1994, saw potential for saving resources through the shared use of "service-providing machines" [1], the authors reach the conclusion that a general resource-saving potential can be realized by "use rather than own" schemes, as long as the framework conditions for using the service do not cancel out the savings achieved. This is apparent in the analysis of the selected case studies: textile swapping, tool hire and chemical leasing. Negative impacts on resource efficiency could be, for example, the resources required within a transaction for transportation and/or packaging or the overuse of products [42].

In the following, this article focuses on analyzing the resource efficiency potentials of "use rather than own" schemes. The paper shows that a general resource-saving potential can be realized by "use rather than own" schemes, depending on the application field and the framework for implementation and that it is suitable for making a positive contribution to achieving the Factor 10 target by playing an important role in changing consumer patterns. Therefore, the paper also demonstrates that current results are, in general, in line with those given by Schmidt-Bleek [ibid.]. The recommendations for action and research topics shall be formulated with a focus on political actors, in addition to other stakeholder groups. After all, consumers can only be encouraged to change to a more resource-conserving lifestyle if, alongside the provision of more resource-efficient products and services, innovative policy instruments are in place that show consumers and entrepreneurs which options for action are available to pursue a more resource-efficient lifestyle that support them and offer the right incentives.

2. METHODOLOGICAL APPROACH

The aim of the present analysis was to contribute to the current debate on "using rather than owning" with a focus on resource efficiency. In the process, emphasis was placed on discussions about the resource efficiency potentials of new use concepts and the possibilities of promoting and disseminating the actual idea.

The findings and discussion thereof presented below are based on a methodological approach using a combination of desk research, case studies, expert interviews and an expert workshop.

First of all, an analysis of the Internet and documents was undertaken in order to identify private and commercial forms and business models related to the idea of "using rather than owning".

Case studies were conducted to analyze the extent to which "using rather than owning" schemes actually lead to more resource-conserving economic activity. The case studies were chosen within a multi-stage selection process. The type of communication and trade relations, resource efficiency potentials, data availability, market maturity and cultural relevance were considered to be relevant criteria. On this basis, the authors teamed up with the client and selected the following case studies:

- Textile swapping (consumer-to-consumer);
- Tool hire (business-to-consumer);
- Chemical leasing (business-to-business).

The selected case studies—textile swapping, tool hire and chemical leasing—were qualitatively described and assessed with regard to resource consumption and potential savings based on the analysis of documents. The analysis and presentation were undertaken according to the following criteria:

- Resource use and efficiency potential;
- Other environmental impacts;
- Feasibility;
- Economic significance and transferability;
- Communicability.

Eight structured, problem-centered expert interviews were conducted with representatives of various "use rather than own" schemes and with scientists who had previously explored this subject matter.

Recommendations for action, research topics and research funding requirements were derived from the knowledge gained from the case studies and expert interviews. These recommendations were finally evaluated at an expert workshop. The results of the expert workshop were taken up and incorporated into the study. In the process, particular importance was attached to gaining experts from all aspects of society (the political sector, the private sector, academia and non-governmental organizations), to enable as many perspectives as possible to be integrated into the study.

The present analysis and the discussion of the findings shed light on the resource efficiency potentials of (new) use concepts connected to the idea of "using rather than owning" or that give priority to ownership-substituting services. In addition, recommendations are given on how to promote and disseminate the idea of "using rather than owning".

3. CASE STUDIES

The environmental impact of "use rather than own" schemes has been investigated in the past within a vast array of studies [54,55,56,57]. In this connection, most of the studies focused on individual environmental indicators or consumption figures, such as carbon emissions or water consumption. The findings of some of these studies are summarized in Table 1, emphasizing the fact that the environmental impact is not always positive, but can also be negative in some circumstances [58].

Table 1. Summary of the environmental impact of "use rather than own" schemes [58].

Environmental impact of "use rather than own" schemes	
Positive	**Negative**
• Extension of useful life, use of durable products • Use of energy-efficient and/or powerful appliances • Maximization of device utilization • Consideration of technical/ecological progress • Promotion of recyclable construction design • Economies of scale and benefits of specialization	• Greater wear and tear from normal use • Overuse • Accelerated withdrawal from service of rental products that are still in working order • (Too) long of a use of inefficient appliances • Additional resource consumption to extend useful life and durability • Additional transportation
Environmental impact due to changes in demand	
Positive	**Negative**
• Demand reduction due to greater cost transparency • Avoidance of mispurchases	• Easier access to the product, due to the absence of purchase costs • Stimulation of the desire for property • Increased demand in other areas of consumption, due to savings in income

It was also ascertained in a wide range of previous studies that it is impossible to generally claim that "use rather than own" schemes are "resource-efficient", because individual "use rather than own" schemes need to be considered and analyzed in a highly differentiated manner. Ecological side-effects are revealed, such as when "use rather than own" schemes lead to excessive wear and tear or when users gain easier access to a product, inciting them to purchase goods. However, the tendency can also be formulated that "use rather than own" schemes lead to a more efficient use of material goods and, hence, a more efficient use of resources when certain framework conditions are observed, for example, by using durable products or enhancing device utilization.

Against this backdrop, the problematic nature of generally claiming that "use rather than own" schemes are "resource-efficient" is illustrated. However, their resource-conserving aspects can only be identified on a case-by-case basis. The problematic nature of the quantification shall be presented using the following case studies and assessments formulated as to whether or not resource efficiency potentials can be expected.

3.1. Textile Swapping

Textile manufacturing occurs in mass production, representing approximately six percent of the total consumption of resources in Germany. In this country, each person purchases around 26 kg of textiles annually, half of which is clothing. The global average figure is approximately eight kilograms of clothing. In Germany, the consumption of foreign products dominates the textile and clothing sector. Around 90 percent of all items of clothing purchased here were produced abroad; 881,000 tons of textiles are imported to Germany annually.

Potentials with regard to resource consumption are heavily dependent on the framework conditions in this case study. Depending on the type of fiber (for example, cotton, viscose, hemp, silk and wool) or leather (both mineral tanned leather and vegetable or synthetically tanned leather), type of cultivation and technique used and any finishing processes that may be applied, potentials can differ hugely [56].

Before an item of clothing can be marketed, it passes through the lifecycle phases of fiber production, textile production, textile refinement and finishing. The ready-to-wear item of clothing is sold to the customer, who wears it, cares for it and finally disposes of it [56]. Textile swapping intensifies resource consumption during the "use/textile care" phase, because this use phase of the textile chain is extended if the item of clothing is passed on to another user. With many textiles, the use phase is the phase that requires the most energy and is heavily dependent on user behavior. If we take the example of a cotton T-shirt, up to 80% of the energy in the production and use phases and water consumed can be assigned to laundry care. This phenomenon is also highlighted in the following Table 2, showing the results of the analysis of material intensities (MI) and material input for certain service units (MIPS) of an investigation from 2004, taking the example of a cotton T-shirt.

Table 2. Results of the analysis—material intensities (MI) and material input per service unit (MIPS) of a cotton T-shirt [59].

MI	Abiotic material	Biotic material	Erosion earth-work	Water	Air
Production	2.00 kg	1.20 kg	233.00 kg	14,800.00 kg	12.50 kg
Use	117.35 kg	0.00 kg	Not specified	2,719.60 kg	27.44 kg
Disposal	0.15 kg	0.00 kg	Not specified	0.40 kg	0.06 kg
Total	119.50 kg	1.20 kg	233.00 kg	4,200.00 kg	40.00 kg

Note: Resource consumption of a black cotton T-shirt by Hess Natur weighing 171 grams (service unit "worn 100 times": manufacture + 100 × drying + 100 × ironing)

The result of the analysis of the cotton T-shirt enables a qualitative comparison to be made between swapped and newly produced clothing: in the event of a textile swap, "only one" production and disposal is incurred per product with multiple service (use). The additional input caused by the exchange (factor of transportation, packaging, and so on) must then be added to this. In the case of a newly purchased product, several products have to be produced and disposed of to achieve the same large number of service units. Production and disposal efforts must be added to the use expenditure per daily cycle, which remains the same in the cotton T-shirt comparison. According to Table 2, production and disposal expenditure predominates the consumption of resources and can, therefore, be considered as having resource-saving potential. However, some of the resource savings can be lost, due to the input of resources caused by the hand-down and the use phase, depending on how intensively these are pursued [59]. Long transport distances can also cancel out any resource efficiency potentials. In an extreme case, therefore, the resource-saving potentials generated by the swap can be cancelled out by a resource-intensive hand-down/swap and the form of transport. In general, however, it must be noted that textile swapping promises resource-saving potential in the areas of production and disposal, because no additional product needs to be manufactured [59].

The analysis demonstrates that a general resource-saving potential can be accomplished by textile swapping, as long as the framework conditions surrounding the exchange do not cancel out the savings achieved by the more efficient use of the textiles. Negative effects on resource efficiency could be the resources used for transportation and packaging in the course of the transaction or an overuse of the textiles through too frequent laundry/care cycles, for instance. The example of the cotton T-shirt shows that approximately 80% of resource consumption is caused in the area of care, due to water consumption. However, it remains to be seen whether the speculation that resource savings are achieved by passing on items of clothing, leading to the recipient refraining from purchasing a newly produced product, does, in fact, hold true.

3.2. Tool Hire

The presentation of the resource-saving potential of this type of "use rather than ownership" must be viewed in a highly differentiated manner. The reason for this is that the potential is dependent on the product group, the performance features of the device, its durability, the frequency of use, the maximum useful life, transportation distances for delivery and procurement by the customer and the modes of transport used, meaning they can vary accordingly. Owing to the inadequate and outdated data available, in this context, only estimates can be formulated that merely enable tendencies towards potential savings to be determined.

However, it can be assumed that positive effects with regard to resource consumption can generally be achieved in the case of rarely used devices. In his study on "Öko-Rent im Bereich "Heimwerken, Baueigenleistung und Gartenpflege" (Eco renting in the area of DIY and gardening), for example, Siegfried Behrendt and Frank Behr [60] identified savings with regard to resource consumption in the case of rarely used equipment. Thanks to short-term rental by service providers, rarely used devices are used more intensively than before, there are no purchase costs and since the devices are more durable and of a better quality, the maximum useful life of the device can be used in line with its purpose.

This conjecture can be illustrated taking the example of energy demand: the energy consumed during the production of a petrol-powered scarifier is around 3500 MJ. Extrapolated to 100 appliances, a reduction potential of 192,500 MJ would be yielded with a non-exhausted maximum useful life of 350 hours compared to sole use. This means that the production-related material flows could be reduced by around 87.5% in the event of rental (with a few uses per year). The same, of course, applies to any other device that is offered for hire [60].

The reduction in quantity, therefore, depends on whether or not the maximum number of operating hours or useful life is reached following use by a single household. Here, again, the example of the scarifier clearly shows that the device is not nearly used efficiently. After all, the appliance is used on average for only 50 hours over a period of 15 years. In other words, there are 350 more hours available until the maximum capacity of utilization of the device is achieved. There is only potential for savings by sharing devices if the maximum useful life is not exhausted. These interrelations are shown in Table 3 using the example of selected devices.

Table 3. Useful life and unused capacity of selected appliances. Given in operating hours, estimates based on information provided by manufacturers and users [60].

Devices	Average useful life	Maximum possible useful life	Unused capacity
Drill	45 h in 15 years*	300 h in 15–25 years	255 h*
Lawnmower	375 h in 15 years	400–600 h in 15 years	25–225 h
Scarifier	50 h in 15 years	400 h in 15 years	350 h*

Note: * = rough estimate.

Schmidt-Bleek also supported this hypothesis by mentioning the example of the lawnmower in 1994, stressing the low utilization rate: a lawnmower is used between five and 20 times a year; after a while, a new one is then purchased. This process is repeated five to 10 times in a person's lifetime [1]. In view of the aforementioned table, his hypothesis that a lawnmower is not used according to its maximum useful life in everyday use is confirmed.

Behrendt's and Behr's study [60] also demonstrated that the ecological advantage of renting tools within a "use rather than own" scheme is that a rarely used device does not need to be purchased especially. The customer merely rents it for the time required to perform the work. Due to multiple use, rental appliances are usually utilized more effectively. This is compounded by the fact that service providers usually use high-grade professional equipment that is designed to be durable and is suitable for heavy duty applications. As a result, resources are saved in the manufacture of devices, and emissions and quantities of waste are reduced.

Nevertheless, tool hire can also lead to an undesirable ecological "side effect", such as when collaborative use of rental tools leads to excessive wear and tear and overuse of the product. According to Behrendt and Behr, therefore, in the case of tool hire, service providers ensure that durable, top-quality appliances are offered and that these are used according to their maximum useful life [60].

Renting do-it-yourself equipment generally has the potential to reduce resources and negative environmental effects. In practice, however, ecological aspects play a relatively insignificant role, or none at all, in motivating consumers to exploit these possibilities. Instead, in the event of the alternative use of goods, economic, logistical and informational aspects (with regard to instructions on how to operate the device and how it functions and concerning the products available for rent) are decisive for consumers with regard to whether a device is ultimately purchased, hired or nor procured. Whether an ecologically effective impact is achieved in terms of resource consumption in the individual case is generally dependent on the particular framework conditions of the respective rental situation and usage requirements. Depending on the individual case, hiring goods can either be beneficial or involve drawbacks.

3.3. Chemical Leasing

Every year, over 50 million tons of chemicals are used in Germany, the majority of which concerns value-creation chains in the chemical industry in which reactions occur with fixed quantities of substances and recipes [61,62,63]. By leasing chemicals, companies' economical use of chemicals cannot only optimize and minimize, but also reduce, the use of raw materials, chemicals and energy, contributing to a responsible use of resources. After all, the rising quantity of chemicals produced and used constitutes a growing problem in this industry. This quantity has multiplied over the past twenty years and puts pressures on the environment and human health. In addition, large-scale use leads to the shortage of important non-renewable raw materials.

According to the UBA, around 10 million tons of chemicals could be leased annually [61]. The UBA was able to estimate the potential savings for the use data of chemicals listed below that are relevant when it comes to chemical leasing (ibid).

Table 4 shows the rough estimates of the reduction potential of relevant chemicals in the event of chemical leasing. These figures are not only of interest to purchasers, but also to manufacturers. Specific statements cannot be made at present, because more detailed market surveys have yet to be presented. UBA estimates that in around one per cent of the potential applicable cases for chemical leasing, an average reduction in a quantity of up to 20% could be achieved (ibid.). In Germany, this results in total potential savings of around 10,000 to 20,000 tons per year. Up to

20% of this potential is expected to be realized over the next five years. This would equate to an annual reduction in quantity of approximately 2000 to 4000 tons [61].

Table 4. Reduction potential of relevant chemicals [61].

Chemical	Use in t	Estimate of reduction potential in t
Solvents	7,000,000	7,000–14,000
Paints and lacquers	1,500,000	1,500–3,000
Adhesives	500,000	500–1,000
Plant protection products	50,000	50–100
Disinfectants	50,000	50–100

All in all, the study identified other major case-specific environmental impacts that could be reduced in the event of leasing chemicals. From the environmental perspective, reductions arise in the quantity of chemicals used due to more efficient use. This reduction leads, for example, to less waste from residues and surpluses [61,62,63].

According to the Federal Environment Agency, environmental and health-related improvements could be achieved in all of the known cases of successfully applying chemical leasing. The use of chemicals was reduced and their handling enhanced [61,62,63].

These enhancements concern, amongst other things:

- Lower quantities of waste;
- Less contamination of waste water with chemicals;
- Fewer air emissions;
- Improved workplace conditions;
- Risk avoidance/reduction from handling chemicals.

It follows that the chemical leasing business model harbors great potential for saving resources. At the same time, it must be noted that these assessments can, of course, vary considerably, depending on the particular example. Nevertheless, the overall impression gained is that chemical leasing harbors high to medium estimates of potential.

4. RESULTS AND DISCUSSION

As already presented in other studies [30,54,55,56,57,60,61] and confirmed by the present analysis, the general statement that "use rather than own" schemes are "resource-efficient" is not applicable. The findings of the analysis illustrate that "use rather than own" systems may be associated with negative ecological side-effects caused, for example, by any transportation services or packaging material required. At the same time, however, the cases analyzed also clearly convey the fact that "use rather than own" schemes can contribute to a more efficient use of material goods and, hence, to a more efficient use of resources, if certain framework conditions are observed, for example, by using durable products or enhancing device utilization.

The results of the analysis also emphasize the need to make distinctions when considering different product groups: the example of the cotton T-shirt revealed how relevant the use phase of products is and how resource intensity varies, because the greatest consumption of (biotic and abiotic) resources is caused by water consumption in the area of care and production. Renting do-it-yourself equipment generally harbors the potential to reduce resources and negative environmental effects; however, the potential for reducing resource consumption is greater in the case of rarely used devices. Additionally, the same applies to the chemical leasing business model: the analysis confirms a great potential for saving resources, even though these assessments can, of course, vary considerably, depending on the particular example.

The aforementioned MIPS concept based on Schmidt-Bleek [1] constitutes an indicator to assess and compare the environmental implications of products, processes and services throughout the entire lifecycle (from extraction, production and use to waste/recycling). On the basis of the MIPS concept, the service life and usage intensity of products are equally relevant key properties, because the resource consumption of a product that is material-intensive in the production or disposal phase, for example, can be optimized by extending the use phase [1,31]. "Use rather than own" schemes, therefore, offer the possibility to achieve a reduction in resource consumption, with the satisfaction of needs level unchanged, by increasing the total number of service units (by swapping, for example). In other words, the longer a product is retained in the use phase, the lower the product's total material footprint (ibid.). According to this, endeavors should be made to prolong and intensify the use phase, as shown also by the findings of the present analysis (ibid.).

Contrary to our cultural consciousness of society that many "service-providing machines" only please us if we actually own them, the analysis undertaken by Leismann *et al.* [42], shows that, due to the whole host of existing offers, any products and services can be borrowed, rented, leased or exchanged for the duration of use, which also show signs of resource efficiency potentials. Thus, product sharing is a relevant example of use concepts that, considered comprehensively, reduce material flows [15,31,36,39].

Against the backdrop of the present results, once again, the problematic nature of a general claim that "use rather than own" schemes are "resource-efficient" is highlighted. However, as explained, their resource-conserving aspects can only be determined for individual case analyses. At the same time, it is emphasized that considerable efforts are still required in order to be able to provide the necessary data and facts, infrastructure and information. Accordingly, there is a great need for research. In order to enhance the resource efficiency potentials of "use rather than own" schemes, the following recommendations can be derived.

4.1. Identifying "Use Rather Than Own" Schemes and Tapping Potential

Existing schemes and those currently under development are to be systematically assessed against the backdrop of the investigation results based on resource efficiency criteria. To this end, suitable assessment tools are required, such as the MIPS concept devised at Wuppertal Institute [1]. This tool is based on the consideration of resource consumptions throughout the lifecycle, from raw material extraction through production, distribution and use to recycling or disposal. In this connection, any potential displacement or rebound effects are included in the examination. This way, various (conventional or ownership-substituting) schemes can at least be allocated approximate values on resource consumption, revealing which business model is more resource-efficient. The data could be made available via tracking codes or apps, offering consumers guidance. The following priority research questions requiring funding can be derived from the above discussions:

- How and to what extent can specific resource efficiency potentials be achieved by "use rather than own" schemes along the entire value-creation chain;
- Which ownership-substituting schemes in the B2B (business-to-business), B2C (business-to-consumer) and C2C (consumer-to-consumer) areas make sense from an ecological or resource-conserving and, also, social perspective;

- Which potential displacement or rebound effects result from the utilization of "use rather than own" schemes;
- Which resource-intensive hot-spots can be identified in the various scheme types, and what measures can be taken to optimize them?

In addition to expanding basic knowledge about resource consumption, additional aspects must be considered if the intention is to disseminate ownership-substituting services. The research questions and funding requirements identified in the investigations are addressed in the following section.

4.2. Raising Awareness of "Use Rather Than Own" Schemes as a Consumption Option

Since the utilization of "use rather than own" schemes depends on the attitudes, degree of awareness and knowledge of those who offer and use the schemes, the need for action must be formulated for the areas of image and awareness-raising work and information and educational activities.

Amongst other things, the focus here is on resolving issues concerning not only the capability of the new forms of use to tie in with the existing symbolism involving ownership, but also current social trends (for example, the declining importance of ownership amongst young adults). Image and awareness-raising campaigns could reflect upon social thought/action patterns. In addition, they are suitable for accentuating the positive aspects associated with "use rather than own" concepts and emphasizing the burdensome obligations connected to ownership.

What is more, many users are unaware of existing service providers and schemes. This deficiency could be resolved by providing sources of information matching demand to supply. It appears appropriate to set up an Internet platform and to create an information brochure in print form, showing the range of schemes within the region.

In addition to practiced routines, knowledge about the existence of alternative forms of use and the effects associated with them are decision-relevant in the selection of consumer choices. In order to create an appropriate knowledge base, the topic of "using rather than owning" must be integrated into current educational systems and formats [52]. The open didactic development of the topic in the form of devising experimentally oriented teaching/learning modules and media formats for different target groups could play a major role here [52,64]. Against this backdrop, the following research questions that require funding are given as examples:

- Image and awareness-raising work: How can cultural barriers (for example, commitment to ownership, negative associations concerning ownership-substituting services) be dismantled? How should image campaigns that aim to change values and behavior be designed;
- Information and communication: Which preferences and obstacles concerning the utilization of "use rather than own" schemes can be identified? Which target groups are receptive to which offers? What elements must a communication strategy that takes up and positively attends to preferences and obstacles (according to specific target groups) contain;
- Educational work: What content must be made didactically accessible to enable systemic interrelationships to be experienced and to promote the ability of potential users to make judgements? What competencies do members of the teaching staff require, and where in the education system can priority connecting factors for mediation be found? Which formats are most suitable for which target groups?

In order to establish ownership-substituting services in society on a broader scale, additional factors are required alongside raising awareness and creating knowledge, namely the stimulation of both the provider/supply side and the demand side by way of accompanying activities. The expansion of the infrastructure and the advisory structure, innovative projects and cooperative activities can make a major contribution in this direction, as described in the following paragraph.

4.3. Expand Infrastructure, Initiate Innovative Projects and Enter into Collaborative Activities

An infrastructure that facilitates advisory services (for example, start-up consultancy, specialist information), practical everyday accompaniment (for example, testing schemes) and the implementation of (funded) projects and that is geared towards both providers and users could support the dissemination of "use rather than own" schemes. A point of reference for such an infrastructure could be local authorities or neighborhoods (for example, waste avoidance centers, re-use enterprises) [39].

New constellations of stakeholders can additionally have a positive effect on the market success of "use rather than own" schemes (for example, by spreading the scheme, facilitating access to target groups, exchanging information and solving problems together). If providers of different "use rather than own" services join forces to make a "branded community" with its own corporate design (for instance, a logo as an "umbrella brand"), the concept of using without owning and of social interaction could be promoted jointly. The following research questions and funding requirements result from this state of affairs:

- Expansion of infrastructure: Which facilities are suitable, and how should their awareness of the topic be raised? How should such a contact point be designed and the range of tasks and communication (for example, for specific target groups) prepared;
- Innovative constellations of stakeholders: In addition, the extent to which the trend of swapping or sharing that is currently booming amongst private consumers can be transferred to the relationship between companies should be investigated.

In addition, a positive effect could be achieved by accompanying this package of measures with an incentive scheme tailored towards ownership-substituting services, as well as guidelines offering providers and users legal certainty, as shown below. Especially analyzing public libraries, Hal R. Varian in the *Journal of Industrial Economics* (2000) already argued that it is not necessarily true that sharing of goods is bad for original producers, because the price of the good that should be shared would be much higher than the book would cost for single purchase [35]. Thus, incentives must especially be created for companies so that they make "using rather than owning" offers.

4.4. Creating Incentives and Legal Certainty for Ownership-Substituting Services

Trust coupled with transparency are two fundamental prerequisites for the utilization of "use rather than own" schemes. This is the case for regional offers and, in particular, for Internet-based services. Credibility and trust in the seriousness of the offer and in the participants is achieved by information gleaned from rating systems. In this respect, the development and advancement of customer/user rating systems is an important aspect. Trust in individual schemes can also be enhanced if independent organizations investigate and certify the quality of the scheme based on specific criteria.

Addressees for incentive schemes to promote "use rather than own" schemes can be found on both the provider and the user side. For providers, support measures from free start-up consultation to start-up support would be conceivable. Tax advantages (for example, depreciation provisions) and state subsidies could offer further incentives. On the consumer side, the demand for "use rather than own" schemes could be linked to tax relief (for example, reduced value-added tax) or achieved by promoting user communities.

Additional incentive schemes could aim to: further develop the ecological tax reform, introduce a material input or resource tax, internalize disposal and recycling costs and reward high waste recovery rates.

With regard to policy, framework conditions must be created that give providers and consumers legal certainty. Gaps in legislation need to be closed and a transparent legal situation created. Standard warranty and liability rules, assistance in drafting contracts (for example, drawing up standard or model contracts) and support in clarifying insurance-related issues, for instance, are conceivable. Needs for research requiring funding can be identified in the following areas:

- Rating systems: Which confidence-building measures are pertinent, and how can they be integrated? Which evaluation methods are suitable for assessing offers directionally (regional/web-based)? What role can certification play;
- Monetary/immaterial incentives: Which measures play a key role in dismantling barriers for consumers and entrepreneurs;
- Legal framework conditions: How can legal and financial obstacles (for example, commercial, tax, warranty, planning law, and so on) be overcome for entrepreneurs who wish to develop or use a "using rather than owning" scheme? How can price economics be shaped in favor of "using rather than owning"?

P. Söderholm and J.E. Tilton also conclude from their analysis of material efficiency in an economic perspective that incentives should play a central role in a policy to effectively promote resource efficiency. They argue: "that environmental externalities and information failures, rather than concerns over depletion and growing resource scarcities, provide the main justification for policies promoting material efficiency. Policy makers should thus opt for regulatory measures that target the relevant market failures (e.g., environmental damages, absence of internalized environmental costs, false information and asymmetric lack of information, innovation-related market imperfection) as closely as possible" [51].

Prices are a relevant aspect for decisions, both on the side of producers and consumers. Because as long as environmental costs are not internalized, prices for products remain accordingly lower and prices for services are higher, it will be hard to promote "using instead of owning" schemes. Additionally, people tend to ascribe high symbolic value to the ownership of goods and, thus, a cultural shift is required "to place value on having a need met as opposed to owning a product" [3]. Central barriers are seen in consumers' reservation towards consumption without ownership and producers have to consider, e.g., organizational change, formation of prices and shifting back risks into their own business, which have, so far, been born by consumers. To handle these tasks and the possible lack of previous experience, time, capital and information are required. Incentives here can help to overcome barriers both on the side of consumers and producers [29,51,65,66].

5. CONCLUSIONS

Similar to Schmidt-Bleek, who in 1994 saw potential for saving resources through the shared use of "service-providing machines" [1], the analysis shows that a general resource-saving potential can be realized by "use rather than own" schemes, as long as the framework conditions associated with using the service do not cancel out the savings achieved. This is apparent in the analysis of the selected case studies: textile swapping, tool hire and chemical leasing. Negative impacts on resource efficiency could be, for example, the resources required within a transaction for transportation and/or packaging or the overuse of products. "Using rather than owning" can lead to the optimization of the resource consumption of products that, for example, are material-intensive in the production phase, by extending the use phase.

In addition, the investigation results clearly indicate that, besides expanding basic knowledge concerning data and facts about resource consumption and how to generate them, other aspects must also be taken into account if ownership-substituting services are to be disseminated. On the one hand, there needs to be a change in attitude in society leading to a loss in the symbolic strength of ownership. Enhancing the image and the level of information amongst (potential) providers and users about "use rather than own" schemes and the framework conditions associated with them can contribute to this. The structural entrenchment of a consultancy infrastructure that goes well beyond merely providing information (for example, neighborhood-based re-use centers, start-up consultation, and so on) can also give important impetus to disseminating supply and demand in the area of ownership-substituting services. This can be done by enabling schemes to be experienced, offering both potential providers and users a testing ground. Experimentally oriented teaching/learning modules and media formats, prepared for different target groups, would be suitable for use in different areas, such as academic and vocational education. Furthermore, incentive schemes (for example, start-up support, tax advantages for providers and users, promotion of user communities), the subject of legal

certainty for providers and users (for example, standard warranty and liability rules, assistance in drafting contracts and the clarification of insurance-related issues) and research promotion set guidelines that are suitable for positively stimulating supply and demand for ownership-substituting services.

To summarize, it can be concluded that "use rather than own" concepts alone will undoubtedly not suffice to reduce resource consumption to the extent necessary. It can be assumed, however, that they can make an economically relevant contribution, particularly because, according to forecasts, above all, Internet-based schemes will continue to expand further and play an important role in changing consumer patterns, due to the wide use and networking opportunities offered by the Internet. The reputation of flexible access to products or services and affiliation to (Internet-based) social networks or the social additional benefit associated with specific schemes are being enhanced, particularly amongst younger population groups. It is a trend within which the well-tried logics of ownership begin to totter or become displaced. In this connection, however, it is important to consider resource consumption and resource efficiency potentials in a differentiated manner. However, the principles underlying "use rather than own" schemes are suitable for making a positive contribution to achieving the Factor 10 target.

ACKNOWLEDGMENTS

We would like to thank Heinrich-Böll-Stiftung e.V. and Naturschutzbund Deutschland (NABU) for their financial support and contextual cooperation within the study.

REFERENCES

1. Schmidt-Bleek, F. *Wieviel Umwelt braucht der Mensch—MIPS, das Maß für ökologisches Wirtschaften*; Birkhäuser: Basel, Switzerland, 1994.
2. Weizsäcker, E.U.V.; Lovins, A.B.; Lovins, L.H. *Faktor Vier: Doppelter Wohlstand, halbierter Naturverbrauch. Der neue Bericht an den Club of Rome*; Droemer Knaur: München, Germany, 1995.
3. Lettenmeier, M.; Rohn, H.; Liedtke, C.; Schmidt-Bleek, F. *Resource Productivity in 7 Steps: How to Develop Eco-Innovative Products*

and Services and Improve Their Material Footprint; Wuppertal Institute for Climate, Environment and Energy: Wuppertal, Germany. Available online: http://epub.wupperinst.org/frontdoor/index/index/docId/3384 (accessed on 29 April 2013).

4. Liedtke, C.; Wiesen, K.; Teubler, J.; Bienge, K.; Greiff, K.; Lettenmeier, M.; Rohn, H. Resource intensity analysis at micro level: Measuring dematerialization at product, company and household level. *Resources* **2013**. Submitted for Publication.

5. Mancini, L.; Lettenmeier, M.; Rohn, H.; Liedtke, C. Application of the MIPS method for assessing the sustainability of production-consumption systems of food. *J. Econ. Behav. Organ.* 2012, 81, pp. 779–793. Available online: http://www.sciencedirect.com/science/article/pii/S0167268111000357 (accessed on 20 April 2013).

6. Ritthoff, M.; Rohn, H.; Liedtke, C. Ressourcenproduktivität von Produkten und Dienstleistungen. Wuppertal Institute for Climate, Environment and Energy: Wuppertal, Germany, 2002.

7. Samus, T.; Lang, B.; Rohn, H. Assessing the natural resource use and the resource efficiency potential of the Desertec concept. *Sol. Energy* **2013**, *87*, 176–183.

8. Schmidt Bleek, F.; Bierter, W. *Das MIPS Konzept. Weniger Naturverbrauch, mehr Lebensqualität durch Faktor 10*; Droemer Knaur: München, Germany, 1998.

9. Federal ministry for the Environment; Nature Conservation and Nuclear Safety (BMU). *Programme for the Sustainable Use and Conservation of Natural Resources*; BMU: Berlin, Germany, 2012. Available online: http://www.bmu.de/fileadmin/bmu-import/files/pdfs/allgemein/application/pdf/progress_en_bf.pdf (accessed on 29 April 2013).

10. Federal Government. *Perspektiven für Deutschland. Unsere Strategie für eine Nachhaltige Entwicklung*; Federal Government: Berlin , Germany, 2002.

11. Lettenmeier, M.; Göbel, C.; Liedtke, C.; Rohn, H.; Teitscheid, P. Material Footprint of a Sustainable Nutrition System in 2050—Need for Dynamic Innovations in Production, Consumption and Politics. In Proceedings of 6th International European Forum (Igls-Forum) on System Dynamics and Innovation in Food Networks, Innsbruck, Austria, 13–17 February 2012; pp. 484–598.

12. Lettenmeier, M.; Liedtke, C.; Rohn, H. Roadmap to lifestyles of low resource consumption—New perspectives on sustainable transformation processes on the level of households. In *Resources*; 2013; Submitted for Publication.

13. Liedtke, C.; Buhl, J.; Ameli, N. Designing value through less by integrating sustainability strategies into lifestyles. *Int. J. Sustain. Des.* 2013; in press. Available online: http://www.inderscience.com/info/ingeneral/forthcoming.php?jcode=ijsdes (accessed on 26 April 2013).

14. Liedtke, C.; Buhl, J.; Ameli, N. Microfoundations for sustainable growth with eco-intelligent product service-arrangements. *Sustainability* **2013**, *5*, 1141–1160.

15. Liedtke, C.; Hasselkuß, M.; Welfens, M.J.; Nordmann, J.; Baedeker, C. Transformation Towards Sustainable Consumption: Changing Consumption Patterns Through Meaning in Social Practices. In Proceedings of the 4th International Conference on Sustainability Transitions, Zurich, Switzerland, 19–21 June 2013.

16. Liedtke, C.; Lettenmeier, M.; Mancini, L.; Urbaneja, D.M. *Resource consumption by private households*; Wuppertal Institute for Climate, Environment and Energy: Wuppertal, Germany, unpublished work; 2013.

17. Welfens, M.J.; Liedtke, C.; Rohn, H. Living Lab: Research and Development of Sustainable Products and Services Through User-Driven Innovation in Experimental-Oriented Environments. In Proceedings of the ERSCP-EMSU Knowledge Collaboration & Learning for Sustainable Innovation Conference, Delft, the Netherlands, 25—29 October 2010.

18. Bringezu, S.; Bleischwitz, R. *Sustainable Resource Management. Trends, Visions and Policies for Europe and the World*; Greenleaf Publisher: Sheffield, UK, 2009.

19. Liedtke, C.; Baedeker, C.; Rohn, H.; Hasselkuß, M.; Grinewitschus, V. Sustainable LivingLabs—European Research Infrastructure for the User-Integrated Development of Sustainable Product and Service Innovation (SusLabNWE). Proceedings of the 17th International Sustainable Innovation Conference, Bonn, Germany, 29–30 October 2012; Available online: http://www.re-ad.dk/karch/files/39618923/SI12_Proceedings_Papers_2012_10_24_.pdf (accessed on 23 July 2013).

20. Liedtke, C.; Welfens, M.J.; Rohn, H.; Nordmann, J. LIVING LAB: user-driven innovation for sustainability. *Int. Sustain. High. Edu.* **2012**, *13*, 106–118.

21. Rohn, H.; Wiesen, K.; Lettenmeier, M.; Pastewski, N. Quantitative Benefits of Sustainable Innovation: Resource Efficiency Potentials of Technologies, Products and Strategies. In Proceedings of the Sustainable Innovation 2010 Conference, Rotterdam, the Netherland, 8–9 November 2010.

22. Rohn, H.; Wiesen, K.; Lettenmeier, M.; Pastewski, N. Sustainability Through Innovative Technologies, Products and Strategies with High Resource Efficiency Potentials: Results from Current Research Studies in Germany. In Proceedings of the ERSCP-EMSU Conference Knowledge Collaboration & Learning for Sustainable Innovation, Delft, the Netherland, 25–29 October 2010.

23. Talwar, S.; Wiek, A.; Robinson, J. User engagement in sustainability research. *Sci. Public Policy* **2011**, *38*, 379–390.

24. Botsman, R.; Rogers, R. Beyond zipcar: Collaborative consumption. *Harvard Business Review*, October 2010. Available online: http://hbr.org/2010/10/beyond-zipcar-collaborative-consumption/ (accessed on 23 July 2013).

25. Botsman, R.; Rogers, R. *What's Mine is Yours: The Rise of Collaborative Consumption. How Collaborate Consumption is Changing the Way of Life*; Harpercollins: London, UK, 2011.

26. Schmidt-Bleek, F.; Tischner, U. *Produktentwicklung, Nutzen Gestalten—Natur Schonen*; Wirtschaftskammer: Vienna, Austria, 1995.

27. Baedeker, C.; Liedtke, C.; Welfens, M.J.; Busch, T.; Kristof, K.; Kuhndt, M.; Schmitt, M.; Türk, V. *Analyse Vorhandener Konzepte zur Messung des Nachhaltigen Konsums in Deutschland Einschließlich der Grundzüge eines Entwicklungskonzeptes*; Wuppertal Institute for Climate, Environment and Energy: Wuppertal, Germany, 2005. Available online: http:// wupperinst.org/ uploads/tx_wupperinst/messung-nachh-konsum. pdf (accessed on 29 April 2013).

28. Hirschl, B.; Konrad, W.; Scholl, G.; Zundel, S. *Nachhaltige Produktnutzung. Sozial-ökonomische Bedingungen und ökologische Vorteile alternativer Konsumformen*; Institut für ökologische Wirtschaftsforschung (IÖW): Berlin, Germany, 2001.

29. Baines, T.S.; Lightfoot, H.; Steve, E.; Neely, A.; Greenough, R.; Peppard, J; Roy, R.; Shehab, E.; Braganza, A.; Tiwari, A.; *et al.* State-of-the-art in product service-systems. *J. Eng. Manu.* **2007**, *221*, 1543–1552.

30. Tukker, A. Eight types of product-sevice system: eight ways to sustainability? Experiences from suspronet. *Bus. Strat. Env.* **2004**, *13*, 246–260.

31. Bierter, W.; Stahel, W.R.; Schmidt-Bleek, F. *Öko-intelligente Produkte, Dienstleistungen und Arbeit. Wuppertal Spezial*; Wuppertal Institute for Climate, Environment and Energy: Wuppertal, Germany, 1996.

32. Scholl, G. Eine Ressourcenschonende Konsumkultur. In *Oekom e.V.—Verein für Ökologische Kommunikation. Rohstoffquelle Abfall. Wie aus Müll Produkte von Morgen Werden Oekom*; Nutzen statt Besitzen: Munich, Germany, 2012; pp. 92–96.

33. Schumpeter, J. The Business of Sharing. Available online: http://www.economist.com/node/17249322/print (accessed on 23 July 2013).

34. Scott, D.A. *Sharing to Advantage: A New Paradigm for Business. Newsletter Strategy & Innovation from Harvard Business School*; Harvard Business School: Cambrigde, MA, USA, 2004.

35. Varian, H.R. Buying, Sharing and renting information goods. *J. Ind. Econ.* **2000**, *48*, 473–488.

36. Stengel, O. *Suffizienz: die Konsumgesellschaft in der ökologischen Krise, Dissertationsschrift, Wuppertaler Schriften zur Forschung für eine nachhaltige Entwicklung*; Oekom: Munich, Germany, 2011.

37. Stengel, O. Weniger ist schwer. Barrieren in der Umsetzung suffizienter Lebensstile–und wie wir sie überwinden können. *GAIA* **2011**, *20*, 614–624.

38. Welfens, M.J.; Liedtke, C.; Nordman, J. Sustainable Consumption: Between Unsustainable Reality and People's Willingness to Act. In Proceedings of the ERSCP-EMSU Knowledge Collaboration & Learning for Sustainable Innovation Conference, Delft, the Netherlands, 25–29 October 2010.

39. Felson, M.; Spaeth, J.L. Community structure and collaborative consumption: a routine activity approach. *Am. Behav. Sci.* **1978**, *21*, 614–624.

40. Wuppertal Institute for Climate, *Environment and Energy. Sustainable Germany in a Globalised World*; Birkhäuser Verlag: Basel, Switzerland, 1996.

41. Stahel, W. *Vertiefungsstudie zu Langlebigkeit und Materialrecycling im Bereich der Produkte*; Ministry for the environment: Stuttgart, Germany, 1991.

42. Leismann, K.; Schmitt, M.; Rohn, H.; Baedeker, C. *Nutzen statt Besitzen. Auf dem Weg zu einer ressourcenschonenden Konsumkultur*; Heinrich-Böll-Stiftung: Berlin, Germany, 2012.

43. Hertwich, E.G. Consumption and the rebound effect: An industrial ecology perspective. *J. Ind. Ecol.* **2005**, *9*, 85–98.

44. Kristof, K.; Süßbauer, E. Material Efficiency and Resource Conservation. *Handlungsoptionen zur Steigerung der Ressourceneffizienz im Konsumalltag*; Wuppertal Institute for Climate, Environment and Energy: Wuppertal, Germany, 2009. Available online: http://ressourcen.wupperinst.org/ downloads /MaRess_AP12_2.pdf (accessed on 26 April 2013).

45. European Commission (EC). *A Resource—Efficient Europe-Flagship Initiative under the Europe 2020 Strategy*; European Commission: Brüssel, Belgium, 2011. Available online: http: //ec.europa.eu/resource-efficient-europe/pdf/resource_ efficient_europe_en.pdf (accessed on 26 April 2013).

46. European Commission (EC). *Roadmap to a Resource Efficient Europe. Communication from the Commission to the European Parliament*; European Commission: Brussels, Belgium, 2011. Available online: http://ec.europa.eu/environment/resource _efficiency/about/roadmap/index_en.htm (accessed on 27 April 2013).

47. Geels, F.W.; Schot, J.W. Typology of sociotechnical transition pathways. *Res. Policy* **2007**, *36*, 399–417.

48. German Advisory Council on Global Change (WBGU). *World in Transition—A Social Contract for Sustainability*; WBGU: Berlin, Germany, 2011. Available online: http://www. wbgu.de/fileadmin/templates/dateien/veroeffentlichungen/hau ptgutachten/jg2011/wbgu_jg2011.pdf (accessed on 26 April 2013).

49. Schneidewind, U.; Scheck, H.; Augenstein, K.; Baedeker, C.; Beuermann, C.; Bleischwitz, R.; Böhler, S.; Bringezu, S.; Fischedick, M.; Jordan, N.D.; *et al. Transitions towards Sustainability. Rethinking the Wuppertal Institute Research*

Perspective; Wuppertal Institute for Climate, Environment and Energy: Wuppertal, Germany, 2011.

50. Schneidewind, U.; Singer-Brodowski, M. *Transformative Wissenschaft. Klimawandel im deutschen Wissenschafts- und Hochschulsystem*; Metropolis-Verlag: Marburg, Germany, 2013.

51. Söderholm, P.; Tilton, J.E. Material efficiency: An economic perspective. *Resour. Conserv. Recycl.* **2012**, *61*, 75–82.

52. Welfens, M.J; Liedtke, C.; Schaefer, I. Encouraging sustainability–educational program for civil society. *Int. Textb. Res.* **2008**, *2*, 639–674.

53. Seiler-Hausmann, J.D.; Liedtke, C.; Weizsacker, E.U. *Eco-efficiency and Beyond: Towards the Sustainable Enterprise*; Greenleaf Publisher: Sheffield, UK, 2004.

54. Erdmann, L. Quantifizierung der Umwelteffekte des privaten Gebrauchtwarenhandels am Beispiel von eBay. In *Wiederverkaufskultur im Internet. Chancen für nachhaltigen Konsum am Beispiel von eBay*; Behrendt, S., Blättel-Mink, B., Clausen, J., Eds.; Springer: Heidelberg, Germany, 2011; pp. 127–158.

55. Scholl, G.; Bietz, S.; Kristof, K.; Otto, S.; Reisch, L.; Rubik, F.; Süßbauer, E. *Consumer-Oriented Approaches to Foster Resource Efficiency*; European Commission: Wuppertal, Germany, 2010.

56. Scholl, G. Product-Service Systems: Taking a Functional and a Symbolic Perspective on Usership. In *System Innovation for Sustainability 1: Perspectives on Radical Changes to Sust*; Greenleaf Publishing in association with GSE Research: Sheffield, UK, 2008; pp. 255–270.

57. Tukker, A.; Huppes, G.; Suh, S.; Heijungs, R.; Guinée, J.; de Koning, A.; Geerken, T.; Jansen, G.; van Holderbeke, M.; Nielsen, P. *Environmental Impacts of Products*; European Commission: Seville, Spain, 2006.

58. Scholl, G. *Marketing nachhaltiger Dienstleistungen. Bedingungen der Übernahme und Empfehlungen zur Vermarktung von eigentumsersetzenden Konsumpraktiken*; Metropolis Verlag: Marburg, Germany, 2009.

59. Paulitsch, K.; Rohn, H. Nackte Tatsachen: Warum das T-Shirt ökologisch schlechter ist als sein Ruf. In *Der ökologische Rucksack: Wirtschaft für eine Zukunft mit Zukunft*; Schmidt-Bleek, F., Ed.; Hirzel: Stuttgart, Germany, 2004; pp. 68–78.

60. Behrendt, S.; Behr, F. *Öko-Rent im Bereich Heimwerken, Baueigenleistungen und Gartenpflege*; WerkstattBericht No. 41; Institut für Zunftsstudien und Technologiebewertung (IZT): Berlin, Germany, 2000.

61. BiPRO/Federal Environment Agency (UBA). Chemical Leasing—Beispiel für Ressourcen- und Materialeffizienz. In Proceedings of Background Paper for a Workshop, Berlin, Germany, 6 June 2011.

62. Lahl, U.; Zeschmar-Lahl, B. *Going Green: Chemie—Handlungsfelder für eine ressourceneffiziente Chemieindustrie*; Heinrich-Böll-Stiftung: Berlin, Germany, 2011.

63. Federal Environment Agency (UBA), *Chemikalienleasing als Modell zur nachhaltigen Entwicklung mit Prüfprozeduren und Qualitätskriterien anhand von Pilotprojekten in Deutschland*; UBA: Dessau-Roßlau, Germany, 2010.

64. Stengel, O.; Liedtke, C.; Baedeker, C.; Welfens, M.J. Theorie und praxis eines bildungskonzepts für Nachhaltigkeit. *Umweltpsychologie* **2008**, *12*, 29–42.

65. Harms, S. Besitzen oder Teilen. Carsharing—Sozialinnovativ Und Kulturell Selektiv? Möglichkeiten und Grenzen Einer Nachhaltigen Mobilität. In *Sozialwissenschaftliche Analyse des Car-Sharings*; Steding, D., Herrmann, A., Lange, M., Eds.; Rüegger-Verlag: Zürich, Switzerland, 2003.

66. Scholl, G. Product Service Systems. Taking a Functional and a Symbolic Perspective on Usership. In Perspectives on Radical Changes to Sustainable, Consumption and Production; Proceedings of Sustainalbe Consumption Research Exchange, Copenhagen, Denmark, 20–21 April 2006; pp. 25–43.

7

CHAPTER

Behaviour Change in the UK Climate Debate: An Assessment of Responsibility, Agency and Political Dimensions

Shane Fudge* **and Michael Peters**

Research Group on Lifestyles, Values and Environment (RESOLVE), Centre for Environmental Strategy, University of Surrey, Guildford, Surrey, GU27XH, UK

ABSTRACT

This paper explores the politics around the role of agency in the UK climate change debate. Government interventions on the demand side of consumption have increasingly involved attempts to obtain greater traction with the values, attitudes and beliefs of citizens in relation to climate change and also in terms of influencing consumer behaviour at an individual level. With figures showing that approximately 40% of the UK's carbon emissions are attributable to household and transport behaviour, policy initiatives have progressively focused on the facilitation of "sustainable behaviours". Evidence suggests however, that mobilisation of pro-environmental attitudes in addressing the perceived "value-action gap" has so far had limited success. Research in this field suggests that there is a more significant and nuanced "gap" between context and behaviour; a relationship that perhaps provides a more adroit reflection of reasons why people do not necessarily react in the way that policy-makers anticipate. Tracing the development of the UK Government's behaviour change agenda over the last decade, we posit that a core reason for the limitations of this programme relates to an excessively narrow focus on the individual. This has served to obscure some of the wider political and economic aspects of the debate in favour of a more simplified discussion. The second part of the paper reports findings from a series of focus groups exploring some of the wider political views that people hold around household energy habits, purchase and use of domestic appliances, and transport behaviour-and discusses these insights in relation to the literature on the agenda's apparent limitations. The paper concludes by considering whether the aims of the *Big Society* approach (recently established by the UK's Coalition Government) hold the potential to engage more directly with some of these issues or whether they merely constitute a "repackaging" of the individualism agenda.

Keywords: environmental policy; climate change; agency; behaviour; lifestyles

1. INTRODUCTION

Environmental issues have become more central to government decision-making in the UK in recent years, gaining a noticeably higher profile in relation to the traditional hierarchy of policy. The effects of industrial oil spills, ozone depletion, atmospheric pollution, and more recently the risks posed by global climate change, have all served to inform the political agenda in increasingly visible ways. A series of energy white papers during the last decade have been among the higher profile policy statements reflecting the UK Government's intention to address the urgency of climate change through mainstream policy. This intent was confirmed in 2006 by the appearance of the government financed *Stern Review* which provided a comprehensive economic, social and environmental hypothesis of future scenarios should the UK fail to address the causes of climate change. Even more significantly, the 2008 Climate Change Bill—incorporating the UK government's pledge to oversee the transition to a society which is based on an 80 per cent reduction in greenhouse gas (GHG) emissions by 2050—clearly indicates a more central role for environmental issues in consideration of the UK's present and future policy agenda.

The practical difficulties of reaching increasingly stringent UK targets for CO_2 emission reductions have encouraged policy-makers to embrace and promote "bottom-up" solutions in order to address, for example, patterns of consumption and lifestyles such as those associated with travel, eating habits, leisure practices and patterns of living. As a 2004 Department for Environment, Food and Rural Affairs (Defra) document points out:

The environmental agenda has traditionally been focused on regulating point sources of pollution, for example from industrial plant. The future environmental agenda is about dealing with the myriad ways in which we put strains on the environment by how we produce, what we produce and the ways in which we consume. Our overarching goal is to be able to continue to pursue economic growth with all the benefits it brings without damaging the environment at home or oversees [1] (p. 23).

Lorenzoni *et al.* [2] show that the last decade in particular has been characterized by the search for a more radical shift in policy through which to address these developments—largely resulting from political acknowledgement of the growing complexities of how to integrate effective sustainability measures in policy.

Building the Big Society [3] is the most recent political statement on how the UK Government intends to address these issues through a new localism agenda in which citizens, communities and local government are given "...the power and information they need to come together, solve the problems they face and build the Britain they want" [3]. (1) According to Scott [4] the *Big Society* approach is an attempt to embed climate change (and the challenge of addressing it) across civil society, integrating energy as a core *political* concern, and engaging people into the design and implementation of policy, as integrated facets of the coalition Government's vision for sustainability.

The crux of this paper lies in the suggestion that limitations in many of the policies developed in the UK around energy and climate to date, relate to an underlying emphasis on individuals—rather than on the Government, government agencies or companies. This policy emphasis suggests that it is individuals, as agents of change, who are going to have to be the driving force behind reductions in greenhouse gas emissions [5]. This paper considers some of the reasons why attempts to forge this synthesis have been instrumental in driving environmental policy in the UK in recent years, grounding politics in serving the needs, preferences and agency of individuals as an integral element of "third way citizenship". In the discussion section we assess the complexities of delivering this renewed focus on local level responsibility and action in the light of recently conducted empirical work with members of the general public, and provide fresh insights into the comparative influence of structural, political, financial, psychological, social/cultural and knowledge factors on the adoption of pro-environmental energy behaviour at an individual level.

2. GOVERNANCE, THE INDIVIDUAL, AND THE "RISK SOCIETY"

Theorists of contemporary social and political change, including Putnam and Giddens [6,7] have made the point that the role and concept of western citizenship has undergone significant change in recent times. Giddens in particular has argued that policy initiatives must now develop concurrently with what has become a more atomized, and indeed "individualized" society. By this, he argues that people have become much more reflexive in terms of the choices and decisions that they make. Giddens' work had had a particular influence on UK policy since 1997 [8], informing what Callinicos [9] has described as "...a dialectical transcendence of past political polarities and the integration of a new form of market economics and progressive social policies".

For similar reasons, Beck [10] has suggested that it is apparent that the role of agency has come to assume a much greater role in contemporary policy-making as well as within the broader political spectrum. Finlayson [11] suggests that this position reflects broader current trends in both academia and politics regarding the ideological status of "agency" in relation to "structure". Giddens makes the particular point that the influence of modernist institutions such as the welfare state, educational establishments, and the role of governance itself, must now be much more receptive to the risk-or *reflexive* stage of modernity-where the possibilities for new choices or life chances must be engaged by policy makers. He suggests, for example, that areas such as healthcare and social exclusion have witnessed a greater focus on the prescription of individual agency away from state-led responsibility. Williams [12] explains these changes with reference to the changing relationship between the individual and welfare state provision:

Central to a new paradigm of welfare is an emphasis on the capacity of people to be creative, reflexive human beings; that is to be active agents in shaping their lives, experiencing, acting upon and reconstituting the outcomes of welfare policies in various ways [12].

Developing this argument, Giddens states that: "the classical welfare state developed in a society where scarcity was the main social problem, especially in the context of the immediate post-war period. But in many circumstances in post-industrial societies we are dealing, not with scarcity of resources, but with issues of lifestyle" [7] (p. 135). He suggests that a growing concern with environmental degradation can be traced to the significance of living in a "post-scarcity society".

Most ecological issues, including global climate change, are not to do with scarcity of resources, but with the profligate use of them. Traffic congestion and pollution are good examples. Los Angeles once upon a time looked like the city of the future, maximizing the effective use of space in relation to individual mobility. But with the multiplication of car ownership it has become a social and ecological dead end. The main freeways are choked with cars for much of the day, and are often almost at a standstill. In spite of the rigorous control measures, levels of air pollution are high. European cities, which were not designed for car travel, are in many cases just as clogged up with traffic and polluted [7] (p. 135).

Giddens reasons therefore that invariably solutions to environmental problems depend upon lifestyle change on the part of individuals, and that this could not be imposed from the "top" without substantial difficulties. He argues that the role of governments and other concerned agencies is to develop a combination of incentives and sanctions that will have a tangible influence on behaviour. The political drive towards encouraging a more sustainable society has observably tried to tap into this ethos.

3. WHAT IS "BEHAVIOUR CHANGE"?

Growing urgency in policy circles on the need for more effective strategies to reduce carbon emissions in both production and consumption cycles has seen the development of a stronger focus on agency through the development of "behaviour change" initiatives. This has become a central aspect of climate change mitigation in the UK, particularly over the last 5–10 years.

Stating that "there is increasing international acceptance that climate change is a serious threat to human well-being and environmental integrity" Whitmarsh [13] argues:

In the UK, the Labour Government has identified climate change as a priority issue, and positioned itself as a global leader in addressing it. Public education to enlist societal support for and involvement in mitigation efforts is a key element of the UK Government's climate change strategy. Since the early 1990s, there has been several government information campaigns intended to educate the UK public about climate change and to encourage personal energy conservation [13] (p. 1).

In the UK situation climate change was not originally a priority for the Labour Government when it came to office in 1997 [14]. There was an assumption that the structural changes associated with the "dash for gas"—which had seen a significant reduction in the UK's greenhouse gas emissions—meant that the issues could be "managed" through a continuation of the *Market for Energy* strategy that had been bequeathed by the previous Conservative administration. This encouraged the new government confidently to sign up to the Kyoto Protocol in 1997, and also to commit to a new national target of a 20% reduction in GHG emissions by 2010. As King [15] reasons, it was largely this situation that encouraged the Labour Government to position itself as a global leader in addressing the challenge of climate change. However, this strategy encountered substantial obstacles almost immediately, as the UK's carbon emissions began to increase again during the mid-1990s. Policy-makers were forced to acknowledge that structural shifts informed by energy privatization were now being eroded, necessitating the need for a shift in emphasis towards a consumption based policy strategy which, it was thought, might have the capacity to deal more effectively deal with growth in road transport use and air travel [16] and also increasing energy demand in housing [17].

The parameters by which the UK Government hoped to align "behaviour change" in individuals with the complexities of climate change in policy was first articulated, and synthesized diagrammatically, in the 2005 Sustainable Development strategy [18]. Chapter 3 of the strategy, in particular, reflected a substantially different view of what it meant to change behaviours than had ever been in mainstream policy before. The "diamond model" (or "4 Es" model—see Figure 1) intended to provide "...a framework for thinking about the different approaches policy-makers can take to influence a behaviour, and how to balance these to produce an effective package of interventions which 'catalyse' change. The model suggests using a mix of interventions to Enable, Engage, Exemplify and Encourage" [19] (p. 13). In essence, the model was intended as an accessible summary of the multiplicity of intervention possibilities, and so explicitly aimed to broaden policy horizons in this area.

The UK Government's *Community Action* 2020—*Together We Can* (included in the 2005 Sustainable Development Strategy) encapsulated the increased focus on behaviour change, setting out the terrain in which policy makers believed this could be made to come about. While the term "behaviour change" suggests an individualized approach to policy making, the "framework for behaviour change" attempted to clarify different influences on behaviour and, more importantly, where the leverage for change might occur. The diamond model itself was therefore located within what might be described as a "Russian doll" model of policy making, pointing the way towards coordination between regional, community and individual levels of policy making, as opposed to traditional top-down approaches. Reducing the acknowledged problem of energy demand and carbon emissions emanating from UK households for instance, would now be couched within the requirements of what was outlined in the previous section of this paper, and Giddens' ideas around a "third way citizenship", where there are rights as well as responsibilities in modern democratic societies.

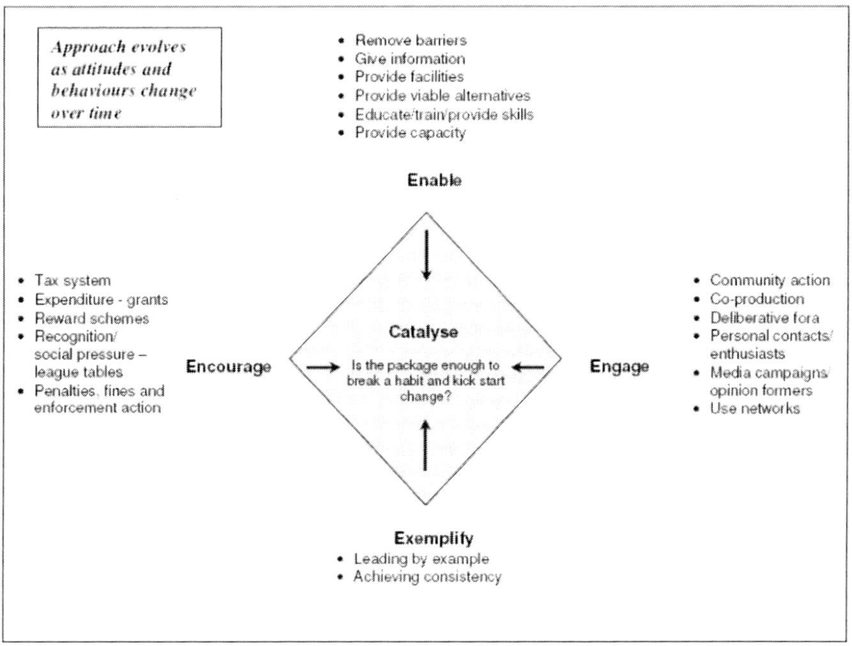

Figure 1. The UK Government's "Framework for Behaviour Change" [18] (p. 26).

Concurring with this argument, Miliband (UK Secretary of State for Environment, Food and Rural Affairs, May 2006–June 2007) [20] (p. 347) set out an argument for engaging citizens and mobilizing communities as an essential aspect of targeting energy demand, where "44% of all emissions are by individual households, most of which comes from four transactions: electricity and gas in our homes, and car and air travel". The UK Government acknowledged that reliance on "technological fixes" alone would only go so far in relation to revised environmental aims and that effective policies needed to embrace the complex interaction between the scientific, economic and social aspects of energy use. With an overall rationale running through this programme of encouraging "the appropriate behavioural responses amongst the UK public via communication strategies and economic measures" [13] (p. 13), the four dimensions of the diamond model were viewed as inter-connected elements of an overall strategy. They are explained below:

- *Enable*. As Figure 1 illustrates, one of the most important ways through which the UK Government hoped to drive change at a behavioural level was to be as an *information provider* in order to encourage the individual consumer to make more informed choices in their purchasing habits. Thus for instance, the development of energy labeling on products, government led media campaigns such as *Act on* CO_2, local government led environmental awareness raising programmes and various other internet sites where individuals can calculate their carbon footprints are all examples of providing information to both individuals and groups to encourage more informed choices on the consequences of their personal energy use. One of the principal rationales behind this point of the diamond model drew upon the economic argument that a market for household energy efficiency investments such as loft insulation, cavity wall insulation and double glazing can develop more effectively once the appropriate price signals are identified and addressed by policy makers.

- *Engage*. Enabling consumers to make more informed choices in their personal energy use was seen by the UK Government as being closely linked to the need to engage their attention in the first place. For example, it was proposed that awareness raising campaigns which are embedded at a local level are far more likely to resonate with individuals if led by local authorities [21]. To this end it was hoped that that information on climate change for instance, would be more effective through dissemination by local authorities than a centrally delivered message; integrating it within existing links between local political jurisdiction and service provision. It has been argued that much of the progress in the level of kerb-side recycling that now takes place in the UK, can be attributed to the establishment of mandatory recycling targets concomitant with increased waste funding for local government [22]. This has enabled local authorities to implement improved infrastructures and collection facilities with the result of enhancing (and easing) household participation.

- *Encourage*. As outlined above, the UK Government felt that providing appropriate regulation could enable the market to be harnessed in pursuit of behaviour change objectives. Thus for instance, changes to vehicle excise duty had been put in place in the UK in order to encourage the purchase of smaller, less polluting cars. Various congestion charge schemes had also been developed in order to encourage less "unnecessary" journeys by private car. The *London Congestion Charge*, for example, has been the largest of its kind ever undertaken by a capital city and a part of the rationale behind it had been to act as a disincentive to private car use in inner London and to encourage more widespread use of private transport and cycling, thereby reducing congestion and contributing to environmental goals. Surplus profit from the charge has also been invested in improvements to London's public transport infrastructure.

- *Exemplify*. The diamond model's final dimension effectively framed the first three aims (enable, engage, encourage) by proposing that the UK Government must "lead the way" in encouraging a more sustainable society; in other words, leading by example. The 2008 *Climate Change Bill* has been perhaps the clearest illustration of these aims where the UK Government set a longer-term target of an 80 per cent reduction in emissions by 2050; punctuated by a series of interim targets by which political leaders will be accountable themselves. The practice of government (nationally and locally) was here considered also to be part of the aim to "exemplify" sustainability aims in relation to more strategic design and management of its own buildings and operations.

By enacting the strategy embodied in the diamond model, a core aim was to "capture" some of the fundamental behavioral norms which were felt to motivate individuals in modern society, in order to catalyze change at the level of consumption habits and practices. Policy makers were hopeful that an emphasis on consumer demand would ultimately be effective in encouraging systemic change—the theory being that markets often respond and adapt to changes in patterns and trends in UK consumption practices. It was intended that this approach would also complement more direct macro policy initiatives, such as carbon trading.

In order to gain further insights into lifestyle diversity among the population and to extend the foundations of the diamond model, Defra went on to formulate the "Framework for Pro-environmental Behaviours" [23]. This considered the response (in terms of willingness and capability to act) of population clusters to 12 headline environmental goals, encouraging behavioural changes and subsequent impact reduction at an individual level. As Scott [4] points out:

...clusters of the population referred to as "positive greens" are generally willing and capable, in contrast to those that lack awareness of environmental issues and are part of the poorer population. Tailored approaches are required to target the different segments. Segments with high ability and willingness to act will need a different approach to segments unwilling to act. An insight like this will allow policy makers to maximize the effectiveness of their policies.

4. A DILEMMA BETWEEN CITIZENSHIP AND BEHAVIOUR CHANGE?

Whitmarsh [13] argues that there is so far little evidence to suggest that behaviour change as a political strategy has been particularly successful in steering consumption trends and associated carbon emissions in the UK towards more sustainable outcomes. She states that recognition of this was partly responsible for the UK Government's revision of domestic targets on carbon emissions. The principal indicator of progress in the behaviour change strategy, according to Whitmarsh, has been through political monitoring and auditing of carbon dioxide emissions in different domains of consumption. These consumption domains have, in turn, been extrapolated from measures of energy consumption within each sector:

...energy consumption in the UK has continued to rise in recent years. Energy use in transport is increasing the most rapidly; domestic energy consumption has risen slightly; and industrial energy demand is declining. Social surveys also show a rise in car use and an increase in the proportion of two-car households [13] (p. 13).

There have been numerous reasons offered as to the relative failure so far of policies which have been aimed at changing consumer behaviour in the UK. For example, O'Neill and Hulme [22] (p. 402) suggest that “climate change is an issue that is difficult to connect with in a tangible way at individual level”, while Lorenzi and Pidgeon [24] assert that the issue itself is “remote both in space and time and it is perceived as affecting other communities and future generations”. Whitmarsh [11] (p. 14) suggests that “government exhortations to reduce energy consumption will continue to go unheeded if they are incongruous with the social and physical context of everyday life”.

Shove [25] also argues that the UK Government emphasis on behaviour change in policy has, ultimately, been limited-particularly in its objective of directing the “captured” complexity of human behaviour to increasingly ambitious environmental targets. Significantly, she suggests that the influence on human behaviour through the structural role of institutions, practices and cultural norms is often underplayed in favour of an overemphasis on the individuals' willingness to “make the right choices”. Importantly, Shove points out: “it is clear that lifestyles, especially in the west, will have to change if there is to be any chance of averting the long-term consequences of resource depletion, global warming, the loss of biodiversity, the production of waste or the pollution and destruction of 'natural' environments" [25] (p. 1) However, she postulates that policies designed to promote sustainable consumption have in general remained focused upon "an extraordinarily narrow understanding of human behaviour". Despite political rhetoric to the contrary, she suggests that policy initiatives have all too often subsumed the complex, social and cultural dimensions of agency in favour of a model of human behaviour underpinned by the "rational individual"; an approach which is ultimately insufficient because the issue of "lifestyles" is invariably approached as an individual phenomenon, devoid of the influence of social and cultural drivers:

To put Brundtland's famous definition another way, future generations will encounter a much degraded world if present trends continue. Apparent agreement on this point disguises important theoretical divisions regarding the conceptualization of behaviour, lifestyles and consumption. Are "lifestyles" in some sense "chosen" or are they better seen as ways of life, that is as part of the social fabric... What is the relation between "behaviour"—what people do and what they think? Is consumption an expression of taste, or a moment in a complex system of social, cultural and material reproduction? [25] (p. 1).

Shove's work highlights one of the greatest difficulties for policy makers in terms of a direct focus on individual behaviour change as a way in which to encourage the shift to a low-carbon economy. That is, the definition of consumption—and what motivates people to consume in the ways that they do—itself lies at the heart of the problem. The work of Harvey [26] provides a useful guide on changes in UK political economy and how they have been able to influence social and cultural change. Harvey suggests that consumption practices in the UK from the post-war period can be traced to wider changes in political economy which have encouraged the influence of choices, tastes and preferences around a particular "market-based" form of citizenship. Although these changes, in turn, have inevitably influenced the ways in which "collective" issues (such as environmental, social and political concerns) have come to be viewed and understood, there seemingly remains a general reluctance amongst much of the UK population to change behaviour. Why should this be so?

While O'Neill and Hulme [27] point out that there is widespread recognition of the urgency of climate change, with "99% of citizens in the UK recognizing the terms 'climate change', 'greenhouse effect' or 'global warming'", only a minority of citizens routinely undertake pro-environmental actions in their daily lives to enable substantial reductions in consumption and energy demand. The following section of the paper explores some of the issues which frame this debate through recent findings from 12 focus group discussions that formed part of three complementary research projects exploring viewpoints on people's everyday energy behaviour, attitudes towards the environment, sustainability issues and links among these topics.

5. EMPIRICAL STUDY

This section describes and analyses some key findings to emerge from a series of twelve focus groups comprising members of the general public; carried out between December 2008 and October 2010. The groups were convened as part of the empirical phase of three complementary research projects that operated within the "Energy and Carbon Governance" theme of the Research Group on Lifestyles, Values and Environment (RESOLVE) at the University of Surrey.

5.1. Objectives

The principal objective of the focus group research was to explore the ways in which people relate to their own "agency" with respect to: (1) Household energy use and purchasing patterns; (2) The use of domestic appliances; and (3) Transport habits. The purpose of pursuing these themes with the participants was to shed light on some of the issues which continue to face policy makers in their attempts to implement an effective "environmental contract" with UK citizens through behaviour change initiatives. In particular the discussions were guided to focus on:

- the degree of political intervention; the benefits and drawbacks associated with different levels;
- the role and responsibility of business and industry; and
- the extent to which structural shifts can be balanced with an increased emphasis on individual behaviour change.

5.2. Approach and Methods

In accord with the recommended sample size for focus group research [28], each group recruited 10-12 adult participants. The samples themselves were stratified in respect of two primary selected variables: "stable" and "transition" consumer groups, and then sub-stratified according to income (income was used for recruitment as a proxy for "social patterns and lifestyles"—key variables which were explored with the participants as part of the focus group discussion guide), age and gender. The detail of this sampling is summarized in Table 1.

Table 1. Focus group sampling details.

	Consumer type	Income	Gender	Age
Group 1	Stable (S)	Low-mid (L-M)	~5 men (M) 5 women (W)	Mixed range from 25–45
Group 2	Stable (S)	Mid-high (M-H)	~5 men (M) 5 women (W)	Mixed range from 46–75
Group 3	Transition (T)	Low-mid (L-M)	~5 men (M) 5 women (W)	Mixed range from 25–45
Group 4	Transition (T)	Mid-high	~5 men (M) 5 women (W)	Mixed range from 46–75
Group 5	Stable (S)	Low-mid (L-M)	~5 men (M) 5 women (W)	Mixed range from 46–75
Group 6	Transition (T)	Mid-high	~5 men (M) 5 women (W)	Mixed range from 46–75
Group 7	Stable (S)	Low-mid (L-M)	~ 5 men (M) 5 women (W)	Mixed range from 25–45
Group 8	Transition (T)	Low-mid (L-M)	~5 men (M) 5 women (W)	Mixed range from 46–75
Group 9	Stable (S)	Low-mid (L-M)	~5 men (M) 5 women (W)	Mixed range from 25–45
Group 10	Stable (S)	Mid-high (M-H)	~5 men (M) 5 women (W)	Mixed range from 46 – 75
Group 11	Transition (T)	Mid-high (M-H)	~5 men (M) 5 women (W)	Mixed range from 25–45
Group 12	Transition (T)	Mid-high (M-H)	~5 men (M) 5 women (W)	Mixed range from 25–45

For the purpose of recruitment we used the following definition specification:

"Stable" = Adults (including those in rented accommodation) who have:

[and/or]

- not moved home in the last 10 years;
- not made substantial alterations to their property (in terms of build/rebuild or repair) in the last 10 years.

"Transition" = Adults who have:

and/or {

- moved home during the last 2 years;
- are planning to move during the coming 2 years;
- Have made substantial alterations to their property (in terms of build/rebuild or repair) in the last 10 years;
- Are currently making substantial alterations to their property or plan to make substantial alterations to their property during the coming 2 years.

While representativeness is not itself an essential aspect of focus group research, it was decided that the participant samples should be drawn from different local authority areas in order to offer a degree of spatial differentiation. This included different types of location from predominantly "urban" to deeply "rural" settings, and also attempted to capture a range of cultural diversity:

- Groups 1, 5, 7 and 8: Surrey, Guildford;
- Groups 2 and 6: West Midlands, Birmingham;
- Group 3: East Sussex, Brighton;
- Group 4: Berkshire, Slough;
- Group 9: Shropshire, Shrewsbury;
- Group 10: London, Richmond;
- Groups 11 and 12: London, Islington.

Four themes were chosen to structure the schedule of questions for each focus group. The first three themes focused on key domestic energy issues, *i.e.*, domestic energy use, household appliances, and travel by car. An additional category, designed to elaborate on "wider issues", was also included to address issues relating to "governance", "trust" and "responsibility". Each topic was subdivided into a set of eight or nine questions alongside a series of "prompts". The prompts were introduced in order to stimulate discussion where necessary; and to encourage participants to expand on the questions themselves-which may well be independent of their individual knowledge territory. It also served to encourage a degree of reiteration to the discussion guide, enabling questions to be explored in a number of different ways, thus maximizing participants' responses to the same themes.

5.3. Results

Key findings from the twelve focus groups are presented in the following subsections, grouped around the core themes of "convenience", "comfort", "knowledge/information", "responsibility" and "regulation". In accordance with anonymity guarantees given to the participants, direct quotations are ascribed categorically (consistent with Table 1), *i.e.*, "SM, L-M, 25–45, Guildford" refers to a male participant in one of the Guildford focus groups, between twenty-five and forty-five years of age, and representing the "stable" consumer type category of the sampling frame.

5.3.1. Convenience

The issue of convenience was considered to be an important factor in participants' decisions with regard to both domestic energy use and purchase of appliances—almost always overriding potential environmental consequences. In relation to this, there was a strong impression from the majority of participants that ownership of certain appliances and products was almost "non-negotiable" and that white goods such as washing machines, cookers and fridges were a "right" for individuals to possess:

There isn't a replacement for some things that are so very convenient. For example, a tumble dryer ...there is not an alternative unless you stick them [clothes] on the radiator and by definition you're having radiators on all day to get them dry (SM, L-M, 25–45, Birmingham).

Some participants argued that the proliferation of electrical goods that we have seen in the last few years should also be accepted as being essential to modern living. Interestingly, while some individuals argued that they "did what they could" in relation to environmental messages from the UK Government (such as switching off appliances fully or purchasing energy saving appliances where possible) it was suggested that the quantity of these goods in the modern household often made this difficult in respect of changing behaviour:

Well, we never used to have them we when we were youngsters...sort of DVD players and stuff like that, they weren't around...you had a record player. It's still the same sort of thing but there's more on the market than there ever was (SM, M-H, 46–75, Slough).

The continued popularity of the private car as an accepted "lifestyle convenience" was strongly articulated by participants in all of the focus groups during discussions on people's transport habits. There was a general perception across the groups that people are attached to private car use for a range of predominantly psychological reasons; not only in relation to convenience, but also in terms of individual feelings of freedom, and comfort:

I like the independence of a car (TF, L-M, 25–45 Birmingham).

I love my car. I couldn't be without it (TF, L-M, 25–45 Guildford).

It was generally considered by many of the focus group participants that barriers to more widespread use and acceptance of public transport could be linked to the idea of "self-sufficiency". Issues of long waiting times; a lack of privacy; perceived differences in cost; and a lack of comfort were viewed as significant issues in this regard. Most participants argued the case that car use appealed directly to the daily concerns and practicalities of peoples' everyday lives; making the focus one of "individuality" rather than say a "collective" concern for the environment or for energy conservation in general.

5.3.2. Comfort

Both comfort and convenience emerged as lifestyle priorities for participants in all of the focus groups when asked about home energy use practices. There was a clear suggestion that "cultural" ideas of comfort and warmth-articulated by almost emotive responses such as "the sensation of heat" and "needing to feel warm"—were argued by participants to be almost non-negotiable aspects of modern-day living. Several participants from across the groups pointed out that they were more likely to turn their home heating up rather than to put on extra clothing. Additionally, many stated that they were more likely to leave heating at constant levels than to adjust it to different times and conditions. Some participants made the point that they would be prepared to trade higher bills if their own ideas relating warmth were to come into tangency with costs. Interestingly, these viewpoints did not seem to be linked to the different income levels represented in each group—participants across all income levels argued that they would be prepared to pay higher costs on their heating bills if it meant that they were able to stay warm:

"I would say that comfort comes before bill (TM, M-H, 46–75, Guildford).

I'd pay anything to be warm if I was cold. If it's in the winter and it's cold, it would be [heating temperature practice adopted] how warm it is (SF, M-H, 46–75 Birmingham). "

It was noticeable that participants in all groups generally argued that both energy efficiency and environmental considerations are secondary considerations to being comfortable. Even participants who had undertaken renovation work such as wall and roof insulation; window replacement; installation of solar panels; and replacement of heating systems with more efficient designs, argued that comfort and cost savings related to better energy efficiency are a higher priority for them than environmental concerns.

Similarly, in terms of travel decisions, comfort emerged as a key issue across all of the focus groups. In addition to factors of convenience many felt that the private car offered the most comfortable way of travelling. There was a general perception that public transport services would need to be greatly improved (particularly in terms of comfort) in order to encourage greater use by the general public. Participants complained for instance, that during peak travel times on train journeys, they often had to stand up in overcrowded carriages, making for uncomfortable journeys.

5.3.3. Knowledge and Information

Corroborating the findings of O'Neill and Hulme [26], it was clear that all focus group participants had awareness—in principal—of the salience of energy and environmental issues in relation to adapting society to the constraints of the planet. When asked about initiatives established by the UK Government during the previous decade, all participants were familiar with the *London Congestion Charge*, the *Warm Front Grant* and the *Home Energy Conservation Act.* Many suggested that the public, generally, have a greater understanding of environmental issues today as a result of efficiency ratings on electrical appliances; educational programmes in schools; government information campaigns; and television and media messages. There was acknowledgement however, that this "knowledge" does not necessarily translate into action (admittedly even in the participants' own lives) together with a general perception that policies providing information alone are likely to be insufficient to modify everyday behaviour on a widespread scale.

Some participants expressed a lack of trust in the information underpinning many of the policies that have been developed to address environmental issues, and as a result considered themselves less willing to act upon it:

It's always struck me...these incentives, you know...you feel that they're doing it to try and stop people using cars and things but clearly, look at the congestion zone—it's just as chock-a-block now as it's always been. So people distrust government because they feel that every initiative they bring out is geared to make money (SM, L-M, 46–75, Brighton).

Other participants were distrustful of the scientific evidence for the existence of climate change and environmental degradation:

I mean it's happening, absolutely, but I'm not convinced it's brought on solely by human activity. I'm sure we've had an influence on it but I think it was going to happen anyway just as it has done a million times before you know...Ice Age etc., etc., (TM, M-H, 46–75, Richmond).

5.3.4. Who is responsible?

While there was some agreement among the focus group participants of a need for the UK to become more sustainable, it was noticeable that there was no real consensus on where responsibility for this progress should lie. Concurring with the policy drive to encourage greater individual responsibility, some participants (although a minority) reasoned that the barriers, and also the opportunities for real change, need to be encouraged at the level of individuals:

Well, ultimately it's all of us...ultimately it's the consumer (SM, L-M, 25–45, Brighton).

I don't know. I suppose the argument is if less and less people buy these products the demand is going to be less and then the carbon footprint (SF, L-M, 25–25, Islington).

While others pointed to the influence of businesses, and the role that they could—or should—play, there was a general consensus that the onus should be on the UK government to take the lead:

I don't think anybody else has got the authority but the government unless they set up a separate body to take control of sustainability (SM, L-M, 46–75, Shropshire).

Government-they're elected to govern the country aren't they? Even if you are not happy with the government in there, the majority of people want the government to govern (SF, M-H, 46–75, Islington).

Interestingly however, this viewpoint was tempered with a measure of distrust in politicians and contemporary governing mechanisms from several participants. Some felt that one of the main problems in putting over effective political messages on sustainability and environmental responsibility is that the messages are invariably inconsistent and often contradictory. These participants, for example, focused on the government's sanctioning of expansion to the UK transport infrastructure and airport runways while simultaneously promoting sustainability ideals. Some also argued that politicians themselves need to "put their own houses in order" before asking the rest of the nation to behave in more environmentally responsible ways. For example, it was felt that although that UK Government had a very influential role to play in encouraging a more sustainable society, the message was likely to be diluted due to a widespread distrust in the formal political agenda:

They all have to lead by example—but they don't all have to drive their massive big cars do they? (SF, M-H, 25–45, Slough).

It was also felt that the UK government, on its own, does not carry the necessary level of political weight needed to bring about the changes desired. It was argued that the ways in which influence is dispersed amongst political institutions, business and consumer power need to work together much more closely (*i.e.*, in a "joined-up" approach) towards sustainability as a common goal than they do at present:

Over the years, the government has foisted all the responsibility onto private companies, whereas it's a government responsibility to get these things up and running (TM, L-M, 25–45, Guildford).

They've privatized all the energy companies so the energy companies...their profits go to the shareholders, whereas if it's nationalized they'd invest (TF, M-H, 46–75, Richmond).

5.3.5. Should there be More Regulation?

Despite reservations on political leadership in the UK, some of the focus group participants suggested that the complexity of factors influencing contemporary lifestyles necessitates a measure of political intervention to encourage the adoption of more sustainable choices in society. It was suggested that there have been previous examples of societal changes that have worked over the long-term as a direct result of political intervention:

Well, I think the government, or a body such as the government, has got to sort of make the changes happen in terms of saying "this is what you must do...there's no choice in it (TM, L-M, 25–45, Brighton).

When they wanted everyone to change from leaded petrol to unleaded petrol it never happened until they made it cheaper. If you want people to change their habits you've got to put economics in there. If you want people to save power, put a tax on it... (SM, M-H, 25–45, Shropshire).

The area of transport drew mixed responses from participants with regard to whether there should be more regulation. While there was a general awareness of the negative consequences of environmental damage caused by car use, there was reluctance for more punitive measures being introduced for car users. Many participants argued that there was a clear need for the government to address current negative connotations associated with use of public transport. While participants pointed out that public transport did not offer the same psychological attractions as the private car, it was argued that greater public investment might go some way towards increasing the attractiveness of these modes of transport.

While there was a general trend across the focus groups in favour of technological change as opposed to individual behaviour change, some participants suggested that a more sustainable future would only be enabled through a combination of behavioural change *and* technological innovation:

I think it'll be a mix...it'll be some technological answers that will offer perhaps replacement for sources that we've got at the moment but they might come at a price and therefore people will start to change their behaviour because it's becoming too expensive, something like that. It will be one or the other and you won't...it won't be people changing their behaviour just morally (TM, M-H, 46–75, Slough).

Some participants made the point that more "user friendly technology" was also needed to increase the visibility of energy consumption and encourage individuals to understand the energy and environmental implications of their purchasing choices. It was suggested for example, that consumers are often reluctant to use electronic temperature controls and water pumps, owing to a perception that they are too complicated to operate easily.

6. DISCUSSION AND CONCLUDING REMARKS

The study of lifestyles as a subject of academic inquiry has intensified in recent times, owing in part to the growing debate around sustainable consumption and to the increased significance of behaviour change as a set of policy initiatives. The practical difficulties of reaching increasingly stringent targets on the UK's CO_2 emissions have seen policy-makers attempting to engage more directly with individual lifestyles and patterns of consumption, particularly those associated with travel, eating habits, and leisure practices.

This paper has argued that there are clear lines to be drawn between behaviour change as an agenda *per se* and the more general political shift that has taken place in recent years regarding the role of agency in policy making. In the UK the emphasis has shifted, particularly over the last decade, from "top down" governance towards encouraging citizens to adopt pro-environmental lifestyle choices. The "diamond model", for example, was developed by policy makers precisely in order to capture the essence of citizenship "rights and responsibilities" through a broad-based range of interventions. The primary intention for this model, from the UK Government's perspective, was to provide a sufficiently far-reaching framework through which to galvanise agency and to direct behaviour towards environmental policy aims and objectives.

However, the UK's behaviour change agenda has arguably proven largely ineffectual to date where, in particular, it has been difficult for policy-makers to reach beyond the relatively small section of society who are already routinely engaged in pro-environmental habits. The challenge of realizing a broader level of connection continues to be particularly problematic for policy makers at all levels. It has been suggested that a key reason for this obstacle to engagement relates to the ways in which agency is influenced by a complex interaction of factors. Individuals articulate their own choices; they have their own reasons for doing what they do. Their actions are often neither explainable nor justifiable in a "rational economic maximiser" sense, and can be unpredictable vis-à-vis feelings of moral responsibility and obligation.

Whilst the issues that emerged from the focus group data considered in this paper are not particularly new in themselves—and are perhaps too small scale to generalize more widely—they nevertheless provide interesting insights into why an emphasis on behaviour change in isolation from other influences will continue to deliver minimal results without a more radical political agenda shift. With current figures showing that approximately 40% of carbon emissions are attributable to household and transport practices in the UK, engaging citizens in more sustainable lifestyles is one of the biggest challenges to UK government initiatives on climate change. The focus group discussions raised a number of interesting questions around wider issues that may either encourage or discourage the kind of agency responses explored in the first half of the paper. It would be reasonable to suggest that policies so far have yet to tap into this sense of political agency—one which, as Dobson [29] has argued is able to resonate with people as citizens rather than as consumers.

The *Big Society* agenda [30] is the latest attempt to address some of the more intractable problems that have been encountered so far on finding a balance between government, business, communities and individuals that will "deliver the reform, fairness and change Britain needs". The policy agenda itself has been outlined as developing around the following five areas:

- To give communities more powers (localism and devolution).

  One of the principal objectives here is to encourage a more "organic" agency response by encouraging higher levels of social learning between individuals within their communities. Here there is recognition that rather than engaging with the "usual suspects", community developed strategies might be able to encourage a more collective response to energy and climate issues.

- To encourage people to take an active role in their communities.

It is hoped that by engaging people more directly in the issues that affect them, they will become empowered through a greater sense of ownership. For instance, a key aim in this regard is to encourage more decentralized energy generation which could be owned and run by communities themselves.

- To transfer power from central government to local government.

  Part of the *Big Society's* overarching objective is to address issues of "trust" in relation to the role of government and business. Changes in the UK's planning laws, for instance, in part recognise that local authorities might be better placed to oversee sustainability initiatives at the infrastructural level. It is also hoped that a continued devolvement of responsibility down to the local level might encourage "grassroots" politics around energy and climate issues.

- To support co-ops, mutuals, charities and social enterprises.

  The Coalition Government has pledged to encourage the creation of co-operatives, "mutuals", charities and social enterprises, and is committed to support these groups in realizing greater involvement in the running of public services. Again, it is hoped that both individual and community entrepreneurship will encourage a more bottom-up approach to sustainability.

- To publish government data (open, transparent government).

  In relation to environment and sustainability targets in the UK, the new government hopes to engender a greater sense of trust in what the machinery and mechanisms of governance are able to deliver, for instance, on national carbon emission reduction targets.

Mulugetta *et al.* [31] (p. 7541) point out: "it is clear that no single intervention can deliver the level of systemic change required to address climate change and energy security". One of the main ways in which the UK Government has proposed addressing carbon reduction targets is through strong, co-coordinated efforts from a variety of different stakeholders, with increased emphasis on community-led governance and a greater role for locally driven energy initiatives. It is worth bearing in mind the relevance of the *Big Society's* localism agenda in relation to the introduction of Feed in Tariffs and the Renewable Heat Incentive—both of which are likely to usher in new actors, including households, cooperatives, housing associations and schools, into the energy generation market. In addition to the behavioural aspects of the debate, there would seem to be a greater recognition now that policies which encourage changes in individuals will take the low carbon transition only so far. As Mulugetta *et al.* [31] (p. 7541) reason: '...significant efforts are needed on many fronts, involving both small and large scale, implementing various ownership and delivery models, and deploying a wide range of low carbon technologies at the demand *and* supply ends'.

Public opinion on some of these issues was revealed through the focus groups findings, particularly in relation to participant responses around questions on "where responsibility for the move to a more sustainable society should lie"; "the degree of political intervention that is deemed desirable"; "the role and responsibility of business and industry"; and "the extent to which structural change might be balanced with the increased emphasis on individual change". It was found that while individuals are generally more informed on the urgency of environmental issues and in many respects more "enabled" now than in recent history (in terms of infrastructural and support provision), many still remain reluctant to change their own behaviour, preferring the comfort and convenience that is often associated with less environmentally sustainable lifestyle choices. The group discussions did however emphasize the need for a more open debate, involving members of the public, around the scope and nature of citizen responsibilities in the transition to a sustainable society.

In relation to these responsibilities many of the focus group participants felt that the current lack of connection and engagement is closely aligned to uncertainty surrounding the role of the individual with regard to the function of UK Government and business interests. Others argued that they were already "doing their bit" and that there was a responsibility on other agencies to play their part. There was general consensus around the notion that a lack of widespread engagement at an individual level could also be attributed to a lack of trust in many of the environmental messages emanating from the UK Government and from scientific experts. It is argued that many of the observations made during those discussions provide an illustration of the multifaceted relationship between structural, political, financial, psychological, social/cultural and knowledge issues—influencing consumption habits and energy-related choices in ways that have so far eluded the grasp of policy makers. We suggest that an over-emphasis on the "rational agency" of individuals in the development of these policies draws attention to some of the limitations of behaviour change in isolation from the wider, structural influences on individual decision-making.

The UK's Climate Change Act puts a legal imperative on the government to cut greenhouse gas emissions by 80% of their 1990 levels by 2050, with a mid-term target of 34% reduction by 2020. Reaching these targets will require strong, coordinated efforts from a dynamic combination of government bodies, institutions, public and private actors, community groups and individuals. Some observers suggest that the recently established *Big Society* agenda is an attempt to locate (individually and collectively) the political citizen at the local level—one who is more engaged with the issues outlined above through an increased emphasis on community level policy making. Further research will be needed to examine this shift of emphasis and its effectiveness (potential and actual) in enabling broader societal-political engagement in sustainable consumption and behaviour change at local and national levels.

REFERENCES

1. HM Government. Delivering the Essentials of Life: Defra's Five Year Strategy. 2004. Available online: http://www.defra.gov.uk/corporate/about/what/5year-strategy/documents/5year-strategy.pdf (accessed on 21 May 2011).
2. Lorenzoni, I.; Pidgeon, N. Public views on climate change: European and USA perspectives. *Clim. Change* **2006**, *77*, 73–75.
3. The Cabinet Office. *Building the Big Society*; The Cabinet Office: London, UK, 18 May 2010. Available online: http://www.cabinetoffice.gov.uk/news/building-big-society (accessed on 21 May 2011).
4. Scott, F. Big society: What does it mean for environmental action? *Inside Track*, 2010, 26, pp. 1–18. Available online: http://www.respublica.org.uk/sites/default/files/Inside Track_26.pdf (accessed on 18 February 2011).
5. Goodall, C. *How to Live a Low-Carbon Life*; Earthscan: London, UK, 2007.
6. Putnam, R. *Bowling Alone*; Simon and Schuster: New York, NY, USA, 2000.
7. Giddens, A. *The Third Way: The Renewal of Social Democracy*; Polity Press: Cambridge, UK, 1998.
8. Fudge, S.; Williams, S. Beyond left and right: Can the third way deliver a reinvigorated social democracy? *Crit. Sociol.* **2006**, *32*, 53–76.
9. Callinicos, A. *Against the Third Way: An Anti-Capitalist Critique*; Polity: Cambridge, UK, 2001.
10. Beck, U. *World Risk Society*; Polity Press: Cambridge, UK, 1999.

11. Finlayson, A. *Making Sense of New Labour*; Lawrence and Wishart: London, UK, 2003.

12. Williams, F. Agency and structure revisited. In *Social Exclusion and Social Work*; Barry, M., Hallett, C., Eds.; Russell House Publishing: Lyme Regis, UK, 1999.

13. Whitmarsh, L. Behavioural responses to climate change: Asymmetry of intentions and impacts. *J. Environ. Psychol.* **2008**, *29*, 13–23.

14. Helm, D. *Energy, the State, and the Market*; Oxford University Press: Oxford, UK, 2004.

15. King, D. Climate change science: Adapt, mitigate or ignore? *Science* **2004**, *303*, 176–177.

16. Royal Commission. Report on Environmental Pollution. 2000. Available online: http://www.rcep.org.uk (accessed on 9 February 2011).

17. Jones, E.; Leach, M.; Wade, J. Local policies for DSM: The UK's home energy conservation act. *Energy Policy* **2000**, *28*, 201–211.

18. HM Government. *Securing the Future: The UK Government Sustainable Development Strategy*; HMSO: Norwich, UK, 2005. Available online: http://www.sustainabledevelopment.gov.uk/publications/pdf/strategy/SecFutcomplete.pdf (accessed on 26 January 2011).

19. Department for Energy, Food, and Rural Affairs. *Behaviour Change: A Series of Practical Guides for Policy-Makers and Practitioners, Number 1. Sustainable Resource Use in the Home Summer 2006*; Department for Energy, Food, and Rural Affairs, Centre for Sustainable Development, University of Westminster: London, UK, 2006. Available online: http://randd.defra.gov.uk/Document.aspx?Document=SD14002_3798_INF.pdf (accessed on 14 February 2011).

20. Miliband, D. A greener shade of red. In *Politics for a New Generation*; Pearce, N., Margo, J., Eds.; Palgrave: London, UK, 2007; pp. 337–350.

21. DECC. *The UK Low Carbon Transition Plan: National Strategy for Climate and Energy, ISBN 9780108508394*, July 2009. Available online: http://www.decc.gov.uk/en/content/cms/publications/lc_trans_plan/lc_trans_plan.aspx (accessed on 29 January 2011).

22. Perrin, D.; Barton, J. Issues associated with transforming household attitudes and opinions into materials recycling: A review of two recycling schemes. *Resour. Conserv. Recycl.* **2001**, *33*, 61–74.

23. Department for Energy, Food, and Rural Affairs. *A Framework for Pro-Environmental Behaviours Report*; The Stationary Office: London, UK, 2007. Available online: http://www.defra.gov.uk/evidence/social/behaviour/documents/behaviours-jan08-report.pdf (accessed on 2 February 2011).

24. Lorenzi, I.; Nicholson-Cole, S.; Whitmarsh, L. Barriers perceived to engaging with climate change among the UK public and their policy implications. *Global Environ. Change* **2007**, *17*, 445–459.

25. Shove, E. Changing Human Behaviour and Lifestyle: A Challenge for Sustainable Consumption? Department of Sociology, University of Lancaster: Lancaster, UK, 2003. Available online: http://www.psi.org.uk/.../shovechanginghumanbehaviourandlifestyle-200308.pdf (accessed on 21 January 2011).

26. Harvey, D. *The Condition of Postmodernity*; Blackwell: Oxford, UK, 1997.

27. O'Neill, J.; Hulme, M. An iconic approach for representing climate change. *Global Environ. Change* **2009**, *19*, 402–410.

28. Kreuger, R.A. *Focus Groups: A Practical Guide for Applied Research*; Sage: London, UK, 1988.

29. Dobson, A. Environmental citizenship and pro-environmental behaviour. *Rapid Research and Evidence Review*; The Sustainable Development Research Network, Policy Studies Institute: UK, 2010. Available online: http://www.sd-research.org.uk (accessed on 7 February 2011).

30. Cabinet Office. *Building the Big Society*; Cabinet Office: London, UK, 2010. Available online: http://www.cabinetoffice.gov.uk/news/building-big-society (accessed on 4 February 2011).

31. Mulugetta, Y.; Jackson, T.; van der Horst, D. Carbon reduction at community scale. *Energy Policy* **2010**, *38*, 7541–7545.

8

CHAPTER

Combining Life Cycle Thinking with Social Theory: Case Study of Compact Fluorescent Lamps (CFL) in the Philippines

Marlyne D. Sahakian

The Graduate Institute of International and Development Studies, Rue de Rothschild 20, Geneva, 1207, Switzerland

ABSTRACT

Resource depletion remains central to human economic activity with resulting negative consequences for the local and global environment. Material and energy consumption patterns are also increasing globally, as developing countries follow the trail blazed by more industrialized countries. Consumers play a role in shifting towards more sustainable forms of consumption. However, consumer-oriented public-policy measures are often restricted to informational campaigns based on moral and price arguments. A multidisciplinary approach to sustainable consumption must go beyond this limited vision of consumers if transitions toward more environmentally friendly consumption patterns are to be made possible. Both a biophysical and social understanding of consumption is necessary. This paper proposes a systemic approach to consumption studies, combining an assessment of consumption patterns with an understanding of the drivers behind them. The concepts will be illustrated using a case study of the government-led promotion of compact fluorescent lamps (CFL) in Metro Manila, the Philippines. Conclusions will include general policy-recommendations.

Keywords: sustainable consumption; compact fluorescent lamps (CFL); life cycle thinking; rebound effect; the Philippines

1. INTRODUCTION

The purchase and usage of products and services by consumers are steadily increasing around the world, with developing countries and their growing middle class following in the path of more industrialized countries. With a rise in affluence, consumers are said to climb a protein and energy ladder to more resource-dependent lifestyles. The question of equity is also worth raising: with limited global resources, including finite fossil fuels, industrialized countries as a whole—as well as pockets of elite groups in less developed countries—are consuming more than their fair share of the natural resource pie. Policy-makers are now calling for a decoupling of economic growth and resource use from environmental degradation, with international efforts underway to address greenhouse gas emissions and biodiversity loss.

The focus of this paper is on understanding consumption, defined here as the purchase and usage of products and services, as being at the nexus of environmental studies and social studies. On the one hand, there is a need to determine existing consumption patterns and priorities for better resource management. This requires a biophysical understanding of consumption that considers the environmental impacts of resource usage over life cycles in a systemic manner and at different scales. On the other hand, it is also critical to grasp the drivers behind those patterns. For this, a social understanding of consumption is necessary, a viewpoint that considers all human and economic activity as embedded in social relations [1].

Current global initiatives to address sustainable consumption and production, such as the UNDP and UN DESA-led Marrakech process, focus more on stakeholder participation than on setting priorities based on scientific research on resource usage patterns and trends. In terms of reaching consumers specifically, policy-makers at the national and local level often apply measures that are limited to the view of consumers as rational decision-makers, sensitive to moral and price arguments. Information campaigns alone do not always lead to so-called rational choices, however, or seemingly rational choices may not lead to the intended outcomes. A multidisciplinary approach to sustainable consumption must go beyond this vision of consumption and consumers, if transitions towards more environmentally friendly consumption patterns are to be made possible.

This paper proposes a systemic approach to consumption studies. The main research question is to determine how life cycle thinking and social theory can be combined to provide insights on how transitions to more sustainable lifestyles could be made possible, from a policy perspective. The focus of this paper is on environmentally significant consumption, one aspect of sustainability. An overview of this conceptual framework will be provided below, and then applied to the case of compact fluorescent lamp (CFL) lighting in Metro Manila. Conclusions will include policy recommendations in this context, as well as a general discussion on the strengths and limits to this approach.

2. CONCEPTUAL FRAMEWORK

Transitions towards more environmentally sustainable lifestyles should involve two approaches: firstly, an assessment of consumption patterns is necessary, drawing on a biophysical and life cycle approach to consumption. Secondly, once priority areas have been established from an environmental perspective, there is a need for a better understanding of what drives these consumption patterns—or the attitude and actions of consumers, which can be apprehended through a social and cultural approach to consumption. The following sections provide an overview of these two complementary approaches.

2.1. A Biophysical and Life Cycle Approach to Consumption

In its biophysical definition, consumption involves human material and energetic provisioning from resources that draw and depend on ecosystem services. While production processes also consume resources, for the purpose of this article the term 'consumption' refers to domestic or household consumption. In ecological economics, economic activity is placed squarely within the environmental system and, therefore, all human activity is subordinate to thermodynamic natural laws and takes place within the limits of the Biosphere, in the sense given to the word by Russian scientist Vladimir Ivanovich Vernadsky (1863–1945)—an open system on which all life depends [2,3,4,5,6]. Unlike what is often asserted by neo-classical economists, resource depletion and pollution cannot be externalized, distinguishing ecological economics from environmental economics. The former does consider biophysical realities and environmental limits.

A close relative of ecological economics, industrial ecology, addresses "anthropogenic complex and coupled systems" [7]. Consumption is significant from an environmental perspective when patterns of resource consumption (the rate and scale of material and energy flows) lean towards exhausting non-renewable resources, or the use of renewable resources beyond their regenerative capacity, and pollution which overwhelms the absorptive capacity of both local and global ecosystem services [8]. Methods used in industrial ecology, such as life cycle analysis, evaluate the resources and energy used in products and services throughout their trajectory, from the extraction of primary resources to final disposal, and envisions ways of slimming down the industrial metabolism [9]. In environmental Life Cycle Analysis (LCA), assessing the impact of a product or service is based on the evaluation of a functional unit, or the quantified performance of a product system based on product utility (1,000 wash cycles, for example, an aspect we will return to later). Economy-wide methods such as Material and Energy Flow Analysis and Environmentally-Extended Input-Output methods are also employed to gauge the physical scale of the economic activities of societies.

These approaches represent a shift away from environmental perspectives of the 1960s and 1970s that focused more on the end of the pipe. In the United States, for example, early environmental regulations were ratified following public and media concern for overflowing landfills, chemical spills and other visible environmental problems. Today, more and more emphasis is being placed on understanding the complete life cycle of products and services, with attention shifting from production processes to consumption patterns and trends.

The following definition of environmentally significant consumption from a biophysical perspective offers a helpful summary:

Consumption consists of human and human-induced transformations of materials and energy. Consumption is environmentally important to the extent that it makes materials or energy less available for future use, moves a biophysical system toward a different state or, through its effects on those systems, threatens human health, welfare, or other things people value. ([10]: p. 20)

Princen went a step further in defining consumption as a "using-up" of resources, with over-consumption including ethical questions such as unequal access to resources ([11]: p. 348). Furthermore, consumption is not a static activity and must take into consideration rates of throughput, growth, scale and patterns of resource use ([12]: p. 3). Thus far, this definition of consumption comprises all economic activity, from the extraction of natural resources to production, distribution and storage, public and private usage, and disposal, but can also include forms of consumption outside of the realm of economic activity (e.g., gathering mushrooms in the forest) and even as a non-activity, including the non-usage of products and services.

While industrial ecology was born in the context of industrialized countries (see [13] for the first use of the term and [14] for its history), researchers have more recently considered socio-economic factors and the specific context of developing countries in relation to resource use [15,16,17,18] and energy usage specifically [19,20]. Efforts are underway to measure the social impact of products and services throughout their life cycle (see [21] for an overview of guidelines towards Social LCA), to not only reduce resource use and emissions, but also improve the socio-economic performance of products. Shifting the focus away from products to consumers, it is less evident to understand how consumers—seen as individuals, household units, social groups or citizens—might be compelled to change their actions and attitudes. In the editorial section of two special issues on sustainable consumption in the *Journal of Industrial Ecology*, Hertwich underlined a need for more research focused on understanding the consumer and consumption patterns, particularly in developing countries [22], and Tukker, Cohen, Hubacek and Mont argued for the need to bridge a gap between an understanding of consumers and the policy measures needed for sustainable lifestyles [23]. The following section outlines how a social and cultural approach to consumption can help better understand consumers, leading to policy recommendations later in this paper.

2.2. A Social and Cultural Approach to Consumption

Sociologists and anthropologists have a long history of theorizing consumption, as seen by an explosion of books in the 1980s [24,25,26,27]. Economic anthropology offers a specific view of consumption that "asks why people want things, not just how they set about to satisfy those wants" ([28]: p. 37). This article builds on economic anthropologist Richard Wilk's framework, which proposes three perspectives—including social, cultural and individual choice forms of consumption—that are each relevant to understanding consumption but also limited in, and of, themselves. Wilk therefore argues for a "multigenic" approach that combines all three perspectives, which is elaborated below and combined with new elements from marketing approaches.

Social forms of consumption "reveal the ways that consumption serves to maintain and challenge the boundaries of social groups, including nations, classes, genders and ethnic groups" ([29]: p. 7). The concepts of status, lifestyles and standards of living are tied to this perspective. The first social theorist of consumption was undoubtedly Thornstein Veblen [30], who coined the term "conspicuous consumption" to define forms of lavish spending on products and services for the display of wealth and for communicating a social position. Following Veblen's line of thinking but using extensive ethnographic materials from France, Pierre Bourdieu [31] took consumption a step further, seeing it as a means for class distinction and therefore political control. He argued that taste judgments are tied to class positions and interest calculations, thus limiting the range of options available to consumers who are neither free agents nor entirely structured by society. As Shove and Warde [32] have argued, forms of inconspicuous consumption—such as bathing or commuting—can be particularly relevant to questions of environmental degradation, and should therefore not be dismissed.

In marketing, advertising campaigns often tap into this social approach to understanding consumption, conveying group characteristics through products that incite consumers to aspirational lifestyles. A shift began to take place in marketing strategies of the 1990s, influenced in part by anthropologists and sociologists joining marketing departments. Up until then, consumption was seen as being driven from the top-down by affluent consumers who are then emulated by lower classes, to follow Veblen's line of thinking [30]. Consumption was also considered as being controlled by production industries and their marketing agencies, following the arguments of Adorno and Horkheimer [33], who saw media and production systems as manipulating the masses into passivity. Malcolm Gladwell in "The Coolhunt" [34], however, noted that fashion trends were also being set and established as 'cool' in the streets before being picked up by 'coolhunters' who used them to inform marketing and production strategies.

Gladwell explains a process by which trends can be diffused to different types of consumers, using the following marketing terminology borrowed from sociologist Everett M. Rogers' work, *Diffusion of Innovations* (1962) [35]: the 'innovator' is the person who finds a pair of old All Star Converse's in a flea market (the canvas and rubber shoe first produced in 1917 for basketball players); the 'early adopters' are the immediate followers of the trend that will try to hunt down their own pair; the 'early majority' are the millions who buy into the trend "jumping in because the really cool people have already blazed the trail" ([34]: p. 78); with the 'late majority' joining the bandwagon last (assuming products are affordable to the masses). For products that embody cool and for Gladwell, the process could not have happened the other way round: a marketing campaign designed by Converse and directed at consumer masses would not have convinced the 'innovator', who in turn would not have influenced the 'early adopter', and so forth. The conclusion drawn from this analysis by Gladwell is that the cool aspect of products is constantly changing, but "Cool people, on the other hand, are constant" (p. 82). As Rogers summarized: "Diffusion is the process by which an innovation is communicated through certain channels over time among members of a social system" ([35]: pp. 5–6). This is consistent with social marketing efforts that seek to engage people through social networks (neighborhood groups, word of mouth, *etc.*), which can be more effective and credible than mass marketing (advertisements, promotions, *etc.*). See [36] for details on how community-based social marketing can foster sustainable lifestyles.

Regardless of whether consumption trends are driven from the top-down or bottom-up, or whether they are conspicuous or not, social forms of consumption place a focus on people and their interactions in society. The focus of cultural forms of consumption is less on people, and more on the goods and products themselves. This second perspective, proposed by Wilk, sees consumption as a form of symbolic behavior with goods coded for communication that express meaning and identity, beyond their practical uses or functional purpose. From the UK, in the same period as Bourdieu, anthropologist Mary Douglas and economist Baron Isherwood [37] saw goods as functioning in a "live information system"—carrying meaning that is not fixed, but rather constantly in transit and in relation to other goods [25]. In France, Jean Baudrillard also offered a symbolic approach to understanding objects [38] as well as a critique of consumerism [39]. This perspective also appears in certain marketing tactics: a car, for example, is often advertised in relation to a graduation diploma and symbolizes a period of life that represents a sense of achievement and freedom (in certain societies). A nuance to the cultural theory of consumption, however, is also needed. For example, a street child in Manila, seen wearing a t-shirt with a black swastika, has neither the choice nor notion of what he is wearing, and people around him may also not understand the political connotations of the logo. Therefore, not all forms of consumption may be intended to communicate meaning, and not all consumers may be equipped to de-code meaning.

Finally, Wilk does not exclude the individual choice forms of consumption that draw from social psychology and behavioral economics and consider the mechanisms by which individuals satisfy so-called needs. In this approach, "needs are produced internal psychological and cognitive processes, leading to choices within a marketplace of possibilities" [29]. One main assumption in public policy is that individuals make consumption choices based on a "price and information" formula, or that individuals have a need for the right price and are swayed by having access to the best information. This strategy was used to "catch a consumer" in post-1950s US and UK marketing techniques (Russel W. Belk in [40]; Frank Mort in [41]). Promotional activities today continue to attract consumers with discounts and sales, and environmental information campaigns prove the prevalence and pervasiveness of this perspective in policy-making. Several authors have argued that information and prices alone do not lead to behavior changes among consumers [42], which can be translated at the policy level into eco-labeling and eco-tax schemes that are often too simplistic [43]. An approach that focuses solely on communicating cost savings or energy efficiency messages to individual consumers tends to ignore the collective aspect of consumption [44], but can be part of a more comprehensive strategy.

As we will see later in this paper, the value of such an approach depends on the social and cultural weight of specific products and services. In the purchase of a car, the cultural and social aspect may play more of a role in influencing consumption decisions than in the purchase of a light bulb. Buying a convertible car most likely costs more and does not relate to the functional aspect of mobility, for example, as social and cultural factors may be more at play. Price does play a role, as does information, but not in the same way for all products and services.

3. APPLYING THE CONCEPTS: THE EXAMPLE OF HOUSEHOLD LIGHTING IN METRO MANILA

In this section, a case study on the public sector promotion of compact fluorescent lamps (CFLs) in Metro Manila, the Philippines, will be used to illustrate how a conceptual framework that combines a life cycle and social approach to consumption can be used to better understand consumption patterns and drivers.

This case study is based on several months of fieldwork in the Philippines between 2005 and 2008, and is part of a larger study that considered other forms of direct energy consumption, including private transport and cooling. The research on which this paper is based involved 30 semi-structured interviews with consumers from different socio-economic groups, age, educational level and gender. Interviews were conducted in homes, while observations took place in both private and public spaces. The interview sample was gathered from three neighborhoods of different socio-economic standing: a former squatter community in Tondo; middle-income houses and apartments in Malate;

and the gated communities of the affluent in Makati. Questions ranged from attitudes towards lighting, cooling and transport, to energy, electricity and environmental issues in general. Interviews were transcribed and fieldnotes were gathered in order to facilitate interpretation, or to uncover the purpose and meaning behind words and actions CFL marketing and distribution tactics were also observed.

Incandescent light bulbs are among the household electrical appliances that have transitioned from novelty to normality over the last one hundred years (see Elizabeth Shove's work [45] for insights into how everyday practices are constructed as normal and ordinary over time). Turning on a switch to instantly illuminate a space is something that is done by millions of people all over the world on a daily basis, without a second thought. Lighting is less significant that cooling in terms of the rate of energy consumption, but presents an interesting case study because of the high frequency of usage: over 95% of households nationwide use some form of lighting. There is nothing conspicuous about this form of consumption, and yet it is environmentally significant as it draws on a coal-dependent electricity grid and replaces more traditional forms of fuel that are now seen as less convenient (for example, jetropha was traditionally burnt for lighting in Manila).

The technology of the incandescent bulb has changed very little since its original conception. Today, new forms of lighting technology are available on the market, including light-emitting-diode (LEDs) lamps, and the CFL bulb. The CFL bulb, which is more commonly used at the household level than the LED, gives off light by passing electricity through mercury vapor, which in turn produces an ultraviolet light that is absorbed by a phosphor coating inside the lamp, causing it to glow. The presence of mercury in CFLs means that special considerations need to be in place for recuperating and managing the waste stream of old bulbs. These bulbs have a longer life span than incandescent bulbs (lasting eight- to nine-times longer) and are more energy efficient (using a quarter of the electrical power needed for an incandescent bulb, e.g., an 18–20 watt CFL is equivalent to a 75 watt incandescent bulb). There is a drawback: CFL bulbs are more expensive to purchase (typically five- to six-times the cost). The cost-saving for the household is in their electricity bills and while the initial cost of the CFL bulb is higher than the traditional bulb, it is less expensive over the course of its life cycle as it does not have to be replaced as often as the incandescent bulb.

Because of the greater energy efficiency in CFL usage, governments around the world have passed measures to phase out incandescent light bulbs, either voluntarily or through legislation. In the Philippines, the campaign to transition away from incandescent light bulbs is known as SWITCH to CFL and was launched jointly by the government of the

Philippines and the Asian Development Bank (ADB). How could a life cycle and social understanding of consumption help guide the way to more environmentally sustainable forms of lighting consumption in the case of Manila? The following section applies the concepts to this case study, and is followed by policy implications in the context of the Philippines.

3.1. The Switch to CFL in Manila: A Life Cycle Perspective

CFL bulb usage is promoted as being energy efficient, yet the production and transport of CFL bulbs, as well as their final disposal, must also be considered in a LCA. From the perspective of ecological economics, the resource depletion and pollution related to CFL bulbs cannot be externalized. CFL bulbs require more material inputs during production processes, and do not contribute to a slimming-down of the industrial metabolism. CFLs are currently not produced in the Philippines—thus incurring energy inputs necessary for their transport into the country. No LCA on the switch to CFLs was conducted in the context of the Philippines prior to this initiative. Opportunities for slimming-down the metabolism of CFLs upstream—during the manufacturing and transportation phase—might have been identified.

However, transport and manufacturing energy requirements were found to be minimal as compared to the energy savings during the usage phase in a study of CFLs in the context of Australia [46]. In the same study, the potential environmental impact of mercury waste from CFLs was also found to be insignificant. CFL bulbs carry approximately four milligrams of mercury per bulb, but because coal-powered electricity plants also release mercury, the benefit of reducing coal-powered electricity consumption outweighs the problem of mercury waste. However, mercury waste remains a health risk when improperly managed.

In the Philippines, as in many developing countries, open dumpsites have been most commonly used in the last few decades, often operated without a license, and are part of the daily lives of thousands of people who live by the landfills and derive their livelihood from collecting recyclables. Non-recycled waste in Manila ends up in semi-controlled landfills (such as the Payatas landfill), illegal open landfills (such as Pier 18), and the natural environment, including waterways (such as the Pasig river and the Manila bay). Household waste segregation has been part of environmental advocacy campaigns for many years. With the passage of the Ecological Solid Waste Management Act in 2001 (RA 9003, [47]), responsibility for household waste segregation was driven down to the *barangay* level, or the smallest governmental unit in the Philippines.

The overall objective of RA 9003 is to decrease the total volume of waste that reaches landfills and this has been achieved to a great extent because of the economic value of recyclables, as well as Metro Manila's access to the sea and the nearby Chinese market. According to a 2004 study by the Asian Development Bank, Metro Manila produces approximately 6,700 tonnes of garbage per day of which only 720 tonnes is retrieved for recycling and composting [48]. CFL bulbs that are not segregated out of the waste stream can therefore pose a toxic hazard when left in the natural environment or in open dumpsites—particularly because poorer populations continue to live in close contact with this waste (based on my observations and interviews at the Smokey Mountain landfill in Tondo, which has been out of use since the 1990s, the surrounding community grows vegetables directly on the waste).

In the press coverage around the launch of the Switch to CFL campaign—which received much media attention as the first initiative of its kind in Asia—the question of recycling was raised: the Department of Energy (DOE) in the Philippines is said to buy back used CFLs and recycle their toxic mercury content. There are thousands of people involved in recycling in Manila, from scavengers more politely called individual waste workers, to cooperatives and micro-enterprises, to larger-volume operations and exporters. It would require a massive effort to engage all those involved in waste collection and segregation to sell the CFL bulbs back to the DOE. The management of the CFL waste stream and recuperating mercury before final disposal seems less clear in this context where so many players are involved.

In terms of energy efficiency, an evaluation of the eco-efficiency and environmental impact of CFL bulbs must take into consideration the regional electricity mix and related energy sources involved in CFL usage. As the Republic of the Philippines is made up of islands, energy sources and electricity mix should be calculated by region or greater island area. At a regional level and for Luzon—the northernmost group of islands in the Philippines and home to Metro Manila—residential sector demand represented the highest share of total energy demand in 2007. Household energy consumption in Metro Manila draws from the Luzon energy grid, more dependent on coal-powered energy and natural gas than other parts of the country. In 2007, coal-fired plants in Luzon accounted for 27% of the total national mix, and for 2006, coal-powered energy represented 14,417,796 MWh of the national total demand of 16,837,096, or 85.6% of national demand. Carbon emissions for a region also need to be placed in relation to energy sources: for Metro Manila, recent reports developed under the Kyoto Protocol's Clean Development Mechanism for waste-to-energy projects in Manila refer to an emission factor of 0.557 kg CO_2e/ kWh for the Manila grid [49], slightly higher than the Filipino average of 0.523 kg CO_2/ kWh, which can be explained by a higher reliance on coal in Manila's electricity mix.

From a life cycle perspective and drawing from industrial ecology, CFL bulbs in their usage phase are more efficient that the traditional incandescent bulb. However, because electricity use in general is highly dependent on coal-powered electricity in Metro Manila, the goal must be to reduce overall electricity consumption. This can be achieved through technical innovations and more eco-efficiency per unit of production, but only if electricity consumption overall doesn't increase. CFL bulbs also pose a problem in terms of final disposal. Finally, because electricity in Manila is dependent on coal-powered energy, it would be significant to determine how lighting consumption patterns change with the introduction of a new technology from a biophysical perspective, and whether this leads to lower electricity usage overall. This is a question we will return to later in this paper.

3.2. The Social and Cultural Meaning of Lighting, and the Role of Influencers

As we saw earlier, a social understanding of consumption means recognizing the role of people and their interactions in society as one driving force for consumption patterns and trends. While CFLs have been researched in terms of technical efficiency, little empirical research exists on relating the uptake of this new technology to socio-economic factors [50]. In this section, we will focus specifically on how social interactions can affect change.

In an interview, an elderly couple explained how their daughter was responsible for their switch to CFL in their home. The daughter had studied environmental issues, had heard about the new bulbs and uses them in her own home, and therefore took the initiative to make the change at her parents' home. To use Gladwell's terminology, as the 'early adopter', she then influenced the 'early majority'.

This type of influencing can also happen on a mass scale, through the use of the media: in the Philippines, celebrities—including models, actors, TV show personalities or members of the wealthier families—are often invited to promote a given message, service or product. Celebrities campaign for everything from family planning to environmental issues in the Philippines, but the influence of celebrities is also global in scope—as images and ideas are communicated through the Internet, as well as TV and radio programs. When I asked one woman (in the 45–54 years age bracket) if she had made the switch to CFLs in her home, she stated:

I did! See, because I watch Oprah. And she said change all your lights so I did. I changed most of them. I heard it this year in one of the shows. She had someone talking about that, and they said that it really saves energy (...) Oprah convinces me of everything (laughter).

For many, a light bulb has very little symbolic value. It is what is known in marketing as a low involvement product: most people in industrialized countries spend less time thinking about what type of light bulb to purchase than they would for the purchase of a new car, as we have already noted. The consumption of products with less of a symbolic and cultural value can more easily influenced by the individual-approach to consumption: for example, among the lower income groups interviewed, the higher initial cost of CFLs was seen as prohibitive and represents a barrier to change. Cost is not the only issue, however. Those who had purchased cheaper versions of this form of lighting expressed disappointment over product longevity (the Chinese brands were perceived to not last very long), leading to mistrust over the product features (a similar conclusion was drawn for the Indian market, see [51]). On store shelves, Chinese brands are offered at a lower cost than brands such as Philips and GE. A cost incentive could act as a driver for CFL consumption, but this strategy alone will not address the question of brand credibility and consumer trust.

During this fieldwork, many interviewees admitted to not remembering any commercials for light bulbs and only buying new bulbs on an annual basis. However, another couple told me that they had first seen CFLs at a friend's house, who had proudly explained their energy saving qualities, showing that these new bulbs could also serve as objects for display, communicating the environmental concern of their owners. Lighting has the potential to become a cultural form of consumption for some, with the CFL a carrier of symbolic meaning.

3.3. Lighting, Rational Choice and the Rebound Effect

Before mass-produced incandescent bulbs, people read, studied or worked by candlelight. Today, our standard of what constitutes appropriate reading light has changed. In an interview, one man (in the 45–54 years age bracket) explained his transition to energy efficient light bulbs in his home:

But I just told my wife, I need two not one. I said, "Don't use one use two". Because in one room di ba parang ganyan *instead of using, she put one for here and one there, one there. But when I work, it's a little dark, I had to put on a two. Anyway it's economical so I said just open both all the time anyway. Anyway it's consuming very little. But it's bad for the eyes to be using only one CFL, there has to be two at a time for a room like this.*

A young couple (24–34 years old) also explained how they use light for safety reasons:

Sometimes we leave on the lights because it shows people that we're home, it's a safety thing. In the kitchen. When we leave or when we're asleep. But it's an energy saving light bulb.

To use LCA terminology, the functional utility of the light bulb is not solely for lighting, but also for safety, which poses the question of how to measure this functionality, and how to find less energy-intensive alternatives that address this particular "cultural energy service" [52].

What is most telling in the quotes above is that people seem to have understood the message of energy and economical savings with the new CFL bulbs, but their actions lead to the overall consumption of more energy (which might only become apparent later, on the monthly electricity bill). This presents a significant issue in terms of energy reduction: perceptions of energy- and economic-savings per light bulb or per production unit can lead to the practice of adding light bulbs to the household or the increased usage of a bulb by extending the time it is turned on. This is what is known as the rebound effect or what Edgar Hertwich also called the ripple effect [53]: an increase in overall consumption despite energy efficiency technological improvements.

In the examples above, there are two driving forces behind the expressed need for additional lighting when switching to more energy-efficient bulbs: the first is that the new bulbs do not give off the same luminosity as the traditional bulbs, and therefore more bulbs are needed. A new design or moving up to a higher wattage could improve this aspect, but a more dangerous reasoning is in the second driver: that if households can save energy and electricity costs by switching to more energy efficient bulbs, then adding new sources of lighting is possible. This is a seemingly rational decision that goes against the purpose of energy-efficient technology. In both examples, lighting also serves other functions that cannot necessarily be addressed by technology alone, but rather a change in external factors (such as safety) and in perceptions (what is considered "normal" light intensity).

4. POLICY IMPLICATIONS

Based on life cycle thinking and from a biophysical perspective, switching household consumption to CFLs would represent an improvement on natural resource usage and pollution compared to incandescent bulbs so long as the following criteria are met: the CFL bulb longevity is up to standard, the dumping of mercury in landfills is avoided, and overall lighting usage doesn't increase over time per household, leading to what has been described earlier as the rebound effect. For the first criteria, some respondents approached through fieldwork expressed feelings of mistrust towards product longevity, which translates to a loss of credibility for certain brands. From a policy perspective, the Philippines must raise their standards in terms of the types of CFL bulbs that can be imported and made available on their markets. In terms of addressing the issue of recycling, the DOE should communicate a clear buy-back strategy for used CFL bulbs, which is currently not the case. Recycling is not free in terms resource usage, and should be seen as a last resort—reducing overall energy consumption should be the main goal. There is also another issue, that of government mistrust: in all interviews, research participants spoke of high levels of corruption in the public sector and general mistrust of politicians. Partnering with the private sector or other institutions would be beneficial in order to lend credibility to any efforts to promote CFL waste segregation and recycling. In both these examples, insights drawn from fieldwork have led to identification of barriers and opportunities that can inform policy-making.

In terms of communicating the energy-efficiency of CFL bulbs, it is not only the medium that presents a problem given general mistrust of the public sector, but also the message: consumers should be given the full picture through an introduction to life cycle thinking when it comes to their household electricity consumption, or a deeper understanding of material and energy used throughout a product's life cycle. Educational campaigns—through school systems, neighborhood associations, celebrity endorsement or other credible sources—must focus not only on the cost-saving aspect of energy-efficient light bulbs, but on the coal-dependent and polluting aspect of Manila's electricity mix. An informational campaign based on advertising alone may not be able to achieve this. None of the respondents interviewed could provide an accurate description of the energy sources for their electricity, with the exception of two respondents working on energy issues.

As noted by Elizabeth Shove, it is ultimately the systems of provision that shape what people do: institutional change the Philippines means changing the "contexts of action" [54] by adding more renewable energy to the electricity mix, for example, or addressing the question of safety. From a life cycle perspective, the problem of household electricity consumption in Metro Manila must start upstream and cannot be addressed through technical solutions alone. CFL bulbs may reduce household electricity consumption, but electricity consumption will increase overall in Manila as households continue to rise in affluence. Public policy must focus on energy sources for a capital region that continues to grow, in terms of population and infrastructure development.

Meters at the household level that record electricity usage for specific household appliances would be effective in helping consumers understand the energy consumption of their lighting needs. These efforts could help reduce the rebound effect and have already been identified as a viable solution for other cities in Asia [55]. In 2009, "smart meters" were deployed to residential homes in Manila, but are cost prohibitive for a large part of the population. In low-income housing developments, electricity meters for apartment units would be a good start. Including environmental objectives in smart meter technology is not merely a question of technology, however, and would need to involve "a powerful shift in the regulatory and institutional frameworks within which utilities and manufacturers are configuring the functionalities of smart meters" [56].

A lack of interest in light bulbs as a low-involvement product, coupled with a higher purchase price of CFLs, represent a barrier to entry for the CFL market, particularly for poorer populations. But this lack of cultural meaning can also be seen as an opportunity: if people have no preference for the type of light bulb they use, it could be easier to promote the new bulbs. Where products and services have low social and cultural value, approaches that focus on price and information could be more effective if combined with a broader social understanding of consumption that yields some of the insights discussed above. Efforts to give away free CFL bulbs seem particularly relevant: by testing a new type of lighting device, you may be more apt to purchase that bulb in the future, as long as the product delivers on its promise (e.g., bulb longevity). The SWITCH campaign has succeeded in giving out free CFLs in poorer neighborhoods, thanks to support from the Asian Development Bank. Influencers could also continue to be engaged in campaigns that would give a cultural meaning to CFL bulbs, promoting them as objects of display. But to avoid the rebound effect, additional measures must be taken, such as household energy meters and education on life cycle thinking, as mentioned above.

5. CONCLUSIONS

This article has brought together Wilk's multigenic approach to understanding consumption as a combination of social, cultural and individual choice approaches, with a biophysical understanding of consumption. It represents a small bridge between social and environmental studies, but one that merits to be expanded upon. Patterns of consumption can be better assessed and prioritized in order of environmental significance, but the drivers of those patterns should also be revealed. For the former, quantitative research is both useful and necessary. For the latter, fieldwork based on observations and interviews with consumers can yield valuable insights into how people relate to various products and services.

The campaign to switch to energy-saving CFL bulbs in the Philippines provides a case study example for understanding how life cycle thinking and social theory can shed light on opportunities for more environmentally-friendly consumption. The functional utility of a product such as the light bulb, for example, can only be uncovered by understanding what secondary lighting functions are important to consumers, such as perceived household safety and reading comfort. Fieldwork can therefore provide useful insights for the design of LCA, while also uncovering the barriers and opportunities for change. This means finding ways to build bridges between disciplines to form multidisciplinary teams, which is not always easy given the different backgrounds and approaches of researchers. Such an effort may be deemed cost- and time-prohibitive, particularly in the context of developing countries, but even a simplified approach—as was the case in this CFL example—can reveal key insights to move policy recommendations in the right direction.

Ultimately, life cycle thinking and social theory have in common a systemic approach that attempts to see the full picture when it comes to understanding consumption patterns and drivers. This approach would certainly be helpful in tackling the question of private transportation and travel, for example, two energy-intensive consumption areas that are also tied up in cultural and social meaning. Combining macro-level data with micro-living insights is not without complexity, but such a multi-disciplinary approach is necessary for understanding how transitions to more sustainable lifestyles could be made possible.

ACKNOWLEDGEMENTS

The author is grateful for the insightful feedback from Isabelle Schulte-Tenckhoff and Julia K. Steinberger on an earlier version of this article. She would like to thank Suren Erkman for introducing her to industrial ecology, as well as Anthony S.F. Chiu for his generous guidance and support during fieldwork in Manila. She is also appreciative of the feedback from the anonymous reviewers.

REFERENCES

1. Polanyi, K. The Economy as Instituted Process. In *Trade and Market in the Early Empires*; Polanyi, K.C.M.A., Pearson, H.W., Eds.; Free Press: Glencoe, IL, USA, 1957; pp. 243–270.
2. Boulding, K.E. The Economics of the Coming Spaceship Earth. In *Environmental Quality in a Growing Economy*; Jarrett, H., Ed.; Resources for the Future/Johns Hopkins University Press: Baltimore, MD, USA, 1966.
3. Daly, H.E. On economics as a life science. *J. Polit. Econ.* **1968**, *76*, 392–406.
4. Georgescu-Roegen, N. *Analytical Economics: Issues and Problems*; Harvard University Press: Cambridge, MA, USA, 1966.
5. Georgescu-Roegen, N. *The Entropy Law and the Economic Process*; Harvard University Press: Cambridge, MA, USA, 1971.
6. Martinez-Alier, J. *Ecological Economics: Energy, Environment and Society*; Blackwell: Cambridge, MA, USA, 1987.
7. Fischer-Kowalski, M.; Hertwich, E.; Lifset, R. Strategies and Tools for Refashioning the Social Metabolism: IE as a Key to the Transition to Sustainability. In Proceedings of the 2009 ISIE Conference on Transitions toward Sustainability, Lisbon, Portugal, 21–24 June 2009.
8. Daly, H.E. *Beyond Growth: The Economics of Sustainable Development*; Beacon Press: Boston, MA, USA, 1996.
9. Ayres, R.; Simonis, U.E. *Industrial Metabolism: Restructuring for Sustainable Development*; United Nations University Press: Tokyo, Japan, 1994; p. 390.
10. Stern, P.; Dietz, T.; Ruttan, V.; Socolow, R.; Sweeney, J. *Environmentally Significant Consumption: Research Directions*; Committee on the Human Dimensions of Global Change, National Academy Press: Washington, DC, USA, 1997; p. 143.
11. Princen, T. Consumption and environment: Some conceptual issues. *Ecol. Econ.* **1999**, *31*, 347–363.

12. Princen, T.; Maniates, M.; Conca, K. *Confronting Consumption*; The MIT Press: Cambridge, MA, USA, 2002.

13. Frosch, R.A.; Gallopoulos, N.E. Strategies for Manufacturing. *Sci. Amer.* **1989**, *261*, 144–152.

14. Erkman, S. Industrial ecology: An historical view. *J. Clean. Prod.* **1997**, *5*, 1–10.

15. Binder, C.R. *The Early Recognition of Environmental Impacts of Human Activities in Developing Countries*; Federal Institute of Technology Zurich (ETHZ): Zurich, Switzerland, 1996.

16. Binder, C.R.; Mosler, H.J. Waste-resource flows of short-lived goods in households of Santiago de Cuba. *Resour. Conserv. Recyc.* **2006**, *51*, 265–283.

17. Erkman, S.; Ramaswamy, R. *Applied Industrial Ecology: A New Platform for Planning Sustainable Societies: Focus on Developing Countries with Case Studies from India*; Aicra Publishers: Bangalor, India, 2003; p. 159.

18. Liu, J.; Savenije, H.H.G. Food consumption patterns and their effect on water requirement in China. *Hydrol. Earth Syst. Sci.* **2008**, *12*, 887–898.

19. Pachauri, S. An analysis of cross-sectional variations in total household energy requirements in India using micro survey data. *Energ. Policy* **2004**, *32*, 1723–1735.

20. Sathaye, J.; Tyler, S.R. Transitions in household energy use in urban China, India, the Philippines, Thailand, and Hong Kong. *Annu. Rev. Energ. Environ.* **1991**, *16*, 295–335.

21. Andrews, E.S.; Barthel, L.P.; Tabea, B.; Benoît, C.; Ciroth, A.; Cucuzzella, C.; Gensch, C.O.; Hébert, J.; Lesage, P.; Manhart, A.; Mazeau, P. *Guidelines for Social Life Cycle Assessment of Products*; UNEP/SETAC Life Cycle Initiative: Paris, France, 2009.

22. Hertwich, E.G. Editorial: Consumption and industrial ecology. *J. Ind. Ecol.* **2005**, *9*, 1–6.

23. Tukker, A.; Maurie, J.; Cohen, K.H.; Mont, A.O. Editorial: Sustainable consumption and production. *J. Ind. Ecol.* **2010**, *14*, 1–3.

24. Appadurai, A. *The Social Life of Things: Commodities in Cultural Perspective*; Cambridge Studies in Social & Cultural Anthropology: New York, NY, USA, 1986.

25. McCracken, G. *Culture and Consumption: New Approaches to the Symbolic Character of Consumer Goods and Activities*; Indiana University Press: Bloomington, IN, USA, 1988.

26. McKendrick, N.; Brewer, J.; Plumb, J.H. *The Birth of a Consumer Society*; Hutchinson: London, UK, 1983.

27. Rutz, H.J.; Orlove, B.S. *The Social Economy of Consumption*; University Press of America: Lanham, MD, USA, 1989.

28. Wilk, R.; Cliggett, L.C. *Economies and Cultures: Foundations of Economic Anthropology,*, 2nd ed.; Westview Press: Cambridge, MA, USA, 2007.

29. Wilk, R. Consumption, human needs, and global environmental change. *Global Environ. Change* **2002**, *12*, 5–13.

30. Veblen, T. *The Theory of the Leisure Class*; Penguin Group: New York, NY, USA, 1994/1899; p. 400.

31. Bourdieu, P. *La Distinction Critique Sociale Du Jugement*; Les Editions de Minuit: Paris, France, 1979; p. 670.

32. Shove, E.; Warde, A. Inconspicuous Consumption: The Sociology of Consumption and the Environment. Available online: www.comp.lancs.ac.uk/fass/sociology/papers/shove-warde-inconspicuous-consumption.pdf (accessed on 10 September 2009).

33. Adorno, T.; Horkheimer, M. The Culture Industry: Enlightenment as Mass Deception. In *Dialectic of Enlightenment*; Continuum, J., Ed.; Herder and Herder: New York, NY, USA, 1944.

34. Gladwell, M. The Coolhunt. *The New Yorker: Annals of Style*, 17 March 1997.

35. Rogers, E.M. *Diffusion of Innovations*, 4th ed.; The Free Press: New York, NY, USA, 1995.

36. McKenzie-Mohr, D.; Smith, W.; Smith, W.A. *Fostering Sustainable Behavior: An Introduction to Community-Based Social Marketing*; New Society Publishers: Gabriola Island, BC, Canada, 1999.

37. Douglas, M.; Isherwood, B. *The World of Goods: Towards and Anthropology of Consumption*, 1996th ed.; Basic Books: New York, NY, USA, 1979; p. 169.

38. Baudrillard, J. *Le système des objets*; Gallimard: Paris, France, 1968.

39. Baudrillard, J. *La société de consommation, ses mythes, ses structures*; Denoël: Paris, France, 1970.

40. Miller, D. *Acknowledging Consumption: A Review of New Studies*; Routledge: London, UK, 1995.

41. Nava, M.; Blake, A.; MacRury, I.; Richards, B. *Buy This Book: Studies in Advertising and Consumption*; Routledge: London, UK, 1997.

42. Barr, S.; Gilg, A.W. A conceptual framework for understanding and analyzing attitudes towards environmental behaviour. *Geogr. Ann.* **2007**, *89 B*, 361–379.

43. Cohen, M.J.; Murphy, J. *Exploring Sustainable Consumption: Environmental Policy and the Social Sciences*; Elsevier: Oxford, UK, 2001.

44. Randles, S.; Warde, A. Consumption: the view from theories of practice. In *Industrial Ecology and Spaces of Innovation*; Green, K., Randles, S., Eds.; Edward Elgar: Cheltenham, UK, 2006; pp. 220–237.

45. Shove, E. *Comfort, Cleanliness and Convenience: The Social Organization of Normality*; Berg: Oxford, NY, USA, 2003.

46. Parsons, D. The Environmental impact of compact fluorescent lamps and incandescent lamps for Australian conditions. *Environ. Eng.* **2006**, *7*, 8–14.

47. *Ecological Solid Waste Management Act of 2000*; Congress of the Philippines: Manila, the Philippines, 2001; Republic Act No. 9003; p. 231.

48. Asian Development Bank. *The Garbage Book: Solid Waste Management in Metro Manila*; Metro Manila Solid Waste Management Project: Makati City, the Philippines, 2004; p. 96.

49. *Makati South Sewage Treatment Plant Upgrade with On-Site Power, Version 4*; Clean Development Mechanism, Simplified Project Design Document for Small-Scale Project Activities: Manila, the Philippines, 2009.

50. Mills, B.F.; Schleich, J. Why don't households see the light? *Resour. Energy Econ.* **2009**.

51. Kumara, A.; Jainb, S.K.; Bansalc, N.K. Disseminating energy-efficient technologies: A case study of compact fluorescent lamps (CFLs) in India. *Energ. Policy* **2003**, *31*, 259–272.

52. Wilhite, H.; Lutzenhiser, L. Social loading and sustainable consumption. *Advan. Consum. Res.* **1999**, *26*, 281–287.

53. Hertwich, E.G. Consumption and the rebound effect: An industrial ecology perspective. *J. Ind. Ecol.* **2005**, *9*, 85–98.

54. Shove, E. Gaps, barriers and conceptual chasms: Theories of technology transfer and energy in buildings. *Energ. Policy* **1998**, *26*, 1105–1112.

55. Tyler, S.R. Household energy use in Asian cities: Responding to development success. *Atmos. Environ.* **1996**, *30*, 809–816.

56. Marvin, S.; Chappells, H.; Guy, S. Pathways of smart metering development: Shaping environmental innovation. *Comput. Environ. Urban Syst.* **1999**, *23*, 109–126.

9

CHAPTER

Exploring Perceptions of Raspberries and Blueberries by Italian Consumers

Vincenzo Girgenti *, Stefano Massaglia, Angela Mosso, Cristiana Peano and Filippo Brun

Department of Agricultural, Forest and Food Sciences, University of Turin, Largo Paolo Braccini 2, 10095 Grugliasco (TO), Italy

ABSTRACT

Consumers can be important active contributors to a sustainable society by selecting foods that are produced respecting environmental and socially ethical standards. In the fruit sector, sustainability issues are often associated with imprecisely defined concepts such as "locally grown", "freshness" and "local product". This study has investigated raspberries (*Rubus idaeus* L.) and blueberries (*Vaccinium corymbosum* L.) purchases in order to identify how berry fruits choice attributes are ranked by consumers in two Italian Regions, using a choice experiment (best-worst methodology). Twelve attributes—that indirectly refer to the concept of environmental sustainability—have been investigated. According to the preferences expressed by our sample of retail purchasers (n = 669), the results show that the reasons for the purchase of berries are associated with numerous parameters among which freshness and product origin are the most important and price was not ranked as so relevant. These findings indirectly testify the consumer attention towards the sustainability of local production and the link between sustainability and territory. Therefore, we can presume that the improvement of consumer familiarity with attributes such as "locally grown" and "local product" could support more eco-friendly consumption of raspberries and blueberries.

Keywords: berry fruits; consumer acceptance; best-worst methodology; choice attributes; sustainability

1. INTRODUCTION

Trends and Aspects of the Consumption of Raspberries and Blueberries in Italy

Consumers are increasingly interested in food quality, broadly defined. In addition to expecting higher dietary, health and hygiene standards from the products that they purchase [1], consumers also consider the equity, fair trade, sustainability and ethical sphere of products [2]. This is also true for fruits and vegetables, which are increasingly valued as an important part of the diet, as their regular consumption has been associated with the prevention of several different diseases [3]. In fact, concern for dietary health impacts is now considered as important as taste in assessing the quality of a product [4]. Other important drivers include the procedures for fruit production, processing and sustainability, as well as the purchase of local products, particularly among European consumers [5]. As a result of this progress, food consumption behaviour in the European Union (EU) appears to be rapidly evolving, and is consequently becoming more difficult to understand and predict [6].

Raspberries and blueberries are a good example of the cultural dynamism that has characterised the evolution of food consumption in Italy. They demonstrate how the image of a product, which has always been considered niche, can potentially be considered as part of daily fresh fruit consumption, in addition to improving agricultural sustainability [7].

Peano et al. [8] emphasised that neither eco-labelling nor providing environmental information can be a goal in itself, but that these approaches are a means of creating a production system, consumption attitude and a more environmentally friendly market. However, before retailers can implement a new marketing strategy they must firstly develop an understanding of the determinants of consumer purchases. The development of trends in consumer demands opens up new possibilities for adding value and differentiating specific products.

Raspberries (*Rubus idaeus* L.) and blueberries (*Vaccinium corymbosum* L.) were chosen for this study as they are important fresh products in Italy, and have been constantly cultivated and grown since 1980. Italy is among the leading European producers, producing 2000 and 1550 tons of raspberries and blueberries, respectively, per year [9]. In Italy, the domestic consumption of fruit and vegetables at the national level is characterised by a negative trend (-6.1% for 7 reference years between 2007 and 2013), while the consumption of berry fruits has increased in volume by (+156.3%) and in value (+206.6%) [10]. There are several contributing factors that have allowed berry fruits to penetrate the Italian market, including an increase in their use in both private households and the food service industry (restaurants, bars and ice-cream shops), the association of these fruits with high nutritional and natural value [11,12], an increase in consumption during the traditional summer period (June to September) due to improved storage techniques [13] and an increase in imports from countries within and outside of Europe [14]. Despite this, the rate of market penetration in this category decreased by approximately 24% in 2012, with an average of 2.7 annual purchases per family [15], composing only 1.5% of the sale value within the fruit sector.

The consumption of berries in Italy is still low compared to that in the UK, where they represent 7.6% of the total purchased fruit [16] with a market penetration of 50% and an average of 10.4 annual purchases per family. Berries are considered a specialty in Italy. It is often difficult to define the fruits that fit into this category, as there is no unique definition of specialty foods. However, several organisations have their own definition of this category [17]. Within the myriad of definitions of specialty foods, it is possible to identify three fundamental characteristics, including a premium price, high quality and limited distribution. Other important features that are commonly included are the production methods, supply chain and symbolism. Murphy et al. [18] propose a definition of specialty foods that is well suited to the objectives of our study, and which combines these features:

"Specialty foods are considered as products outside the mainstream possessing specific qualities, which differentiate them from standard foods. These qualities are derived from a combination of at least two of the following features: (1) Exclusiveness: the product is produced on a small scale and is therefore only available in limited quantities; (2) Processing: the product has at least undergone primary processing using non- industrial artisan techniques; (3) Distinctiveness: the distinctiveness of the product arises from a combination of all or some of the following attributes: extraordinary packaging, premium price, renowned origin, and/or its unique design."

In order to increase the consumption and production of raspberries and blueberries in Italy, it is necessary to predominantly include large-scale points of sale, which already contribute to the biggest increase in sales [15]. The aim is to activate tangible pathways for enhancement, both within and outside of these points of purchase, that intercept the consumer in everyday life and contribute to "constructing" his or her shopping basket of choice [17], based on that achieved previously by South American producers in large-scale retail stores in the UK [19].

It is necessary to understand how the knowledge of the consumer (what and why they are consuming a particular producer) can influence the future economic and marketing strategies of both the producer and retailer, also considering that these relationships should not be designed in a unique way. In fact, several consumer segments and niches differ widely and are ever-changing. Income, demographic variables and lifestyle are no longer sufficient in the categorisation of consumers [20]. This is particularly evident in the food industry, where the differentiation and overload of food supply, increased budget, migrations, globalisation and lifestyle changes, particularly in working habits, have altered food consumption patterns. Senauer [21] remarked that the decision making unit for food consumption is increasingly becoming individualised, rather than focusing on the household. Currently, consumer choices and behaviours are affected by attributes and the quality of goods, in addition to the cultural, social, personal and psychological characteristics of individuals. Only a multi-disciplinary approach can succeed in explaining the behaviour of the modern consumer [20]. The opening of new markets and the reorganisation of existing markets is strongly driven by the introduction of new products and more sustainable production technologies [7]. Based on these considerations, the objective of this study was to assess the importance of 12 consumption attributes for berry fruits (raspberries and blueberries) in two Italian regions (Piedmont and Liguria). Using a choice experiment, this study identifies the way in which these attributes are ranked by consumers, considering the potential environmental and/or regional effects that may drive choice differences between the two investigated areas.

2. RESEARCH METHODOLOGY

2.1. Blueberry and Raspberry Quality Attributes

The 12 attributes assessed in this study were selected using two different approaches. The first approach used was the "Delphi" method [22], where 10 experts (producers' marketing managers and retail buyers) were interviewed twice to obtain convergent opinions on the major characteristics of the raspberry and blueberry markets. The second approach, concerning the choice of attributes, included an in-depth review of articles published in international journals. The attributes chosen were:

Freshness: In investigations focusing on specific fruits, such as apples, freshness has been shown to be one of the primary choice criteria for consumers [23,24]. As berries have a shorter shelf life, the consumer evaluates the freshness of the product at the moment of purchase [19,25,26,27,28];

Product origin: Numerous marketing studies have shown that the assessments made by consumers are significantly influenced by their knowledge of the origin of the products. For the consumer, information about the geographical origin can serve to identify both the product and the quality [22,29,30];

Organic label: Organic certification is recognised in various studies as an attribute that positively influences the choice of the consumer at the moment of purchase [31,32,33,34,35];

Health benefits: Research conducted on the psychology of consumption suggests that one of the main attributes driving the choice for buying raspberries and blueberries is the health benefit associated with their consumption [12,27,36,37,38];

Seasonality: Traditionally, the consumption of raspberries and blueberries has been closely linked to their harvesting season [19,33];

Appearance: The appearance of fruit is one of the attributes that most influences choice at the time of purchase. Retail stores and retailers at traditional street markets make their selections based on visual criteria before selling fruit and vegetables [28,39];

Locally grown: For companies, information regarding the region of origin is a means for differentiation. This provides a competitive advantage if appreciated by the consumer. Furthermore, food is closely related to territory and has strong traditional and symbolic connections with its place of origin, resulting from its interactions with the natural resources and the lifestyles of the inhabitants [28,30,40,41,42,43];

Packaging: Initially used for the purpose of containment and protection, packaging is now seen by retailers and brand owners as a potential platform for communication with consumers. Environmental sustainability influences the customer's expectations regarding retail products and their packaging [16,44,45];

Labelling (producer and/or retailer): Relying on a guarantee is one of the possible strategies in situations of risk or lack of information [38];

Quality certifications: Retail suppliers are required to provide quality certifications [46];

Price: In general, price is a key element in the purchasing decision of consumers. It can also be used as an indicator of quality when a consumer does not have enough information to evaluate a product. Price can also be important in situations of risk, as purchasing cheaper products reduces financial risk, while a particularly high price protects against poor quality [28,47];

Brand knowledge: The brand is an extrinsic quality indicator, as it allows the consumer to identify the product and connect with it through past experiences or information about the manufacturer (or seller) [38].

Each of these chosen attributes, with the exception of price, were clustered into five categories, shown in Table 1, obtained by adapting the four dimensions of food quality detailed by the "Total Quality Food Model" [48], in addition to the future trends of consumption described by Lappo et al. [5].

Table 1. Categories representing emerging cues in fruit perceived quality and consumer choice.

Sensory	Safety and Health Benefits	Convenience	Sustainability and Processing	Country and Region of Origin
Freshness	Health benefits	Packaging	Organic labelling	Product origin
Appearance	Quality certification	Labelling (producer and/or retailer)	Seasonality	Locally grown
		Brand knowledge		

Adapted from Grunert [48] and Lappo et al. [5].

The price was not included in this classification, consistent with studies by Grunert [4] and Lopez Galan et al. [49]. These previous studies emphasised that food demand not only is driven by the price of a product and the income of the consumer, as stated by classic economic theory, but is also increasingly driven by more complex and heterogeneous attributes. Therefore, it may be useful to consider the price elasticity of the demand for fruits and berries. Andreyeva et al. [50] stated that the elasticity of demand for the price of fruit is 0.7 on average, suggesting that the demand for fruit reacts in a less proportional way to price changes.

Sobeková et al. [51] reported an elasticity range of 1.25–1.88 for berry fruits, arguing that price was not a major driver in the choice of individual purchases, as purchase of berries is often sporadic and in small quantities. Furthermore, they determined that price did not have a significant impact on the level of household spending.

2.2. Data Collection

Data were collected in supermarkets within the urban areas of Turin and Genoa (medium-sized Italian towns), in order to obtain data from consumers who had just bought berries. A total of 669 consumers participated in the study, which was conducted during the summer of 2014. The berry fruit marketing data [15] show that the main sales channel for raspberries and blueberries is large-scale retail, which comprises approximately 60% of the Italian market. Face-to-face interviews were conducted using paper questionnaires (see Appendix A) using an intercept survey method, choosing people who had just bought berries and alternating, whenever possible, between genders. The interviews were conducted from Monday to Sunday over 2 weeks in two time slots (10:00 a.m. to 12:00 p.m. and 4:00 p.m. to 6:00 p.m.), to intercept different types of consumers. Before beginning the questionnaire, the respondents were briefed on the research and the selected attributes.

2.3. Measurement of the Importance of Attributes Using Best–Worst Scaling

The best–worst scaling (B–W) methodology was introduced by Finn et al. [52] and more recently formalised by Marley et al. [53]. It consists of a measuring technique in which respondents are asked to choose their favourite attribute (the best) and their least favourite attribute (the worst) from a set of attributes. We adopted this methodology due to the possibility of identifying associations between sensory attributes and consumer choices in the preference data, as suggested by Jaeger et al. [54]. Different advantages such as the use of a dimensional range for the importance of the attributes were reported. The B–W methodology avoids the problem of bias that may occur from differences in the use of rating scales between respondents. While all acceptance and preference methods have been reported to be comparable, B–W scaling allows for improved discrimination between attributes. This method has also been reported to be slightly easier to use, thereby improving the ability of the consumer to provide accurate hedonic responses [55]. This method also offers the best way to determine the level of importance that the interviewee assigns to each attribute [53,56,57,58]. The B–W scale methodology has previously been used to analyse and discuss different scientific topics, including ethical beliefs and wine and food marketing values [42,56,57,58,59,60,61]. Two limitations of the method need to be highlighted. The first limitation of this method is its relativism, as additional information needs to be elicited in order to anchor the scale results. Such information would also allow for easier comparison to values from traditional rating scales [54,62]. The second limitation is that this methodology requires a greater cognitive effort [62], and may be considered more confusing than numerical scales [63]. We acknowledge these limitations and, therefore, in our study we have only made comparisons among specific attributes and not within their levels. This also limited the difficulties associated with the maximum difference scaling (MaxDiff) questionnaire in understanding the mechanism of response [64].

2.4. Questionnaire Design and Data Analysis

The questionnaire was divided into two parts (see Appendix A). The first part examined the socio-demographic characteristics of the respondent through standard questions (residence, gender, age, household, level of study, work and income) [65]. The second section focused on the 12 attributes chosen for the B–W scaling. In order to implement the experimental design, it was necessary to choose how many times each attribute should be presented to respondents, as well as the number of attributes included in each set of choices. Orme [66] recommended that a range of 3–5 attributes should be included in each set of choices, and that each attribute should be presented to the respondent between 3 and 5 times. According to these recommendations, we chose to include 4 attributes per set, and to present each attribute three times within the questionnaire. The following Equation (1) was used to determine the nine subsets:

$$N^{\circ}\ SET = \frac{ATT \times FR}{SET} \tag{1}$$

where ATT represents the total number of attributes, FR represents the frequency of appearance of each attribute and SET is the number of attributes per set.

MaxDiff designer (v.2.0.2; Sawtooth Software, Orem, UT, USA) was used to assign each of the 12 attributes to 4 different versions of the questionnaire. Each of these versions comprised nine subsets, each including four attributes (see Appendix B and Appendix C). Using the MaxDiff Designer software we performed a series of simulations using different combinations of attributes to obtain the best experimental design [65,66]. The design meant that each attribute was used 3 times on average, and that each pair of attributes appeared together an average of 3.27 times (standard deviation 0.44). Overall, this was an almost balanced design. Methods such as latent class (LC) and hierarchical Bayes (HB) estimation do not require a perfect balance [54]. A two-way balance was favoured in this study design, meaning that it was directed towards the frequency at which paired combinations of attributes appeared together. As the average B–W scores take positive and negative values, and therefore sum to zero, they are often perceived as difficult to interpret. For instance, in the case of importance measurement, a negative B–W value does not indicate negative importance, but rather low (below average) importance. In order to allow a more intuitive interpretation of the results, we rescaled the B–W score to adopt a square root ratio approach that standardises the square root ratio scale to importance weights, which add to 100 per cent. Therefore, each root value (i = 1, ..., n) needs to be weighted by a factor, given in Equation (2):

$$\text{Weighting factor importance scale} = \frac{100}{\sum_{i=1}^{n} \sqrt{\frac{B}{W}}} \qquad (2)$$

where B is the number of best score, W is the number of worst score and i is the total number of observations.

Rescaling can be applied for the total sample or the subsamples, such as segments, to allow an easier comparison than using raw B–W scores [48]. The total responses for each best and worst attribute were calculated using Sawtooth MaxDiff (SSI-version 8.4.6; www.sawtoothsoftware.com) using the cyclical algorithm, k(k − 1)/2 (were k is the total number of attributes) making possible paired comparisons. An estimation analysis of the scores was performed using SPSS (version 21.1, Armonk, NY, USA). In order to understand whether one attribute was preferred to another within the same sample of respondents, we performed a repeated measures *t*-test with two tails to compare the rescaled scores for the attributes identified by each individual respondent.

3. RESULTS AND DISCUSSION

3.1. Socio-Demographic Characteristics

The socio-demographic characteristics (Table 2) of the respondents (n = 669 observations) revealed that the majority were women and people over the age of 45.

Table 2. Demographic characteristics of the respondents.

		Piedmont (%)	Liguria (%)	Frequency
		n = 43	n = 57	n = 669
Gender	Women	81	62	470
	Men	19	38	199
Age	<30 years old	9	14	79
	Between 30 and 45 years old	31	35	220
	Between 46 and 55 years old	21	20	139
	>55 years old	39	31	231
Household composition	1	16	10	90
	2	40	39	243
	3	32	35	195
	≥4	12	16	141
Educational status	Primary school	4	6	40
	Lower secondary school	10	7	39
	Upper secondary school	46	41	308
	Master's degree	40	46	282
Occupation	Housewife	10	9	58
	Unemployed	6	6	35
	Employee	52	45	323
	Entrepreneur	12	18	111
	Retired	14	15	108
	Student	6	7	34

A small proportion of interviewees (13.5%) lived alone, with a higher proportion living in pairs (36.3%). Respondents who claimed to have a family consisting of 3 persons were about one-third of the total (29.0%) and those who have a family of 4 or more persons made up more than 50% of the sample. The majority had a master's degree (42.2%) or upper secondary education (46.0%), making our sample somewhat biased when compared to the national schooling rate. Regarding occupation, employed individuals composed approximately half of the interviewees (50.5%), self-employed (16.6%) and retired (16.2%) individuals composed approximately one third of the sample, and the remaining respondents were students and job seekers. We observed a higher frequency of women sampled in Piedmont when he demographic characteristics between the two subsamples (Piedmont and Liguria) were compared, however, there were no significant differences for the other analysed parameters.

3.2. Importance of Raspberry and Blueberry Attributes

The number of times that each attribute was chosen as being the best or worst, the difference between these two values (best *minus* worst) and the average rescaled score for each attribute (from an estimate of the MaxDiff score function of the HB software SSI) are presented in Table 3.

It is evident that the most important attribute, according to the respondents, was the freshness of the berries, which presented the highest average value for the rescaled scores (13.072). Furthermore, this attribute was significantly different from all other attributes. Cardello and Schutz [24] reported that the type of food influences the judgement of freshness, and that characteristics related to the description of freshness depended on the food considered. Similarly, a study on apples by Péneau et al. [23] found that consumers assigned remarkable importance to *freshness*, and when asked to specify the meaning of this term, they answered *crispness* and *juiciness*. These results support the assumption of Bourne [67] that textural properties, such as firmness, often represent the freshness of a product.

Table 3. Best-worst scale rating for attributes of raspberries and blueberries.

Category	Attributes	Best	Worst	B–W	Rescaled Score
		n	*n*	*n*	(%)
Sensory	Freshness	804	306	498	13.072
	Appearance	390	510	−120	7.245
Safety and health benefits	Health benefits	571	458	113	9.210
	Quality certifications	443	571	−128	7.322
Convenience	Labelling	501	451	50	8.266
	Packaging	371	653	−282	6.749
	Brand knowledge	367	587	−220	6.496
Sustainability and processing	Seasonality	549	495	54	8.722
	Organic labelling	512	461	51	8.541
Country and region of origin	Locally grown	441	547	−106	9.658
	Product origin	634	428	206	7.284
-	Price	429	545	−116	7.435

We did not organise a panel test in the current study. Therefore, the responses of consumers were derived from their general preferences, which are associated with the memory of their experience and not a sensory evaluation.

Péneau [68] reported that appearance is of high importance in perceiving the freshness of strawberries. From our analysis, however, a close relationship between these two attributes was not evident.

The rescaled score of 6.496, obtained for the brand knowledge attribute, was the minimum value observed in this study. This was close to the value observed for packaging, both of which are part of the macro category of "convenience". Roosen et al. [69] indicated that it is often difficult and expensive for manufacturers of agricultural products to highlight their product quality with a brand. In fact, a survey performed in Germany showed that the brand was not important to consumers purchasing steak, and this also applied to dairy products [70]. All other attributes had a value of below 10 and did not differ significantly.

The results for the Piedmont and Liguria subgroups are presented in Table 4 and Table 5, respectively. These two subsamples were compared using the raw score and the standard deviation. As previously mentioned, the most important attribute for consumers in both regions was the freshness, and the least important attribute was the packaging. Furthermore, in the Piedmont subgroup, the freshness of the product was given the highest absolute value. The attribute that differed the most between the two areas was the labelling attribute, which was given a score of 9.467 in the Piedmont subgroup and 6.519 in the Liguria subgroup. The values for the other attributes evaluated were relatively similar between the regions, meaning that the consumer behaviour was not very divergent.

Table 4. Best–worst scale rating for attributes of raspberries and blueberries in the Piedmont subsample.

Category	Attributes	Best	Worst	B–W	BW Average	Standard Deviation	Average
		n	*n*	*n*	Raw Score		Rescaled Score (%)
Sensory	Freshness	427	103	324	1.158	0.825	11.362
	Appearance	164	226	−62	−0.178	0.540	6.906
Safety and health benefits	Health benefits	195	179	16	0.152	0.670	9.607
	Quality certifications	208	271	−63	−0.317	0.863	7.520
Convenience	Labelling	177	236	−59	−0.261	0.906	9.497
	Packaging	186	262	−76	−0.244	1.120	6.090
	Brand knowledge	142	269	−127	−0.392	0.405	7.111
Sustainability and processing	Seasonality	219	243	−24	−0.176	0.516	9.344
	Organic labelling	241	166	75	0.254	0.758	7.829
Country and region of origin	Product origin	301	144	157	0.624	0.746	9.047
	Locally grown	188	240	−52	−0.242	0.868	7.553
_	Price	153	262	−109	−0.377	0.532	8.134

Table 5. Best-worst scale rating for attributes of raspberries and blueberries in the Liguria subsample.

Category	Attributes	Best	Worst	B–W	BW Average	Standard	Average
		n	*n*	*n*	Raw Score	Deviation	Rescaled Score (%)
Sensory	Freshness	377	203	174	0.483	0.641	10.886
	Appearance	226	284	−58	−0.231	0.462	7.100
Safety and health benefits	Health benefits	376	279	97	0.202	0.680	9.272
	Quality certifications	235	300	−65	−0.109	0.426	7.490
Convenience	Brand knowledge	225	318	−93	−0.213	0.535	9.777
	Packaging	324	215	109	−0.473	0.682	6.923
	Labelling	185	391	−206	0.215	0.480	6.519
Sustainability and process	Seasonality	330	252	78	0.209	0.402	9.028
	Organic labelling	271	295	−24	−0.083	0.584	7.656
Country and region of origin	Product origin	333	284	49	0.095	0.722	9.425
	Locally grown	253	307	−54	−0.108	0.469	7.645
	Price	276	283	−7	0.013	0.362	8.279

From the raw scores, it is evident that three attributes (freshness, health benefits and product origin) were more influential in purchase decisions. By contrast, five attributes had scores that were below average (negative raw score) for both regions, including appearance, locally grown, packaging, quality certification and brand knowledge. Consumers from Liguria, unlike those from Piedmont, assigned a positive weight to seasonality, while consumers from Piedmont were more receptive to the processing aspects. In fact, the organic labelling attribute received a positive score by Piedmont consumers, while seasonality and brand received positive scores in the Liguria region. It is necessary to highlight, as stated by Evera Qendro [71], that the term "organic" has many meanings and is often associated, or confused, with terms such as "green", "ecological", "environmental", "natural" or "sustainable" [72]. Consumers attribute different meanings to the term "organic" and, similarly, the factors that make one product organic may not be organic for another, which influences purchasing decisions in unpredictable ways. In our study, consumers from Liguria assigned high importance to the seasonality of berries. Similar results have also been reported in strawberries from a German study [73], in which locally grown strawberries were preferred to imported strawberries. The same authors [73] stated that the reasons for this choice by consumers may have been the idea that these berries were fresher, with a shorter storage period than imported strawberries. Such considerations can also be applied to our results. Finally, consumers from the two regions assigned a similar importance to the price attribute.

3.3. Emerging Cues in Fruit Perceived Quality and Consumer Choice

The "Total Quality Food Model" developed by Grunert [48], applied in a study by Lappo et al. [5], showed that the taste and preference of consumers in food consumption were the principal purchase drivers. The attributes used in the B–W analysis were grouped into five categories (see Section 2.1), and the authors assigned four different levels of relevance (quite relevant, relevant, very relevant or extremely relevant) in accordance with responses obtained during the survey (Table 6).

Table 6. Comparison of the five classes with weight, as assigned by the authors.

Sensory ****	Safety and Health Benefits ***	Convenience *	Sustainability and Processing **	Country and Region of Origin **
Freshness	Health benefits	Packaging	Organic labelling	Origin
Appearance	Quality certification	Labelling (producer and/or retailer)	Seasonality	Locally grown
		Brand knowledge		

* Denotes categories deemed to be quite relevant; ** relevant; *** very relevant or **** extremely relevant, as assigned by the authors.

For the attributes included in the "convenience" category, there was little importance assigned by the consumers analysed in our study. The packaging of berry fruits is not considered to have any added value, as the consumer is accustomed to buying berries in different types of clamshell packaging [44,45]. In fact, extrinsic information, such as packaging, branding and labelling, can significantly alter our experience of food through the process of "sensation transfer", in which these attributes contribute to our sensory perception of a product [74]. Furthermore, compared to unbranded products, consumers perceive products that are branded as blackberries to be more reliable, of higher quality, and with less chance of not meeting expectations. Nevertheless, most fresh fruit products are sold unbranded, and existing marketed fruit brands are not particularly well-known by consumers, as confirmed in our study. The advantages of forming new names and brands are, in fact, lower than those of trusted brands [75].

Some consumers are willing to pay a premium price for organic and biotech-free products, as well as products produced with concern for equitable income distribution, animal welfare and/or the environment, even if these products look and taste the same as products without these attributes, as measured by sensory analysis [76]. In our study, an analysis of the "sustainability and processing" category suggests that only Piedmont consumers preferred organic products. This result was expected, as consumers often associate berry fruits with wild berries. In general, consumers believe these products to be grown in hilly or mountainous areas, and therefore, consider berries to be more sustainable by default [14].

Recently, the "safety and health benefits" and "country and region of origin" categories have become more important in their influence on consumer purchases, as confirmed in our study. One factor that has contributed to the growth in the market for fresh berries is the consumer recognition that berries are high in phytochemicals, associated with desirable effects on human health and protection against disease. The most commonly cited reasons for the preference of locally produced food items are related to the quality, personal health of the consumer, food safety, care for the environment and support of the local economy. Therefore, the interest in locally produced food is linked to the perception that berries are sustainable local products, unlike foods that are produced far from the consumer [77].

The consumers analysed in our survey identified that their primary criteria were in the "sensory" category, even if they paid attention to social and environmental concerns. In fact, the "freshness" attribute was considered the most important for both regions analysed. This result could be confirmed with a supporting study that combined panel and/or consumer testing with a consumer analysis study [23].

4. CONCLUSIONS AND SUGGESTIONS FOR FUTURE RESEARCH

This study investigated the perception of raspberries and blueberries by consumers in two regions of Italy. The results, obtained using the B-W method, indicated that freshness was the most important determinant in consumer choice for both areas. This finding is consistent with previous studies on apples and strawberries [23,68]. The price of the berries did not rank within the most relevant attributes for either region investigated. This result agrees with that previously reported by Mezzetti et al. [78], which showed that, in general, the price of a product was not important for the consumer when choosing vegetables and fruit. When the consumption preferences of consumers in the two regions were compared, it was evident that Ligurian consumers, unlike consumers from Piedmont, preferred seasonal berry fruits and products that showed labels from the producer or retailer. Moreover, these two choice attributes appeared to be associated. Liguria consumers, who preferred seasonal products, tended to buy products from a neighbouring area of production (e.g., Piedmont), giving rise to a loyalty mechanism. The results from our study may be useful for raspberry and blueberry producers in Piedmont, which, especially in rural hilly and foothill areas, are well suited for the production of berries [14,79]. An increase in demand could generate further cultivation, having a positive impact on the sustainability of such fragile territories, both economically and socially. Berry cultivation is labour-intensive and environmentally friendly, due to the limited use of pesticides [7,80]. In order to promote cultivation, existing marketing strategies could be combined with a specific communication campaign focussing on the production areas and their close proximity. In this way, seasonal and local products, and thus fresh products, could be offered to consumers that appreciate these attributes, in addition to an awareness of their sustainability. In fact, this study clearly shows the increasing consumer attention towards the sustainability of food production and the link between sustainability and territory. These associations could be used to create or enhance the value of territorial systems, contributing to their sustainable development, especially due to economic activities, which are often led by young entrepreneurs [81]. An additional marketing strategy could be based on further promoting the health benefits of berry fruits, which are already widely recognised by consumers and supported by numerous scientific studies [73,82,83]. The current study has contributed to increasing our knowledge of berry fruits, as little is known about the consumer preference for raspberries and blueberries in the scientific literature. However, our study has some limitations that should be considered in further research. First, our study was limited to a specific country (Italy) within the EU, and therefore, should be repeated in other European countries to confirm the results. In addition, regarding the methodology of this study, a more detailed characterisation of consumer profiles should be performed in order to provide more specific and targeted marketing recommendations, especially as we collected socio-demographic data from consumers. Moreover, the B–W methodology proved to be a useful tool in evaluating consumers' preferences, as previously used in other studies in the agribusiness sector [22,64]. The main positive feature of this study was the ability to discriminate between the importance of each choice-attribute, providing clear and simple answers about the attributes that the respondents considered to be more or less important. Future research should focus on better identifying the consumers, as well as conducting a survey that includes other attributes, such as taste and flavour, which were not included in this study as they require consumer and panel tests.

ACKNOWLEDGMENTS

The authors would like to thank the producers, professionals and consumers that participated in this research project. This research was supported by the private company Ortofruititalia soc.coop. S.R.L.—(Saluzzo CN, Italy) and the Lagrange Project of the ISI foundation funded by the CRT foundation.

AUTHOR CONTRIBUTIONS

Vincenzo Girgenti, Stefano Massaglia and Filippo Brun designed the research, interpreted the results and wrote the paper. Stefano Massaglia, Angela Mosso and Cristiana Peano collected data, collaborated in the literature review, performed the research and checked the results. All of the authors read and approved the final manuscript, analysed the data and contributed to the discussion.

CONFLICTS OF INTEREST

The authors declare no conflict of interest.

REFERENCES

1. Bryla, P. The role of appeals to tradition in origin food marketing. A survey among Polish consumers. *Appetite* **2015**, *91*, 302–310.
2. Arnold, C. *The Ethical Sphere, in Ethical Marketing and the New Consume*; John Wiley & Sons, Inc.: Hoboken, NJ, USA, 2012.
3. World Health Organization (WHO). *Reducing Risks, Promoting Healthy Lives*; WHO Technical Reports; World Health Organization: Geneva, Switzerland, 2002.
4. Grunert, K. How changes in consumer behavior and retailing affect competence requirements for food producers and processors. *Econ. Agrar. Recur. Nat.* **2006**, *6*, 3–22.
5. Lappo, A.; Bjørndal, T.; Polanco, J.F.; Lem, A. Consumer Trends and Preferences in the Demand for Food. Available online:https://brage.bibsys.no/xmlui/bitstream/handle/11250/

166728/A51_13.pdf?sequence=1 (accessed on 26 February 2016).

6. Grunert, K.G.; Brunsø, K.; Bredahl, L.; Bech, A.C. Food-Related Lifestyle: A Segmentation Approach to European Food Consumers. In *Food, People and Society: A European Perspective of Consumers' Food Choices*; Frewer, L.J., Risvik, E., Schifferstein, H.N.J., von Alvensleben, R., Eds.; Springer: New York, NY, USA, 2001; pp. 211–230.

7. Peano, C.; Baudino, C.; Tecco, N.; Girgenti, V. Green marketing tools for fruit growers associated groups: Application of the Life Cycle Assessment (LCA) for strawberries and berry fruits ecobranding in northern Italy. *J. Clean. Prod.* **2015**, *104*, 59–67.

8. Girgenti, V.; Peano, C.; Baudino, C.; Tecco, N. From "farm to fork" strawberry system: Current realities and potential innovative scenarios from life cycle assessment of non-renewable energy use and green house gas emissions. *Sci. Total Environ.* **2014**, *473–474*, 48–53.

9. Food and Agriculture Organisation of the United Nations: Agricultural Statistical Database. 2016. Available online: http://www.fao.org/economic/ess/ess-publications/ess-yearbook/en/#.VzOJgmPwHrY (accessed on 15 February 2016).

10. Centro Servizi Ortofrutticoli (CSO): Piccolo Frutti—Report. 2012. Available online: http://www.csoservizi.com/dettagli_documento.php?id=1350 (accessed on 10 December 2015).

11. Paredes-Lòpez, O.; Cervantes-Ceja, M.K.; VignaPerez, M.; Hernandez-Perez, T. Berries: Improving human health and healthy aging and promoting quality life—A review. *Plant Foods Hum. Nutr.* **2010**, *65*, 299–308.

12. Wang, S.Y.; Chen, H.; Camp, M.J.; Ehlenfeldt, M.K. Genotype and growing season influence blueberry antioxidant capacity and other quality attributes. *Int. J. Food Sci. Technol.* **2012**, *47*, 1540–1549.

13. Briano, R.; Giuggioli, N.R.; Girgenti, V.; Peano, C. Biodegradable and compostable film and modified atmosphere packaging in postharvest supply chain of raspberry fruits (cv. Grandeur®). *J. Food Process. Preserv.* **2015**, *39*, 2061–2073.

14. Di Palma, R. Piccoli Frutti, Grandi Risorse: Lamponi, Mirtilli, Ribes & Co. Available online: http://www.pr.camcom.it/portale/comunicazione/riviste-e-pubblicazioni/contenuti-riviste-e-pubblicazioni/parma-economica/archivio-parma-economica-

2011-1/Piccoli%20frutti,%20grandi%20risorse_%20lamponi,%20ribes,%20mirtilli%20-%20Co..pdf (accessed on 1 February 2016).

15. SG Marketing Piccoli Frutti Grandi Opportunità 2013. Available online: http://www.sgmarketing.it/it/news/Piccoli_frutti_grandi_opportunita-4 (accessed on 28 January 2016).

16. Koutsimanis, G.; Getter, K.; Behe, B.; Harte, J.; Almenar, E. Influences of packaging attributes on consumer purchase decisions for fresh produce. *Appetite* **2012**, *59*, 270–280.

17. Wycherley, A.; McCarthy, M.; Cowan, C. Speciality food orientation of food related lifestyle (FRL) segments in Great Britain. *Food Qual. Preference* **2008**, *19*, 498–510.

18. Murphy, A.; Meehan, H.F.; O'Reilly, S.; Bogue, J. A ten-year Delphi forecast of the Irish speciality food market. *J. Int. Food Agribus. Mark.* **2002**, *14*, 67–83.

19. Cassani, G. Saving at the Italian farmers' markets: An investigation on fruit and vegetables items. *Riv. Econ. Agrar.* **2012**, *2*, 37–60.

20. Fabris, G. *Il Nuovo Consumatore: Verso Il Postmoderno*; Franco Angeli: Milano, Italy, 2003; pp. 1–259.

21. Senauer, B. *The Food Consumer in the 21th Century: New Research Perspectives*; University of Minnesota: Minneapolis, MN, USA, 2001; Volumes 1–3, pp. 1–25.

22. Dekhili, S.; Sirieix, L.; Cohen, E. How consumers choose olive oil: The importance of origin cues. *Food Qual. Preference* **2011**, *22*, 757–762.

23. Peneau, S.; Hoehn, E.; Roth, H.R.; Escher, F.; Nuessli, J. Importance and consumer perception of freshness of apples. *Food Qual. Preference* **2006**, *17*, 9–19.

24. Cardello, A.V.; Schutz, H.G. The concept of food freshness: Uncovering its meaning and importance to consumers. In *Freshness and Shelf Life of Foods*; Cadwallader, K.R., Weenen, H., Eds.; American Chemical Society: Washington, DC, USA, 2003; pp. 22–41.

25. Haffner, K.; Rosenfeld, H.J.; Skrede, G.; Wang, L. Quality of red raspberry *Rubus idaeus* L. cultivars after storage in controlled and normal atmospheres. *Postharvest Biol. Technol.* **2002**, *24*, 279–289.

26. Wang, S.Y.; Lin, H. Antioxidant activity in fruits and leaves of blackberry, raspberry, and strawberry varies with cultivar and developmental stage. *J. Agric. Food Chem.* **2000**, *48*, 140–146.

27. Bustos-López, M.D.P.; Spadaro, D.; Garibaldi, A.; Gullino, M.L. Effect of different conservation strategies on plant health and quality of blueberries. *Prot. Colt.* **2013**, *2*, 58–59.

28. Cavard, P.; Moreau-Rio, M.A. *Le Comportement du Consommateur Dans Ses Achats de Fruits et Légumes: Lieux d'Achat, Modes de Vente*; Ctifl: Montreuil Sous Bois, France, 2013; pp. 1–47.

29. Al-Sulaiti, K.I.; Baker, M.J. Country of origin effects: A literature review. *Mark. Intell. Plan.* **1998**, *16*, 150–199.

30. Aichner, T. Country-of-origin marketing: A list of typical strategies with examples. *J. Brand Manag.* **2013**, *21*, 81–93.

31. Aertsens, J.; Verbeke, W.; Mondelaers, K.; van Huylenbroeck, G. Personal determinants of organic food consumption, A review. *Br. Food J.* **2009**, *111*, 1140–1167.

32. Viganò, E.; Mariani, A.; Taglioni, C.; Torquati, B. Consumers and alternative channels of organic food: The case of Organised Demand and Supply Groups (GODO) of AIAB-Umbria. *Econ. Agro-Aliment.* **2012**, *1*, 173–194.

33. Janssen, M.; Hamm, U. Governmental and private certification labels for organic food: Consumer attitudes and preferences in Germany. *Food Policy* **2014**, *49*, 437–448.

34. Rousseau, S. The role of organic and fair trade labels when choosing chocolate. *Food Qual. Preference* **2015**, *44*, 92–100.

35. Hu, W.; Woods, T.; Bastin, S. Consumer acceptance and willingness to pay for blueberry products with nonconventional attributes. *J. Agric. Appl. Econ.* **2009**, *41*, 47–60.

36. Lim, T.K. Vaccinium corymbosum. In *Edible Medicinal and Non-Medicinal Plants*; Springer: Dordrecht, The Netherlands, 2012.

37. NCX Drahorad Piccoli Frutti, un Successo Favorito Anche dal Marketing di Prodotto. Available online: http://www.ncx.it/2013/10/30/piccoli-frutti-mirtilli-marketing-uk-cile/ (accessed on 25 January 2016).

38. Mitchell, V.W.; Greatorex, M. Risk reducing strategies used in the purchase of wine in the UK. *Eur. J. Mark.* **1989**, *23*, 31–46.

39. Chironi, S.; Ingrassia, M.; Sgroi, F. Study of some aspects of the blonde oranges demand by Cluster Analysis. The Case of Ribera

DOP oranges and potential market strategies. *Econ. Agro-Aliment.* **2012**, *1*, 217–233.

40. Tragear, A.; Kuznesof, S.; Moxey, A. Policy initiatives for regional foods: Some insights from consumer researc. *Food Policy* **1998**, *23*, 383–394.

41. Chambers, S.; Lobb, A.; Butler, L.; Harvey, K.; Traill, W.B. Local, national and imported foods: A qualitative study. *Appetite* **2007**, *49*, 208–213.

42. Di Trapani, A.M.; Sgroi, F.; Testa, R. The short supply chain: A possible strategy for improving the competitiveness offarm. *Econ. Agro-Aliment.* **2013**, *2*, 35–49.

43. Memery, J.; Angell, R.; Megicks, P.; Lindgreen, A. Unpicking motives to purchase locally-produced food: Analysis of direct and moderation effects. *Eur. J. Mark.* **2015**, *49*, 1207–1233.

44. Almenar, E.; Hernandez Munoz, P.; Lagaron, J.M.; Catala, R.; Gavara, R. Advances in packaging technologies for fresh fruit and vegetables. In *Advances in Postharvest Technologies of Horticultural Crops*; Noureddine, B., Norio, S., Eds.; Research Signpost: Kerala, India, 2006; pp. 87–112.

45. Gomez, M.; Consuegra, D.M.; Molina, A. The importance of packaging in purchase and usage behavior. *Int. J. Consum. Stud.* **2015**, *39*, 203–211.

46. Marescotti, A.; Brazzini, A. L'utilizzo degli standard privati di qualità nella gdo italiana. Il caso dello standard Global G.A.P. *Econ. Agro-Aliment.* **2014**, *1*, 63–83.

47. Simon, H.; Zatta, D.; Fassnacht, M. *Price Management. I: Strategia, Analisi e Determinazione del Prezzo*; Franco Angeli: Milano, Italy, 2013.

48. Grunert, K.G. Food quality and safety: Consumer perception and demand. *Eur. Rev. Agric. Econ.* **2005**, *32*, 369–391.

49. Lopez-Galan, B.; Gracia, A.; Barreiro-Hurle, J. What comes first, origin or production method? An investigation into the relative importance of different attributes in the demand for eggs. *Span. J. Agric. Res.* **2013**, *11*, 305–315.

50. Andreyeva, T.; Long, M.W.; Brownell, K.D. The Impact of Food Prices on Consumption: A Systematic Review of Research on the Price Elasticity of Demand for Food. *Am. J. Public Health* **2010**, *100*, 216–222.

51. Sobekova, K.; Thomsen, M.R.; Ahrendsen, B.L. Market trends and consumer demand for fresh berries. *Appl. Stud. Agribus. Commer.* **2013**, *7*, 11–14.

52. Finn, A.; Louviere, J.J. Determining the appropriate response to evidence of public concerns: The case of food safety. *J. Public Policy Mark.* **1992**, *11*, 12–25.

53. Marley, A.A.J.; Louviere, J.J. Some probabilistic models of best, worst, and best–worst choices. *J. Math. Psychol.* **2005**, *49*, 464–480.

54. Jaeger, S.R.; Jørgensen, A.S.; Aaslyng, M.D.; Bredie, W.L.P. Best–worst scaling: An introduction and initial comparison with monadic rating for preference elicitation with food products. *Food Qual. Preference* **2008**, *19*, 579–588.

55. Heina, K.A.; Jaeger, S.R.; Carr, B.T.; Delahunty, C.M. Comparison of five common acceptance and preference methods. *Food Qual. Preference* **2008**, *19*, 651–661.

56. Auger, P.; Devinney, T.M.; Louviere, J.J. Using best–worst scaling methodology to investigate consumer ethical beliefs across countries. *J. Bus. Ethics* **2007**, *70*, 299–326.

57. Goodman, S.; Lockshin, L.; Cohen, E. *Examining Market Segments and Influencers of Choice for Wine Using the Best–Worst Choice Method*; Revue Internationale des Sciences Sociales—Special Wine Marketing Edition; ESKA: Cairn, France, 2008; pp. 94–112.

58. Cohen, E. Applying best worst scaling to wine marketing. *Int. J. Wine Bus. Res.* **2009**, *21*, 8–23.

59. Cohen, S.H.; Neira, L. Measuring preference for product benefits across countries: Overcoming scale usage bias with Maximum Difference Scaling. In Proceedings of the ESOMAR Latin America Conference, Amsterdam, The Netherlands, 1–3 October 2003.

60. Lee, J.A.; Soutar, G.; Louviere, J. The best–worst scaling approach: An alternative to Schwartz's values survey. *J. Pers. Assess.* **2008**, *90*, 335–347.

61. Loose, S.M.; Lockshin, L. Testing the robustness of best worst scaling for cross-national segmentation with different numbers of choice sets. *Food Qual. Preference* **2013**, *27*, 230–242.

62. Lusk, J.L.; Briggeman, B. Food values. *Am. J. Agric. Econ.* **2009**, *91*, 184–197.

63. Cohen, S.; Orme, B. What's your preference? *Mark. Res.* **2004**, *16*, 32–37.

64. Boshier, R.; Mohapi, M.; Moulton, G.; Qayyum, A.; Sadownik, L.; Wilson, M. Best and worst dressed web courses: Strutting into the 21st Century in comfort and style. *Distance Educ.* **1997**, *18*, 327–349.

65. De Magistris, T.; Groot, E.; Gracia, A.; Miguel Albisu, L. Do Millennial generation's wine preferences of the "New World" differ from the "Old World"? A pilot study. *Int. J. Wine Bus. Res.* **2011**, *23*, 145–160.

66. Orme, B. S.S.I Web V.8.3, Sawtooth Software. Available online: www.sawtoothsoftware.com/downloadPDF.php?file=SSI_Web_Documentation.pdf (accessed on 12 October 2016).

67. Bourne, M.C. *Food Texture and Viscosity: Concept and Measurement*, 2nd ed.; Academic Press: New York, NY, USA, 2002.

68. Peneau, S.; Brockhoff, P.B.; Escher, F.; Nuessli, A. Comprehensive approach to evaluate the freshness of strawberries and carrots. *Postharvest Biol. Tech.* **2007**, *45*, 20–29.

69. Lusk, J.L.; Roosen, J.; Fox, J.A. Demand for beef from cattle administered growth hormones or fed genetically modified corn: A comparison of consumers in France, Germany, the United Kingdom, and the United States. *Am. J. Agric. Econ.* **2003**, *85*, 16–29.

70. Profeta, A.; Balling, R.; Roosen, J. The relevance of origin information at the point of sale. *Food Qual. Preference* **2012**, *26*, 1–11.

71. Evera Qendro, A. Albanian and UK Consumers' Perceptions of Farmers' Markets and Supermarkets as Outlets for Organic Food: An Exploratory Study. *Sustainability* **2015**, *7*, 6626–6651.

72. Hutchins, R.K.; Greenhalgh, L.A. Organic confusion: Sustaining competitive advantage. *Nutr. Food Sci.* **1995**, *95*, 11–14.

73. Bhat, R.; Geppert, J.; Funken, E.; Stamminger, R. Consumers Perceptions and Preference for Strawberries—A Case Study from Germany. *Int. J. Fruit Sci.* **2015**, *15*, 405–424.

74. Skaczkowski, G.S.; Durkin Kashima, Y.; Wakefield, M. The effect of packaging, branding and labeling on the experience of unhealthy food and drink: A review. *Appetite* **2016**, *99*, 219–234.

75. Varela, P.; Ares, G.; Giménez, A.; Gambaro, A. Influence of brand information on consumers' expectations and liking of powdered drinks in central location tests. *Appetite* **2016**, *99*, 219–234.

76. Codron, J.M.; Grunert, K.; Giraud-Heraud, E.; Soler, L.G.; Regmi, A. Retail Sector Responses to Changing Consumer Preferences. Available online: http://www.ers.usda.gov/media/872095/aib794e_002.pdf (accessed on 18 February 2016).

77. Feldmann, C.; Hamm, U. Consumers' perceptions and preferences for local food: A review. *Food Qual. Preference* **2015**, *40*, 152–164.

78. Mezzetti, B.; Leonardi, C. Determinanti della qualità delle produzioni ortofrutticole. *Ital. J. Agron.* **2009**, *1*, 103–113.

79. Beccaro, G.; Giacalone, G.; Bounous, G.; Baudino, M. An overview on berry fruit industry in Piedmont (Italy). *Acta Hortic.* **2002**, *585*, 259–262.

80. Tecco, N.; Baudino, C.; Girgenti, V.; Peano, C. Innovation strategies in a fruit growers association impacts assessment by using combined LCA and s-LCA methodologies. *Sci. Total Environ.* **2014**, *568*, 253–262.

81. Grivins, M.; Tisenkopfs, T.; Stojanovic, Z.; Ristic, B. A Comparative Analysis of the Social Performance of Global and Local Berry Supply Chains. *Sustainability* **2016**, *8*, 532.

82. Little, C.; Aqueveque, C.; Aguilera, J.M. Producer–Consumer Misalignment as a Possible Cause for New Food Failure: Empirical Evidence from Chile. *J. Int. Food Agribus. Mark.* **2015**, *27*, 228–253.

83. Schnettler, B.; Miranda, H.; Sepulveda, J.; Denegri, M.; Mora, M.; Lobos, G. Preferences for Berries Among Consumers in Southern Chile: Blueberries Are Produced but Are They Consumed? *J. Food Sci.* **2011**, *76*, 458–464.

10
CHAPTER

Food Leftover Practices among Consumers in Selected Countries in Europe, South and North America

Kadri Koppel[1,*], Federica Higa[1], Sandria Godwin[2], Nelson Gutierrez[3], Roman Shalimov[4], Paula Cardinal[5], Brizio Di Donfrancesco[1], Miriam Sosa[6], Angel A. Carbonell-Barrachina[7], Loreida Timberg[8] and Edgar Chambers IV[1]

1. The Sensory Analysis Center, Kansas State University, Manhattan, KS 66503, USA

2 Department of Family and Consumer Services, Tennessee State University, Nashville, TN 37209, USA

3 Centro Surcolombiano de Investigación en Café (CESURCAFE), Facultad de Ingeniería, Universidad Surcolombiana, Neiva 660003, Colombia

4 Tochka Rosta, 1 Kvesisskaya str., 18, Trade Center Bld, Moscow 127220, Russia

5 Comisión de Investigaciones Científicas Provincia de Buenos Aires (CIC), Instituto Superior Experimental de Tecnología Alimentaria (ISETA), 9 de Julio, Buenos Aires 6500, Argentina

6 Consejo Nacional de Investigaciones Científicas y Técnicas (CONICET), Instituto Superior Experimental de Tecnología Alimentaria (ISETA), 9 de Julio, Buenos Aires 6500, Argentina

7 Departamento Tecnología Agroalimentaria, Escuela Politécnica Superior de Orihuela, Universidad Miguel Hernández de Elche, Orihuela 03312, Alicante, Spain

ABSTRACT

Foodborne illnesses may be related to many food production factors with home practices of consumers playing an important role in food safety. Consumer behavior for handling food leftovers has been studied, however little work on comparisons among countries has been published. The objective of this study was to investigate home food leftover practices of people from North American, South American, and European countries. Surveys were conducted with approximately 100 or more consumers in Argentina, Colombia, the United States, Estonia, Italy, Russia, and Spain. The participants responded to questions related to the length of time different types of food leftovers; such as meat, fresh salads, or restaurant dishes would be kept refrigerated or would be left at room temperature before refrigeration. Researchers also investigated how consumers would determine if the food was still safe for consumption. Potentially risky behaviors were observed in all seven countries. For instance, 55.8% of Estonians, 25% of Russians and 25.8% of Argentinean participants left food out at room temperature for several hours before storing in the refrigerator. Furthermore, 25%–29% of Colombian, Estonian, and Spanish consumers would look, smell, and taste leftovers to determine its probable safety. Correct handling of leftovers is an important aspect of consumer food safety. Although the surveys cannot be representative of all consumers in each country, they do provide an initial overview of comparative practices for handling leftovers among different countries. This provides government and educators with information on potential universal and unique consumer food safety issues related to handling leftover foods among various countries.

INTRODUCTION

Poor food handling may result in a large number of foodborne illnesses in many countries [1]. Although food handling risks can be reduced during production, the consumer has the ultimate responsibility for the safe storage and preparation of food eaten in the home. To reduce foodborne illnesses, consumers need to implement proper food handling practices. Moreover, a large portion of consumers underestimate or are unaware of the risk of contracting foodborne diseases from improper practices related to handling food at home [2].

Food safety guidelines are abundant in the United States [3], but less often in other countries. There are general food safety guidelines available by the World Health Organization that have been translated into several languages [4]. However, it is not clear how widespread the knowledge of these guidelines are by consumers. Government and educational websites in many countries do not mention the availability of educational food safety programming to consumers and little data has been published showing widespread adoption and use of the guidelines in health campaigns. Contrary to food companies that must follow legislative requirements, consumers are not supervised when handling food and have to make decisions based on prior knowledge, experience, convenience, and practicalities. This can constitute a public health problem, especially when cross-contamination involves pathogens such as *Escherichia coli*, *Salmonella*, or *Campylobacter*. In Europe and North America, more than half of the registered food infections are contracted at home [1]. Pathogenic bacteria have been found in home-cooked meals [5] and can grow rapidly even if food is stored following proper temperature guidelines [6].

Some of the issues with food leftovers that may result in foodborne illnesses include using containers that the food was cooked or served in to store leftovers, the time and storage conditions used for leftover foods, and the initial cooking and reheating processes used. Bruhn and Shutz indicated that half of the participants in their survey sometimes stored food in large containers where the food was prepared, while only two-thirds reported using smaller containers for storage, which is the recommended practice [7]. Furthermore, consumer sociodemographic backgrounds may have an influence as well. For example, males and young participants felt less responsibility for their own safety when preparing food than women or older people [2]. Marklinder et al. also found differences between older and younger participants when it came to the amount of days leftovers were stored, showing that older people tended to save food for fewer days [1]. Kwon et al. (2008) and Terpstra et al. (2005) observed older consumers and found that practices were different than those of younger participants [8,9]. In addition, Cody et al. found that women stored leftover food better than men [10]. Furthermore, Kwon et al. found that education level had an influence when deciding the safest way to store leftovers [8].

Cody et al. reported that several food safety practices, including storing leftovers correctly, declined from 2008–2010 in the United States [10]. This indicates that consumers need to be continuously informed about proper food-handling practices. Some studies have compared food safety practices across countries. For example, egg- and poultry-related practices were studied in Asian countries [11], in European countries [12], and in North and South America [13]. No studies were found that investigated how leftover food practices differ among countries. This type of information may be useful when developing food safety-related consumer messages around the world. Various pan-governmental and educational organizations develop and promote guidelines for food safety that transcend countries, but have little actual comparative data from a single country to rely on; particularly when it comes to consumer food-safety issues.

The objective of this study was to understand consumer behavior towards food leftover storage in selected countries from North and South America (Argentina, Colombia and the United States) and Europe (Estonia, Italy, Russia and Spain), particularly as it is related to:

1. times various foods might be left out before storage as leftovers;
2. times various leftover foods typically are stored in the refrigerator; and
3. how consumers determine if leftover foods are still good to eat.

2. MATERIALS AND METHODS

2.1. Questionnaires and Data Collection

The questionnaires were originally created in English, then translated into Italian, Estonian, Russian, and Spanish by native speakers, and back-translated into English to ensure the information the questionnaires were gathering matched across countries. The questionnaires were answered by participants either online or at a central location, using paper surveys that were handed to the consumers to be completed.

Questions concerning demographic information such as: gender, age (≥35 and <35 years old), educational level (high school education or less; some college education or a higher degree), and household income (categories equivalent as determined by each country (low: <$25,000; medium: $25,000–$50,000; high: >$50,000) and were included at the end of the questionnaire (Table 1).

Table 1. Participant demographics in percentages by country.

Demographic Segmentation %	USA (n = 239)	Argentina (n = 100)	Colombia (n = 99)	Estonia (n = 113)	Italy (n = 94)	Russia (n = 100)	Spain (n = 99)
Gender							
Male	26.9	0.0	32.3	15.0	16.1	14.0	51.5
Female	73.1	100.0	67.7	85.0	83.9	86.0	48.5
Age							
18–34	56.3	23.0	53.0	8.0	39.4	30.0	39.4
≥35	43.7	77.0	46.0	92.0	60.6	70.0	60.6
Education							
Less than college	11.4	59.0	72.0	8.0	17.0	17.0	8.1
Some college courses or more	88.6	41.0	27.0	92.0	83.0	83.0	91.9
Income							
Low	24.7	52.0	90.9	64.6	22.5	19.0	23.7
Medium	26.4	27.0	8.1	31.0	52.8	67.0	42.3
High	48.9	21.0	1.0	4.4	24.7	14.0	34.0

Questions regarding leftover storage investigated how leftover foods were stored when a meal is cooked in the household; food storage frequency; time food is left out at room temperature before being refrigerated; containers used to store leftovers in refrigeration and time certain leftovers (meat dishes, vegetables, fresh salad, cooked pasta, desserts, fruits, restaurant dishes) could be stored before spoilage occurred; and how leftover safety was determined by the consumers.

2.2. Respondents

About 100 participants in each country were surveyed and they were selected according to a pre-screening survey. The consumers were over 18 years old; involved in food shopping, cooking, and storing food in the households—primary or shared responsibility for shopping, cooking, and storage—and they had to own a refrigerator for food storage. Similar criteria has been used in studies by Koppel et al. that investigated Asian consumer food safety practices [11] and European consumer food safety practices [12].

Respondents (Table 1) completed the questionnaire from the United States (from the states of Kansas, Missouri and Tennessee), Argentina (Buenos Aires province), Colombia (Huila, Neiva region), Italy (Lecce area), Estonia (Tallinn area), Russia (Moscow area), and participants from Spain (Alicante area). Most consumers were recruited from established consumer databases (USA—Kansas and Missouri—Argentina, Estonia, and Spain) or mall intercept (Russia); but some consumers were a convenience sampling from the local area (USA: Tennessee—parents of local school children, faculty, staff, students at two local colleges; Colombia—homemakers and office workers; Italy—local e-mail server and snowball sampling or word of mouth). Consumers were divided by age (<35 and ≥35) because other studies of food safety behaviors have found differences in younger and older consumers [1,2,8,9]. It should be noted that the studies, although conducted predominantly by university researchers, did not target students and attempted to avoid student areas or populations during recruiting. The limited number of consumer sampling procedures did not cover each category of the population, but provides an initial insight into the behavior of a general population for leftover foods in each country.

2.3. Data Analysis

Data analysis was performed using frequencies, percentages, and the CHITEST Excel function (Microsoft Excel 2010; Microsoft, Redmond, WA, USA) to study differences among countries and differences based on sociodemographic information within and among countries.

3. RESULTS

3.1. Consumer Demographics

The respondents represented a mixture of genders, ages, education, and income levels (Table 1). In most countries studied, a mixture of males and females were recruited; however in Argentina, all of the respondents were female. In addition; in Estonia, Italy, and Russia, ≤16% of respondents were male. Although this may be because of sampling, this more likely is because of food purchasing, preparation, and storage behaviors (the qualifying criteria) in those countries typically done by females. Thus, the low percentage of males completing the survey in those countries is not surprising. The age distribution of the respondents was not evenly distributed among countries; particularly in Estonia, where the percentage of people in the survey is heavily skewed towards over 35 and clearly appears to have been impacted by the sampling procedure. To the extent that age impacts decisions on leftovers can be a confounding affect with countries in this study. Education levels among the respondents was higher (some college or more) in the United States, Italy, Estonia, Russia, and Spain than in other countries; in part reflecting the country; in part reflecting the communities in which the surveys were conducted, and in part reflecting the differences in survey methodology used in various locations. Income of the respondents was distributed over the three categories in most countries; although in Colombia, the majority of the respondents declared their income as "low" and in Estonia, most respondents declared their income as "low" or "medium"—both most likely related to the in-country decisions on what constituted a low, medium, or high income compared to the dollars set for the United States.

3.2. Behavior of Saving Leftovers

The participants were asked if and how often they usually saved leftovers (Table 2). In all countries, most participants (>80%) saved leftovers always or sometimes (Table 2). Only 13.1% of Colombian, 5.1% of Spanish, and 6% of Russian participants indicated they never saved leftovers. Women tended to save leftovers more frequently than men, except for Russia and Spain, where the behavior for saving food was similar for both genders (Figure 1). This may be caused by several factors, such as men cooking less than women, or perhaps women being responsible for saving leftovers after a meal.

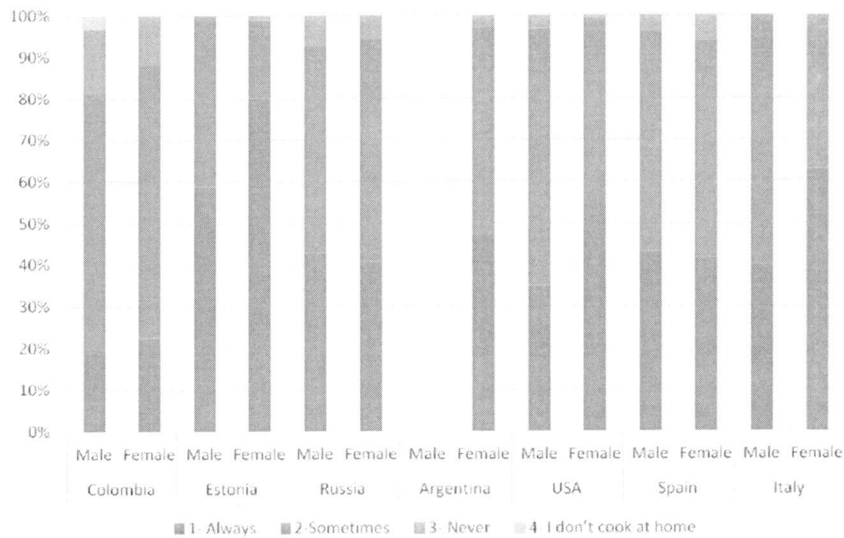

Figure 1. When you cook at home, do you usually save your leftovers? Results presented for women and men in each country, by percentage.

Table 2. When you cook at home, do you usually save leftovers? Results given in % of respondents.

Answers:	USA	Colombia	Argentina	Estonia	Italy	Spain	Russia	*p*-Value
Always	49.6 *	21.2	47.0	77.0	59.1	42.4	41.0	0.000
Sometimes	49.1	64.6	50.0	22.1	40.9	52.5	53.0	0.001
Never	1.3	13.1	3.0	0.9	0.0	5.1	6.0	0.000
I do not cook at home	0.0	1.0	0.0	0.0	0.0	0.0	0.0	0.276
p-value (overall)								0.000

* Values shown in bold are statistically significantly different among the countries according to chi-square test ($p < 0.05$).

Almost half of participants saved leftovers with a frequency of two to seven days per week (Table 3). Participants in Russia and Argentina were an exception, where 57% and 56% of the participants respectively saved food leftovers only once a week or never (Table 3). Estonian and the United States respondents tended to save their leftovers more frequently. Marklinder et al. found that older Swedish participants tended to save foods for shorter days than did younger participants [1]. This was not necessarily the case in this study, however. In most of the countries studied, it was found that younger and older people tended to save leftovers in a similar fashion, although the proportion of older respondents who saved leftovers for four or more days was larger in Colombia, Estonia, and the United States (Figure 2).

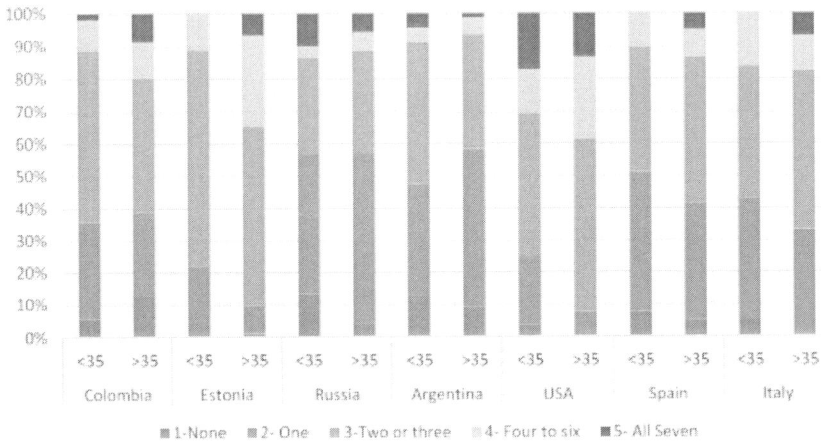

Figure 2. If someone were to look in your refrigerator each day for a week, on how many of the seven days do you think they would find leftover food in your refrigerator? Results presented for respondents aged <35 and ≥35 in each country, by percentage.

Table 3. If someone were to look in your refrigerator each day for a week; how many of the seven days do you think that they would find leftover food in your refrigerator? Results given in % of respondents.

Answers:	USA	Colombia	Argentina	Estonia	Italy	Spain	Russia	*p*-Value
None	**2.1**	9.1	10.0	0.9	**2.1**	6.1	7.0 *	0.003
One	**15.8**	**28.3**	**46.0**	9.7	**35.1**	**39.4**	**50.0**	0.000
Two or three	47.9	47.5	37.0	56.6	45.7	42.4	31.0	0.122
Four to six	**18.8**	**10.1**	**5.0**	**26.5**	**12.8**	9.1	**5.0**	0.000
All seven	**15.4**	5.1	**2.0**	6.2	4.3	3.0	**7.0**	0.000
p-value (overall)								0.000

* Values shown in bold are statistically significantly different among the countries according to chi-square test ($p < 0.05$).

3.3. Time Food is at Room Temperature

Participants were asked how long leftovers were left out before storing them in the refrigerator after cooking for a holiday meal. A holiday meal was chosen specifically for this study because it represents a time when many people gather and people may tend to leave food out for snacking over the course of the day. Also, more people may eat the leftovers at a later time, resulting in a greater potential for foodborne illness. About half of the participants in the United States, Spain, Russia, Italy, and Argentina indicated that they let food sit at room temperature between half an hour and an hour (Table 4). In Colombia, 39.4% of participants left food out for up to two hours before storing it in the refrigerator.

Table 4. You have prepared food for a holiday meal and there is food left over. How long do you generally leave it out at room temperature before putting in the refrigerator? Results given in % of respondents.

Answers:	USA	Colombia	Argentina	Estonia	Italy	Spain	Russia	*p*-Value
Within half an hour	14.2	9.1	30.7	4.4	22.3	41.8	34.0 *	0.000
Within one hour	36.9	25.3	23.8	8.0	31.9	26.5	17.0	0.000
Within two hours	25.3	39.4	8.9	19.5	29.8	14.3	12.0	0.000
Within three to four hours	12.0	15.2	5.9	11.5	6.4	8.2	11.0	0.367
If people are still there, I let it sit until they leave, which may be many hours later	6.9	8.1	24.8	55.8	8.5	7.1	25.0	0.000
I never store leftovers in the refrigerator	0.4	2.0	1.0	0.0	1.1	2.0	1.0	0.831
I never cook a holiday meal	4.3	1.0	5.0	0.9	0.0	0.0	0.0	0.003
p-value (overall)								0.000

* Values shown in bold are statistically significantly different among the countries according to chi-square test ($p < 0.05$).

In the United States, most people older than 35 (60.6%, Figure 3) stored food within an hour from preparation; while for Argentina, 30.4% of participants younger than 35 years old left food out for several hours. Both in Argentina and Colombia, the majority of participants over 35 did not leave food out for periods longer than two hours (Figure 3).

Italy, Spain, and Russia showed similar results to those in North and South American countries, where the majority stored food within one hour. On the other hand, for Estonian participants, 55.8% indicated that they left food out for longer periods of time, which may be many hours after the meal was prepared. The majority of these respondents were participants over 35 years old (Figure 3). A similar response was selected by 24.8% of Argentinian and 25% of Russian respondents.

Italian participants, with less than college education, saved food within one hour (43.7%); and 31.6% of people, with some college education, saved leftovers within two hours. However, 12.5% of Italian respondents, with less than college education, let food sit out for several hours; while 7.6% of people, with some college education, did the same thing. In Russia, most participants saved food within half an hour (34%); but people with college education left food out for longer periods (27.7%) than people with less than college education (11.7%).

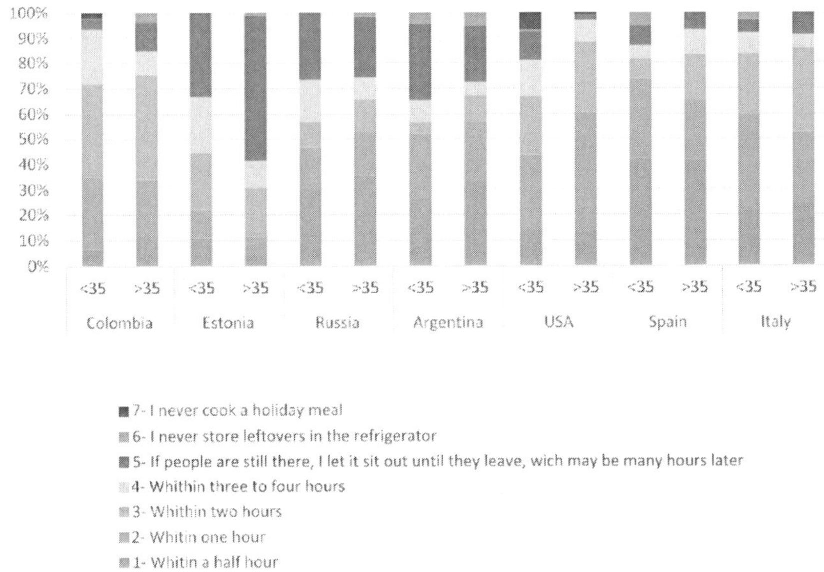

Figure 3. You have prepared food for a holiday meal and there is food left over. How long do you generally let it sit out at room temperature before putting it in the refrigerator? (Select one.) Results presented for respondents aged <35 and ≥35 in each country, by percentage.

By income, 40.9% of high-income Italian consumers had food at room temperature for two hours, while medium- and the majority of low-income respondents left food out for an hour from preparation. According to several studies, young adults take more risks when it comes to food safety, such as eating raw foods of animal origin [8,14,15,16]. On the other hand, Terpstra et al. indicated that older people lacked knowledge about how long food should be stored [9]. Altekreuse also reported that men and people with higher socioeconomic status tend to take more risks [16], while Klontz reported the same behavior for participants with an education lower than high school level [14]. The results from this study indicated that sociodemographic indicators may not predict behavior in a similar way in different countries.

3.4. Containers for Storing Leftovers

Participants were asked about the way they usually saved food leftovers. Participants from the United States and Italy stored leftover food mainly using special containers, and plastic or aluminum wrap as a second choice. Similarly, the majority of Estonian participants indicated the use of a special container to store food as the most popular option, but as the second option; they indicated using the container in which the food was cooked in (Table 5). The majority of people with high incomes (55.5%) chose plastic or aluminum foil as a first option, while medium or low incomes preferred special containers or the container in which food was served in.

Table 5. How do you usually store leftover food in the refrigerator? (Check all that apply.) Results given in % of respondents.

Answers:	USA	Colombia	Argentina	Estonia	Italy	Spain	Russia	p-Value
In the container in which was cooked	9.2	15.2	3.9	16.4	2.5	7.3	11.0 *	0.000
In the container in which was served	11.2	20.7	17.2	25.8	9.2	14.6	21.0	0.000
In containers I have especially for leftovers	60.7	41.5	60.9	36.4	62.2	64.2	49.0	0.000
In plastic or aluminum wrap	18.9	22.6	18.0	21.3	26.1	13.8	19.0	0.000
p-value (overall)								0.000

* Values shown in bold are statistically significantly different among the countries according to chi-square test ($p < 0.05$).

The majority of Argentinian participants (60.9%) saved food in special containers (Table 5). For participants under 35, the second most popular storage was to save food in the container in which food was served (17.85%), while people over 35 preferred to save leftover food in plastic or aluminum foil (21%). As a second choice, people with less than a college education (16.9%) and people with low incomes (19.7%) indicated that they saved food in the container which food was served, while people with higher education level (21.1%)—as well as with medium (20%) and high (21.9%) incomes—indicated using plastic or aluminum foil to store leftovers.

Similarly, in Russia, the most frequent option was to use special containers for all respondents. However, a second frequent option for males was using the container which the food was cooked (28.6%), while females (20.9%) preferred plastic or aluminum foil. In Colombia, males and females indicated that they handled leftovers differently. While most of the women (49.1%) chose to use containers specially designed to store food, men had no preference (Figure 4).

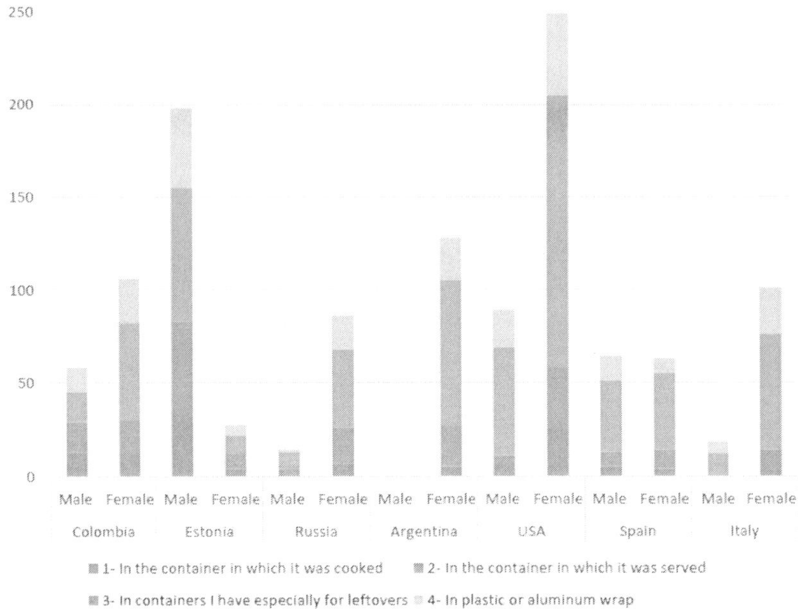

Figure 4. How do you usually store leftover food in the refrigerator? (Check all that apply). Results presented for males and female in each country, by count.

Participants in Spain indicated they use special containers as the most frequent option for food storage, but the second most frequent option varied between sociodemographic groups. Males (20.3%), participants over 35 (15.3%), and high-income participants (21.1%) chose plastic or aluminum foil, while females (16.94%), participants under 35 (20%), and low- and medium-income participants (23.3% and 18.9%) chose using the container which the food was served.

3.5. Time Food Can Be Stored before Spoiling

Respondents were asked how long they thought certain leftovers; such as meat dishes, vegetable dishes, fresh salads, cooked pasta, desserts, fruits, and restaurant dishes can stay in the refrigerator before spoiling. The results varied quite a bit depending on the food category.

3.5.1. Meat Dishes

Terpstra et al. found that although most of the consumers in their study perceived meat a risky product when considering storage time, about half of them stored meat dishes for a longer period than the one recommended in the guidelines [9]. The United States Food Safety and Inspection Service (FSIS) guidelines suggest storing leftovers for a maximum of 3–4 days in the refrigerator [17]. Most participants in this study indicated that they thought meat dishes can be stored for 3–4 days in the refrigerator (Table 6). A total of 12.4% of the United States, 5.1% Colombian, 5% of Argentinian, and 5% of Russian respondents indicated they thought that meat dishes can be stored for up to a week.

Table 6. How long do you think certain leftovers can stay in the refrigerator before spoiling? (Check one box from each row). Results given in % of respondents.

	Answers:	USA	Colombia	Argentina	Estonia	Italy	Spain	Russia	*p*-Value
Meat	1–2 days	40.3	67.7	71.0	46.9	76.1	60.2	58.0 *	0.000
	3–4 days	45.5	27.3	20.0	50.4	22.8	37.8	36.0	0.000
	1 week	12.4	5.1	5.0	2.7	1.1	2.0	5.0	0.000
	Do not know	1.7	0.0	4.0	0.0	0.0	0.0	1.0	0.040
	Does not matter	0.0	0.0	0.0	0.0	0.0	0.0	0.0	-
p-value (overall)									0.000
Vegetables	1–2 days	27.9	77.8	76.0	35.4	62.8	67.7	57.0	0.000
	3–4 days	50.6	17.2	17.0	57.5	34.0	25.3	37.0	0.000
	1 week	17.6	5.1	0.0	7.1	3.2	6.1	6.0	0.000
	Do not know	0.9	0.0	7.0	0.0	0.0	1.0	0.0	0.007
	Does not matter	3.0	0.0	0.0	0.0	0.0	0.0	0.0	0.601
p-value (overall)									0.000
Fresh Salad	1–2 days	60.9	78.8	87.0	87.6	79.6	89.9	83.0	0.040
	3–4 days	29.2	17.2	6.0	8.0	16.1	9.1	15.0	0.000
	1 week	6.4	4.0	1.0	3.5	3.2	1.0	2.0	0.133
	Do not know	1.3	0.0	6.0	0.9	1.1	0.0	0.0	0.043
	Does not matter	2.1	0.0	0.0	0.0	0.0	0.0	0.0	0.002
p-value (overall)									0.000
Cooked pasta	1–2 days	23.8	46.5	61.0	30.1	60.2	42.9	46.0	0.00
	3–4 days	42.4	48.5	32.0	51.3	34.4	52.0	37.0	0.150
	1 week	29.0	5.1	3.0	17.7	3.2	4.1	14.0	0.000
	Do not know	2.6	0.0	4.0	0.9	1.1	1.0	2.0	0.374
	Does not matter	2.2	0.0	0.0	0.0	1.1	0.0	1.0	0.212

p-value (overall)									0.000
Dessert	1–2 days	**14.7**	**48.5**	**31.0**	**36.3**	**47.3**	**45.5**	**66.0**	0.000
	3–4 days	**37.5**	**37.4**	**49.0**	**50.4**	**48.4**	**46.5**	**25.0**	0.041
	1 week	**42.2**	**11.1**	**17.0**	**9.7**	**4.4**	**8.1**	**7.0**	0.000
	Do not know	3.0	3.0	1.0	3.5	0.0	0.0	2.0	0.054
	Does not matter	2.6	0.0	2.0	0.0	0.0	0.0	0.0	0.296
p-value (overall)									0.000
Fruit	1–2 days	**19.0**	**5.1**	**9.0**	**9.7**	**21.3**	**20.2**	**23.0**	0.002
	3–4 days	**31.6**	**18.2**	**45.0**	**30.1**	**43.6**	**22.2**	**31.0**	0.004
	1 week	**41.1**	**76.8**	**44.0**	**54.9**	**31.9**	**53.5**	**27.0**	0.000
	Do not know	**6.1**	**0.0**	**2.0**	**2.7**	**2.1**	**4.0**	**17.0**	0.000
	Does not matter	2.2	0.0	0.0	2.7	1.1	0.0	2.0	0.308
p-value (overall)									0.000
Restaurant dishes	1–2 days	68.8	90.9	58.0	75.2	72.7	75.8	62.0	0.135
	3–4 days	**25.1**	**6.1**	**4.0**	**8.8**	**3.4**	**14.1**	**10.0**	0.000
	1 week	**3.5**	**3.0**	**3.0**	**0.9**	**0.0**	**1.0**	**2.0**	0.000
	Do not know	**2.6**	**0.0**	**32.0**	**15.0**	**23.9**	**9.1**	**26.0**	0.000
	Does not matter	**0.0**	**0.0**	**3.0**	**0.0**	**0.0**	**0.0**	**0.0**	0.000
p-value (overall)									0.000

* Values shown in bold are statistically significantly different among the countries according to chi-square test ($p < 0.05$).

3.5.2. Vegetables, Fresh Salad, Fruit

Most of the respondents indicated 1–2 days as a safe storage time for vegetables, while 17.6% of the United States participants indicated storing vegetable leftovers for up to a week (Table 6). The safe practices for vegetable storage vary by the source and quality of the vegetables. In comparison to meat dishes, it is perhaps somewhat easier to determine whether vegetables have deteriorated in quality. The majority of the participants indicated that fresh salads could be stored for 1–2 days before spoiling would occur (Table 6). Most of the respondents from all countries indicated that one week was the period of time that fruit could be stored before spoiling.

3.5.3. Pasta

The majority of the participants indicated that pasta could be stored for 1–4 days before spoiling would occur (Table 6). However, a total of 29% of the United States and 17.7% of Estonian participants responded that they would store cooked pasta for up to a week. Whether this practice is risky or not, depends somewhat on the type of pasta dish. For pasta dishes with sauces, the safe storage time may be shorter; while for pasta alone, this may not be true. Aside from the storage time, the consumers should also follow safe reheating guidelines [17].

3.5.4. Desserts

In most of the countries, participants indicated that desserts could be stored up to four days before spoiling, except for the United States, where 42.2% of respondents stated that this type of food can be stored for up to a week (Table 6). Depending on the dessert ingredients and cooking method, this may either be considered a safe or a risky behavior.

3.5.5. Restaurant Dishes

The majority of the consumers indicated that restaurant dish leftovers are safe to store for up to four days in the refrigerator. This question elicited a large percentage of "do not know" responses. Of all Argentinian, Russian, Estonian and Italian participants, 32%, 26%, 15%, and 23.9% respectively, indicated not knowing how long to store restaurant dish leftovers (Table 6). More than 30% of Russian participants with college education and 44% of less than college participants in Estonia indicated not knowing how many days restaurant dishes could be stored before spoiling. Perhaps this may also be associated with the frequency the participants in that country are used to eating out at restaurants. In some countries, such as the United States, eating out at restaurants and bringing home leftovers from that meal may be a more common practice than in others.

A total of 32% of Argentinian participants did not know how long restaurant dishes could be stored before spoiling (Table 6). This segment of consumers included 38.9% of people over 35 years old, 39% with less than college education, 36.5% with low income and 33.3% with medium income.

3.6. Determining Leftovers' Safety in the Refrigerator

Respondents were asked how they determined whether a leftover is still safe to eat when they did not know how long it had been stored in the refrigerator. In the United States (47%), Argentina (58%), Italy (38%), and Spain (61%), the majority of respondents indicated that when not knowing how long the leftover had been stored, they just threw it in the garbage without trying to determine if it could be eaten or not (Table 7). In Colombia (10%) and Russia (12%), this percentage was much lower. In Russia, most of the consumers (38%) answered that they smelled the leftover to determine if it was bad. In Estonia (35%) and Colombia (33%), most of the consumers looked at and smelled the leftover to determine if the leftover could still be consumed. Surprisingly, 22%–29% of the respondents in Estonia, Italy, and Colombia indicated that they looked, smelled, and tasted the leftover to determine safety. This could place many consumers at risk for foodborne illnesses. The practices were similar by age, except for Colombia, where younger people tended to look, smell, and taste the leftover before deciding if it was safe to consume (Figure 5).

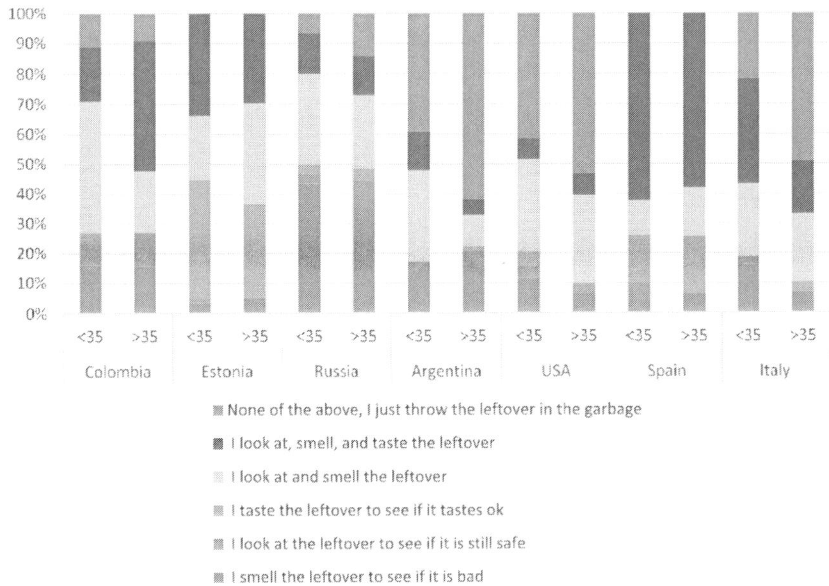

Figure 5. If you find a leftover in the refrigerator and do not know how long it has been in there, how do you determine if it is still safe to eat? (Select one). Results presented for respondents aged <35 and ≥35 in each country, by percentage.

Table 7. If you find a leftover in the refrigerator and do not know how long it has been in there, how do you determine if it is still safe to eat? Results given in % of respondents.

Answers:	USA	Colombia	Argentina	Estonia	Italy	Spain	Russia	*p*-Value
I smell the leftover	8.9	16.2	15.2	4.4	10.6	5.0	38.0 *	0.000
I look at the leftover	3.7	9.1	4.0	0.9	1.1	4.0	7.0	0.047
I taste the leftover	2.8	2.0	1.0	0.0	2.1	0.0	4.0	0.247
I look at and smell the leftover	30.5	33.3	15.2	35.4	23.4	16.0	26.0	0.017
I look at, smell, and taste the leftover	6.9	29.3	7.1	27.4	24.5	14.0	13.0	0.000
None of the above	47.2	10.1	57.5	31.9	38.3	61.0	12.0	0.000
p-value (overall)								0.000

* Values shown in bold are statistically significantly different among the countries according to chi-square test ($p < 0.05$).

4. DISCUSSION

The results on behavior of leftover holiday meals presented some interesting results. The majority of the respondents stored the leftovers in less than two hours, as suggested by FSIS [17]. However, the results also show at least 15%–20% exhibiting problem behaviors (storage after more than two hours) in Italy, Spain, and the United States and over 60% admitting this in Estonia. That suggests this problem behavior is still common around the world, but much more common in some locations than others. This behavior can pose risks from a food safety standpoint of view, but it is likely difficult to change from a social standpoint of view. Holiday meals are typically social gatherings. Clearing the table of dishes can indicate the end of the eating occasion and, at the same time, social occasion. It would be interesting, for future studies, to look deeper into these situations to determine the type of interventions or guidelines needed to change the consumer behavior.

Leftover storage results indicated that more than half of the respondents in all of the countries studied used special containers to store leftovers from meals. Bruhn et al. found that two-thirds of the participants in their study used small containers to store food, while the remaining one-third preferred to use containers in which the meal was prepared [7]. Smaller containers are preferred over larger ones, in order to allow food to cool faster in the refrigerator. The United States Food Safety and Inspection Service (FSIS) suggests that consumers wrap leftovers or store leftovers in special containers [17]. These were the most common ways to store leftovers for the participants in this study in all of the countries. However, it should be noted that 9.2% of the United States, 11.0% of Russian, 15.2% of Colombian, and 16.4% of Estonian respondents indicated they stored the leftovers in the container in which the food was cooked in, and this could potentially cause food safety issues. Thus, work related to increasing consumer awareness of this necessary practice should continue.

The respondents were asked to indicate how they determined if the leftover was still safe to eat. Large portions of the consumers looked and smelled the leftovers. Surprisingly, large proportions of the respondents answered that they "looked, smelled, and tasted the leftovers". A total of 6.9% of the United States respondents, 7.1% of Argentinian, 13% of Russian, 14% of Spanish, 24.5% of Italian, 27.4% of Estonian, and 29.3% of Colombian consumers indicated that they used most of their senses to determine leftover safety. Tasting leftovers to determine if they are spoiled is a potentially risky practice because the leftover being tasted may already be spoiled. Consumer guidelines do not actually indicate anything about determining safety of the leftovers using senses, including tasting. This may be an area for future studies to further investigate.

Respondents were asked how long they thought certain leftovers; such as meat dishes, vegetable dishes, fresh salads, cooked pasta, desserts, fruits, and restaurant dishes, can stay in the refrigerator before spoiling. Marklinder et al. found that leftovers were kept for a maximum of three days [1], and FSIS suggests for consumers to store leftovers for 3–4 days [17]. Kosa et al. reported consumer refrigeration practices in the United States; showing that owning refrigerator thermometers and keeping the refrigerators clean and at the correct temperatures, were practices that also varied in subpopulations [18]. In another country, Italy, the researchers found that 21.5% of the refrigerators were not holding the correct storage temperature, even though the consumers knew what the temperature should be [19]. Most participants in this study indicated that they thought meat dishes and restaurant dishes can be stored for 3–4 days in the refrigerator (Table 6). A total of 12.4% of the United States, 5.1% Colombian, 5% of Argentinian, and 5% of Russian respondents indicated they thought that meat dishes can be stored for up to a week. A total of 32% of Argentinians, 26% of Russians, 15% of Estonians, and 23.9% of Italian respondents selected the "do not know" option for storage of restaurant leftovers. This indicates some potentially risky practices when it comes to meat dishes, storage of restaurant dishes, and later usage. This may be related to the typical frequency of eating at restaurants. However, one thing to point out is that in the United States, the consumer is provided with a lot of food safety related information, such as guidelines from the FSIS, and different outreach programs. In other countries, this may or may not be the case, depending on resources available for consumer education and food safety-related research. Of course, these may come in different languages. For example, in Russia and Spain, some guidelines exist; though consumer education programs are scarce [20,21]. Thus; this study is not only looking at specific consumer behaviors and knowledge on food safety, but it is also pointing out that there are considerable food safety-related educational materials available that could be adopted in different countries. The approach to sharing all of these materials is yet to be determined and up for discussion.

Naturally, this study comes with limitations. Key among them is the limited sample size of the populations in each country, which cannot possibly represent all the consumers in that country. We do not suggest this is an exhaustive study, but rather should be viewed as a first look at cross-countries similarities and differences among consumer behaviors related to leftover foods. In addition, there are many socioeconomic and cultural differences among these countries that can have an enormous impact on behaviors. This research is not intended to be a study of those cultural impacts nor to identify particular cultural norms. Rather, it was the intent to simply describe the results of the study in terms of potential differences among countries and generalized sociodemographic behaviors. Further research is needed to study particular social or cultural influences on food safety behaviors.

5. CONCLUSIONS

This study focused on how consumers handled leftover foods in different countries: the United States, Argentina, Colombia, Estonia, Italy, Spain, and Russia. Several similarities were found, such as preference of choosing special containers for storing leftovers (by the majority of respondents), and a majority of women being the ones that usually stored leftovers more often than men. Further, most participants indicated they stored leftovers for a time period that is similar to the guidelines (3–4 days). However, some risky behaviors were identified in all countries; such as the time that food is left out before being stored, and storing certain types of leftovers for several days longer than they should be kept (in some cases up to a week). Of considerable concern is that a portion of consumers were tasting leftovers to determine safety—a risky practice. Those areas of concern appear to be the weak points that need further assessment for education within individual countries and worldwide.

ACKNOWLEDGMENTS

This research was supported, in part, by a grant from the United States Department of Agriculture, GRANT 10980553, Project #TENX-2011-06512 titled "Development and evaluation of science-based messages to improve consumers' storage handing and preparation of poultry and poultry products".

AUTHOR CONTRIBUTIONS

Authors Koppel and Chambers IV conceived and designed the experiments. Godwin, Koppel, and Chambers composed the questionnaire. Koppel and Higa analyzed the data. Data was collected by Timberg in Estonia, Shalimov in Russia. Di Donfrancesco in Italy,

Carbonell-Barrachina in Spain, Godwin, Koppel, and Chambers in the United States, Sosa and Cardinal in Argentina, and Gutierrez in Colombia. Koppel, Higa, and Di Donfrancesco wrote the manuscript. All co-authors helped edit the manuscript.

Conflicts of Interest: The authors declare no conflict of interest.

REFERENCES

1. Marklinder, I.; Magnusson, M.; Nydahl, M. CHANCE: A healthy lifestyle in terms of food handling and hygiene. *Br. Food J.* **2013**, *115*, 223–234.
2. Redmond, E.C.; Griffith, C.J. Consumer perceptions of food safety risk, control and responsibility. *Appetite* **2004**, *43*, 309–313.
3. United States Department of Agriculture. Food Safety Education. Available online: http://www.fsis.usda.gov/wps/portal/fsis/topics/food-safety-education (accessed on 4 August 2016).
4. World Health Organization. Five Keys to Safer Food Programme. Available online: http://www.who.int/foodsafety/consumer/5keys/en/ (accessed on 4 August 2016).
5. Beumer, R.R.; Kusumaningrum, H. Kitchen hygiene in daily life. *Int. Biodeter. Biodegr.* **2003**, *51*, 299–302.
6. Rocourt, J.; Cossart, C. Listeria monocytogenes. In *Food Microbiology: Fundamentals and Frontiers*; Doyle, M.P., Beuchat, L.R., Monville, T.J., Eds.; ASM Press: Washington, DC, USA, 1997; pp. 337–352.
7. Bruhn, C.M.; Schutz, H.G. Consumer Food Safety Knowledge and Practices. *J. Food Saf.* **1998**, *19*, 73–87.
8. Kwon, J.; Wilson, A.N.S.; Bednar, C.; Kennon, L. Food Safety Knowledge and Behaviors of Women, Infant, and Children (WIC) Program Participants in the United States. *J. Food Protect.* **2008**, *71*, 1651–1658.
9. Terpstra, M.J.; Steenbekkers, L.P.A.; de Maertelaere, N.C.M.; Nijhuis, S. Food Storage and disposal: Consumer practices and knowledge. *Br. Food J.* **2005**, *107*, 526–533.
10. Cody, M.M.; Gravani, R.; Smith Edge, M.; Dooher, C.; White, C. International Food Information Council Foundation Food and

Health Survey, 2006–2010, Food Safety: A Web enabled Survey. *Food Protect. Trends* **2012**, *32*, 309–326.

11. Koppel, K.; Sowonsichon, S.; Chitra, U.; Lee, J.; Chambers, E., IV. Eggs and poultry purchase, storage, and preparation practices of consumers in selected Asian countries. *Foods* **2014**, *3*, 110–127

12. Koppel, K.; Timberg, L.; Roman, S.; Vazquez-Araujo, L.; Carbonell-Barranchina, A.A.; Di Donfrancesco, B.; Chambers, E., IV. Purchase, storage, and preparation of eggs and poultry in selected European countries. *Br. Food J.* **2015**, *117*, 749–765

13. Koppel, K.; Sosa, M.; Gutierrez, N.G.; Cardinal, P.; Godwin, S.L.; Cates, S.C.; Chambers, E. Consumer practices for purchase, storage, and preparation of poultry and eggs in selected North and South American countries: A pilot study. *Vitae* **2016**, *23*, 58–64.

14. Klontz, K.C.; Timbo, B.; Fein, S.; Levy, A. Prevalence of selected food consumption and preparation behaviors associated with foodborne disease. *J. Food Protect.* **1995**, *58*, 927–930. [

15. Altekruse, S.F.; Street, D.A.; Fein, S.B.; Levy, A.S. Consumer Knowledge of Foodborne Microbial Hazards and Food-Handling Practices. *J. Food Protect.* **1995**, *59*, 287–294.

16. Altekruse, S.F.; Yang, S.; Timbo, B.B.; Angulo, F.J. A Multi-State Survey of Consumers Food-Handling and Food-Consumption Practices. *Am. J. Prev. Med.* **1999**, *16*, 216–221.

17. FSIS. Leftovers and Food Safety. Available online: http: //www.fsis.usda.gov/wps/portal/fsis/topics/food-safety-education/get-answers/food-safety-fact-sheets/safe-food-handling/leftovers-and-food-safety/ (accessed on 2 June 2016).

18. Kosa, K.M.; Cates, S.C.; Karns, S.; Godwin, S.L.; Chambers, D. Consumer Home Refrigeration Practices: Results of a Web-Based Survey. *J. Food Protect.* **2007**, *70*, 1640–1649.

19. Vegara, A.; Festino, A.R.; Di Ciccio, P.; Constanzo, C.; Pennisi, L.; Lanieri, A. The management of the domestic refrigeration: Microbiological status and temperature. *Br. Food J.* **2014**, *116*, 1047–1057

20. AESAN. Agencia Española de Seguridad Alimentaria y Nutrición. Prevention of Foodborne Illnesses.online: http://www .aecosan.msssi.gob.es/AECOSAN/web/para_el_consumidor/secci on/para_saber_mas.htm (accessed on 5 August 2016).

21. GOST. Foodstuffs. Information for Consumers. General requirements. Available online: http://ozpp.ru/standard/gosty/gostr510742003/ (accessed on 5 August 2016).

11

CHAPTER

The Impact of an Epidemic Outbreak on Consumer Expenditures: An Empirical Assessment for MERS Korea

Hojin Jung*, Minjae Park, Kihoon Hong and Eunjung Hyun

College of Business Administration, Hongik University, 94 Wausan-ro, Mapo-gu, Seoul 121-791, Korea

ABSTRACT

In this paper, we investigate the effect of an epidemic outbreak on consumer expenditures. In light of scanner panel data on consumers' debit and credit card transactions, we present empirical evidence that outbreaks cause considerable disruption in total consumer expenditures with significant heterogeneity across categories. Our findings strongly imply that customers alter their behaviors to reduce the risk of infection. The estimated effect of an epidemic outbreak is qualitatively different from that of other macroeconomic factors. The implications of this research provide important guidance for policy interventions and marketing decisions aimed at sustaining economic growth.

1. INTRODUCTION

Infectious diseases have become more challenging and more complex to control. For example, the Ebola outbreak in West Africa, one of the deadliest occurrences of an epidemic, has killed more than 11,000 people in six countries since its first report in March 2014 [1], and SARS, which originated in China in 2002, has infected over 2700 people and triggered an unprecedented campaign across nations to prevent its spread [2].

Inevitably, on top of the direct medical costs of treating patients and implementing different controls for diseases, epidemics have devastating effects on the economy. Restrictions on the transportation of people and goods, commonly imposed in areas where the risk of infection is high, significantly disrupt outputs and exports, and the seeds of future growth are often hindered by undercuts in investment as investors lose their confidence in the market.

Apart from the impact of an epidemic outbreak on production and investment, a considerable negative influence to be noted is that an extreme event often imposes negative shocks on consumer expenditures at the other end. In particular, consumers often avoid travel and shun public places in an attempt to reduce the risk of getting infected, and this disruption in consumption influences the economy considerably. Consistently, conventional wisdom about the effect of a macroeconomic factor, such as gasoline prices and business cycles, is that a key mechanism by which a macroeconomic factor impacts the economy is through disruption of goods and services [3].

Accordingly, understanding the indirect, but strong effects of epidemics on consumers' willingness to buy would provide important implications and guidance for policymakers, as well as practitioners aiming to counteract disruption in the economy. However, little research has investigated how an epidemic outbreak affects individual shopping behaviors and consumption. Instead, studies have generally focused on the total burden of epidemics on populations based on aggregate data [4,5,6].

The attention to individual consumer behaviors has been limited largely because microdata that would enable the measurement of indirect and behavioral effects of epidemics are not widely accessible to academics. Extant studies on extreme events heavily relied on aggregate spending data, which are generally measured at low frequencies, such as on a monthly or quarterly basis, and often subject to revision. Given this limited availability of microdata, attempts to assess the economic impact of epidemics without an understanding of individual consumers' behaviors can provide only limited implications, because changes in these microeconomic variables are a root of these individual behaviors [7].

In this paper, we explore the economic effect of an epidemic outbreak and provide substantive empirical evidence on how epidemic outbreaks impact the consumption and shopping behaviors of consumers. Using scanner panel data on individual consumers' debit and credit card transactions, we found that the outbreak of an epidemic caused a substantial disruption in consumer expenditures with considerable heterogeneity across expenditure categories. In particular, consumers dramatically cut down expenditures at traditional shopping channels, but exhibited a substantial increase in e-commerce spending.

Our findings are particularly relevant in that the consumers' response to the epidemic was attributable to a psychological factor, fear of contagion, rather than budgetary constraints. Considering the increasing challenges posed by infectious diseases given advances in transportation efficiency, our paper provides important implications for policy and interventions meant to sustain the economy when epidemics occur. For example, the improved policy environment for establishing and maintaining the e-commerce channel would lessen consumers' fear of contagion from purchasing goods and services and may help manufacturers and retailers retain their sales. For the realization of sustainable economic growth with increasing concerns about more complicated epidemic outbreaks, of particular importance is the establishment and adoption of e-commerce as an alternative shopping channel.

The paper proceeds as follows. Section 2 explains the outbreak whose effects we will explore in this paper and discusses the related literature on the economic impact of extreme events. Section 3 describes the data. Section 4 presents preliminary analyses and their results. Section 5 provides the estimation methods and results. Finally, Section 6 discusses the implications of our findings, and Section 7 concludes.

2. BACKGROUND

2.1. The MERS Outbreak in Korea

An outbreak of Middle East respiratory syndrome coronavirus (MERS) in South Korea began in May 2015. The outbreak started when a single male from South Korea who had traveled to the Middle East returned and transmitted the infection to the Korean population, in what became the largest outbreak of MERS outside the Middle East. The death toll from the outbreak was 36, with 186 confirmed cases; more than 6500 people in the country were isolated for the possible exposure to the disease. The last new case was reported on 5 July, and the last (36th) death from MERS was announced on 10 July. Figure 1 presents the number of deaths and confirmed cases [8].

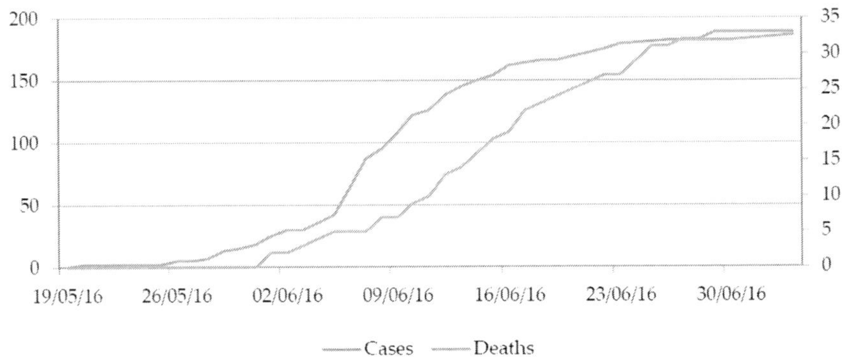

Figure 1. Number of cases and death tolls.

The government was highly criticized for underestimating the danger of MERS and withholding the names of health facilities where MERS victims had been treated and visited in the early stage of the outbreak [9,10,11,12]. In accordance with widespread MERS fear, over 2200 schools were temporarily closed, and many patients canceled hospital appointments apparently out of fear of being exposed to the disease [13].

Given the failure to effectively contain MERS, the South Korean government cut the country's economic growth forecast for 2015 to 3.1% from the 3.8% projected in the previous year. More specifically, compared to those during the same period in the previous year, retail shops in South Korea faced a 3.4% decrease in sales, and department stores experienced a 16.5% decrease in sales [14], according to the Minister of Strategy and Finance. The outbreak also raised international concerns, which led to over 100,000 canceled tourist visits to the nation [14]. In response, a stimulus package of over $13.5 billion was passed, and a 0.25-percentage-point cut in interest rates was offered by the Central Bank to help cushion the economic fallout from the outbreak [15].

2.2. Related Literature

A rich body of literature in economics and marketing explores the impact of macroeconomic factors. For example, researchers describe how firms change their decisions regarding innovation and advertising during a recession with the particular focuses on the effectiveness of these proactive actions [7,16,17] and examine the effect of business cycles on consumer confidence in the context of durable goods and private label sales [7,18,19,20]. These studies are, however, typically based on industry- or firm-level sales data and, therefore, provide little information about individual responses to changes in macroeconomic factors [21].

As scanner panel data measured at low frequencies have become more widely available to academics, much attention has been paid to more disaggregate data to address the effects of macroeconomic factors on different variables of interest. For example, Gicheva, Hastings and Villas-Boas [22] and Ma *et al.* [21] explore the impact of gasoline prices on consumer shopping behaviors using daily scanner panel data and reveal that consumers exploited different avenues to save money on grocery shopping.

Yet, these studies focus on business cycles or gasoline prices, which are qualitatively different from the outbreak of an epidemic. More specifically, unlike epidemic outbreaks, macroeconomic factors, such as business cycles or gasoline prices, impact the economy mainly through disrupting consumers' ability to buy rather than their psychological willingness to buy. For example, consumers become more price-sensitive as a result of the increasing financial hardship resulting from rising gasoline prices [23,24,25] and rely on a wide range of efforts to save money [21,22]. Consequently, less is known about how the population responds to a transitory extreme event, such as epidemic outbreaks, and how a psychological factor (fear of contagion), rather than budgetary constraints, influences consumer behaviors.

In one of the few exceptions in the literature addressing an extreme event using high-frequency data, Galbraith and Tkacz [26] investigate the economic burden of September 11 on consumption based on daily debit and credit card data. However, their results are subject to a strong restriction in that the data were also aggregated over individual consumers and categories and, therefore, provided limited implications about the effect of an extreme event on individual consumer behaviors. In turn, it is still an open question how the substantive changes in consumer expenditures occurred as a result of an extreme event.

Our paper contributes to these streams of research in the following respects. We explore the economic effect of an extreme event by analyzing how an epidemic outbreak influenced consumers by disrupting psychological willingness to spend. The detailed information on credit and debit cards transactions allowed us to comprehensively determine how changes in shopping behaviors arose from the fear of contagion, which is qualitatively different from other macroeconomic factors. Accordingly, our results have explicit and direct implications for policymakers and managers focused on maintaining sustainable economic growth.

3. DATA

Our data come from a mobile phone application design and development firm in Korea. The company developed a household account book application that automatically records credit and debit card transactions. The application's bookkeeping is based on text messages its users receive from credit card companies and banks. The application is available only in Korea and provided free of charge.

The available information for each transaction in the data included customer identifiers, date, time, amount paid and the name of the retail store. Additionally, retailer types and categories of expenditures were identified based on retail-store names and recorded by the data provider. The data included a variety of expenses, ranging from expenditures at restaurants, grocery stores and cafes to payments for gas and electronics. Although the data do not specify the list of products purchased in a given transaction nor show information about prices or promotions at stores, the extensive range of our data provided us with extremely detailed information on consumers' shopping behaviors and expenditures on goods and services.

Our data included the records of retail transactions of 11,225 customers. However, among these 11,225 customers, the complete transaction data throughout 2014 and 2015 were available only for 1521 customers. The remaining 9704 customers did not remain registered for the application throughout the sample period due to late registration or dropping out of the service. These customers, on average, remained active only for 67 days and exhibited less than two transactions per month. Thus, we restrict our attention to the 1521 customers.

Table 1 summarizes the shopping behaviors of the 1521 customers. An average customer in this group engaged in 12.33 transactions and spent 633,863 won per month. More specifically, grocery expenditures made up the largest share of total expenditures, followed by expenditures on food outside the home and gasoline/transportation. Such an expenditure pattern is highly similar to that observed in the U.S., where expenditures on food account for a large component after housing expenditures. Table 2 describes the composition of our data and shows that, given that our data collection was based on a mobile phone application, most customers were below 50, and customers in their 20s and 30s accounted for 72.25% of the focal sample.

Table 1. Number of monthly transactions and expenditures.

	Monthly Transactions	Monthly Expenditures (in Won [1])/Share of Total Expenditures	(in U.S. Dollar)
Recreation and Culture	1.62	24,960/3.93%	21.33
Food Outside the Home	2.41	89,767/14.16%	76.72
Department Store	4.57	65,577/10.34%	56.04
E-Commerce	4.27	34,001/5.36%	29.06
Health/Medical Expenses	2.35	67,714/10.68%	57.87
Grocery Stores	2.61	97,337/15.35%	83.19
Gasoline/Transportation	2.57	87,606/13.82%	74.87
Others	3.90	166,900/26.33%	142.64
Sum	12.33	633,862	541.76

[1] The won is the Korean currency, and $1 is approximately equal to 1170 won as of 26 March 2016.

Table 2. Number of customers.

Age	N
20s	389
30s	710
40s	344
50s	62
60 and above	16
Sum	1521

As a sample that is not representative of the general population can produce erroneous inferences, such a sample composition therefore does raise concerns about the generalizability of our results. However, in the absence of systematic research on the economic burden resulting from a transitory extreme event, our data provide an opportunity to conduct such research. Moreover, the distinctive nature of our data, which capture consumers' purchase and consumption behaviors in considerable detail, provides a comprehensive understanding of customer shopping behaviors not offered by data in other formats. Thus, the current data still provide important implications for practitioners and policymakers regarding sustainable growth in different industries. Nonetheless, we will address this particular aspect of our data later in this paper, after our empirical findings and their implications are discussed in detail.

4. PRELIMINARY ANALYSIS

Using our data on credit and debit card purchases, we plotted weekly transactions from January 2014 to August 2015 in Figure 2 with a trend line. The first overarching point in Figure 2 is that the transaction volume exhibited steady growth, far exceeding the growth of the Korean economy. For example, total expenditures of the sample customers in the data increased from 5.85 billion won in January 2014 to 6.64 billion won in September 2015, exhibiting the standard deviation of 0.315 billion won. It is not clear how this pattern arose. This may have been due to the actual growth in debit and credit card transactions, as our sample consists of relatively young customers whose expenditures tend to rise quickly. On the other hand, the growing volume in credit and debit card transactions may have been due to the increased adoption of text services provided by credit and debit card companies. Upon finding the persistent pattern in the data, we understand the importance of this growth in the transaction volume and explicitly controlled for it in later analyses, although the primary purpose of our research did not include the identification of causes for this particular aspect.

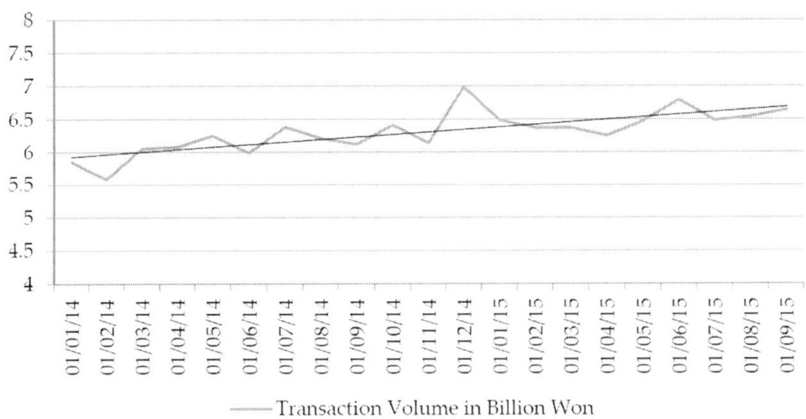

Figure 2. Transaction volume

Beyond the growth in transaction volumes in 2014 and 2015, another noteworthy point in Figure 2 is that there was high variability around the Christmas holiday, followed by a considerable drop in January. This clear pattern in our data from South Korea is consistent with common behavioral patterns found in other parts of the globe [26]. In particular, in December 2014, the transaction volume was 7.71% and 13.68% higher, respectively, than in November 2014 and January 2015. We also took this holiday effect into account when evaluating the impact of the MERS outbreak in Korea and explicitly addressed the time trends in our empirical analysis.

Finally, most interesting is our finding that the transaction volume exhibited a significant drop beginning in June 2015. More specifically, the transaction volume in won decreased from 6.79 billion won in June to 6.48 billion won in July. This is particularly interesting in that, first, the period during which the drop occurred coincided with the period during which the MERS outbreak took place in Korea, and second, a considerable drop was not observed during the summer of 2014.

To understand how such a slowdown in transaction volume occurred in May and June of 2015, we examined the underlying components of expenditures. If the decrease in transaction volume arose from the disruption of consumption due to the fear of infection, it should have been limited to transactions through channels customers considered risky to use. On the other hand, if the drop in the transaction volume in May and June of 2015 was not systematically related to the outbreak, no particular differences should be observed in transaction volumes across categories.

Among nine categories defined by the data provider, we restricted our attention to three that were appropriate for comparison. In particular, we chose two categories that customers would be likely to associate with the risk of contagion and one category that they would not. Figure 3 summarizes the changes in consumer expenditures in these categories between 2014 and 2015. Interestingly, across categories, consumer expenditures exhibited significantly different patterns. Consumers reduced their expenditures at department stores and on food outside the home. By contrast, e-commerce expenditures dramatically increased in May and June of 2015.

Together with the disruption of expenditures at department stores and on food outside the home, the hike in the e-commerce transaction volume supports the argument that the considerable decrease in transaction volume was primarily attributable to consumers' fear of contagion. This negative impact of the epidemic outbreak on consumer sentiments and behaviors was thus qualitatively different from that of other macroeconomic factors. Upon finding notable patterns in consumer expenditures, we developed formal models to investigate how the fear of infection influenced consumers, which we describe in the next section.

Table 3. Estimation results for Model 1. MERS, Middle East respiratory syndrome coronavirus.

Variable		Variable	
MERS	−0.0731 ** (0.0135)	Holidays	0.0996 ** (0.0186)
Year Dummy	0.0469 ** (0.0200)	February	0.0315 ** (0.0127)
March	0.0413 ** (0.0123)	April	0.0499 ** (0.0122)
May	0.0551 ** (0.0121)	June	0.0584 ** (0.0122)
July	0.0650 ** (0.0118)	August	0.0689 ** (0.0117)
September	0.0647 ** (0.0118)	October	0.0759 ** (0.0159)
November	0.0712 ** (0.0159)	December	0.0611 ** (0.0200)
Dependent Variable Mean	11.4485 ** (0.0091)		
Number of Observations	138,410	Number of Consumers	1521
Durbin–Watson Statistic	1.5417		

Note: Standard errors are shown in parentheses. * $p < 0.05$; ** $p < 0.01$.

5. MODELS AND RESULTS

5.1. Total Expenditures

Based on credit and debit card transactions information, we explored the effect of the MERS outbreak in Korea with the focus on the changes in consumer total expenditures. The dependent variable is therefore total expenditures per week, and the model is of the following form:

$$\log Exp_{it} = \alpha_0 + \alpha_1 I^t_{MERS} + AX_{it} + \varepsilon_{1it} \quad (1)$$

where Exp_{it} is consumer i's total expenditures during week t and I^t_{MERS} is the dummy indicating whether a new case of MERS had been reported in week t, to identify if week t is during the outbreak. Finally, X_t is a set of controls for time trends, including dummies for year, month and Christmas holidays (last three weeks of December). The explanatory variables can be grouped into two sets. The first set estimates the effect of the outbreak, which is of central interest to our research, and the second set, variables indicating time periods and holiday seasons, controls for time trends and the holiday effect, addressed in the preliminary analysis.

Note that the model is specified in log-linear form, and therefore, coefficients are provided in percentages rather than absolute terms, following other studies that explore the macroeconomic effect on consumer expenditures (e.g., [21]). This is because we observed considerable variation in the magnitude of the expenditures across consumers and over time. However, we noted that the Box–Cox test reveals that the current log specification did not fit best (Table A1). Thus, we provided the estimation results for the model in the linear specification later in this subsection.

The model is estimated by an ordinary least squares regression. We allowed for first-order autocorrelation in the error terms, ε_{it}^{1}, as the Durbin–Watson test of the *d* statistics shows that the hypothesis of no first order serial correlation can be rejected, as shown in Table 3.

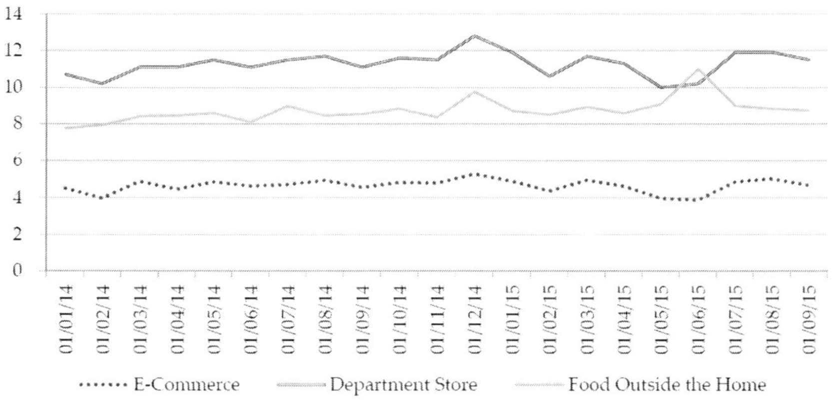

Figure 3. Transaction volume in billion won by category.

To aid interpretation of the coefficient estimates, note that the estimate of α^1, the coefficient of our primary interest, measures the effect of the outbreak on consumer expenditures. Based on the considerable drop in expenditures during the MERS outbreak, described in the previous section, we expected a negative effect of I_{MERS}^{t}.

Table 3 reports estimation results. Consistent with our expectation, the estimate of α^1 is statistically significant and negative. The results imply that customers lowered their expenditures by 7.31% during the outbreak. Such a considerable drop in consumer expenditures is as large as the effect of other macroeconomic factors. For example, Ma *et al.* [21] predicted that a 100% increase in gasoline prices would reduce grocery expenditures by 6%, as consumers would switch from national brands to private labels [27] and shift their spending from one store format to another to save money [28,29,30]. This presents strong empirical evidence that the disruption of consumption, resulting from the fear of infection, is important enough to be relevant. Turning to variables controlling for the time trends and the holiday effect, Table 3 reveals that the effects were all statistically significant and intuitive. For example, during the holiday season, consumer expenditures increased by more than 9.96%, consistent with our findings in the preliminary analysis.

Having identified the significant effect of the MERS outbreak, we checked the robustness of the results. First, we replicate the analysis using a different variable to describe the effect of the outbreak. In particular, we used the number of new deaths in week *t* as a variable, hypothesizing that the disruption of consumption due to the fear of contagion might increase with the number of deaths. Second, while a number of economics and marketing studies employs the log-linear specification to examine consumer expenditures, we recognized that the model in a linear specification had a better fit in describing the impact of the MERS outbreak in our data. Therefore, using the number of new deaths reported during the week to describe the MERS effect and a linear model specification, we developed two additional models in the following forms:

$$\log Exp_{it} = \beta_0 + \beta_1 Death_t + BX_{it} + \varepsilon_{2it}, \quad (2)$$

$$\text{and } Exp_{it} = \gamma_0 + \gamma_1 I^t_{MERS} + \Gamma X_{it} + \varepsilon_{3it}. \quad (3)$$

Again, β^1 and γ^1 are the variables of our key interest and measure the effect of the MERS outbreak on consumers' expenditures.

The results are reported in Table 4. The estimates of β^1 and γ^1 turned out to be statistically significant and negative in all replications, indicating that the effect of the MERS outbreak is significant. More specifically, customers, on average, reduced their expenditures by 1.24%, or by 43,517 won per week, for a unit increase in the number of deaths during the outbreak. Remember that, on average, 5.14 new deaths were reported per week during the outbreak and that total expenditures of an average customer were approximately 158,465 won ($135.44). Then, the current estimation results are fairly similar to the previous findings.

Table 4. Estimation results for Models 2 and 3.

Variable	Model 2	Model 3
Infection/MERS	−0.0124 ** (0.0001)	−43,517 ** (11,058)
Holidays	0.0603 ** (0.0186)	62,040 ** (17,192)
Year	0.0497 ** (0.0199)	4369 (1,069)
February	0.0445 ** (0.0127)	9229 (10,395)
March	0.0468 ** (0.0123)	14,833 (9753)
April	0.0562 ** (0.0122)	13,677 (9683)
May	0.0598 ** (0.0120)	24,559 ** (9540)
June	0.0579 ** (0.0130)	25,534 ** (9657)
July	0.0698 ** (0.0118)	37,544 ** (9302)
August	0.0726 ** (0.0117)	46,102 ** (9237)
September	0.0734 ** (0.0117)	50,064 ** (9259)
October	0.0717 ** (0.0158)	40,765 ** (12,611)
November	0.0837 ** (0.0158)	61,065 ** (12,485)
December	0.0795 ** (0.0199)	47,347 ** (17,270)
Intercept	11.4707 ** (0.0089)	330,939 ** (9283)
Number of Observations	138,410	
Number of Customers	1521	
Durbin–Watson Statistic	1.6285	

Note: Standard errors are shown in parentheses. * $p < 0.05$; ** $p < 0.01$.

To sum up, after explicitly controlling for the time trends and heterogeneity across individual customers, we found converging empirical evidence that the MERS outbreak significantly disrupted consumer consumption. These results are consistent with past studies on macroeconomic factors, such as business cycles and gasoline prices. Yet, the findings we report here are particularly important, upon finding the descriptive evidence that the effect of the MERS outbreak arose from the fear of contagion. The effect could therefore differ from those of other macroeconomic factors in how consumer expenditures are influenced. Therefore, we address the underlying reason for the effects of this extreme event on consumer expenditures in the next section.

5.2. Expenditures in E-Commerce and Other Categories

To understand how the large change in expenditures arose more comprehensively, we examine how customers altered their expenditures in the different categories. Based on the preliminary findings that the considerable decrease in transaction volume was attributable to the psychological factor, quantifying changes in customer expenditures in different categories would further assure the importance of the establishment and adoption of e-commerce as an alternative shopping channel for sustainable economic growth during epidemic outbreaks.

Following the previous specification we employed to investigate total expenditures, we attempted to explicitly control for the heterogeneity in the effect of the MERS outbreak across the categories and developed the separate category-expenditure models in the following specification. This specification allowed us to identify mutually exclusive marginal effects of the MERS effect on consumer expenditures across categories, without imposing a restriction on the distributions of error terms for different categories. Similar to previous analyses, we allowed for first-order autocorrelation in the error terms, ϵcit. Based on the behavioral patterns presented in Section 4, the main goal of our investigation is to quantify the differences in adjustments customers made across categories.

$$\log Exp_{cit} = \zeta_{0c} + \zeta_{1c} I^{t}_{MERS} + Z_c X_{it} + \varepsilon_{cit}\ 0 \tag{4}$$

Table 5 gives the coefficient estimates of expenditure models for five categories and their standard errors (see Table A2 for other estimation results). First, focusing on three categories we examined in the preliminary analysis, coefficient estimates of ζ_{1c} in Table 6 are intuitive and consistent with our expectation. In particular, during the outbreak, consumers reduced their expenditures at department stores to the greatest extent by 18% and lowered expenditures on food outside the home by 8.24%. This statistically and economically significant negative effect is highly consistent with the behavioral patterns described in the preliminary analysis and with the report by the Minister of Strategy and Finance.

Table 5. Estimation results for Model 4.

	Recreation/Culture	Food Outside	Department Store	E-Commerce	Grocery Stores
MERS	−0.0687 ** (0.0184)	−0.0824 ** (0.0112)	−0.1801 ** (0.0214)	0.0524 ** (0.0154)	0.0014 (0.0242)
Holidays	0.2120 ** (0.0342)	0.1821 ** (0.0214)	0.1521 ** (0.0252)	0.1243 ** (0.0345)	−0.0241 (0.0324)
Year	0.0447 (0.0326)	0.0452 ** (0.0214)	0.0458 ** (0.0211)	0.0435 ** (0.0185)	0.0445 ** (0.0154)
February	0.0245 (0.0147)	0.0351 ** (0.0127)	0.0324 ** (0.0112)	0.0421 ** (0.0254)	0.0421 ** (0.0157)
March	0.0289 (0.0154)	0.0368 ** (0.0123)	0.0368 ** (0.0103)	0.0487 ** (0.0241)	0.0465 ** (0.0159)
April	0.0324 * (0.0165)	0.0362 ** (0.0122)	0.0388 ** (0.0121)	0.0512 ** (0.0214)	0.0457 ** (0.0154)
May	0.0387 ** (0.0147)	0.0498 ** (0.0120)	0.0412 ** (0.0123)	0.0568 ** (0.0254)	0.0512 ** (0. 0165)
June	0.0412 ** (0.0189)	0.0479 ** (0.0130)	0.0468 ** (0.0120)	0.6125 ** (0.0256)	0.0564 ** (0.0175)
July	0.0462 ** (0.0210)	0.0508 ** (0.0118)	0.0598 ** (0.0121)	0.0621 ** (0.0241)	0.0621 ** (0.0156)
August	0.0456 ** (0.0187)	0.0526 ** (0.0117)	0.0624 ** (0.0118)	0.06752 ** (0.0258)	0.0645 ** (0.0154)
September	0.0501 ** (0.0214)	0.0634 ** (0.0117)	0.0675 ** (0.0119)	0.0702 ** (0.0265)	0.0654 ** (0.0165)
October	0.0561 ** (0.0231)	0.0617 ** (0.0158)	0.0721 ** (0.0158)	0.0758 ** (0.0294)	0.0712 ** (0.0164)
November	0.0645 ** (0.0185)	0.0637 ** (0.0158)	0.0757 ** (0.0125)	0.0854 ** (0.0241)	0.0784 ** (0.0154)
December	0.0504 ** (0.0231)	0.0605 ** (0.0199)	0.0694 ** (0.0188)	0.0798 ** (0.0184)	0.0684 ** (0.0157)
Intercept	8.1054 ** (0.0087)	9.4049 ** (0.0089)	9.0909 ** (0.0098)	8.4314 ** (0.0089)	9.1230 ** (0.0093)
Observations	138,046	137,658	138,392	138,064	138,401
Customers	1521	1521	1521	1521	1521
Durbin-Watson Statistics	1.7852	1.6851	1.5136	1.7295	2.0403

Note: Standard errors are shown in parentheses. * $p < 0.05$; ** $p < 0.01$.

Even more important is the finding that, by contrast, consumers increased their e-commerce expenditures by 5.24%. This significant increase in e-commerce expenditures together with the disruption of expenditures at the above two traditional channels, where shopping would be accompanied by the risk of contagion, ensure that the MERS outbreak impacted consumers' sentiments and consumption to a significant extent and led consumers to switch to e-commerce to prevent possible exposure to the disease.

Turning to consumer expenditures in other categories, Table 5 suggests that, during the MERS outbreak, consumers reduced their spending on recreation and culture by 6.87% and maintained relatively persistent expenditures on groceries. The null effect of I^t_{MERS} on grocery expenditures may appear inconsistent with our prediction, but remember that groceries are often considered less affected by macroeconomic factors because they cannot be postponed [7]. Thus, we conclude that the estimation results of category expenditure models are intuitive.

In general, studies on macroeconomic factors and their effects on consumer shopping behaviors and consumption have focused on the disruption of economic abilities to explain decreases in spending and changes in store and brand choices. However, the findings we report here indicate that epidemics influence consumer behaviors through the fear of infection and psychological willingness to spend. Our results strongly suggest a qualitative difference between the effect of epidemic outbreaks and the effects of other macroeconomic factors, such as business cycles and gasoline prices. We believe our findings suggest an important implication for sustainable growth in the economy, which we will discuss in a greater detail in the next section.

6. IMPLICATIONS

In this study, we addressed the effect of an epidemic outbreak on consumer expenditures. Using scanner panel data on individual consumers' debit and credit card transactions, we found that the outbreak of an epidemic caused a substantial disruption of consumer expenditures. However, the negative effect was not prevalent across all categories of expenditures, and the significant drop in expenditures was limited to traditional shopping channels, which consumers are likely to consider risky during an outbreak. By contrast, consumers switched to e-commerce to prevent the possible exposure to the disease.

Based on our empirical findings, one implication we can consider for manufacturers and retailers is that they may lessen the considerable negative shocks of epidemic outbreaks by developing and improving e-commerce as an alternative shopping channel. In many industrialized countries, a significant share of the population uses the Internet, and the rate of online shopping adoption has been persistently growing. For example, among adults in the United States, 84% use the Internet [31], and over half (57.4%) of the U.S. population shopped online during 2015 [32]. A similar pattern was observed in Korea, in that, among population ages three and above, 83.6% used the Internet and 51.3% have bought products or goods online by desktop, mobile, tablet or other online devices in 2014 [33].

Despite the considerable increase in the adoption of e-commerce, however, e-commerce still makes up only a minor share of total retail sales. For example, only 7.1% of total retail sales were made through e-commerce in the U.S., and the expenditures through e-commerce constitute the lowest share of the total expenditures, following the expenditures on culture and recreation. One account that can explain the relatively small volume of transactions made through e-commerce is that online retail is still restricted to big names and that only a limited share of small stores are selling products online [34]. This is largely because attracting customers in an online environment is often considered much more challenging than in a traditional business environment [35], as lack of trust, one of the most frequently-cited reasons for consumers not purchasing through e-commerce, could be more problematic for small retailers [36].

It is beyond the scope of our paper to do a complete counterfactual analysis. However, we suggest that our empirical findings would be useful for understanding the effect of policies that influence the e-commerce adoption, and a back-of-the-envelope calculation can give some context to our results. For example, suppose that the transaction volume made through e-commerce increased to 10% from 5.36% of the total retail sales, based on the improved policy environment for e-commerce adoption. Such a growth occurred at the expense of department stores, and their retail share decreased to 5.7% from 10.34% of the total retail sales. Then, our findings suggest that the decrease in expenditures at department stores would have remained at 55.12% of its current level.

The implications we provide in this subsection are important particularly for developing countries, where internet access to information networks is expensive and policies promoting trust confidence among e-commerce participants are not yet compatible with international norms. Yet, we caution that our approach in this section is largely descriptive and that the account we propose may not be well suited for conclusive validation and testing based on our data. Furthermore, our analysis should be interpreted with some care, because it does not represent what is commonly considered to motivate individuals and firms to accept e-commerce services [37,38,39,40]. Instead, our primary objective in this discussion is to propose a particular implication for practitioners and policymakers and to stimulate further research to investigate our argument.

7. CONCLUSIONS

Through a series of analyses, we addressed the effect of an epidemic outbreak on consumer expenditures. Our empirical investigation presented empirical evidence that the outbreak of an epidemic caused a substantial disruption of consumer expenditures, while the negative effect was not prevalent across all categories of expenditures. Our findings are particularly important, in that studies on macroeconomic factors have generally focused on the disruption of economic abilities. However, such an explanation is not appropriate for predicting the effect of an epidemic outbreak, which results from fear of contagion. As a result, the implications of our research provide important guidance for policy intervention and marketing decisions for sustainable growth in the economy despite the more challenging and more complex epidemic outbreaks.

We note the limitation of our study. As the data collection was based on credit and debit card transactions, the data do not contain the information on cash payments and withdrawals, and therefore, the implications we make in this paper may not be eligible when customers engage in a different type of payment method. Moreover, customers in the sample can be considered self-selected given the nature of the data, and the estimation sample is fairly small. Although it is likely that the decision of adopting the household account book application is positively correlated with the adoption of online shopping, ensuring that the composition of our data neither exaggerate the negative shock of the epidemic outbreak on total expenditures nor overstate the consumers' adjustment we found in our empirical analyses, as a result, our results must be interpreted with caution. However, in the absence of systematic research on the economic burden resulting from an epidemic outbreak, we consider our data as a useful alternative to the existing sources and believe that our findings are important for practitioners and policymakers regarding sustainable growth in different industries.

ACKNOWLEDGMENTS

The authors thank their research assistant, Janice Choi, for her contribution to this work. This work was supported by the Hongik University new faculty research support fund.

AUTHOR CONTRIBUTIONS

Kihoon Hong conceived and designed the empirical model; Eunjung Hyun analyzed the data; Hojin Jung and Minjae Park wrote the paper.

Conflicts of Interest: The authors declare no conflict of interest.

Table A1. Box–Cox test statistics.

Dependent Variable	Restricted Log Likelihood	Likelihood-ratio Statistic Chi-Squared	p-Value
$\frac{1}{Exp_{it}}$	−660,362.85	1.3×10^5	0.000
Exp_{it}	−623,973.29	59,917	0.000
$\log Exp_{it}$	−603,792.15	19,554	0.000

Table A2. Expenditure models for other three categories.

Variable	Health/Medical Expenses	Gasoline/Transportation	Others
MERS	−0.0125 (0.0152)	−0.0236 (0.0237)	−0.1243 (0.0198)
Holidays	−0.0018 (0.0048)	0.0024 (0.0149)	0.1425 (0.0145)
Year	0.0257 (0.0114)	0.0389 (0.0122)	0.0421 (0.0135)
February	0.0235 (0.0112)	0.0421 (0.0142)	0.0314 (0.0148)
March	0.0287 (0.0114)	0.0485 (0.0174)	0.0402 (0.0143)
April	0.0307 (0.0121)	0.0501 (0.0175)	0.0423 (0.0163)
May	0.0348 (0.0128)	0.0512 (0.0176)	0.0487 (0.0147)
June	0.0317 (0.0111)	0.0542 (0.0182)	0.0523 (0.0175)
July	0.0387 (0.0138)	0.0602 (0.0192)	0.0546 (0.0167)
August	0.0410 (0.0128)	0.0621 (0.0188)	0.0578 (0.0158)
September	0.0453 (0.0125)	0.0638 (0.0184)	0.0621 (0.0176)
October	0.0415 (0.0134)	0.0628 (0.0172)	0.0624 (0.0163)
November	0.0487 (0.0121)	0.0701 (0.0178)	0.0638 (0.0175)
December	0.0501 (0.0108)	0.0724 (0.0165)	0.0582 (0.0164)
Intercept	8.674 (0.0144)	9.2452 (0.0108)	10.0214 (0.0088)
Number of Observations	138,298	138,384	138,410
Number of Customers	1521	1521	1521

Note: Standard errors are shown in parentheses. * $p < 0.05$; ** $p < 0.01$.

REFERENCES

1. Ebola: Mapping the Outbreak. Available online: http: //www.bbc.com/news/world-africa-28755033 (accessed on 31 January 2016).
2. evere Acute Respiratory Syndrome (SARS) Multi-Country Outbreak—Update 6. Available online: http://www.who.int/csr /don/2003_03_21/en/ (accessed on 27 April 2016).

3. Hamilton, J.D. *Causes and Consequences of the Oil Shock of 2007–08*; National Bureau of Economic Research: New York, NY, USA, 2009.

4. Bloom, D.E.; Mahal, A.S. Does the AIDS epidemic threaten economic growth? *J. Econ.* **1997**, *77*, 105–124.

5. Gubler, D.J. Epidemic dengue/dengue hemorrhagic fever as a public health, social and economic problem in the 21st century. *Trends Microbiol.* **2002**, *10*, 100–103.

6. Kalia, M. Assessing the economic impact of stress [mdash] The modern day hidden epidemic. *Metabolism* **2002**, *51*, 49–53.

7. Deleersnyder, B.; Dekimpe, M.G.; Sarvary, M.; Parker, P.M. Weathering tight economic times: The sales evolution of consumer durables over the business cycle. *Quantit. Mark. Econ.* **2004**, *2*, 347–383.

8. Middle East Respiratory Syndrome Coronavirus (MERS-CoV)—Republic of Korea. Available online: http://www.who.int/csr/don/07-july-2015-mers-korea/en/ (accessed on 31 January 2016).

9. Fear in the Air. Available online: http://www.economist.com/news/asia/21653731-fear-air (accessed on 31 January 2016).

10. Mers Prompts Hong Kong to Declare 'Red Alert' on South Korea Travel. Available online: http://www.newsweek.com/mers-prompts-hong-kong-declare-red-alert-south-korea-travel-341093 (accessed on 31 January 2016).

11. South Korea Replaces Health Minister Criticized over MERS Outbreak. Available online: http://www.reuters.com/article/us-health-mers-southkorea-idUSKCN0Q90JJ20150804 (accessed on 31 January 2016).

12. South Korean Schools Reopen Despite Widespread MERS Fear. Available online: http://newsok.com/article/feed/852330 (accessed on 31 January 2016).

13. Park, J.-M.; Kim, S. Secrecy Surrounding MERS Outbreak Fuels Fear, Confusion In South Korea. Available online: http://www.huffingtonpost.com/2015/06/02/south-korea-mers-outbreak_n_7492380.html (accessed on 31 January 2016).

14. Park, M.; Kwon, K.J.; Kim, J.-E. WHO calls MERS Outbreak a 'Wakeup Call'. Available online: http://edition.cnn.com /2015/06/15/asia/south-korea-mers-outbreak (accessed on 31 January 2016).

15. S Korea Cuts Interest Rates to Record Low Amids Mers Concerns. Available online: http://www.bbc.com/news/business-33089930 (accessed on 31 January 2016).

16. Frankenberger, K.D.; Graham, R.C. Should firms increase advertising expenditures during recessions? *MSI Rep.* **2003**, *3*, 65–85.

17. Srinivasan, R.; Rangaswamy, A.; Lilien, G.L. Turning adversity into advantage: Does proactive marketing during a recession pay off? *Int. J. Res. Mark.* **2005**, *22*, 109–125.

18. Allenby, G.M.; Jen, L.; Leone, R.P. Economic trends and being trendy: The influence of consumer confidence on retail fashion sales. *J. Bus. Econ. Stat.* **1996**, *14*, 103–111.

19. Kumar, V.; Leone, R.P.; Gaskins, J.N. Aggregate and disaggregate secto

20. Lamey, L.; Deleersnyder, B.; Dekimpe, M.G.; Steenkamp, J.-B.E. How business cycles contribute to private-label success: Evidence from the United States and Europe. *J. Mark.* **2007**, *71*, 1–15

21. Ma, Y.; Ailawadi, K.L.; Gauri, D.K.; Grewal, D. An empirical investigation of the impact of gasoline prices on grocery shopping behavior. *J. Mark.* **2011**, *75*, 18–35.

22. Gicheva, D.; Hastings, J.; Villas-Boas, S. Investigating Income Effects in Scanner Data: Do Gasoline Prices Affect Grocery Purchases? *Am. Econ. Rev.* **2010**, *100*, 480–484.

23. Allenby, G.M.; Rossi, P.E. Quality perceptions and asymmetric switching between brands. *Mark. Sci.* **1991**, *10*, 185–204.

24. Du, R.Y.; Kamakura, W.A. Where did all that money go? Understanding how consumers allocate their consumption budget. *J. Mark.* **2008**, *72*, 109–131.

25. Jacobe, D. High gas prices causing consumer spending cuts. *Gallup News Service, (May 24)*. 2016. Available online: http://www. gallup.com/poll/22918/high-gas-prices-causing-consumer-spendingcuts.aspx (accessed on 22 November 2010).

26. Galbraith, J.W.; Tkacz, G. Analyzing Economic Effects of September 11 and Other Extreme Events Using Debit and Payments System Data. *Can. Public Policy* **2013**, *39*, 119–134.

27. Ailawadi, K.L.; Pauwels, K.; Steenkamp, J.-B.E. Private-label use and store loyalty. *J. Mark.* **2008**, *72*, 19–30.

28. Bell, D.R.; Ho, T.-H.; Tang, C.S. Determining where to shop: Fixed and variable costs of shopping. *J. Mark. Res.* **1998**, *XXXV*, 352–369.

29. Bhatnagar, A.; Ratchford, B.T. A model of retail format competition for non-durable goods. *Int. J. Mark. Res.* **2004**, *21*, 39–59

30. Luchs, R.; Inman, J.J.; Shankar, V. *Channel Blurring: A Study of Cross-Retail Format Shopping Among US Households*; working paper; Katz Graduate School of Business, University of Pittsburgh: Pittsburgh, PA, USA, 2007.

31. Perrin, A.; Duggan, M. Americans' Internet Access: 2000–2015. Available online: http://www.pewinternet.org/2015/06/26/americans-internet-access-2000-2015/ (accessed on 27 April 2016).

32. Five 2015 Ecommerce Stats and Trends You Should Know About. Available online: http://www.pixelmedia.com/blog/5-ecommerce-stats-trends-you-should-know-about (accessed on 31 January 2016).

33. Survey on the Internet Usage. Available online: http://isis.kisa.or.kr/board/?pageId=060300&bbsId=10&itemId=327&pageIndex=1 (accessed on 27 April 2016).

34. Online Retailing: Britain, Europe, US and Canada 2015. Available online: http://www.retailresearch.org/onlineretailing.php (accessed on 27 April 2016).

35. Bhattacherjee, A. Acceptance of e-commerce services: The case of electronic brokerages. *IEEE Trans. Syst. Man Cybern. Part A: Syst. Hum.* **2000**, *30*, 411–420.

36. Grabner-Kräuter, S.; Kaluscha, E.A. Empirical research in on-line trust: A review and critical assessment. *Int. J. Hum.-Comput. Stud.* **2003**, *58*, 783–812.

37. Agarwal, R.; Prasad, J. The role of innovation characteristics and perceived voluntariness in the acceptance of information technologies. *Decis. Sci.* **1997**, *28*, 557–582

38. Brancheau, J.C.; Wetherbe, J.C. The adoption of spreadsheet software: Testing innovation diffusion theory in the context of end-user computing. *Inf. Syst. Res.* **1990**, *1*, 115–143

39. Karahanna, E.; Straub, D.W.; Chervany, N.L. Information technology adoption across time: A cross-sectional comparison of pre-adoption and post-adoption beliefs. *MIS Q.* **1999**, *23*, 183–213.

40. Rogers, E.M. *Diffusion of Innovations*; Simon and Schuster: New York, NY, USA, 2010.

12

CHAPTER

Household Debt and Consumption Inequality: The Spanish Case

Gonzalo Paz Pardo[1,†] and José Manuel Sánchez Santos[2]

[1]*University College London, Gower St, London WC1E 6BT, UK; E-Mail: gonzalo.pardo.13@ucl.ac.uk*

[2]*Faculty of Economics, Universidade da Coruña, Campus de Elviña, s/n, 15071 A Coruña, Spain*

ABSTRACT

The aim of this paper is twofold. On the one hand, we attempt to find out whether Spanish households took part in a process of substituting loans for wages during the period before the beginning of the current economic crisis. On the other hand, we try to identify the consequences of such process in the evolution of income and consumption inequalities. The theoretical framework to deal with the above mentioned issues is provided by a review of the economic literature on the determinants of consumer behaviour, namely, on consumption, saving and debt. The empirical study consists of a descriptive analysis, which is focused on two fields. First, we analyze the evolution of consumer credit (both, in aggregate and by income groups) and the savings rates. Second, we compare the values and temporal evolution of income and consumption inequalities. The period under study ranges from 2000 to 2008. Our analysis provides some empirical evidence that supports the hypothesis that financial conditions led to significant effects on the distribution of consumption. This influence is especially significant in the case of consumption inequalities. These inequalities were lower than income inequalities and were kept "artificially" low and stable during the whole period.

Keywords: financial conditions; household indebtedness; consumer credit; income distribution; consumption inequalities

1. INTRODUCTION

The positive macroeconomic effects of a developed and efficient financial system have been well documented in economic literature. For example, King and Levine [1] established a very close correlation between the development of the financial sector in an economy and variables like economic growth, capital accumulation and improvements in the efficiency of the use of physical capital. However, the role of the financial system can also be addressed from the perspective of its relationship to the inequalities in the distribution both of income and consumption. The evolution of inequalities and the causes that explain them are topics with a notable presence in the economic research agenda, yet far fewer studies have attempted to explore the link of this variable with financial conditions.

A priori, a financial system that operates properly, in particular, if financial institutions properly value risk and there are no adverse shocks, could facilitate wide access to credit, allowing individuals to optimize the distribution of their expected income throughout their lives. Under these circumstances, this optimization process does not necessarily have negative macroeconomic consequences. Furthermore, the ease of access could favour the reduction of inequalities, especially those which are established in terms of consumption. This latter kind of influence is consistent with the results of Heathcote, Perri and Violante [2] and Agnello and Sousa [3]. In the first case, the authors provide evidence that access to the financial markets has reduced both the magnitude and the growth of consumption inequalities in terms of consumption in the United States since the 1980s. For their part, Agnello and Sousa [3], based on a panel of 62 countries, conclude that better access to credit also reduced inequalities.

In a similar vein, Barba and Pivetti [4] argue that developments in financial sector development allowed households to meet with loans the demand that they were not able to meet with their wages. This is what these authors call a substitution of debt (loans) for wages. As a consequence of this process, households indebtedness increased sharply, giving rise to concerns about the sustainability of this debt.

In a similar line, Rajan [5] argues that in the United States the increase in inequalities was "hidden" by credit expansion. These inequalities were derived mainly from differences in education, but also from other causes (the process of deregulation, the influx of immigrants, tax cuts for the richest, a minimum wage barely growing, *etc.*). According to this author, with the aim of preventing such an increase in inequalities becoming a social problem, the US authorities supported loans to households with an increasingly lower income, mainly for the purchase of housing. In this way, "inequality was hidden", households felt wealthier and consumption increased.

More recently, Galbraith [6] provides a more detailed analysis about this rise in inequality. This author finds that there are common global patterns in economic inequality across different countries that appear to be very strongly related to major events affecting the world economy as a whole. Particularly, the most important have been changes in financial regimes and changes in systems of financial governance. In his own words: "The economics of inequality is, in large measure, an economics of instability; inequality is the barometer, in many ways, of the instabilities that global credit relationships create" (Galbraith, [6], p. 18).

The private sector's debt and, in particular, households' indebtedness have substantial macroeconomic implications. The important role played by this variable both in the expansionary (before 2008) and recessive phase (from 2008 onwards) of the last business cycle in numerous developed economies has placed households' indebtedness at the centre of the debate regarding the recent financial crisis. In particular, a special emphasis is placed on the role played by high levels of household leverage as a factor influencing the possibilities and the rhythm of the economy recovering in several developed economies after the last recession. In addition, some authors have highlighted that one of the consequences of the increase in households' indebtedness is that they become much more sensitive to changes that might occur in macroeconomic conditions such as a rise in unemployment, increases in interest rates or a fall in the housing price (Debelle, [7]).

According to these kinds of considerations and taking into account that in the economic literature few studies have attempted to explore the implications in terms of inequality of the evolution of households' indebtedness, the main objective of this study is to verify the hypothesis that in the last expansionary phase of the business cycle in the Spanish economy, the increase in household consumption levels was financed mainly through the recourse to borrowing that, in turn, favoured the reduction of inequalities, particularly in terms of consumption.

In this context, the main contribution of this work is to deal with the link between household indebtedness and the evolution of inequalities in Spain since 2000. In principle, this link may have a two-way nature: the evolution of inequalities can act as a determinant of borrowing and, at the same time, rising household debt levels may have distributional consequences for income and consumption.1

Most of the research on inequalities in Spain is unanimous in identifying higher levels of unemployment as the main variable determining factor causing an increase in inequality. Other variables that appear in the literature are the level of GDP, public spending and transfers in the public sector, higher education and inflation.2 In this context, the issue addressed in this work is novel because as far as we know regarding the Spanish case, there is no research on the relationship between financial conditions (deregulation, monetary policy, cost, funding, *etc.*) and economic inequalities. This shortcoming gives our analysis a special interest, to the extent that knowledge of the distributional implications that may arise from the financial conditions is relevant to inform policy decisions.

This paper is organized as follows: Section 2 reviews some of the explanatory hypotheses of the consumer behaviour explaining borrowing and, particularly, consumer demand of credit. Section 3 deals with the evolution of the households' indebtedness and real wage levels in Spain. Section 4 analyses the link between the evolution of households' indebtedness and the degree of income and consumption inequalities. In Section 5, some empirical evidence is provided. Finally, Section 6 draws the main conclusions.

2. ANALYTICAL FRAMEWORK

2.1. Determinants of Consumption and Borrowing Decisions: Beyond the Conventional Explanations

According to the traditional Keynesian formulation of consumption function, the consumption of an individual in a period basically depends on the disposable income in the same period. However, individuals can distribute their consumption throughout their life in the manner they consider appropriate and regardless of their current income, through the use of borrowing (current consumption at the expense of future income) and saving (future consumption at the expense of current income). Following this line, one of the traditional explanations to the households' indebtedness of families has its roots in the theories of the permanent income (Friedman, [15]) and "life cycle" (Ando and Modligliani, [16]; and Modigliani, [17]).

However, when it comes to delving into the causes that explain household behaviour, it is important to explore the role of some factors that can lead individuals to consuming and borrowing, outside or above the levels predicted by the hypothesis of permanent life-income cycle. In order to carry out this type of analysis, it is necessary to go far beyond the assumption of a fully rational consumer in the most orthodox sense of the term. In particular, this type of approach is essential to elucidate whether the existence of a process of substitution of debt for wages is a consumer behaviour that strictly meets the criterion of the maximization of an intertemporal utility function or, by contrast, is explained by other type of reasons.

Authors such as Foster and Magdoff [18], who adopt a more heterodox view, point out that, in the U.S. economy, individuals rely on borrowing as a means of maintaining their standard of living in a context of wage stagnation (or as "desperate" means of increasing their standard of living). According to their approach, it could be argued to some extent that in the late 1990s U.S. economic expansion was "bought" with debt, especially household debt that is mainly related to housing, and to low income households. In the same line, Foster [19] argues that this type of reasoning can be extrapolated to the period 2000–2006 and potentially with many more devastating consequences.

In the context of a model that seeks to explain the effects of income distribution on consumption expenditure, Brown [20] concluded that broader access to credit allowed an increase in the purchasing power of middle-low income groups. Therefore, the removal of the so-called "income constraint" allows consumption and the propensity to consume in individuals by these income groups to increase. Although inequality increases, its potential effect on consumption may be mitigated by the expansion of consumer credit. In this sense, this author warns that U.S. growth dangerously relied on the willingness of a significant segment of the population to borrow at a level that, eventually, could cause them serious financial pressures.

Iacoviello [21] develops a model that attempts to explain the evolution of indebtedness and the degree of wealth and consumption inequalities. The results of this analysis showed that although the changes in the economic cycle affect household indebtedness, the substantial growth of this variable in the United States can only be explained by taking into account the increasing degree of inequality in the income distribution. According to this author, the growth of inequalities in wealth and the slight increasing trend (far less than income inequalities) of consumption inequality can be explained with his model based on the income distribution.

Taking the American case as a reference, Barba and Pivetti [4] argue that the tensions that led individuals to consume "beyond their means" are related to the slow growth of real incomes, the attractiveness of new consumer goods (related to new technologies, *etc.*) and the desire to emulate individuals with higher incomes.

In a later work, these same authors reiterate that the factors most commonly cited as determinants of the last economic and financial crisis (low rates of interest, global imbalances, *etc.*) are not the real causes. On the contrary, the crucial point was an economic scenario characterized by stagnant wages and growing economic inequalities. Under these circumstances, low interest rates fostered the growth of households' indebtedness and, furthermore, economic authorities tried to replace this private debt with public debt, so as to maintain the stability of the financial system (Barba and Pivetti, [22]).3

These points are further illustrated in Rancière and Kumhof [24]. These authors provide a theoretical framework for explaining the connection between inequality, leverage and financial crises. Their model shows how rising inequality in a climate of rising consumption can lead poorer households to increase their leverage. Particularly, according to these authors' model, an increase in the bargaining power of high income households causes them to have higher incomes, which are given back to the rest of the population via loans. This situation allows lower-income households to maintain their consumption levels, but eventually leads to higher leverage and to a higher probability of a financial crisis.

2.2. Liquidity Constraints

Previous explanations based on permanent income-life cycle models and on the desires of individuals to access borrowing from other causes do not always adequately match the reality. Any individual can save whenever he/she so wishes, but not any individual can borrow, because access to borrowing is subject to someone's willingness to lend the funds. It is common for individuals to confront the so-called liquidity constraints (either in terms of the amount they can borrow or the interest rate to be paid), which prevent the theoretical assumptions from being carried out in practice (Shapiro, [25]).

In this area, Campbell and Mankiw [26] argue that consumption is better explained by dividing consumers into two categories: on the one hand, individuals who consume on the basis of their current income and, on the other hand, individuals who consume according to their permanent income. These groups therefore correspond with those who are facing financial restrictions and those that do not, respectively.

From this, it is clear that the existence of restrictions that limit the capacity of certain consumers to freely distribute their consumption over time will be determined by the financial conditions. If for any reason, their credit conditions are particularly favourable, the above mentioned liquidity constraints are reduced and consumption tends to increase (Bacchetta and Gerlach, [27]). In addition, it should be noted that the expansion of the supply of credit not only affects the total volume of consumption, but also its distribution. As credit conditions improve, the credit becomes increasingly available for households with a lower level of income or wealth, which were previously subject to "liquidity constraints".

In this sense, there are numerous studies showing the positive effects that financial deregulation and innovation has had (since the 1980s) in terms of relaxing these restrictions on liquidity. In particular, one of these effects is a rise in the level of consumption that households can access because they are less limited when it comes to borrowing against their future income (Boone, Girouard and Wanner, [28]; Brady, [29]; Brady, [30] and Aron *et al.* [31]). In regard to financial innovation, Brown [32] argues that the expansion of financial engineering (particularly after 1987) played an important role in making consumer credit more widely available and it was crucial for the growth of consumption in the U.S.

In light of the above considerations and insofar as that an expansive monetary policy in general involves more favourable financial conditions, it can be expected that monetary policy also has effects on both levels of consumption and its distribution. By the end of the 1990s, Galbraith [33] pointed out that the growth of inequality in the United States was related to the poor performance of the American economy which, in turn, was the result of inadequate policies, in particular, the interest rates set by the Federal Reserve.

In fact, as regards the redistributive role of the monetary policy, Coibion *et al.* [34] provide some evidence that restrictive monetary policy causes long term increases in inequalities across households (in terms of whole income, labour income, consumption or total expenditure), clarifying that such effects are particularly visible in consumption inequalities.

Finally, it should be noted that a factor that can significantly influence the liquidity constraints is the "wealth effect", which refers to the increase in consumption linked to the rise in the price of financial and real assets. Economic literature dealing with the relationship between asset prices and consumption is profuse.4 Among the arguments put forward, the most relevant one for the purposes of our analysis is that the increase in the price of the assets allows individuals a growing access to credit. This is a way of relaxing the financial constraints faced by households with low levels of income or wealth (Bernanke and Gertler [38]).

In countries like the United Kingdom or the United States, the *Mortgage Equity Withdrawal* (*MEW*) has become a widespread financial practice, a financial transaction which consists of getting a mortgage extension by using the increase in housing value. One of the factors that led to the expansion of this practice was the favourable fiscal treatment that it gets, for example, in the U.S. In the Spanish case, it can be expected that the wealth effect is especially relevant given the well-known fact that it is one of the European countries with the highest homeownership rates (82.2% according to INE data).

Insofar as the liquidity restrictions primarily affect individuals with low levels of income and wealth, the favourable financial conditions that contribute to lifting these restrictions, will have redistributive effects. These effects can be explained because more individuals will be able to distribute their consumption as they wish by means of borrowing. In short, under these conditions, the number of individuals subject to liquidity constraints is reduced and individuals of lower income (and wealth) can increasingly access borrowing, which will favour the reduction of inequalities in terms of consumption.

If this argument is integrated into the above mentioned theories of consumption, if an individual is not restricted to liquidity constraints, he/she can distribute his/her consumption according to the predictions derived from the theories of the permanent life-income cycle. The individual can also, if this is the case, use the debt to try to access higher levels of consumption in comparison with other individuals or access new emergent products. Therefore, via both routes, it seems likely that an individual who is no longer subject to liquidity constraints will increase his/her consumption.

Within the framework of this approach, the objective of this work is to analyze, first, to what extent liquidity constraints were eased in Spain over the period starting at the beginning of the 2000s and, second, the distributional consequences that this may have. This is a matter of special relevance, given that, contrary to what was happening in the expansionary phase of the business cycle, the recent financial turmoil gives rise to a scenario of restrictive financial conditions. In particular, access to credit has been made extremely difficult and, according to the above formulated hypothesis, a growth of inequality, especially in terms of consumption, could be expected.

3. HOUSEHOLD DEBT AND WAGES IN SPAIN

3.1. Households Indebtedness: Components and Evolution

One of the indicators that reveal the magnitude of households' indebtedness in Spain is the ratio volume of loans to disposable income. For purposes of assessing to what extent households borrow so as to finance their consumption, the total debt is divided into two main segments: mortgage debt (in the Spanish case they represent the greatest part of households debt), and non-mortgage debt (consisting of credits and loans to households and other non-mortgage debts. Within this last category, those of greater importance are consumer loans, although, for example, loans and credits for the purchase of securities or other purposes are also included. Moreover, this category can also include some loans not classified as "home loans", but in practice intended for housing. Despite these nuances, in the follow-up, we use this variable as a "proxy" of the funding intended for consumption.

In the Spanish case, the continuous and significant growth of the ratios of both types of debt to households' gross disposable income over the period 2000–2007 is evident (Figure 1).

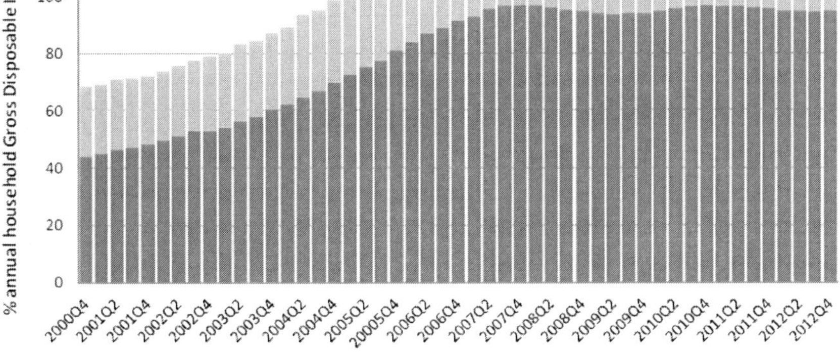

Source: own ellaboration with data from Banco de Espana (BdE) and Instituto Nacional de Estadistica (INE).

Figure 1. Households and Non Profit Institutions Serving Households (NPISH) debt-to-income ratio.

During this period, not only did mortgage debt grow, but the rest of household debt also experienced a sharp expansion (Figure 2).

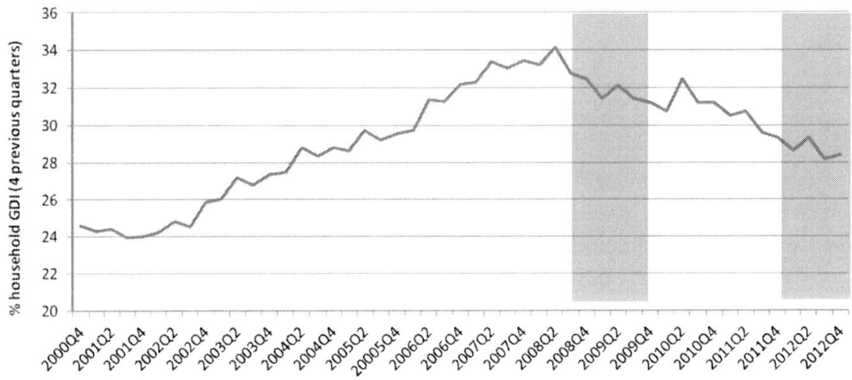

Source: own ellaboration with data from BdE and INE. Shaded areas indicate recessions.

Figure 2. Consumer debt for households and NPISHs.

The above mentioned time path of this variable may be associated with a context of increasing credit demand as well as highly flexible supply of credit conditions (reduction of the liquidity constraints).

In particular, the total volume of non-mortgage debt increased from 24.57% of the households RDB by the end of the year 2000 to 34.13% in the second quarter of 2008. This growth should also be viewed within the perspective of a context of significant increase in the RDB of households (in some years exceeding annual growth rates of 6% in nominal terms). Furthermore, it is interesting to note that this variable has been declining slowly and irregularly since 2008.

The evolution of the credits officially classified by financial institutions as "credit for consumer durables" (an important part of the credits for consumption) in terms of RDB is represented in Figure 3. The evolution of this variable, despite being more irregular, is similar to the previous one. The values are significant and grew until the beginning of 2008, the moment when they collapsed. This crash can be linked to a progressive comeback of restrictions on liquidity as a result of the crisis that affected the European and, particularly, Spanish financial sector.

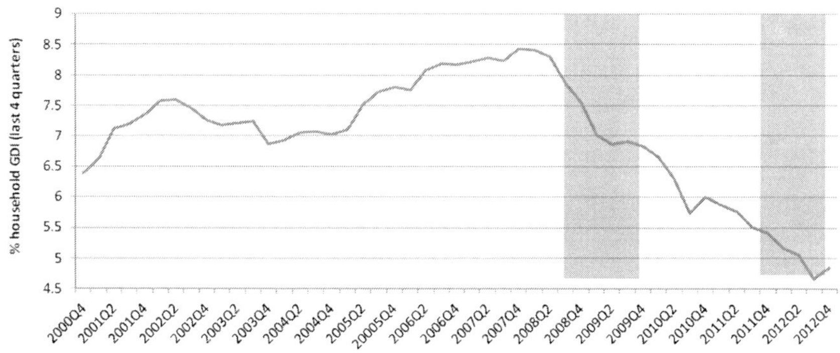

Source: own ellaboration with data from BdE and INE. Shaded areas indicate recessions.

Figure 3. Volume of credit for durable consumption.

The time path of real rates of growth of non-mortgage debt, which we identify with the consumer credit (FINC), presents important similarities with the evolution of consumption (C). The evolution of these variables along with the relative importance of the consumer credit regarding household consumption (FINCF/C) is reflected in Figure 4. This evidence suggests that the tendency of consumer credit growth predicts the evolution of consumption.5

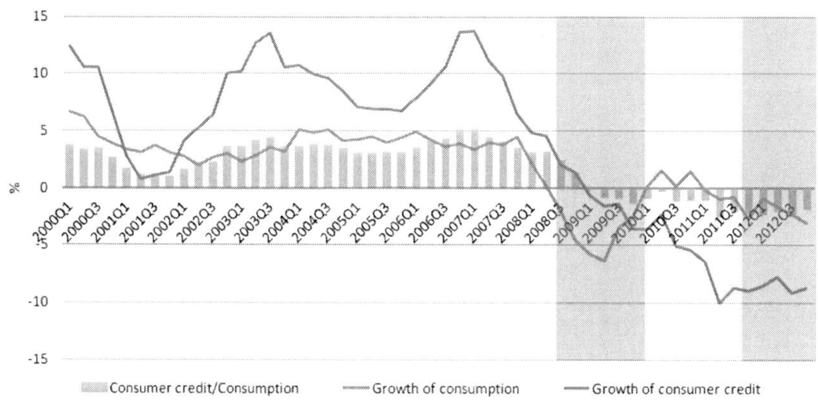

Source: own ellaboration with data from Bank of Spain (BdE). Spanish National Statistics Institute (INE) and Organization for Economic Cooperation and Development (OECD). Growth rates are real and expressed in interannual terms. The ratio consumer credit/consumption is a SMA for the previous 4 quarters. Shaded areas indicate recessions.

Figure 4. Consumption and consumer credit.

3.2. Credit Supply Conditions

As stated in the theoretical argumentation, credit supply conditions play a role in easing the "liquidity constraints" for certain households and, thus, in allowing them to raise their indebtedness.

Credit supply conditions consist of numerous elements, many of which are hard to extract from statistic data. Nevertheless, for illustrative purposes, we chose real interest rates as a representative variable of the credit supply environment.

During the period under study, and mostly because Spain joined the EMU, real interest rates for consumer credit remained at historically low values (Figure 5): credit supply conditions were undoubtedly favorable during the pre-crisis years.

Nevertheless, it should not be ignored that a housing loan is also a way of substituting loans for wages, and that the growth of housing loans was spectacular in Spain between 2000 and 2008 (in terms of disposable income). This kind of consideration could be a first indication that families were actually resorting to borrowing to supplement their current incomes, thus supporting the application of Barba and Pivetti's [4] hypothesis in Spain.

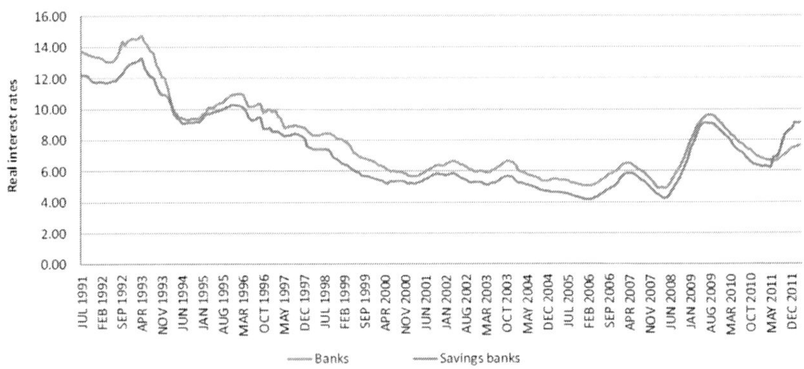

Source: own ellaboration with data from BdE and INE.

Figure 5. Real interest rates for credit consumption.

3.3. Debt by Income Groups

The analysis of the distribution of debt by income groups is relevant, since we would not be talking about a leveling effect of credit if the distribution of the aforementioned indebtedness corresponded basically to higher income individuals. As the Survey of Household Finances (EFF) provides information about households' income, we can break down this analysis by income groups.

First, with regards to liquidity constraints, it is clear from Figure 6 that the lowest income quintile is very liquidity-constrained. For the entire period, over 40% of families in this income quintile who applied for a loan were rejected or given a smaller amount (we also include in this percentage those families who did not apply for a loan because they felt that their application would be rejected). Of course, following the basic logic, liquidity constraints decrease as income increases.

It is also relevant to note the substantial increase in overall liquidity constraints that took place in 2008.

With regard to the percentage of individuals who have outstanding debts, the data in Table 1 are consistent with the earlier analysis for liquidity constraints.

On the one hand, the table shows that households in the first income quintile are liquidity constrained. Throughout the period, less than 20% of these individuals had outstanding debts. On the other hand, the probability that a certain individual is indebted rises with income. This is not surprising: it is a common trend that is reproduced in several countries, as Debelle [7] highlights.

However, the evolution between 2002 and 2008 does reflect a softening of the liquidity constraints (and/or a significant increase in credit demand) for households between the 20th and 60th income percentiles, particularly between the 40th and the 60th. In fact, the probability that a family in this income group is indebted increases by 14.2 percentage points during this period.

If, in addition, we observe the breakdown which is offered in Table 1, it is easy to see that the two types of credit which are more closely related to consumption (personal credit and credit card debts) have significantly grown in middle-income households. In particular, among the central quintile, the proportion of indebted families grows by 5.5 percentage points (consumer credit, 2002–2008) and 8 percentage points (credit card debt between 2005 and 2008). On the other hand, it is also worth mentioning that the proportion of households in the top decile that resorted to consumer credit declined between 2002 and 2008 (−3%).

In summary, these data allow us to appreciate that more and more households used these sources of financing.

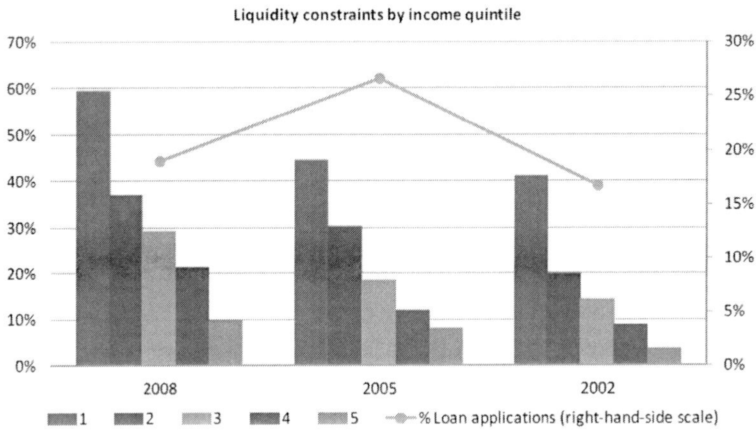

Note: 1 refers to the lowest income quintile. Source: own ellaboration with data from BdE and INE.

Figure 6. Liquidity constraints by income quintile.

Table 1. Percentage of households with outstanding debts.

Year	2002					
Income percentile	0–20	20–40	40–60	60–80	80–90	90–100
Purchase of main residence	7	19	24.6	27.3	28.2	31.6
Purchase of other real estate properties	0.7	2.6	5	9	11.7	18.5
Secured loans	0.6	2.5	4.5	3.6	4.6	6.5
Personal loans	7.3	18.3	24.1	25.5	24	24.6
Other	2	1.9	2	3.2	6.3	4.4
At least one type of debt	15.7	37.6	49.4	54	58.1	64.2
Year	2005					
Income percentile	0–20	20–40	40–60	60–80	80–90	90–100
Purchase of main residence	6.8	21.3	32	35.3	36.8	32.7
Purchase of other real estate properties	0.9	4.3	5.5	12.1	12.9	19.5
Secured loans	1	2.7	5	4.3	4.3	5.3
Personal loans	10	22.4	28	32.1	30.8	30.1
Credit cards	1.5	2	2.5	2.6	1.1	1.5
Other	1.7	2	4.2	2.6	3.6	4.7
At least one type of debt	18.7	42.3	57.5	63	66.5	65.4
Year	2008					
Income percentile	0–20	20–40	40–60	60–80	80–90	90–100
Purchase of main residence	7	20.6	38.4	33.5	33.3	30.1
Purchase of other real estate properties	0.7	3.4	6.6	9.2	15.5	23.3
Secured loans	0.2	1.9	4.3	4.1	3.8	5.7
Personal loans	9	21.9	29.6	29.3	29.8	21.6
Credit cards	2.6	4.3	10.5	11.3	10.4	5.4
Other	1.2	2.1	2.9	3.6	3.3	3.5
At least one type of debt	16.5	42.3	63.6	61.2	68.5	64.7

Source: Banco de España [41] and Banco de España [42].

However, for the purposes of assessing the possible implications that the level and the evolution of household indebtedness may have, the analysis of the percentage of households that have any kind of debt is unavoidably limited. It must be supplemented with information on the magnitude of those debts. Table 2 shows the values of the ratio between household debt and income by income groups.

Table 2. Household debt-to-income ratio.

Year	2002					
Income percentile	0–20	20–40	40–60	60–80	80–90	90–100
Median	104.8	90.6	92.7	67.1	52.5	46
Percentage of households where ratio exceeds 3	34.5	12.4	8.6	3.6	0.9	1.6
Year	**2005**					
Income percentile	0–20	20–40	40–60	60–80	80–90	90–100
Median	137	109.4	113.4	114.3	93.1	59.9
Percentage of households where ratio exceeds 3	42.5	28.3	23.4	15	11.3	4.6
Year	**2008**					
Income percentile	0–20	20–40	40–60	60–80	80–90	90–100
Median	147.7	137	148	95.8	84.6	62
Percentage of households where ratio exceeds 3	34.1	29.7	28.1	21.9	16.3	8.3

Source: Banco de España [41] and Banco de España [42].

According to the data in this table, at first glance we can see that in the Spanish case indebtedness (in terms of household income) is mostly concentrated in the lower income quintiles.6 The highest income decile's indebtedness rates grow from 46% to only 62%. The increase for the lower income quintile is much more remarkable (from 105% to 148%). Other important increases were recorded in the individuals between the 20th and the 60th percentiles. The fact that households of the 60–90 group were the only ones to reduce their debt-to-income ratio between 2005 and 2008 is also noteworthy.

These figures underpin the hypothesis that favorable financial conditions, linked to the increase in credit demand, played a role in the growth of indebtedness in lower income groups. By 2008, the debt-to-income ratio was higher than 130% for all three groups below the 60th percentile.

The evidence that the earlier figures provide can be completed with some relevant information about savings. Indeed, if individuals use debt to increase their revenue beyond their salaries, in order to improve their consumption capacity, it is logical that this behavior will be accompanied by a declining savings rate.

In this sense, the EFF provides data relating to households that spent more than they earned. The percentages, grouped by income quintiles, are shown in Figure 7. As it can be seen from these data, households that spend more than they earn are mostly located in the lower income groups, just the same as with households which borrow for consumption purposes. Actually, consumption credit is the second most common way of compensating the imbalance between spending and income, after "spending savings" and before "family help", as data from the EFF shows.

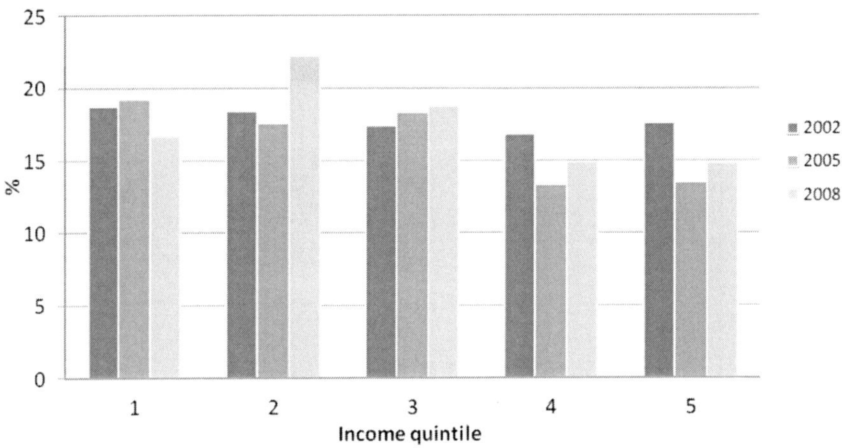

Source: own ellaboration from EFF micro-data.

Figure 7. Households that spend more than they earn (%).

Anyway, the temporal distribution of the EFF and its three-yearly results make it difficult to analyze the evolution of this variable. In 2008, some of the households could be beginning to be affected by the change in the economic cycle. However, it can be observed that dispersion by income quintiles of the percentage of households that "spend more than what they earn" has increased from 2002 to 2008.

3.4. Real Wages and Wage Share

In principle, the evidence collected in the preceding paragraphs is consistent with the idea that resorting to credit generates some kind of an income effect. This effect was especially significant for consumers in lower income groups: because of consumer credit, these consumers could reach higher consumption levels than they had been able to before.

On the other hand, it is relevant to study if a "substitution of loans for wages" is actually taking place. This expression refers to the fact that families get income from debt to complement their salaries, in line with the hypothesis that Foster and Magdof [18] or Barba and Pivetti [4] stated for the U.S.

As Figure 8 shows, during 2000–2007 the participation of workers in the distribution of national income (Compensation of employees/GDP) and the average real wage both recorded almost continuous declines. This is an interesting fact in a period of economic prosperity, but it is along the lines of what happened in the U.S. and has been thoroughly analyzed in the literature. Besides, this downward trend intensified after the first years of the last crisis.

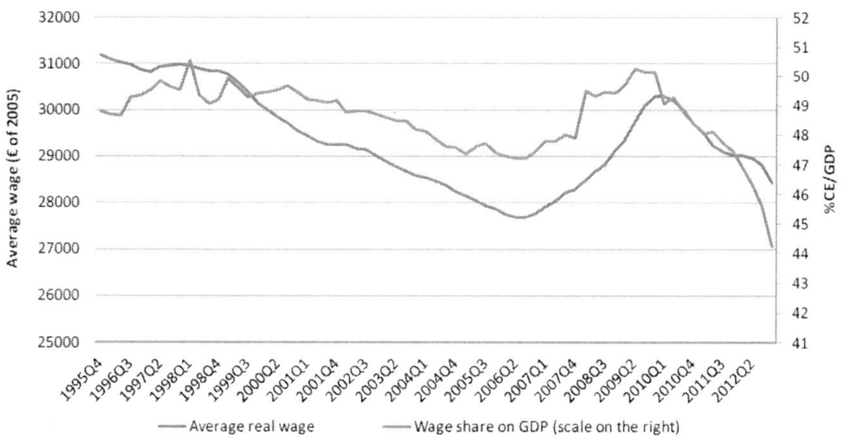

Source: own ellaboration with data from INE and OCDE (deflator: CPI).

Figure 8. Average real wage and wage share in the Spanish gross domestic product (GDP).

According to the data, there is certainly an initial phase of the crisis in which average mean salaries and the wage share clearly increase. The increase in real wages can be explained from a statistical methodology problem. On the other hand, the increase in the GDP wage share is due to the strong fall in corporate profits caused by the crisis itself. However, after this first adjustment period, the downward trend in both cases is unequivocal.7 We can see that ultimately, crises have strong effects on workers: first, the number of employees is affected and, later, the salaries of those who have kept their jobs decline.

In the light of the evolution of these indicators, it seems undeniable that the really high growth rates of consumption, demand and ultimately of output that Spain experienced between 2000 and 2008 could hardly have existed if it were not for the easy access to credit by families, which offered them a way of supplementing their incomes.

Therefore, if we combine these data with the family indebtedness by income segments, the evidence obtained for the Spanish case suggests that the growth of consumption in a period of stagnation in real wages was based on the expansion of credit and in the indebtedness of most of the families with lower income levels.

4. INCOME AND CONSUMPTION INEQUALITY

Since liquidity constraints have been considerably relaxed for an important part of the Spanish households during 2000–2008, and since households have reacted to this situation by increasing their indebtedness (either to level out their consumption throughout their lives or because of any other factor), it should follow that consumption inequalities have grown less or decreased more than income inequalities. If data confirm this, we could be talking about the existence of favorable empirical evidence for a leveling effect of credit.

As a starting point for the analysis of income inequalities in Spain, we use the Gini index data provided by Eurostat (Figure 9). Between 2003 and 2007 (expansion stage), variations are insignificant. On the contrary, from 2008 onwards inequalities grow sharply, a fact which is consistent with the effects that unemployment has on this variable.

From this finding, a possible reading of the fact that inequalities did not decrease during the expansion period is that the new jobs that were created offered low wages. This is consistent with the idea that the recipients of these wages financed increasing levels of consumption with recourse to borrowing.

For the purposes of comparing the evolution of income and consumption inequalities, the information given by the Gini index can be completed with micro-data from the EFF, since this source provides detailed data of both variables (income and consumption) that can be grouped into percentiles of income.

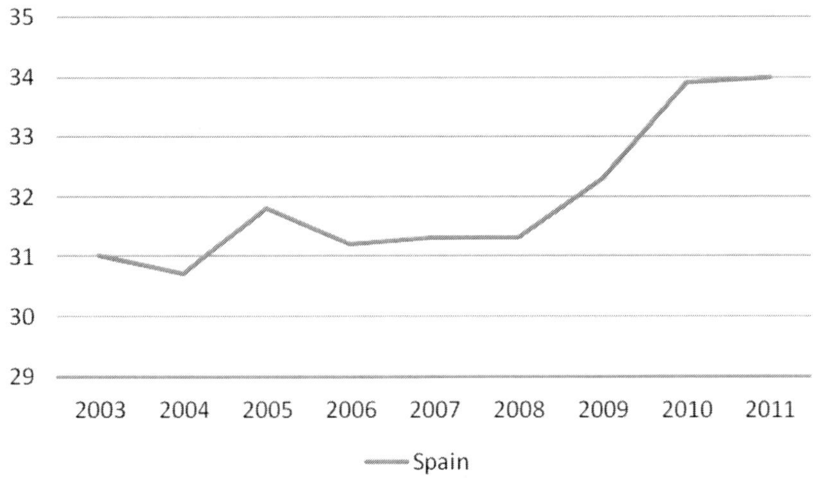

Source: Eurostat.

Figure 9. Gini index for the Spanish economy.

Firstly, we have estimated the values of the S80/S20 indicator in terms of income. This indicator is used according to the Eurostat definition: the ratio of total income received by 20% of the population with the highest income (top quintile) with respect to the total income received by 20% of the population with the lowest income (bottom quintile). Income is understood as adjusted gross income (since the EFF does not provide data about taxes, we cannot calculate disposable income in this case).

This income is what Banco de España understands as "household total income", that is, the sum of work-related income and non-work-related income. When making inequality calculations, it is more appropriate to consider the equivalent gross income, that is, the result of dividing the total household income by the number of its members (weighting as 1 the head of the family, 0.5 the rest of individuals above the age of 14 years and 0.3 the individuals under 14 years living at home). This is the OECD criterion, which is also followed by Eurostat. These weightings exist in order to recognize the economies of scale derived from family life. This way, household income is converted into a "standard income" of "same-size households". The problem inherent in the comparison of very different households is thus solved.

Using the available data from the three waves of the survey, and following the methodology previously described, we have first calculated the income inequality indicator S80/S20 (understanding income as equivalised gross income).

Secondly, we have calculated a S80/S20 indicator for consumption. This indicator is the quotient between the total consumption of the individuals in the highest income quintile and the consumption of the individuals in the lowest income quintile. Logically, for the calculation of consumption, the variable "annual household consumption" has been adjusted in the same way as the annual income.

The results can be seen in Figure 10. The first relevant aspect is that consumption inequality is lower than income inequality. The most basic economic theory points out that marginal propensity to consumption becomes lower as income becomes higher and, therefore, lower income individuals will consume a greater proportion of their income than higher income individuals. On the other hand, the role played by public redistribution in this difference should not be overlooked.8

With respect to the evolution of these indicators, it is clearly visible that consumption inequalities remained almost stable during the period, especially when compared with income inequalities, which increased significantly between 2002 and 2005 and later decreased in 2008's wave.9

However, the indicator S80/S20 could suffer from a problem of lack of generality when measuring the evolution of inequality, given that only the income received by the top and bottom income quintiles, which exhibit particular behaviours derived from their extreme position in the distribution of income, is taken into account for its calculation. For this reason, in order to take into account the totality of the income groups, we also calculated the ratio between the total income of individuals over the median and individuals below the median (S50/S50, adapting Eurostat's terminology to the matter that occupies us).

The values of the S50/S50 ratio, which are logically smaller in value than S80/S20, point in the same direction as the latter and allow us, in general, to extrapolate the aforementioned results.

5. HOUSEHOLD DEBT AND CONSUMPTION INEQUALITY: SOME EMPIRICAL EVIDENCE

In order to conduct a multivariate analysis with the aim of possibly making any causality statement on the influence of household debt on consumption, we estimate a reduced form expression for household consumption. The choice of explanatory variables is based in a wide literature that suggests that a household's consumption in any period depends on a number of factors.10 Particularly, we assume that household consumption depends on current income, wealth, expectations of future income and the ability to smooth consumption in the face of income shocks. Specifically,

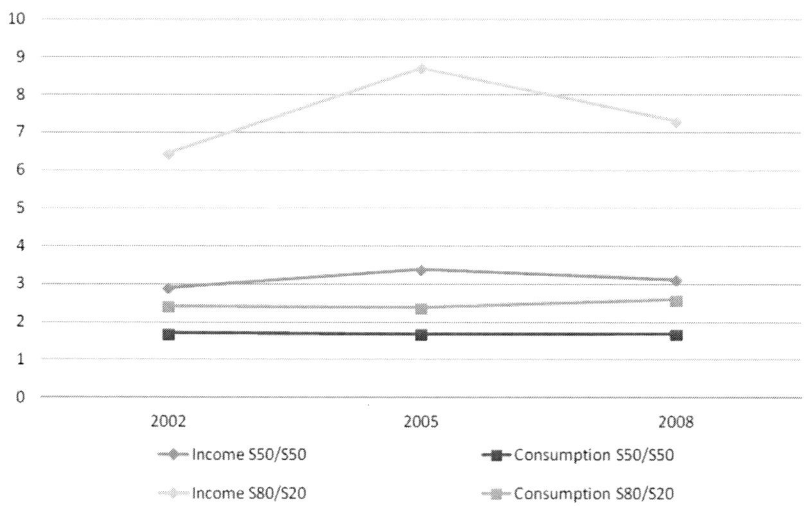

Source: own ellaboration from EFF micro-data.

Figure 10. S80/S20 and S50/S50 income and consumption indicators.

Consum = β_0 + β_1*Labinc* + β_2*Capinc* + β_3*Finwealth* + β_4*Reawealth* + β_5*Incexpect* + β_5 *Debt* + **X** + ε (1)

where, *Consum* is household consumption defined as the sum of durable and non-durable consumption over the 12 months prior to the survey. *Labinc* is the sum of labour income of the household (including proper wages, but also fringe benefits, unemployment benefits or income obtained by unemployed people in other ways). *Capinc* is defined as all other sources of income for the household that are not derived from labor (interest, dividends, *etc.*). It was computed as the difference of total household income and labor income as previously defined. *Finwealth* is the household financial wealth (bank accounts, stocks, bonds, *etc.*). *Realwealth is* the household real wealth (housing, equipment, vehicles, *etc.*). *Incexpect* is a dummy variable that takes value 1 if the members of the household are expecting to have a higher income in the future and 0 otherwise. *Debt* is the sum of the household liabilities (either as a home mortgage or for other reasons). **X** is a vector of socio-demographic variables.

All variables are defined in equivalised terms, following the OECD-modified scale that is used by Eurostat (the first adult is weighted as 1, all other individuals aged 14 or more are weighted as 0.5 and children are weighted 0). For ease of computation, we consider a person to be 14 if he was 14 at the beginning of the year of the survey.

We estimate Equation (1) using an ordinary least squares (OLS) procedure and the results are summarized in Table 3.

For each year we estimate two models: a baseline specification (Model I) in which we include debt such as it was above defined and a modified version of it in which we consider family indebtedness by income segments (Model II).

According to results reported in Table 3, we observe that all the variables proxying household current income and wealth are significant and have the expected sign. Particularly, it is interesting noting that the labor income—mainly wages—influence on households consumption decreases in 2005. Furthermore, in the early 2000s, household debt has a significant and negative effect on consumption. This effect becomes positive from 2005 and its influence seems to increase over time. To some extent, these results for the baseline model are consistent with the hypothesis of a substitution of income for debt in the Spanish economy during the last expansionary phase of the economic cycle.

Table 3. Estimates of the influence of debt on household consumption.

Dependent Variable: Households consumption (*Consum*)						
	2002		2005		2008	
Regressor	**Model I**	**Model II**	**Model I**	**Model II**	**Model I**	**Model II**
Labincome	0.19611*** (0.0192)	0.20035*** (0.019)	0.13117*** (0.009)	0.13358*** (0.009)	0.15198*** (0.0068)	0.15044*** (0.0068)
Capincome	−0.0006 (0.009)	0.00119 (0.009)	0.01833*** (0.005)	0.01971*** (0.006)	0.03828*** (0.004)	0.03759*** (0.0041)
Finwealth	0.02506*** (0.0005)	0.02499*** (0.0005)	0.00684*** (0.0004)	0.0069*** (0.0004)	0.0011*** (0.00039)	0.00114*** (0.00039)
Realwealth	0.01197*** (0.001)	0.01211*** (0.001)	0.00564*** (0.0005)	0.00562*** (0.0005)	0.00029*** (0.00006)	0.00029*** (0.00006)
Incexpect	−803.31‡ (444.19)	−786.71‡ (443.97)	483.08 (303.59)	488.12 (304.36)	−50.667 (284.82)	−19.22 (285.11)
Debt	−0.0313*** (0.005)	−0.0347*** (0.006)	0.00537** (0.003)	0.00318 (0.0028)	0.01473*** (0.0009)	0.01502*** (0.0009)
Debt q2		0.0607** (0.026)		0.0164‡ (0.0088)		−0.00339 (0.007)
Debt q3		0.04701 (0.036)		0.0188 (0.0125)		−0.0114 (0.0084)
Debtq4		0.04693 (0.038)		0.0049 (0.018)		−0.01944‡ (0.012)

Debtq5		0.04208 (0.066)		0.0130 (0.017)		−0.02604 (0.019)
Age	−4.701*** (18.8)	−1.2293*** (19.045)	−78.313 (12.445)	−69.91 (12.57)	66.05*** (11.06)	62.53*** (11.21)
Education	−58.18 (65.87)	−49.903 (66.014)	192.38*** (44.59)	195.52*** (44.72)	401.05*** (37.46)	394.27*** (37.56)
Salaried	−572.22 (556.72)	−563.7 (556.72)	−872.12** (358.63)	−886.20** (358.62)	542.88* (322.64)	557.73* (322.71)
Selfemployed	−1388.7* (742.76)	−1397.24* (742.36)	1434.07*** (485.74)	1475.6*** (486.16)	3185.33*** (451.32)	3176.99*** (451.52)
Unemployed	−1546.83* (900.91)	−1506.54* (903.21)	−1019.36* (618.02)	−1027.77* (618.2)	−132.72 (465.87)	−107.74 (466.41)
Constant	8664.37*** (1248.16)	7929.52*** (1278)	5333.84*** (793.95)	5015.9*** (811.4)	314.35 (732.96)	649.05 (750.69)
Number of observations	2743	2743	3323	3323	3252	3252
F	464.13 (0.0000)	341.40 (0.0000)	187.52 (0.0000)	137.93 (0.0000)	217.4 (0.0000)	159.92 (0.0000)
R^2	0.6515	0.6525	0.3839	0.3849	0.4247	0.4257

*** Significant at 1 % level. ** significant at 5 % level; * significant at 10 % level.

It is worth noting the sharp fall in the value of R^2 in regressions based on 2005 and 2008 samples. It is quite possible that there may be other important factors that influence household consumption besides those captured in the baseline model. Therefore, to draw substantive conclusions about the effect on consumption of changes in household debt, the model specification should be augmented with additional control variables.

In order to obtain some additional evidence of the potential effect on households' consumption of households' indebtedness, we consider an alternative to the baseline specification. With this purpose, in Model II we include five interaction terms: debtq1, debtq2, debtq3, debtq4 and debtq5 that are the result of multiplying debt by a dummy variable that expresses the household income quintile. Indeed, regression in model II examines whether the effect of changing household debt on consumption varies across income quintiles. In other words, by including interactions between debt and income quintiles, we can check whether the regression functions relating debt and household consumption are different for low and high household income levels. As can be seen in Table 3, the difference between the estimated effects across income segments is not statistically significant.

As we have discussed in Section 3, in the Spanish case, indebtedness (in terms of household income) is mostly concentrated in the lower income quintiles. If we combine these data with the results derived from our econometric estimates, we obtain some evidence suggesting that the growth of consumption in Spain over a period of stagnation in real wages was partially based on the expansion of credit and on the indebtedness of most of the families with lower income levels.

6. CONCLUSIONS

The process of growing indebtedness which was experienced by Spanish households in the last expansion phase of the economy and its subsequent correction with the onset of the crisis has had important implications in several fields. This article has mainly focused on the search for clues in a two-way direction: on the one hand, regarding the role played by inequalities in the process of household indebtedness and, on the other hand, regarding the possible distributive consequences of financial conditions.

More specifically, the analysis that has been developed throughout this work allows us to obtain some empirical evidence that, without being completely conclusive, gives some credibility to the hypothesis that consumption inequalities did not respond to variations in income inequalities, but were kept "artificially" low during the period under study. This evidence would be compatible with the existence of a levelling effect of credit during that period, in the sense used by Brown [20] or predicted by the model in Rancière and Kumhof [24].

Our empirical analysis provides some preliminary evidence of the phenomenon of substitution of debt for wages as a determinant of households' consumption in the Spanish economy during the last expansionary phase of the economic cycle. Moreover, the observed differences in the evolution of income and consumption over that period of time can be explained under the hypothesis that within a context of growing income inequality consumption inequality only can be reduced by a general surge in consumption-related borrowing by low and middle-income households. Furthermore, the favorable financial conditions that prevailed during that stage helped to reduce the liquidity constraints that affect mostly lower-income households. This would be a factor that may have contributed to containing the growth of inequalities measured in terms of consumption.

Finally, it should be noted that, if the main hypothesis of this article is true, the end of easy financial conditions since the beginning of the current crisis would make inequalities worse. On the one hand, it would worsen income inequalities because of the already proven effect of unemployment over them, widely covered in literature. On the other hand, it would worsen consumption inequalities because of the main argument developed in this article.

From the point of view of supply, financial conditions are more restrictive nowadays and, from the point of view of demand, many of the factors that drove individuals to finance their consumption with credit have been moderated (for example, it is likely that wealth effect will have changed its sign because of the reduction in the price of real estate assets).

As a result of these factors, families resort less to borrowing in order to finance consumption. Therefore, depending on the extent to which households, especially those of lower income and wealth, are suffering "liquidity constraints" again, they will not be able to distribute their consumption as they would like to. This way, these households would be limited to the use of their current income which, in many cases, has suffered a negative impact. In these circumstances, the future increase in consumption inequalities will be more than likely.

The three available EFF have been conducted between 2002 and 2008, which is too short a time to make any meaningful predictions. In this sense, although the publication of the EFF 2011 will allow a more exhaustive study to be carried out of the changes arising from the new economic situation that Spain faces, it is likely that high household indebtedness will be one of the factors that has aggravated the severity of the effects of the increase of unemployment and the sharp correction in prices of real estate assets on inequalities.

In any case, our findings should be recognized as tentative because we do not yet have any evidence in terms of causality, and the empirical evidence shown could be compatible with other interpretations.

ACKNOWLEDGMENTS

The authors are grateful to the journal editor and three anonymous reviewers for their helpful comments. All remaining errors are our own.

AUTHOR CONTRIBUTIONS

Both authors (G.P.P. and J.M.S.) contributed equally to the work presented in this paper. Particularly, G.P.P. and J.M.S. made substantial contributions to conception and design, acquisition of data and analysis and interpretation of data. Both, G.P.P. and J.M.S. discussed the results and implications and commented on the manuscript at all stages. Finally, G.P.P. and J.M.S. drafted the article and revised it critically for important intellectual content. The order of authors was established following an alphabetical criterion.

CONFLICTS OF INTEREST

The authors declare no conflict of interest.

REFERENCES

1. King, R.G.; Levine, R. Finance and growth: Schumpeter might be right. *Quart. J. Econ.* **1993**, *108*, 717–737.
2. Heathcote, J.; Perri, F.; Violante, G.L. Unequal we stand: An empirical analysis of economic inequality in the United States, 1967–2006. *Rev. Econ. Dyn.* **2010**, *13*, 15–51.
3. Agnello, L.; Sousa, R.M. How do banking crises impact on income inequality? *Appl. Econ. Lett.* **2012**, *19*, 1425–1429.
4. Barba, A.; Pivetti, M. Rising household debt: Its causes and macroeconomic implications—A long-period analysis. *Camb. J. Econ.* **2009**, *33*, 113–137.
5. Rajan, R.G. *Fault Lines—How Hidden Fractures Still Threaten the Global Economy*; Princeton University Press: Princeton, NJ, USA, 2010.
6. Galbraith, J.K. *Inequality and Instability: A Study of the World Economy just before the Great Crisis*; Oxford University Press: New York, NY, USA, 2012.
7. Debelle, G. BIS Working Papers. No 153. Macroeconomic Implications of Rising Household Debt. Available online: http://www.ecri.eu/new/system/files/46+2004_Macroecon_impl_rising_household_debt.pdf (accessed on 15 June 2013).
8. Survey of Household Finances. Available online: http://www.bde.es/bde/en/areas/estadis/Otras_estadistic/Encuesta_Financi/ (accessed on 15 June 2013).
9. Pijoan-Mas, J.; Sánchez-Marcos, V. Spain is different: Falling trends of inequality. *Rev. Econ. Dyn.* **2010**, *13*, 154–178.
10. Farré, L.; Vella, F. Macroeconomic conditions and the distribution of income in Spain. *Labour* **2008**, *22*, 383–410.
11. Bonhomme, S.; Hospido, L. The Cycle of Earnings Inequality: Evidence from Spanish Social Security Data. Available online: http://www.bde.es/f/webbde/SES/Secciones/Publicacio

nes/PublicacionesSeriadas/DocumentosTrabajo/12/Fich/dt1225e.pdf (accessed on 10 July 2013).

12. Ayala, L.; Cantó, O.; Rodríguez, J.G. Poverty and the Business Cycle: The Role of the Intra-Household Distribution of Unemployment. *ECINEQ WP 2011-222*, Available online: http://www.ecineq.org/milano/WP/ECINEQ2011-222.pdf (accessed on 13 August 2013).

13. Addabo, T.; García-Fernández, R.; Llorca-Rodríguez, C.; Maccagnan, A. The Impact of the Crisis on Unemployment and Household Income in Italy and Spain. *ECINEQ WP 2011-235*, Available online: http://www.ecineq.org/milano/WP/ECINEQ2011-235.pdf (accessed on 13 August 2013).

14. Fundación Alternativas 1er Informe sobre la Desigualdad en España. Available online: http://www.falternativas.org/la-fundacion/documentos/libros-e-informes/1er-informe-sobre-la-desigualdad-en-espana-2013 (accessed on 23 September 2013).

15. Friedman, M. *A Theory of the Consumption Function*; Princeton University Press: Princeton, NJ, USA, 1957.

16. Ando, A.; Modigliani, F. The life-cycle hypothesis of saving: Aggregate implications and tests. *Am. Econ. Rev.* **1963**, *103*, 55–84.

17. Modigiliani, F. The life cycle hypothesis of saving, the demand for wealth and the supply of capital. *Soc. Res.* **1966**, *33*, 160–217.

18. Foster, J.B.; Magdoff, H. Working Class Households and the Burden of Debt. Available online: http://monthlyreview.org/2000/05/01/working-class-households-and-the-burden-of-debt/ (accessed on 28 October 2013).

19. Foster, J.B. The Household Debt Bubble. Available online: http://monthlyreview.org/2006/05/01/the-household-debt-bubble/ (accessed on 29 October 2013).

20. Brown, C. Does income distribution matter for effective demand? Evidence from the United States. *Rev. Polit. Econ.* **2004**, *16*, 291–307.

21. Iacoviello, M. Household debt and income inequality, 1963–2003. *J. Money Credit Bank.* **2008**, *40*, 929–965.

22. Barba, A.; Pivetti, M. Changes in income distribution, financial disorder and crisis. In *The Global Economic Crisis: New Perspectives on the Critique of Economic Theory and Policy*;

Brancaccio, E., Fontana, G., Eds.; Routledge: Londres, Argentina, 2011; pp. 81–97.

23. Barba, A.; Pivetti, M. Distribution and accumulation in post-1980 advanced capitalism. *Rev. Keynes. Econ.* **2012**, *1*, 126–142.

24. Kumhof, M.; Rancière, R. Inequality, Leverage and Crises. IMF Working Paper WP/10/268. Available online: https://www.imf.org/external/pubs/ft/wp/2010/wp10268.pdf (accessed on 3 September 2013).

25. Shapiro, M.D. The permanent income hypothesis and the real interest rate: Some evidence from panel data. *Econ. Lett.* **1984**, *14*, 93–100.

26. Campbell, J.Y.; Mankiw, N.G. Consumption, Income and Interest Rates: Reinterpreting the Time Series Evidence. MIT Press. Available online: http://www.nber.org/chapters /c10965.pdf (accessed on 4 November 2013).

27. Bacchetta, P.; Gerlach, S. Consumption and credit constraints: International evidence. *J. Monet. Econ.* **1997**, *40*, 207–238.

28. Boone, L.; Girouard, N.; Wanner, I. Financial Market Liberalisation, Wealth and Consumption. OECD Economics Department Working Papers, No. 308, OECD Publishing. 2001. Available online: http://www.oecd-ilibrary.org/docserver/download/5lgsjhvj80g8.pdf?expires=1405484028&id=id&accname=guest&checksum=51B309767F3E30717E1A3C5FAA8FA1F5 (accessed on 12 September 2013).

29. Brady, R.R. Structural breaks and consumer credit: Is consumption smoothing finally a reality? *J. Macroecon.* **2008**, *30*, 1246–1268.

30. Brady, R.R. Consumer credit, liquidity and the transmission mechanism of monetary policy. *Econ. Inq.* **2010**, *49*, 246–263.

31. Aron, J.; Duca, J.V.; Muellbauer, J.; Murata, K.; Murphy, A. Credit, housing collateral and consumption: Evidence from Japan, the UK and the US. *Rev. Income Wealth* **2011**, *58*, 397–423.

32. Brown, C. Financial engineering, consumer credit, and the stability of effective demand. *J. Post Keynes. Econ.* **2007**, *29*, 429–455.

33. Galbraith, J.K. With Economic Inequality for All. Available online: http://www.njfac.org/gal-ineq.htm (accessed on 30 September 2013).

34. Coibion, O.; Gorodnichenko, Y.; Kueng, L.; Silvia, J. Innocent Bystanders? Monetary Policy and Inequality in the US. Available online: http://www.nber.org/papers/w18170 (accessed on 2 May 2013).

35. Pichette, L. Are Wealth Effects Important for Canada? Available online: http://www.bankofcanada.ca/wp-content/uploads/2010/06/pichettee.pdf (accessed on 23 June 2013).

36. Carroll, C.D.; Otsuka, M.; Slacalek, J. How large are housing and financial wealth effects? A new approach. *J. Money Credit Bank.* **2011**, *43*, 55–79.

37. Case, K.E.; Quigley, J.M.; Shiller, R.J. Comparing wealth effects: The stock market *versus* the housing market. *Adv. Macroecon.* **2005**, *5*, 1–34.

38. Bernanke, B.; Gertler, M. Agency costs, net worth, and business fluctuations. *Am. Econ. Rev.* **1989**, *79*, 14–31.

39. Antzoulatos, A.A. Consumer credit and consumption forecasts. *Int. J. Forecast.* **1996**, *12*, 439–453.

40. Ludvigson, S. Consumption and credit: A model of time-varying liquidity constraints. *Rev. Econ. Stat.* **1999**, *81*, 434–447.

41. Banco De España. Boletín Económico. Encuesta Financiera de las Familias (EFF) 2005: Métodos, Resultados y Cambios entre 2002 y 2005. Available online: http://www.bde.es /f/webbde/SES/estadis/eff/Separata_EFF_2007.pdf (accessed on 23 October 2013).

42. Banco de España. Boletín Económico. Encuesta Financiera de las Familias (EFF) 2008: Métodos, Resultados y Cambios desde 2005. Available online: http://www.bde.es/f /webbde/SES /estadis/eff/eff2008_be1210.pdf (accessed on 23 October 2013).

43. Brzozowski, M.; Gervais, M; Klein, P.; Suzuki, M. Consumption, income and wealth inequality in Canada. *Rev. Econ. Dyn.* **2010**, *13*, 52–75.

44. Browning, M.; Lusardi, A. Household saving: Micro theories and micro facts. *J. Econ. Lit.* **1996**, *34*, 1797–1855.

ENDNOTES

[1]The source of data on which this study is based is the *Encuesta Financiera de las Familias* (Survey of Household Finance) (EFF), a triennial survey developed by the Bank of Spain since 2002 [8]. There are EFF for 2002, 2005 and 2008 [8]. Currently is under development and publication the EFF for the year 2011.

[2]For detailed studies on this topic, see Pijoan-Mas and Sánchez Marcos [9], Farré and Vella [10], Hospido and Bonhomme [11], Ayala, Canto and Rodriguez [12] and Addabo, García-Fernández, Rodríguez-Llorca and Maccagnan [13]. The Informe *sobre la Desigualdad en España* [14], published by *Fundación Alternativas* includes a series of works related to the problems of income distribution and inequality in Spanish society.

[3]More recently, Barba and Pivetti [23] even argue that the trend towards austerity prevailing today in Europe could be understood, in a way, as a continuation of that process of substitution of debt for wages.

[4]As an example can be mentioned Pichette and Tremblay [35], Carroll, Otsuka and Slacalek [36] and Case, Quigley and Shiller [37]. These authors also estimate the wealth effect, trying to discern if the effect associated with financial assets is greater or less than the real assets one.

[5]This observation is in line with the results of authors like Antzoulatos [39] and Ludvigson [40].

[6]Debelle [7] had already pointed out that, usually, higher debt-to-income ratios correspond to lower income groups. He thinks this result is due to the effect of younger families, with not so high incomes, who have just bought a house.

[7]Since the average wage is a statistical mean, it is relevant to know how the variable is distributed. If all wage earners had the same wages, an increase or decrease in employment would have no effect on average wages. However, if the distribution of wages is really dispersed, final effects are very different. In Spain the labor market has a dual structure. On the one hand, we have permanent workers (with higher wages) and temporary workers (with lower wages). At the beginning of a crisis, the first who suffer the effects are temporary workers: they lose their jobs and average wages statistically rise. However, as the crisis goes on, the increase in unemployment lowers nearly all salaries, so average wages decrease again.

[8]Brzozowski, M. *et al.* [43] offer evidence for this for the Canadian case.

[9]It should be noted that the indicators do not exactly match in time. Income data refer to the year before the survey, while consumption data

are associated with the same year in which the survey takes place (specifically, in part to the 12 months before each household answers the questionnaire and in part to multiplying by 12 the average monthly consumption in the moment the survey takes place).

[10]See Browning and Lusardi [44] for an overview about micro-determinants of consumption.

13

CHAPTER

From Consumerism to the Empowerment of Consumers: The Case of Consumer Oriented Movements in France

Sophie Dubuisson-Quellier

Centre de sociologie des organisations (CNRS-Sciences Po), 19 rue Amélie, 75007 Paris, France

ABSTRACT

Political consumerism was developed during the 19th century and expanded at the turn of the century through social movements aimed at empowering civil society in the market. Many of these movements succeeded in building power on the consumption side. Today, we still witness several forms of political consumerism. This contribution explores the possibilities and limits of consumer involvement in sustainable consumption. The main finding of this study of the political organization of consumers is that the market may not be the only arena for changing consumer behavior. Instead, social constraint and political empowerment seem to be rather more efficient.

Keywords: political consumerism; sustainability; consumption

1. INTRODUCTION

Since the World Summit for Sustainable Development, held in Johannesburg in 2002, consumption has been stressed as one of the main issues that developed countries should focus on. States and Non Governmental Organizations have started to mobilize consumers towards a more responsible behavior and have attempted to rely on consumers to achieve more sustainable societies. States and NGOs claim that individual decisions of consumption should be reframed and should focus more on concerns about the decisions' impact on the environment. Consumers are identified as primary agents of environmental change today [1,2], and most sustainable consumption policies are aimed at regulating the consumers' individual choices to orient them towards sustainability [3]. The policies either focus on consumers' waste production or their energy consumption, by providing consumers market incentives or information to make them choose more eco-friendly products. Taxes, educational campaigns, or labelling schemes are the major policy tools of sustainable consumption policies [4].

Most of the relationships between consumption and sustainable development issues have been framed through political consumerism by public actors [2,5,6]. Michele Micheletti proposed a systematic analysis of contemporary political consumerism as a combination of both the public and the private role of consumers, which reconciles the tradition of public virtue in politics with its private virtue. It means that consumers are also citizens, who choose their products in accordance with private preferences and public principles. For Micheletti, political consumerism also provides new modes of expressing involvement in public life through more flexible, network-oriented, and hands-on arenas that allow consumers to combine their daily lives with political concerns. Yet, even though many surveys show that consumers may be highly receptive to ethical or environmental issues, as evidenced in the development of fair trade awareness as an example, evaluations of changes in consumer behavior tend to be misleading.

This framing puts a lot on consumers' shoulders, and in the meantime, ignores some aspects of consumption patterns that cannot be reduced to individual choices. Other scholars working on sustainable consumption issues, have also emphasized the collective aspects of consumption decision; making a plea for a reframing of sustainable consumption to include its social and collective dimensions [4,7,8,9]. Consumption patterns are social practices that cannot be reduced to individual choices [10]. These patterns are deeply rooted in collective norms and provisioning systems [9,10,11]. What could be the relationship between these processes of building norms and political consumerism? Can the consumers' involvement in sustainable development issues contribute to a form of political consumerism that cannot be reduced to individual choices (even though having collective effects), but which could have normative and collective dimensions?

This paper aims to question the relationships between consumption and sustainable development by assessing the consumers' role and involvement as collective, rather than as individual, actors. For this purpose, we need to go back to the history of political consumerism to show that activists, through political consumerism protests, have always contributed to the re-framing of consumption practices and the construction of the consumers' responsibility. Historians have provided several pieces of evidence, which suggest that political consumers have taken several forms. Political consumerism is a longstanding form of collective action. It was developed during the 19th century, with the cooperative movement, and expanded at the turn of the century through various social movements aimed at empowering civil society in the market [12]. Many of these movements succeeded in building power on the consumption side, and were able to achieve certain goals that are not simply related to consumer advocacy [13]. For example, consumers were mobilized by trade unions to circumvent difficulties encountered in strike actions during the 1910s, or to support workers' struggles during the 1950s in the United States [14]. In other situations throughout the 20th century, up until the present day, consumers were called on to support many different causes, from civil rights advocacy, to the defence of social justice, or the protection of the environment. Consumers have thus been built up over time as a political and social force that cannot be ignored.

In political science literature, political consumerism is considered to be a new phenomenon that came from the post-modern critics of society via a network oriented activism. This activism tries to articulate the political concerns involved with everyday life activities [1,2]. It will be shown that political consumerism is as old as market society and that it is deeply rooted in activism that aims at involving consumers in protest activities. These activities are meant to reshape norms, with respect to consumption, in order to include new concerns about civil rights, working conditions, and environmental protection. By putting the analysis of the building of sustainable consumption norms within the larger historical context of political consumerism, one can understand the contribution of social protest in the genesis of new norms. But, as was shown by historians, several types of political consumerism always occur simultaneously: some try to target individual consumers and their purchasing power, others aim to build collective power through protest actions; some are very critical, others accept some kind of institutionalization. These different forms of political consumerism still exist today, and they contribute differently to the genesis of new norms with respect to sustainable consumption. Some types, such as those of fair trade organizations, still target the individual responsibility of consumers. These receive a great deal of media attention, but experience difficulty in stabilizing changes in consumer behaviors. Other types, with less media coverage, such as those of anti-consumption activist groups or of local contract schemes between consumers and producer organizations, gather small numbers of consumers, but are very effective in producing and stabilizing new norms. Both types of political consumerism contribute to the reframing of norms on consumption by including new concerns that aim at achieving sustainability goals.

In the first part of the paper, we will address this issue of the history of political consumerism to show that consumer mobilizations have been organized, both through individual and collective action, in the past to organize consumers' responsibilities toward social problems. The progressive institutionalization of the consumers' movements contributed towards weakening political consumerism, and turned the mobilization of consumers into a defence of consumers' rights and interests.

Today, in both developed and developing countries, we still witness several forms of political consumerism [1]. In the second part of the paper, we present, based on several examples of consumers' mobilizations towards sustainable objectives, some evidence about contemporary forms of political consumerism that aim to enlighten consumers of their responsibilities. Some of this political consumerism emphasizes individual choices and the responsibilities of consumers, while trying to introduce change by modifying the purchasing behaviors of consumers. But there is also, as in other countries, another form of political consumerism that aims at organizing the collective power of consumers. Furthermore, new kinds of appeals to consumer involvement in collective action have emerged within the sustainable development context [5]. Local contracts between producers and groups of consumers organize new forms of governance within local food systems, in which consumers may decide collectively with producers which kinds of modes of production, distribution, and consumption they want to support. In this collective perspective, change does not rely on the responsibilities of individuals, but on the reframing of collective dimensions of consumption. We want to show that the social control coming from the group provides specific incentives for consumers to collectively change their consumption behaviors.

This contribution intends to use the ethnographic interpretation of consumption behaviors [15,16] to explore the possibilities and limits of consumer involvement in sustainable consumption, by analyzing the contemporary conditions of political consumerism. Hence, this issue of political consumerism needs to be assessed through a critical-reflexive approach [17], since this political or resistant behavior of consumers is both shaped by the market (and marketers) and shapes the market; this behavior may be progressively integrated into consumption culture by researchers and marketers [18,19]. Political consumerism, like other consumption patterns stated by Consumer Culture Theory [20], has to be understood as a way for consumers to experience realities. However, political consumerism is more precisely a way of defining consumers' roles and their contributions to the society as a collective project.

In the second part, I will present some elements from the literature of history, which explain the different forms of consumer involvement in the political consumerism of the past. I will then show the main limits encountered by current consumer mobilization. In the third part, I describe the specific characteristics of political consumerism, relative to sustainable development in France, as based on the empirical material from various ethical food movements. In particular, I highlight some attempts to empower consumers in social networks, with respect to how these attempts aimed to trigger change in the consumers' economic and political behavior. The main finding of this study of the political organization of consumers involved in promoting sustainable development is that the market may not be the only arena for changing consumer behavior. On the other hand, social constraint and political empowerment seem to be rather more efficient.

2. FROM A CONSUMER'S POLITICAL POWER TO DISCIPLINED CONSUMERISM

In this part, I describe the historical and institutional conditions for the construction of a consumer identity. Throughout the history of consumer movements in Western countries, we observe, ranging from economic citizenship to an institutionalization of consumer capitalism, the progressive institutionalization of several consumer figures in the political economy. The fragmentation of consumer needs and interests by states, firms, and consumer movements may explain why consumer organizations today are no longer social movements aimed at involving consumers in political action.

2.1. Building Citizens' Rights through Market Action

The market is not only an arena designed to organize peaceful exchanges of products between buyers and sellers; it has also progressively become a place where social groups try—with varying degrees of violence—to express their rights as citizens. To understand political consumerism as collective consumer action, we need to analyze the ways in which solidarity has been built between consumers. Many recent historical studies have provided rich evidence of this. In particular, they show that this solidarity among consumers may have different goals. Two of these goals can be identified as: asking consumers to show collective solidarity with another social group, and building solidarity within a group of consumers in order to defend their rights.

One of the first national boycotts in the United States was organized by the Knights of Labor national trade union at the end of the 19th century, in a specific context where strikes were not considered as effective enough [14]. Boycotts progressively became a means of increasing pressure on the production side, through strong mobilization of consumers on the market side. The American Federation of Labor systematized this idea by publishing a black list of firms that were accused of social dumping. The pressure on firms became so intense that they decided to organize the American Anti-Boycott Association in order to deal with these boycott calls and try to rebuild consumer confidence in the market. In certain circumstances, the attempts to get consumers to show solidarity with workers were, of course, ineffective, especially when workers and unions were demanding very local and specific wage increases. However, trade unions, by empowering consumers, won some legitimacy in building collective action on the market side. One of the main evidences of this power was the table grapefruit boycott organized by César Chàvez during the mid-20th century in the United States. The boycott was launched by the National Farm Workers Association in 1965 to support a strike of Californian farm workers who were demanding access to the labor rights of which they were deprived. The boycott obtained the support of other trade unions, as well as of students in religious groups. Its economic impact was huge, and prices collapsed, forcing farm owners to enter negotiations with the newly-created United Farm Workers Organizing Committee. The final agreement signed in 1970 involved 26 other farm enterprises as well. This boycott showed the capacity of consumers to be involved in strong mobilization for a cause that is not directly their concern. These different examples of consumer-oriented protest, designed by social movement organizations that were not directly concerned with consumption issues, show the contribution of a wide number of social movements toward the framing and re-framing of what the responsibility of consumers should be, with respect to a large number of social issues, including working conditions and rights.

However, on the basis of these examples, we should not see consumers simply as a group that can be mobilized by other social movements whose struggle they support. Consumers also struggle for themselves to defend their rights as citizens and as consumers.

The first examples of consumer mobilization reported by historians were the boycotts and consumer protests during the 18th and the 19th centuries in Great Britain and the United States [21]. Mass boycotts, such as that of British products during the 1760s by American pioneers, contributed to shaping the emerging US nation, as citizens became aware of forming a social group, first of all, as boycotters of British products.

Some of these movements, and especially the free trade movement against slavery, laid the foundations of modern political consumerism by focusing on the political dimension of trade. Consumers became aware of their ability to be members of a social group that could build a new politics of solidarity through the market. As Glickman said, "their understanding of the social consequences of consumption and of the consequent power of long-distance solidarity, while not ends in themselves for these groups, became the means by which modern citizens believed that they could promote social change" [21]. This analysis provides evidence for understanding why different social groups agreed to defend their rights by using market-related protests. For example, during the early 20th century the civil rights movement organized several protests known as the "don't buy where you can't work" and the "spend your money where you can work" campaigns, designed both to build labor rights for African American people and to establish their rights as US citizens. The market became an arena where people could fight for their rights and produce a strong connection between consumption and citizenship.

2.2. The Connection between Consumption and Citizenship

This strong connection between consumption and citizenship has been studied in depth by many historians. In particular, they have shown that it has been jointly produced by states and firms. Frank Trentmann described the shift in consumer politics that may be observed by comparing the social protests in Britain over cheap bread during the early 20th century, and over clean milk after the Second World War [22]. Organized consumers profoundly changed their views about their own action, but also about the policies that should be implemented concerning the production and consumption of these necessities. Whereas in the 1910s, various consumer organizations, such as cooperatives, had a strong radical-liberal perception of consumption, expected the state to provide economic actors with the conditions of free trade, and made the "cheap white loaf" the main icon of this consumer politics. The "pure milk" campaign of the 1940s, on the contrary, demanded strong state involvement in market regulation. Trentmann demonstrates that this shift should be interpreted as a deep transformation of the link between citizenship and consumption. During the free trade campaign, consumers viewed state regulation, and especially protectionism, as an invasion by the state of the domestic (especially the female) sphere. They grounded consumer citizenship in the community self-help system provided by cooperatives, reinforcing civil society as a strong social group, and founding citizenship on autonomy from both firms and the state. These consumer politics evolved towards a more social-democratic approach, as several difficulties arose: privation during the First World War called for a more interventionist food policy, and several official reports on food adulteration and disease required state regulation of the conditions of trade: "For organized consumers, the milk question went to the heart of the need to reform Britain's political economy" [22]. In this new perspective, the state was an essential element of the connection between consumption and citizenship: by protecting consumer's interests, in the name of civil society, it built a new democracy of consumers based on economic citizenship.

Lizabeth Cohen provides a comparable analysis of the US case [13]. As part of the New Deal, the state undertook the responsibility of protecting consumers' interests from workers' and firms' interests, which were already well established, by representing consumers within the administration, and by passing the first significant law regulating consumption. Consumer organizations, such as the famous National Consumers League, believed that it was the state's duty to protect consumers. On the other hand, during and after the Second World War, the state considered as consumers having certain duties, such as accepting restrictions during the war and consuming after the war. These duties became the best way for consumers to express their citizenship, thus completing the construction of a new connection between consumption and citizenship. As described by Lizabeth Cohen, US citizenship was based on the new idea of a Consumer Republic, in which mass consumption was to become the way to increase the country's wealth. Through the market and consumption, a new social contract was built that was based on a specific identity of the consumer. A wide diversity of actors intended to define and protect this identity. These actors, such as consumer unions, the newly created National Associations of Consumers, consumer bureaus within the administration, and of course, marketing departments within firms and universities, organized consumers. The protection of consumers' general interests lay in the hands of each consumer, whose choices had become atomized, autonomous, and a source of both economic growth and citizenship.

The development of the Marshall Plan in Europe contributed to the importation of a new vision for the role of consumption in economic development. Even though the idea of mass consumption would not be used as an element of a democratic ideal before the 1960s in most Western Europe countries, the consumer's role in the reconstruction effort was emphasized by the state both in France and in Great Britain [23].

These different historical studies provide evidence of the social construction of the role of consumers in the political economy. They show, through notions of the economic citizenship of consumers and of a consumer republic, how the state, in agreement with consumer organizations, helps to portray consumers as individuals with specific rights and duties in a democracy. Consumers' social identity stems, above all, from their capacity to choose, purchase, and consume products that have been designed by firms for them. This purchasing creates wealth, while the state and consumer organizations care of the rights of consumers.

2.3. The Atomization of Consumers and the Institutionalization of Consumer Organizations

In these conditions, the role of consumer organizations has evolved profoundly. They may differ from one country to another, but they have all contributed to the atomization of consumers as a group, and to the fragmentation of their need to be protected.

Following the results proposed by Patricia Maclachlan, who compared consumer politics in Great Britain and the United States, and presented an in-depth study of the Japanese case [24], and by Gunar Trumbull, who compared the French and the German cases, three main models of consumer politics can be identified [25].

The United States is characterized by the Consumer Advocates model. The legitimacy of the state to intervene in consumer affairs was settled after Kennedy delivered his famous speech on the four rights of consumers: to be secure, to be informed, to choose, and to express. Observing that the consumer is the only citizen in the economy "without a high-powered lobbyist" [13], the President decided to be that lobbyist, and created the Consumer Advisory Council. In 1973, an independent regulatory agency was asked to establish new protection rights for consumers, and the authority of the Consumer Product Safety Commission, the Federal Trade Commission, and the Food and Drug Administration was extended. These new consumer politics afforded new opportunities for consumer organizations to lobby the government. Within this favourable context, Ralph Nader created his network of audacious consumer advocates, the Raiders. American consumer organizations wielded considerable power through the use of a wide range of tactics (from classical consumer protests, such as boycotts, to expert class action). However, at the same time, the freedom of these organizations was limited because the political administration harnessed the power of these consumer representatives. The segmentation of the consumers' needs by big companies' marketing techniques also limited the leeway of these organizations. The French case is similar to that of the US from the point of view of the state's involvement in consumer protection. This is especially because the French government took its ideas from the American ideology of consumer politics. However, as consumer organizations became stronger during the 1970s, owing mainly to substantial financial support from the state, they also became specific allies of the state with respect to the latter's standardization and information policy. This situation explains why some trade unions and family organizations have developed activities in consumer advocacy in France. This gradual harnessing of the main consumer organizations led to a particular model of consumer protection, which operates through standards and laws. The harnessing also led to a specific and important consumption policy that protected consumers' interests from those of firms, and strongly differentiated the French model from the American one.

In Germany and Great Britain, consumer organizations are less politicized and more inclined to cooperate with both companies and the state. The information model, which characterizes these two countries, stems from strong cooperation between the upstream government and consumer organizations and firms; resulting in regulations that produce fewer constraints for economic actors.

Trumbull uses the term "consumer capitalism" to describe the form of political economy in which consumers' institutionalized interests contribute to defining the terms of public policies and companies' strategies. As observed, this institutionalization depends on the nature of the cooperation between consumer organizations and public authorities, which in turn is connected to the organization of the consumer movement and its relationship with companies. This is why consumers' political models may be so different from one country to the next. But this reality shows that today's consumer's political identity is built at the intersection of business strategies, public policies, and the actions of consumer movements. Part of the representation of consumers' interests has been captured by both the state and by large companies, with the proportion of earlier types of harnessing varying from one country to another. For example, according to Patricia Maclachlan, the Japanese case is an extreme example of the capture process by the state, since some consumer organizations may act as a public policy instrument, while the British case is an example of capture by large companies [24].

For states, companies, and consumer movements, the consumer is portrayed as an individual whose choice must be oriented and equipped with several devices: the market provides consumers with specific needs, while the state and consumer organizations provide them with rights and duties [26]. The three of them contribute to reducing consumer expression within an atomized demand for goods or protection. The consumer movement has evolved into a technical consumer advocacy aimed at defending specific and segmented interests, with regard to specific situations, and for this purpose, uses either the courts [27] or technocratic standardization.

This fine fragmentation of consumer interests with respect to purchasing choices makes the construction of consumers' collective action difficult today. In the second part of this paper, I explore the conditions of a possible involvement of consumers in what could be identified as political action. I will show that most of the attempts to involve consumers in political consumerism target individual responsibility. These attempts provide consumers with labels or market devices to change their individual purchasing behavior. But I would like to stress that there are also some collective experiments, which instead target the collective dimension of consumption.

3. INVOLVING CONSUMERS IN ETHICAL CONSUMPTION IN FRANCE

As in many other countries, consumer organizations in France are strongly institutionalized and are at the core of an impressive consumption policy that makes the French consumer one of the most protected in the world. Yet at the same time, these organizations have to face a major criticism: they are not large grassroots movements, and in a way, one finds it difficult to support the claim that they are representative of consumers. A good example of this difficulty (with respect to the French consumer organizations to claim to act on behalf of consumers) is that these organizations were not identified as the first spokespersons in the development of conditions of sustainable consumption. As in other countries, the idea of the role of the consumer in sustainable development emerged in France at the end of the 1990s, already some time after the Johannesburg Earth Summit, where consumers of Northern countries were blamed by Southern countries for their direct responsibility in the deterioration of the environment. Several NGOs and social movements tried to involve consumers more deeply in what could be a political project on sustainable consumption. They were quickly joined by companies and public authorities. Most of them found it difficult to generate profound changes in consumer behaviors and to establish the conditions of what could be called a political awareness of the consumers' responsibility. Some of them succeeded, as we will see in the last part of this section, but do not use market tactics as much as others groups do. We can thus conclude that the market may not be an arena for consumers' political involvement.

The purpose here is not to assess the different instruments that are used by public authorities to influence consumer behaviors, but to present the role of NGOs and social movement activities in the reshaping of consumption practices.

3.1. Patterns of Political Consumerism in France

French consumers, who wish to change their consumption patterns, in order to be more environmentally friendly, or to show their concern for social justice, have access to a wide range of goods, services, and recommendations. These include advice proposed by public authorities, such as the National Agency for the Environment (ADEME), regarding the use of water, household appliances, energy for the home, transportation in urban areas, or product label identification. This advice is available for consumers in brochures, or on websites, designed by the government, or may be disseminated through the media (e.g., commercials or radio).

Other propositions come from NGOs or companies, which offer labelled products, such as "green" products, organic food, and fair trade products. In France, several green labels exist for products; some have been introduced by the public authorities, while others are private initiatives. "*NF-environnement*" is the French official label for environmentally friendly products. Nineteen types of products may be sold using this label, which is the property of the French Agency for Standardization (AFNOR). This agency is also in charge of the certification for the label. The European eco-label created in 1992 is also used, but less often than in Belgium or Germany. A label for organic foods, the AB Label

(*Agriculture Biologique*), was created in 1985 by the French Ministry of Agriculture, to identify products that comply with the French requirements on organic food production. In France, only 1.8% of the surface area farmed produced organic food in 1995, with a 5% increase since 2004 (Fédération Nationale d'Agriculture Biologique). Finally, other labels from abroad may also be used to sell products. The Forest Stewardship Council (FSC) label is controlled by three types of actors (NGOs working on environmental issues, NGOs working on social justice issues, and companies exploiting or distributing wood) and may be used to sell sustainable wood products in home improvement stores. The Marine Stewardship Council (MSC) label is proposed by the NGO, WWF, and Unilever to certify products that comply with requirements concerning sustainability. In France, about 12 frozen fish products use this private label. The private Max Havelaar trademark is given by the Fairtrade Labelling Organizations (FLO) to products that comply with fair trade requirements. These are the main labels used in France, most of which are available both in supermarkets and in specialized shops (organic food shops and world shops).

Figures produced by the French Agency for the Environment (ADEME) show that total sales in France of eco-labelled products grew from 50 million euros in 1998 to 800 million euros in 2005. But the market share of eco-labelled products may vary widely from one market segment to another. For example, eco-labelled products account for 25% of the market share for garbage bags, but no more than a 1 to 3% market share in most other segments. No figure is available for the market share of organic food products, but sales have been evaluated by the French Agency for organic food at 1.6 billion euros in 2005, with a growth rate of almost 10% per annum. Finally, the fair trade figures supplied by the Max Havelaar Company also show a considerable increase, but remain low: 120 million euros in 2005.

These mixed results show that a substantial increase, in the consumption of what remains a very small share of the market, has to be related to French consumers' sensitivity to political consumerism. A recent survey by the French Center for Research on Living Conditions (CREDOC) [28] on political consumerism shows a gap between what French consumers say about their political involvement through consumption and what they actually do when they shop. In 2006, 44% of French consumers said they cared about companies' ethical involvement while choosing their products, which is 6 points more than in the 2002 survey, and 61% said they would agree to pay 5% more for a product produced by such a company, which is 9 points more than five years earlier. They also said they would be able to boycott products from companies with unethical practices. When asked about their purchases over the past six months,

21% said they had purchased a product for ethical reasons and 30% said they may have done so, but were not absolutely sure. This political choice was more important for high-income consumers (72%) than for low-income consumers (45%). Such a survey has some limits. Most importantly, it is based on statements rather than acts, and therefore cannot describe real consumption patterns regarding political consumerism in France. But it does, nevertheless, show that ethical framing of consumption may be used as common knowledge between consumers, and perhaps as a social norm: consumers claim, (and the more they earn, the more they do so), that they may shop for the environment or for social justice. The high score of answers shows that they have integrated the fact that it is socially and politically correct to show such political involvement in their purchase choices.

These data portray the French situation as a case in which consumers are aware of the power of their purse, but use it sparingly, especially when they are economically constrained. In the next section, I provide a theoretical explanation of the limits of such political involvement of consumers in the marketplace.

3.2. The Limits of Market Action to Build Consumers' Political Awareness of Sustainable Development

It seems important to place the development of a supply of ethical products (fair trade products, organic food, eco-labelled products) within the context of mass consumption.

As described by Lizabeth Cohen [13], the development of a mass consumption economy was a fertile context for the articulation between general interest in growth in the post-war period, and individual interest in spending for consumption. The state, companies, and consumer movements all wanted the best conditions for consumers to spend their money [29], and they all worked at designing and implementing what was to become known as market segmentation. This was a term introduced by Wendell Smith and Pierre Martineau in the late 1950s. With trademarks and distribution chains [30], market segmentation was one of the pillars in the making of mass markets. One of the main assumptions of the principles of market segmentation is that these groups of consumers, or consumption patterns, already exist in society; these groups are kinds of sub-cultures that regularly emerge to bring together individuals and differentiate them from other groups. Even the development of what historians called the consumer society has been described as the social construction of a sub-culture in the 19th century, based on Romanticism, which made consumption a major occupation

[31]. The market appears then as a suitable arena for individuals to express their identities through their consumption choices. Even market specialists acknowledge that markets produce the fragmentation of consumers into isolated groups [32]. From this perspective, each critique of mass consumption society can be reinterpreted as the development of a new sub-culture, which the market ends up supplying. Examples include the hippie or the beat generation cultures. Capitalism is founded on an immense capacity to integrate its own critique [33]. This mechanism has been assessed in depth in consumer studies, especially by authors who have proposed a theory of post-modern consumers based on their huge capacity for reflexivity in their consumption behavior [34,35,36,37].

In France, the first alternative supply proposed to consumers to make them responsible for environmental protection, or for the development of social justice, was proposed by groups formed to challenge some of the conventional market rules. In the 1970s, some fair trade products were sold in specialized shops by *Artisans du Monde*, an NGO, which adopted the new ideology of development based on "trade not aid". The *Biocoop* network, a consumer cooperative, was also developed in the 1970s to organize the retail distribution of newly available organic food production. Most of these groups of producers, importers, sellers, and consumers had the feeling of belonging to a politically involved social group characterized by concerns on environmental or social justice issues.

For many food marketing departments or retailing companies, these positions sounded like a new sub-culture, perfectly congruent with the post-modern consumer concept, and could easily be incorporated into new market offerings. Most supermarkets had a variety of organic products on their shelves by the end of the 1980s, and were selling different fair trade products under the Max Havelaar trademark by the end of the 1990s. The point in this paper is not to establish whether fair trade and organic food are a sub-culture or not, but to show that large companies in food processing and retailing have dealt with them as though they were fruitful critiques that should be incorporated as new market segments. In France today, fair trade products and organic food are still available in specialized stores (*Biocoop* or *Artisans du Monde* shops for example), but are also largely available in supermarkets.

In a former contribution, we showed that consumers learn to choose their products in supermarkets by relying on what we called a "delegation process" [38]. This idea emphasizes the role of certain technical devices to inform and guide consumers, such as trademarks, logos, labels, or certification. As consumers are not able to check the supply chain, they simply rely on some "delegates," which they decide to trust. From this perspective, eco-labels, fair trade, and organic food labels are just some extra "delegates" in the supermarket, which consumers may or may not decide to follow or to trust. In the marketplace, the idea of sustainable, ethical, or political consumption essentially appears as a new market proposition intended for the specific market segments of consumers who are willing to show their responsibility by shopping in a certain way.

However, this does not mean that this consumption is excluded from what is called political consumerism. In other words, the political dimension of consumption does not disappear simply because most ethical consumption is produced by large companies. We agree with the analysis proposed by Michele Micheletti, who has defined such consumption as an individualized collective action [2]. Even when they are expressed in the marketplace and driven by business strategy, consumer choices are politicized. Micheletti shows that in a context where involvement becomes more flexible and network oriented, individuals try to combine their daily life with political causes. Consumption provides a good opportunity for such a combination, since it is driven both by self-interest, like every other purchase choice, and by the general welfare, for the ethical message it contains. The collective dimension of what remains an individual choice depends not only on this post-modern reflexivity theorized by Beck, but also on the aggregating effect of every individual purchase. These two causal factors are summed up in the concept of the ecological and ethical footprint of daily private lives. Additionally, the collective dimension depends on the amount of knowledge that must be translated with respect to the environmental consequences of consumption [6,39]. Many social movements and NGOs promoting ethical consumption, such as Max Havelaar for fair trade, and Biocoop for organic food, make the following type of assumption: consumers' political power will derive from the aggregate effects of their individual purchases, which will help more small producers in the South or support more small organic farmers in the North. Max Havelaar advertisements tend to show this aggregate effect and to use this argument to defend the firm's strategy in contracting with large retailing companies.

Hence, consumption in the marketplace may definitely be a political act for both those who promote it by selling products (such as NGOs, cooperatives, or alternative producers and retailers, or even companies) and those who purchase these products. Why do market shares of ethical products fail to show the level of awareness and involvement in political consumerism described by the survey data? Several theoretical reasons may be proposed. The first is that, as shown by the surveys, this awareness concerns mostly high-income consumers, and economic constraints play a major role in the segmentation between convinced consumers and those reluctant to shop for ethics. Many people may therefore answer positively because they have accepted the necessity of political consumerism as a social norm, but actually think they cannot afford it. However, there is a second reason. The activity of grocery shopping is strongly informed by a wide variety of prescriptions and devices, such as plans, dispositions, and constraints from the consumer's side; trademarks, labels, and packaging from the product side; and prescriptions, commercials, disposals, and sales from the market environment inside and outside the supermarket [40]. This wide variety of devices, combined with that of the supply, contributes to making purchase choices highly erratic and unstable. Prescriptions from the government, fair trade, or organic food labels participate in this diversity of devices, thus contributing to framing and unframing consumers' choices. Purchase choices are always a trade-off, not only between products, but also between devices that are able to inform the choice. Like other purchasing choices, consumption of ethical products in a mass consumption market cannot be anything but unstable.

Earlier I presented two avenues for political consumerism that are proposed to consumers in France: first, through the government's prescriptions and guidelines for changing consumption patterns regarding transportation and the use of energy or water, in home improvement or ordinary consumption; second, through the ethical products supplied by NGOs, cooperatives, alternative producers, and retailers. In the next part, I present a third avenue for consumers' political involvement.

3.3. Consumers' Involvement in Social Movements

Today, several groups seek to involve consumers in collective actions aimed at improving their awareness on ethical or environmental issues [38]. I will present two of them. The first is a social movement organization focused on political consumerism, derived from the anti-globalization movement ATTAC (*Association pour la taxation des transactions financières et pour l'action citoyenne*—Association for the promotion of financial transaction taxation and of citizen activism) and created at the end of the 1990s. This organization, consisting of about a hundred members, only a few of whom are real activists, provides a large range of information to its members on the social, economic, and environmental effects of consumption. The movement is based on a very precise ideology of consumers' responsibility, which fills the gap between two points of view: one in which this responsibility is overemphasized or exaggerated by governments that consider most of the damage to the environment or social justice as a result of consumers' foolish and selfish behavior; and, the second, a view in which this responsibility is minimized, for example, by some fair trade operators who consider that once consumers have bought some fair trade products, they have done their duty. The movement thus positions its prescriptions between what it calls an over- and an under-responsibility of consumers. It attempts to show accurate evidence of the effects of consumers' choices by describing the functioning of mass markets and capitalism, as it is usually portrayed in the anti-globalization arguments. Most of the members and activists of the group are also involved in ecological, anti-advertising, or downsizing movements. The group belongs to international networks that campaign against the effects of capitalism on the environment and social justice (such as Adbusters, Public Citizens, anti-GMO movements) [41]. Its members promote fair trade products and organic foods that are not sold in supermarkets, but in alternative retailing networks. The groups' main opponents are not only large retailing or food processing companies, but also the government, especially when the group considers the public regulations insufficient with respect to the environmental or social justice effects of consumption and production. But as shown by [37], who studied similar groups in the United States, ordinary consumers are also targets of this social movement, especially when the movement denounces consumers' foolish consumption behavior.

This situation tends to establish members' and activists' involvement on the basis of the feeling of adherence to a social group of expert consumers who share knowledge on the capitalist and mass consumption system, and provide one another with accurate advice for their purchase choices. In a sense, these people feel different from other consumers, not only on both moral and ethical grounds, but also with respect to knowledge and awareness. These exchanges of expertise and experience between the different members of the group build an important social constraint, which provides members strong incentive to change their individual behaviors. Most of the organizations' leaders were activists and felt very concerned about sustainable issues. They had already changed their consumption behavior. For them, there is no use of big retailing or chain stores and no use of cars. Additionally, they only consume local organic food and seasonal fruits and vegetables, and only utilize fair trade products. They share services or domestic appliances, reduce their consumption and waste, and find some solutions to reduce their energy consumption. But most of the other members were just aware about some environmental issues and their emergency. Once one entered the organization, they learnt a lot from other members experiences, adopted some solutions (such as the collective buying schemes developed by the group to source local organic products), and some of them were also eager to provide the group with new solutions (such as finding some technical solution to insulate windows to decrease energy consumption), to share they own experiments (with washable diapers, organic home-made washing powder), and to involve themselves in collective campaigns (against GM food, against ionized food) or actions (against advertising). Indeed, the group provides different resources to each individual consumer: practical solutions for consumption, information and expertise on environmental issues, and collective support to share services and assistance. But, the group also provides consumers with new norms on consumption that may be shared, and which can also help to legitimate each individual choice. Indeed, some of the members explain that their new choices about consumption may put them aside from their former groups of friends or relatives, who may think they are becoming too requiring or too critical. For these members, the activist organization provides them with a more similar social context with consumers that share not only their ideas, but also their consumption practices.

But, in the meantime, the group may also be very demanding of each individual, asking him or her to comply with specific norms of consumption. Even though no member has been fired by the group for his or her consumption practices, a member may tease some member that does not adopt the norms, or more often, some members adopt a very drastic compliance with these new norms such that other members may feel social pressure.

This position may sometimes trigger a kind of radicalization within the group, on certain subjects. In such cases, the members in favour of a radical shift in consumer behavior (stop shopping in supermarkets, stop buying unnecessary goods, support alternative farming and production, ride instead of driving) clash with those who prefer a gradual approach. This radicalization may also explain the high turnover in membership, as some members find that the group may be too elitist or demanding on consumers. Another reason for the high turnover stems from the fact that changing practices of consumption may offer few rewards for involvement. As explained earlier, consumer organizations usually wish to collectively defend consumers' individual interests and rights. They are more of an advocacy technocracy than real social movements where activists can derive rewards from their involvement owing to its general interest. The third explanation for the turnover is related to the difficulty of mobilizing through involvement. This involvement often cannot lead to a collective and visible action. Even if all the activists in the movement change their daily consumption habits, this involvement remains thankless and invisible. For example, when many members called for more collective action, the group responded by joining national and international protest campaigns, such as the "Buying nothing day", "the campaign against the abuse of environmental arguments in advertising", the "campaign against the ionization of food" launched by Food and Water Watch, or the campaign against GMOs. But most of all, the group promotes consumers' involvement in networks of local production and consumption of food, especially those built on the model of the US "Community Supported Agriculture" (CSA), the second social movement on political consumerism that we will examine here.

The AMAP system (*Association pour le Maintien d'une Agriculture Paysanne*) was developed in Southeastern France at the end of the 1990s, in collaboration with the anti-globalization movement, ATTAC, and the small farmers' union, *Confédération Paysanne*. The system, inspired by the American CSA and the Japanese *Tekei*, is based on a contract between a small farmer and several consumers, who agree to pay six months in advance for a weekly basket of fruit and vegetables [42]. Today, there are about 200 of these groups of consumers in France. They may also contract with several farmers for the supply, or a wider variety of products, such as bread, milk, eggs, meat, or cheese. Consumers, as members of these groups, are involved in a direct relationship with the farmer: they decide collectively on the biological variety that will be grown, they help the farmer, and they visit the farm two or three times a year. The main aim of the AMAP system is to support small-scale farming activities around cities (green belts). Most of the farmers produce organic food products, but they also may choose, in agreement with their consumers, not to comply with the requirements of certification. As described earlier, this movement allows for the diffusion, within consumer groups, of a learning process that progressively makes most of them relatively knowledgeable on ethical consumption. It also emphasizes the awareness, responsibility, and possibly, the morality of AMAP consumers, compared to that of ordinary consumers. Through information and advice, consumers learn from one another where and how to find products that comply with the ethics of sustainable development, how to improve their home or their use of energy and water, how to collectively organize for transportation or for care services, and so on. As in the social movement described above, the AMAP groups have a high turnover: about 30% of the consumers may exit the system each year, but because of long waiting lists, new consumers enter the group immediately. The two also have in common the fact that they connect this strong involvement of consumers in ethical everyday consumption with their empowerment in local politics. The first group promotes, for example, the diverse involvement of citizen consumers in local decisions, such as the provision of school meals by local farmers instead of large catering companies, the negotiation with public authorities for the allocation of land to small-scale farming instead of real estate development, or the establishment of a farmers' market in the city. The AMAP system provides a useful framework for this empowerment of consumers through learning processes, as well as through the connection between some of the members and other social movement networks (e.g., anti-GMO movement, ecological movement, anti-globalization movement) or other social groups (e.g., parents groups, citizen groups, sports associations).

This political consumerism is then strongly connected, not only with market protest, through boycotts and buycotts, but also with social constraints within consumers' groups and with the political empowerment of citizen consumers in what could be called a food citizenship. As noted above, this political consumerism seems to be highly erratic, but one of its particularities is its connection to more conventional forms of collective and political action: from campaigning and protesting, to lobbying, including voting. Another particularity of this political consumerism is its congruence with the collective dimension of consumption that has been stressed by the theoretical framework on consumption practices [40,43]. This perspective highlights what in consumption choices relates to collective and historical contexts. Indeed, individual practices are deeply rooted in socio-technical systems that are path dependent, and which strongly constrain individuals' choices, as Shove showed for the case of the use of air-conditioning, but also for laundering practices [11]. But these practices are also governed by collective norms that may legitimate individual choices and stabilize these choices [9]. The collective experiment of political consumerism provides interesting initiatives to assess the way change in consumption behavior may come. Changes comes neither from information nor from market incentives, as is usually the case with political consumerism through boycotts and boycott, or though consumer education. Instead, changes come from the production of social norms and constraints within groups.

4. CONCLUSIONS

In this contribution, I have stressed, based on the French case, the specific conditions of contemporary political consumerism. As in many other countries where consumer movements have been captured in the institutionalization of their representations, these movements strongly contribute to extending the functioning of a mass consumption system by organizing an expert and efficient advocacy of consumers' rights. The expression of consumers' political involvement remains possible, in response to various institutional prescriptions and advice or market propositions by NGOs, cooperatives or retailing companies. Through their individual purchases, consumers may show their concern for general-interest issues, such as environmental protection or social justice. These individual choices will aggregate and then have a collective effect by reflecting consumers' awareness of the importance of these issues. However, some studies show that despite the high level of awareness of French consumers, their consumption habits remain misleading [44,45]. I explain this paradoxical situation by demonstrating that markets do not provide a sufficiently stable environment to generate deep and lasting shifts in consumers' behaviors. I propose to focus instead on another type of consumer involvement, that of social movements, which emphasizes consumers' direct responsibility through their buying choices. These movements, such as a group concerned with political consumerism and the system of local production and consumption of food, provide consumers with alternatives for their purchases, through a contract or a list of alternative shops and suppliers, as well as through collective actions, such as protests in national and international campaigns, or involvement in local politics. Even with a high turnover of their membership, these movements produce a stable shift in the consumption behavior of their members, based on strong learning processes about consumption patterns and a broad view of consumers' political responsibility.

This case shows how contemporary forms of political consumerism borrow from former ones. The idea of responsibility in the earlier consumer movements was based on the idea of solidarity between several actors, such as between workers and consumers, or between consumers themselves. In the movements that we explored, solidarity between consumers and farmers, producers, or workers from the South, or between consumers themselves, is the core ideology. In the earliest consumer movements, consumers were fighting for their rights, not only as consumers, but also as potential workers or citizens. In contemporary consumer movements, consumers fight for the rights of several other constituencies, such as future generations, biodiversity, or citizens from the South who do not have the possibility to express themselves. Even the link between citizenship and consumption is strongly reactivated, since most of the prescriptions from both the government and social movements use a rhetoric based on the idea of a disciplined consumer, who must behave individually for the good of the community as a whole. Finally, early and contemporary political consumer movements have in common their combination of a wide variety of tactics, from market tactics such as boycotts and buycotts, to protest and collective action, and also political empowerment. In the specific case of a sustainable consumption paradigm, the French case shows the limits of market tactics in triggering shifts of consumption patterns, and the relative efficiency of consumers' empowerment in political action. The question of whether the market should remain the only and best way to change consumption patterns is worth considering.

The theoretical framework that sees consumption as social practices is provided by several scholars in sociology [7,8,9,10,11]. The framework emphasizes the role of social norms in the shaping of consumption practices. This analytical perspective is of particular interest in assessing the effect of different political consumerism tactics. We showed in this contribution that political consumerism is not a new phenomenon and has always shaped and reshaped consumption norms by imposing consideration of new concerns related to consumption (e.g., civic rights, working conditions, fairness of trade, the environment, biodiversity...). Activists have deeply contributed to this reshaping of consumption norms, as have firms and states. Regarding sustainable development issues, activists from today, in France, and in other countries, are using two forms of political consumerism. The most common relies on individual responsibility, providing consumers with market incentives to change their purchasing choices. Its effects seem to be limited and consumers may not change very radically their consumption behavior through market incentives. Another solution is implemented by social movement organizations that organize groups of consumers and push them to find not only find collective solutions and involvement in protesting, but also in consumption practices. These groups may provide an interesting case to follow in terms of the emergence, sharing, and stabilization of new norms, with respect to consumption practices, and also provide insight into the conditions of implementing sustainable consumption practices.

ACKNOWLEDGEMENTS

This article has benefited from research funded by the French *Agence Nationale de la Recherche* (ANR) and from ongoing collaborative research. The views presented here are the responsibility of the author alone.

REFERENCES

1. *Politics, Products and Markets. Exploring Political Consumerism Past and Present*; Micheletti, M.; Follesdal, A.; Stolle, D. (Eds.) Transactions Publishers: New Brunswick, NY, USA, 2003.
2. Micheletti, M. *Political Virtue and Shopping. dividuals, Consumerism, and Collective Action*; Palgrave: New York, NY, USA, 2003.
3. Cohen, M. Sustainable consumption in national context: An introduction to the special issue. *Sustain. Sci. Pract. Policy* **2005**, *1*, 22–28.
4. Vand den Burg, S.; Mol, A.; Spaargaren, G. Consumer-oriented monitoring and environmental reform. *Environ. Plan. A* **2003**, *21*, 371–388.
5. *Exploring Sustainable Consumption: Environmental Policy and the Social Sciences*; Cohen, M.; Murphy, J. (Eds.) Pergamon: Oxford, UK, 2001.
6. Boström, M.; Klintman, M. *Eco-standards, Product Labeling and Green Consumerism*; Macmillan Publishers: Hampshire, UK, 2008.
7. *The Earthscan Reader in Sustainable Consumption*; Jackson, T. (Ed.) Earthscan: London, UK, 2006.
8. Mol, A.P.J.; Spaargaren, G.; Sonnenfeld, D.A. Ecological modernisation: Three decades of policy, practice and theoretical reflection. In *The Ecological Modernisation Reader. Environmental Reform in Theory and Practice*; Mol, A.P.J., Sonnenfeld, D.A., Spaargaren, G., Eds.; Routledge: London, UK, 2009.
9. Spaargaren, G.; Mol, A.P.J. Greening Global Consumption. Politics and Authority. *Global Environ. Change* **2008**, *18*, 350–359.
10. Warde, A. Consumption and theories of practice. *J. Consum. Culture* **2005**, *5*, 131–153.
11. Shove, E. *Comfort, Cleanliness, and Convenience: The Social Organization of Normality*; Berg: New York, NY, USA, 2003.
12. Bevir, M.; Trentmann, F. *Markets in Historical Contexts: Ideas and Politics in the Modern World*; Cambridge University Press: Cambridge, UK, 2004.
13. Cohen, L. *A Consumers' Republic: The Politics of Mass Consumption in Post-war America*; Vintage Books: New York, NY, USA, 2004.

14. Friedman, M. *Consumer Boycotts: Effecting Change through the Marketplace and the Media*; Routledge: New York, NY, USA, 1999.

15. Arnould, E.J. Towards a Broadened Theory of Preference Formation and the Diffusion of Innovations. Cases from Zinder Province, Niger Republic. *J. Consum. Res.* **1989**, *16*, 239–267.

16. Belk, R.W.; Ger, G.; Askegaard, S. The Fire of Desire: A Multisited Inquiriy into Consumer Passion. *J. Consum. Res.* **2003**, *30*, 326–351.

17. Thompson, C.J. A Re-Inquiry on Re-Inquiries: A Post-modern Proposal for a Critical-Reflexive Approach. *J. Consum. Res.* **2002**, *29*, 142–145.

18. Thompson, C.J.; Arsel, Z. The Starbucks Brandscape and Consumers' (Anticoporate) Experiences of Glocalization. *J. Consum. Res.* **2004**, *31*, 631–642.

19. Thompson, C.J.; Coskuner-Balli, G. Countervailing Market Responses to Corporate Co-optation and the Ideological Recruitment of Consumption Communities. *J. Consum. Res.* **2005**, *34*, 135–152.

20. Arnould, E.J.; Thompson, C.J. Consumer Culture Theory (CCT): Twenty Years of Research. *J. Consum. Res.* **2005**, *31*, 868–883.

21. Glickman, L. *Buying Power. A History of Consumer Activism in America*; The University of Chicago Press: Chicago, IL, USA, 2009.

22. Trentmann, F. Bread, Milk and Democracy: Consumption and Citizenship in Twentieth Century Britain. In *The Politics of Consumption. Material Culture and Citizenship in Europe and America*; Daunton, M., Hilton, M., Eds.; Berg: Oxford, UK, 2001; pp. 129–163.

23. Kroen, S. A political history of the consumer. *Hist. J.* **2004**, *47*, 1–28.

24. Maclachlan, P. *Consumer Politics in Postwar Japan*; Columbia University Press: New York, NY, USA, 2004.

25. Trumbull, G. *Consumer Capitalism. Politics, Product Markets and Firm Strategy in France and Germany*; Cornell University Press: Ithaca, NY, USA, 2006.

26. *The Politics of Consumption: Material Culture and Citizenship in Europe and America*; Daunton, M.; Hilton, M. (Eds.) Berg: Oxford, UK, 2001.

27. Rao, H. Caveat Emptor: The Construction of Nonprofit Consumer Watchdog Organizations. *Amer. J. Sociol.* **1998**, *103*, 912–961.

28. Croutte, P.; Delpal, F.; Hatchuel, G. *Représentations et pratiques de la consommation engagée: évolution 2002–2006*; Cahier de Recherche du CREDOC: Paris, France, 2006.

29. *Getting and Spending. European and American Consumer Societies in the Twentieth Century*; Strasser, S.; McGovern, C.; Judt, M. (Eds.) Cambridge University Press: New York, NY, USA, 1998.

30. Strasser, S. *Satisfaction Guaranteed: The Making of the American Mass Market*; Smitthsonian Books: New York, NY, USA, 1989.

31. Colin, C. *The Romantic Ethic and the Spirit of Modern Consumerism*; Basic Blackwell: Oxford, UK, 1987.

32. Muniz, A; O'Guinn, T. Brand Community. *J. Consum. Res.* **2001**, *27*, 412–432.

33. Boltanski, L.; Chiapello, E. *Le nouvel esprit du capitalisme*; Gallimard: Paris, France, 1999.

34. Holt, D. Why do Brands Cause Trouble? A Dialectical Theory of Consumer Culture and Branding. *J. Consum. Res.* **2002**, *29*, 70–90.

35. Kozinets, R. Can consumers escape the market? Emancipatory illuminations from burning man. *J. Consum. Res.* **2002**, *29*, 20–38.

36. Gabriel, Y; Lang, T. *The Unmanageable Consumer*; Sage: London, UK, 2006.

37. Kozinets, R.; Handelman, J. Adversaries of consumption: Consumer movements, activism, and ideology. *J. Consum. Res.* **2004**, *31*, 691–704.

38. Dubuisson-Quellier, S; Lamine, C. Consumer involvement in fair trade and local food system: Delegation and empowerment regimes. *GeoJournal* **2008**, *73*, 55–65.

39. Klintman, M. Ambiguous framings of political consumerism: Means or end, product or process orientation? *Int. J. Consum. Stud.* **2006**, *30*, 427–438.

40. Dubuisson-Quellier, S. De la routine à la délibération. Les arbitrages des consommateurs en situation d'achat. *Réseaux* **2006**, *34*, 253–284.

41. Dubuisson-Quellier, S.; Barrier, J. Protester contre le marché: du geste individuel à l'action collective. Le cas du mouvement anti-

publicitaire. *Revue française de science politique* **2007**, *57*, 209–237.

42. Lamine, C. Settling the shared uncertainties: Local partnerships between producers and consumers. *Sociol. ruralis* **2005**, *45*, 324–345.

43. *Sustainable Consumption: The Implication of Changing Infrastructure of Provision*; Southerton, D.; Chappels, H.; Van Vliet, B. (Eds.) Edward Elgar Publishing: Cheltenton, UK, 2006.

44. Ozcaglar-Toulouse, N.; Shiu, E.; Shaw, D. In search of fair trade: Ethical consumer decision making in France. *Int. J. Consum. Stud.* **2006**, *30*, 502–514.

45. Sanches, S. Sustainable consumption à la française? Conventional, innovative, and alternative approaches to sustainability and consumption in France. *Sustain. Sci. Pract. Policy* **2005**, *1*, 1–15.

Index

I

L

O

P

R

S

U